THE
HUMAN
FACE
OF
JAPAN'S
LEADERSHIP

THE HUMAN FACE OF JAPAN'S LEADERSHIP

Twelve Portraits

MARTIN E. WEINSTEIN

Foreword by George R. Packard

PRAEGER

New York
Westport, Connecticut
London

Library of Congress Cataloging-in-Publication Data

Weinstein, Martin E., 1934-
    The Human face of Japan's leadership : twelve portraits /
    p.   cm.
    Includes bibliographical references and index.
    ISBN 0-275-93290-7 (lib. bdg. : alk. paper)
    ISBN 0-275-93351-2 (pbk. : alk. paper)
        1. Politicians—Japan—Interviews.   2. Japan—Officials and
    employees—Interviews.   3. Businessmen—Japan—Interviews.
    4. Internationalism.   I. Title.
    DS889.15.W45   1989
    952.04'8'0922—dc19   88-38360

Library of Congress Catalog Card Number: 88-38360
ISBN: 0-275-93290-7
        0-275-93351-2 (pbk.)

First published in 1989

Praeger Publishers, One Madison Avenue, New York, NY 10010
A division of Greenwood Press, Inc.

Printed in the United States of America

The paper used in this book complies with the
Permanent Paper Standard issued by the National
Information Standards Organization (Z39.48-1984).

10 9 8 7 6 5 4 3 2 1

TO MY WIFE, ERIKA MARIANNE,
SKIER, MUSE AND CRITIC

Contents

Acknowledgements

THE RESEARCH for and writing of this study were made possible by a sabbatical leave from the University of Illinois and by additional funds made available by the International University of Japan, and by the Japan Society for the Promotion of Science. My appointment to the Japan Chair at The Center for Strategic and International Studies (CSIS) in Washington, D.C., afforded me the time necessary to complete the manuscript. I would like to express my appreciation to these institutions for their generous support.

I wish to thank the many people in Japan whose hospitality, good humor and willing assistance enabled me to write this book. It is not possible to mention all their names, but I do want to acknowledge the kindness of Mr. Sohei Nakayama, Dr. Saburo Okita, Dr. Toshio Shishido and Professor Chihiro Hosoya, of International University of Japan, Professor Seizaburo Sato of Tokyo University, Professor Tsuyoshi Hasegawa of Hokkaido University, Mr. Mikio Kato, International House of Japan, and Mr. Takao Tominaga, Sanyo Electric Company. Their advice and help were essential.

I owe a special debt to my wife Erika, for transcribing one hundred hours of taped interviews--an enormous task which laid the foundation for this book. I would like to thank Ms. Elizabeth Lynch for formatting the manuscript; Ms. Lona Sato for administrative support, proofreading, and indexing; and Ms. Nancy Eddy, Director of Publications at CSIS, for her counsel and encouragement.

Martin E. Weinstein
Washington, D.C.
January, 1989

Foreword

WITHOUT MUCH fanfare, the Japanese have recovered from their crushing defeat in 1945 to become the world's second largest economy and leading creditor nation. This dramatic rise, which will reshape the international order of the 21st century, did not come as a surprise to those who have watched the Japanese since World War II. But its low-keyed intrusion into our national consciousness has aroused a flurry of speculation about who these people really are, and what they are up to in the long run. Are they friends and allies, grateful for our postwar benevolence, or spiteful competitors, out to avenge their losses in the Pacific?

Many kinds of explanations have been offered for their miraculous success: the tight alliance of business and government in a state-directed capitalist economy (the "Japan Inc." theory); superior management techniques; long-term business strategies "targeting" American industries; emphasis on R&D; excellence in education; docility of labor unions; protected domestic markets; high propensity to save and so forth. All of these are part of the explanation, of course, but Japan's miraculous economic success rests ultimately on sound decisions by qualified individuals. Who, in fact, are the leaders who have guided their nation's phoenix-like miracle from poverty to riches in four decades?

The Japanese themselves have made it hard to answer this question. Their culture dictates that the individuals should subordinate themselves to the group. The nail that sticks up is hammered down, runs an oft-quoted proverb. This emphasis on teamwork, concensus, group goals and self-effacing behavior may well be one of the secrets to their success, but it remains true that complex modern societies require tough decisions by well educated, experienced leaders, and this is especially true in the interdependent global economy in which Japan must operate to maintain its standard of living.

Dr. Martin E. Weinstein has taken an unusual approach--one that would have been virtually impossible for a Japanese scholar/writer. He has conducted penetrating interviews with four leading politicians, four elite bureaucrats, and four highly successful businessmen, connecting their lives to the tumultuous events of their era. His approach reveals the extraordinarily diverse backgrounds and routes to power of today's ruling elite in Japan and goes far to destroy the image of a faceless economic juggernaut, bent on winning a new economic war of the Pacific.

Though they sometimes appear impassive, even inscrutable to foreigners who do not speak their language or understand their traditions, the Japanese are as intensely human, emotional and diverse as any people in this world, and Weinstein captures this aspect while weaving his personalities into the fabric of postwar Japanese history. This is the work of a careful scholar, admirably qualified by his long residence in Japan and his Japanese language ability, to cut through the curtains of anonymity which shield the decision-making process in Japan.

Yet the book, for the general reader, will be an excellent introduction to modern Japanese society. Not since Frank Gibney's early postwar classic, *Five Gentlemen of Japan*, has there been a more revealing study of the human face of modern Japan.

The book is important for another reason. The leaders described here are "young" by Japanese standards: 45-61 years old. It is not until their late sixties or early seventies that Japanese leaders ordinarily reach the apogee of their power and influence. Thus the twelve men described here have critically important roles to play in the future as Japan seeks to adjust itself to rising pressures from the international community to open its markets still further and play by rules that are recognized as "fair" throughout the world.

A theme of Japanese history since the start of the Meiji Period (1868-1912) has been the drive to gain international acceptance and respect. The leaders of the Showa Period (1925-1989) were driven by this quest, and yet they bore the added burden of Japan's unsuccessful efforts to gain an empire after the age of imperialism had passed. How they view their nation's defeat, and their own role in forging a new Japan, is a fascinating aspect of this book. And whether they will prevail in the Heisei Period (1989) over the ever-present forces of nationalism at home and intense competition abroad is by no means certain. Defeated by narrow, isolated and fanatic militarists in the 1930s, Japan's internationalists face continuing opposition from those who would against all odds try to preserve the pristine and "unique" Japanese society and culture against foreign influences. We have in this pioneering work an admirable playguide to what will be a continuing drama whose outcome must be a matter of concern for all of us.

George R. Packard
Dean, School of Advanced International Studies
The John Hopkins University

THE
HUMAN
FACE
OF
JAPAN'S
LEADERSHIP

Introducing
Japan International

WHAT KIND of people will be leading Japan into the 21st century? Who will guide the second most productive industrial economy in the world, a nation based on a tightly-knit, traditional society and a language almost unknown outside Japan? Whoever they are, they will find that the challenge of handling Japan's burgeoning international connections--its foreign markets, overseas investments, raw material suppliers and heavily armed neighbors--will weigh at least as heavily upon them as domestic concerns.

It is widely believed that Japan will continue to be led by its conservative politicians, bureaucrats, and businessmen. This is a book of portraits of twelve Diet members, bureaucrats and businessmen in their forties and fifties, the kind of people who will probably be in leadership positions for the next ten to twenty years. These people, first of all, are trusted members of Japan's elite establishment, whose views will count in building the concensus that determines policy. They are not go-betweens or interpreters who deal with foreigners while others decide. However, these particular future leaders are also members of a growing group of influential Japanese who are proficient at foreign languages and are seasoned practioners of international relations. In Japan, they are called internationalized (*kokusaiteki*).

The main purpose of this book is to give a human face to these future leaders, and by so doing get a better idea of what makes them tick, of the experiences that have shaped their values and their views of Japan and the world. One of the most prevalent and dangerous American misperceptions is the image of Japan as a faceless, impersonal, corporate entity. This notion is inadvertently reinforced by the fact that most of our studies of Japan focus on their policies and organizations, rather than on individual Japanese, and also by the fact that most Japanese consider it bad manners to talk about themselves and their families. At an Aspen Institute seminar in Japan, in November 1984, a number of the Japanese participants complained of American misunderstanding and lack of warmth for Japan. I explained that Americans, who pride themselves on their openness and informality, often find it difficult to warm up to Japanese who are reluctant to talk about personal matters, even with their close friends. I suggested that if the Japanese would sit down and tell me about themselves, their families, their childhood years and memories of the war and Occupation, their educations and careers, I would put together a book that would help Americans to see them as individual human beings.

Two of the Japanese at the Aspen seminar agreed to do that, and one of them, Schunichi Hiraki, a hard-driving, jovial banker appears in this volume. The other participants were selected partly from a long list of internationalized younger leaders whom I had never met before. Their names were suggested by elder statesmen such as Saburo Okita, a former foreign minister, and Sohei Nakayama, retired president of the Industrial Bank of Japan. Others were chosen from a shorter list of acquaintances whom I had met while working in the U.S. embassy in Tokyo in the late 1970s. Consequently, the twelve people whose cooperation made this book possible are not a scientifically selected sample or cross-section. In fact, the purpose of this book is to move away from generalizations, to the details, texture, and richness of individual lives. A study such as this is not going to eliminate conflicts of national or business interests. Hopefully, it will help to eliminate the stereotype of the faceless, inaccessible Japanese, a misperception that could be very damaging in a time of strain or crisis.

Although my purpose is to get beyond generalizations to individuals, the reader may find it useful to first spend a few minutes considering: (1) the historical ideas and images that are shared by Japanese leaders who were born between the late 1920s and the early 1940s; (2) their educational backgrounds; (3) the ruling triumvirate of politicians, bureaucrats, and businessmen; and (4) the meaning of internationalization.

HISTORICAL BACKGROUND: IMAGES AND LESSONS

It is important to know something about their historical ideas and images, because these leaders see themselves as heirs and participants in Japanese history. They are more knowledgeable and conscious of the past than most Americans of their age and status. Their values and actions are shaped by their beliefs about their historical heritage, and the future they are working to build is based on that heritage.

The older leaders in this study, those well into their fifties, entered school before World War II and began to study history at a time when textbooks and media accounts presented glorified versions of Japan's past. Within a few months of the Surrender in August 15, 1945, the American Occupation had ordered that all references in textbooks to Japan's divine origins and victorious wars be deleted. Since the country was so impoverished that it was to take several years to publish new textbooks, the students were simply ordered to take their writing brushes and India ink in hand and to black out objectionable passages. At the same time their teachers, who under American Occupation guidance had organized themselves into the pacificist Japan Teachers Union, began to teach that Japanese history since the late 19th century was a catalogue of evil deeds committed by feudalistic, militaristic men who had led the country to the disaster and defeat of the Pacific War. Their basic message was that Japan's past was bad, and that Japan must start over again and build itself into a peace-loving, democratic country.

The younger leaders, those now in their late forties, did not begin to study history until after the war. They were taught only the latter version. Nevertheless, although the twelve leaders do not agree on all matters of historical fact and interpretation, they are not sharply divided by age. Since they all went on to the university and have read widely on history and public affairs, not only in Japanese but in foreign languages as well, they tend to dismiss any oversimplified, black/white interpretations of human behavior.

They do agree, however, that Japanese history since the middle of the 19th century, when Japan was forced out of its self-imposed isolation by American and European intrusions and began to industrialize, should be divided into three distinct periods. The first of these periods lasted from the overthrow of the Tokugawa government and the beginning of the Meiji era in 1868, until sometime in the 1920s or 1930s. Overall, these were years of successful industrialization, impressive economic growth, victorious wars against China (1894-1895) and Russia (1904-1905), the building of an overseas empire, and the recognition of Japan as a great power. Sometime in the 1920s or 1930s, Japan began to descend into the second period, the Dark Valley that led to the Pacific War, the atomic bombing of Hiroshima and Nagasaki, and to disaster and defeat in 1945. The third period began in the ashes and ruins of that defeat and is still going on. Like the Meiji period, it has been one of extraordinary economic and political transformation and achievement, without the wars and empire building of the late 19th and early 20th centuries.

Japan's future leaders are proud of the Meiji era (1868-1912) and proud of the Japan that has been built since 1945. They know that of the numerous states that have struggled to industrialize since the late 19th century, Japan has been the most successful. They know that the industrialization of the Meiji era laid the foundation for Japan's present economic strength. Moreover, they believe that the Meiji leaders succeeded in industrializing Japan because they had the will and ability to deal with foreigners and to understand and apply Western culture and technology, and at the same time managed to remain firmly attached to traditional Japanese values. In this respect the Meiji leaders are still models for Japan's future leaders.

In order to appreciate the magnitude of Japan's achievements in the Meiji period, one must realize that in 1868 Japan was a feudal, agricultural, subsistence society with a population of about thirty-five million, living on their relatively small, mountainous islands off the coast of Asia. In terms of technology and military power, the country was so backward that in 1853-1854, Commodore Matthew G. Perry was able to force the Tokugawa government to open Japan to foreign trade and residence by boldly steaming into Edo (present day Tokyo) Bay with four black, paddlewheeldriven U.S. warships, and demanding that the government negotiate. Tokugawa officials knew that the guns on Perry's ships could bombard Edo and that they were helpless to defend the city.

The reluctant Tokugawa decision to open Japan to the foreigners led the feudal lords, who had been conquered by the Tokugawa and had been biding their time for 250 years, to believe that the government could be overthrown, and in so doing they initiated a period of domestic turmoil and insurrection. Japan at that time was organized into four classes: a court nobility of several hundred that lived in Kyoto with the imperial family, which had been reduced to dependence on the Tokugawa; the samurai, a class of about two million literate, disciplined soldier-bureaucrats; hard working farmers, who composed the bulk of the population; and at the bottom of the social scale a small class of despised, but affluent artisans and merchants .

The samurai were supported by fixed allowances of rice, but throughout the 19th century many of them had lived beyond their means, had fallen into debt to the merchants, and were impoverished and seething with discontent. They were quick to charge the government with failure to defend the sacred soil of Japan, argued that the Tokugawa had usurped the authority of emperor, and demanded that the barbarian foreigners be expelled and the emperor honored. Satsuma and Choshu, the two largest and most powerful clans that had been conquered in 1603, became the core of an anti-Tokugawa coalition. In 1867-1868, after a decade of intrigue, Choshu openly defied the Tokugawa, defeating a military force sent by the government to punish them and forcing the Tokugawa to abdicate. With the cooperation of Satsuma and two other clans, Tosa and Hizen, and the support of the court nobility, a new government was installed in Tokyo under the nominal authority of the young Emperor Meiji.

Although the fighting and change of government in 1868 is called the Meiji Restoration, implying that Japan had returned to its pure, ancient traditions, the new government soon decided on a fundamental policy of industrialization and modernization. Real power in the new imperial government was exercised by a small group of middle ranking samurai from the successfully rebellious clans together with a few court nobles. By 1873, when the leadership split over the question of whether to go to war with Korea or to concentrate on economic development, most of these men realized that expelling foreign barbarians and conquering Korea were not simply foolish slogans, but were also dangerous distractions from their principal task. They had learned that courage and swordsmanship would not suffice to expel the Westerners who had forced Japan open. The Americans and Europeans possessed the technology and factories to make steamships, powerful guns, railroad trains, and telegraph lines. Being realistic men, the Meiji leaders quickly concluded that unless they mastered the technology of the Westerners, Japan would lose its independence and be carved up, as was happening in China. Their travel to the West and their studies led them to believe that Western technology and military power were outgrowths of Western culture and political organization. If Japan were to survive and flourish in this new world, it would have to be politically unified, its people educated, its economy industrialized, and its military armed with modern weapons.[1]

They decided that the way to accomplish these formidable tasks was to buy Western manufactured goods--from steamships to sewing machines--and then learn to make them, to bring foreign teachers into Japan who could teach engineering, agriculture, and government, and to send students to the West to learn the secrets of their strength. By the middle of the 1870s, the Meiji government, under the leadership of men such as Tomomi Iwakura (court noble), Toshimichi Okubo (Satsuma samurai), Hirobumi Ito (Choshu samurai), Aritomo Yamagata (Choshu samurai), and Shigenobu Okuma (Hizen samurai), had been firmly set on the course of what is now called internationalization.

Many of the new leaders, including Ito, Yamagata, and Okuma, were in their thirties when they rose to the top of the Meiji government in the 1870s, and they retained great power and influence over policy into the early 20th century. This contributed to the continuity and stability of Japanese policy. Probably the most remarkable qualities of the Meiji leaders were their practicality and the openness of their minds. Particularly in the 1870s and 1880s, they

---

1. See Toshimichi Okubo's carefully argued memorandum of early fall 1873, "Reasons for Opposing the Korean Expedition," in Wm. Theodore de Barry, ed., *Sources of Japanese Tradition* (New York: Columbia University Press, 1960), 657-62.

were willing to enthusiastically explore and try out whatever the West had to offer. An example was the opening by the government in 1883 of a Western style club in Tokyo, known as the *Rokumeikan*. Here meetings were held on European music, art, novel writing, western theater, foreign cooking, and dressmaking. The Foreign Ministry officially sponsored tea parties, receptions, dances, and fancy dress balls for foreign diplomats, businessmen, and their ladies. A fancy-dress ball held on April 20, 1887, at the *Rokumeikan* was reported in the popular press, which was critical of the government. The public was shocked by reports and drawings of a Japanese cabinet minister in ridiculous foreign costume, cavorting in public over a dance floor in the arms of a foreign woman, while foreign diplomats waltzed with Japanese ladies, who also wore gowns that immodestly displayed their bare shoulders.[2] A Japanese moralist observed that his country had learned the decadence of the Roman Empire without first reaching its pinnacle of glory.[3]

By the end of the 1880s, the *Rokumeikan* had been closed and the Meiji leaders had decided to try to limit the absorption of Western culture to what was needed to organize an effective, modern state, industry, and military force. Their new slogan was "Western Science-Eastern Ethics." Although they backed away somewhat from their early enthusiasm for Western culture, they admired effective government and technological and military prowess, and they optimistically and vigorously set out to match the West in these attainments. In the system of universal compulsory education that they established as quickly as schools could be built and teachers trained--a task of four decades--young Japanese were trained in foreign languages and Western science and technology in order to build Japan into a prosperous, secure, and respected member of the civilized international society of the late 19th century.

By 1890, after two decades of turmoil and experimentation during which they abolished feudalism, organized a conscript army and suppressed several large-scale insurrections, the Meiji leaders

---

2. Hugh Borton, *Japan's Modern Century* (New York: Ronald Press, 1955), 174.

3. George B. Sansom, *The Western World and Japan* (New York: Random House, Inc., 1950), 370-371. Sansom's account of the cosmopolitan activities of the Meiji leaders is rich in detail, gracefully written and entertaining.

had established a unified, constitutional monarchy, including an
elected legislature modeled on Bismark's Germany. They also had
laid the foundations of an industrial economy. In the 1870's the
government opened textile factories, shipyards, rail lines, foundries,
munition works, and mines. In 1881, most of these fledgling industries were sold to private enterprises at scandalously low prices,
and they subsequently flourished. In fact, the public outcry over the
1881 scandals led the government to promise that a constitution
would be promulgated within a decade.

Eiichi Shibusawa's success as the head of the Tomioka
Spinning Mills is illustrative of the way private industry grew in
Japan. In the 1880s, Shibusawa increased the spindles in his Tokyo
and Osaka factories sevenfold. In 1868, Japan imported only
12,000 bales of raw cotton. By 1888, Japanese spinning mills
imported 158,000 bales.[4]

Comparable gains were made in mining and heavy industry.
Although Japan is very poorly endowed with energy and mineral
resources, there was enough coal available to fuel its infant industries, railroads, and steamships. Foreign engineers were brought in
to open mines, which soon came under Japanese management.
Between 1880 and 1890, coal production increased from 870,000
tons to 2,600,000 tons. Despite the fact that Japan has very little
iron ore, by 1890 the steel mills in northern Kyushu were meeting
40 percent of the country's rapidly growing needs. The beginnings
of a railroad system were in place. Japanese shipyards were building ocean going steel hulls, but marine engines and propulsion machinery were still being largely imported. The Mitsubishi conglomerate, assisted by periodic gifts of ships by the government, had developed the Japan Mail Steamship Company (N.Y.K.) into a
powerful merchant fleet of fifty-eight ocean going vessels.

It should also be noted that by 1890, the Japanese Imperial
Army consisted of six well armed and disciplined divisions, organized into specialized units of infantry, artillery, supply, engineers,
and a general staff modeled on German lines. Conscription and a
body of trained reserves gave these units a combat strength of
274,000 men. Since Japan is an island nation, a navy was believed

---

4. Borton, *Japan's Modern Century*, 155.

to be as essential as an army. Between 1883 and 1889, twenty-three smaller warships were built in Japanese yards for the Imperial Navy. Cruisers were either purchased from the British Navy or ordered from British shipyards. In the early 1880s, Naval schools were largely staffed by British instructors who were replaced by Japanese by the end of the decade. The budgets of the Meiji government between 1877 and 1894 show that approximately one third of government expenditures went to the army and navy.[5]

These were the military forces that decisively defeated China in 1894-1895. In the Treaty of Shimonoseki, ending that war, Japan gained sovereignty over Taiwan (Formosa), and displaced China as the preeminent foreign power in Korea. Russia, fearful that a strong Japan would block its own planned expansion in the Far East, immediately challenged and for a few years succeeded in blocking Japan's attempt to take over Korea.

In 1902, Japan entered into a Far Eastern alliance with Great Britain, at that time the leading naval power in the world and a major force in Asia. Greatly strengthened by this alliance, Japan approached the Czar's government with an offer to divide Korea into a Russian sphere of influence north of the 38th parallel, and a Japanese sphere in the south. Russia refused this division, probably in the expectation that when the Trans-Siberian Railroad reached the Pacific coast, which it was scheduled to do within a few years, Russian military strength and its diplomatic position in the Far East would be greatly augmented. The Japanese government decided to fight Russia before the Trans-Siberian Railroad could be completed. In contrast to China, Russia was a great power, with relatively modern, well armed forces. Americans and Europeans were astonished, therefore, when, in 1904-1905, the Japanese decisively defeated the Russians on land and at sea. In the Treaty of Portsmouth, Russia recognized Japan's paramount interests in Korea, transferred its railroad rights in South Manchuria to Japan, and ceded to Japan the Kurile Islands and the southern half of Sakhalin Island. Japan emerged from the war with Russia as a great power.

---

5. Edwin A. Falk, *Togo and the Rise of Japanese Sea Power* (New York: Longmans, Green and Co., 1936), 125.

The generation of Japanese leaders who are now in their late forties and fifties are proud of the economic, political, and cultural achievements of Meiji Japan, and respect and admire the Meiji leaders. However, their views about the wars with China (1894-1895) and Russia (1904-1905), and the building of Japan's overseas empire, are not as clear. They do not boast about these victorious wars and the empire Japan won, but neither are they apologetic about them.

Based on the sparse discussions we did have on this subject, it seems that in their minds it was only natural that Japan's initial surge of industrialization and modernization culminated in war and overseas expansion. The society of civilized nations, the Americans and Europeans who had coerced Japan out of its isolation, were conquerors and empire builders. In the late 19th century, the Western nations were proud of their armies and navies and believed that a fierce martial spirit was a necessary element of national greatness. Western leaders also believed that it was the moral duty of advanced, civilized nations to enlighten and improve backward, poorer people either by ruling them directly or by absorbing them into commercial spheres of influence. Britain's pride was that the sun never set on its empire. Englishmen, Germans, and Frenchmen were jostling each other in their competition for colonies and trade in Africa and Asia. Americans and Russians, preoccupied with developing their own vast, continental countries, were late entering the contest. As a result of the Spanish-American War (1898), the United States annexed the Philippine Islands and challenged the exclusive European spheres in China with its Open Door policy. Russia pushed into Manchuria and Korea, and following the Boxer Rebellion in Peking in 1900, Russian forces occupied all of Manchuria. How could Japan, given its own military tradition, its geographical propinquity, and its desire to become a member of the society of advanced, civilized nations, be expected to refrain from the military and commercial scramble over Asia?

A major reason why conservative Japanese leaders avoid discussions of the Sino-Japanese and Russo-Japanese wars is that both wars were fought over the control of Korea, and Korea is still a very live issue in Japanese domestic politics. To speak objectively of the policies that led to the colonization of Korea in 1910, is considered by many Japanese to be tantamount to defending "imperialism," "militarism," and the policies that led Japan into World War II.

For Japanese who were born between the late 1920s and early 1940s, Japan's defeat in World War II was a searing, personal experience. In contrast to Americans of their age, they are not a postwar generation. Even the youngest people in this book remember air raids, fires, food shortages, and the trauma of the Surrender. Although children at the time, they all passed through the Dark Valley, and they emerged from it with a number of powerful, lasting lessons. The most obvious lesson, which is enshrined in Article 9 of the Constitution and has become a basic principle of Japanese education, is that Japan cannot and should not be a military power. Japan must channel its energy and talents into peaceful, economic pursuits.

A second lesson is that Japan was plunged into war, disaster, and defeat by men who did not comprehend the United States and Europe, and who did not have a realistic understanding of what they were doing when they started the war. Ryohei Murata, of the Foreign Ministry, put it this way:

"In this century, we had to deal with other countries-- especially your country and the European powers. Not just in trade. We had to understand the interests, the point of view, and the power of these foreign countries. Before the Pacific War, we were not able to do that sufficiently. Our perception of the world based on our culture was perhaps too narrow, too one-sided. That made us unrealistic. We were so unrealistic that we declared war on the United States and took on almost the whole world. (pause) Something was seriously wrong with us, or we could not have done that. So . . . we were defeated and humiliated in the war.

"For my generation, our task has been and still is to recover from that defeat and to make Japan an accepted country in the international community. (pause, very thoughtfully) Perhaps the underlying task is still to correct the cultural and psychological narrowness that led us to war and defeat."

The implication of this lesson is that Japan should be led by people who really know and understand the outside world--by internationalized Japanese.

Applied simultaneously, as they have been for the last forty years, these two lessons have produced a synergistic effect--a peaceful Japanese economic powerhouse that does business all over the world. These lessons also help to explain why a growing number of Japanese who aspire to the highest levels of leadership have made the effort to master foreign languages and have managed to study and live abroad.

EDUCATIONAL MERITOCRACY

After going through a few of the portraits, the reader will notice that with one possible exception, the people in this book all seem to have graduated from one of several prestigious universities, and that their fathers are also university graduates, although their father's alma maters are more varied. In fact, the future leaders are products of a system of educational meritocracy that was established in the Meiji era and then reformed under the American Occupation.

The Meiji leaders believed that in order to industrialize and thrive in the modern world, Japan needed an education system that would produce universal literacy and at the same time channel the most talented, conscientious students into the highest levels of national leadership. Based on French and German models, they set up a system of universal, mandatory elementary schooling, followed by voluntary education at the higher levels. Entrance into the post-elementary schools, including high schools and universities, required passing progressively more difficult entrance examinations. By the early years of this century the most prestigious universities were training the men who were to staff the government bureaucracy and the upper ranks of the business and political worlds.

Tokyo Imperial University and to a lesser extent Kyoto Imperial University were the most difficult schools to enter and were the main training centers for the Higher Civil Service, and also for industry, banking, business and the learned professions. Two private universities in Tokyo, Keio and Waseda, were somewhat less rigorous in their entrance requirements, but still very selective. Whereas the Imperial universities put great emphasis on service to state and society, the private universities took a relatively more liberal, entrepreneurial approach. Very few graduates of Keio and Waseda entered the powerful government bureaucracy. Most went into industry, business, banking, journalism, or party politics.

The grandparents of the people in this book were farmers, small businessmen, and teachers, who realized that the educational meritocracy opened great opportunities. They and their children had the brains and the capacity for hard work that the system demanded. No matter what their social position or wealth, if they could pass the entrance examinations, they would attend the best higher schools and universities. Tuition was very modest, and grandparents, uncles, and aunts could always manage to scrape together the small amount required to keep a bright, young relative in school. Graduation from a leading university was usually tantamount to admission to Japan's ruling elite. Students who had attended the less prestigious higher schools and universities became middle-level bureaucrats and executives, and also fared very well. This education system achieved universal literacy, produced an elite of bright, industrious leaders, and also generated a high level of social mobility in Japan.

Naturally, mobility was greatest in the first two or three decades of this century, when the universities, the bureaucracies, and business worlds were in their early and most rapid stages of growth. By the 1950s and 1960s, the brighter, more ambitious families who had studied and worked their way into the new system in its early years had become an educational gentry. The people in this book are all children of this well educated class. Two come from wealthy families. All come from families in which education was held in the highest esteem. In this respect, the future leaders in this book are typical of Japanese leaders of their age. Although it is difficult to find exact figures, roughly 85 percent are children of the educational gentry. The remaining 15 percent come from poorer, less educated families, and are themselves first generation members of this class.

The educational reforms carried out by the American Occupation did not basically alter the system of entrance examinations and elite universities. They did change the content of education and the values that were stressed, but it should be recognized that even these changes were matters of degree and emphasis. The postwar schools continued to give great importance to society, family, and group obligations and duties. More importance was placed on the dignity and rights of individuals--as long as these new values were harmonized with the old ones.

THE RULING TRIUMVIRATE

The reader may also wish to know how it came about that Japan is governed by a triumvirate of politicians, bureaucrats, and businessmen, what roles these groups usually play in leading the country, and how they relate to each other. We have seen how the Meiji oligarchs, a small group of former clan samurai, formed the core of the Japanese government from the early 1870s until the turn of the century. By the beginning of this century, as a result of industrialization, empire building, and the establishment of constitutional government, a number of powerful interest groups had developed whose leaders controlled the government. These leaders almost all had connections with the Meiji oligarchs and their groups frequently over-lapped and had sharp internal divisions. There was: (1) an entrenched, powerful military group; (2) the top civilian bureaucrats in the Civil Service; (3) the leaders of the major political parties who competed in popular elections for control of the Diet; (4) a small but influential circle of officials at the Imperial Court; and (5) the leaders of rapidly growing and essential industries, banks, and trading houses. From the turn of the century until the end of the Pacific War, these five groups vied for control of the cabinet and national policy.

Early in the Occupation (1945-1952), the Imperial Army and Navy were disbanded and abolished. The 1947 Constitution removed both the military and the Imperial Court from politics. The Occupation ruled Japan through the established civilian Civil Service and left it with more influence than it had enjoyed before the war. Under the new Constitution, which clearly established a responsible, cabinet form of government, the political parties were also greatly strengthened. Their leaders would become prime minister and would select their cabinet ministers from the elected members of the Diet. In 1947, the Occupation decided to support the revival of industry and banking, and very soon money from business contributions had again become the lifeblood of the political parties. It became customary for politicians and bureaucrats to consult with business leaders on policy, and thus, the ruling triumvirate was formed.

The roles of these three groups are neatly described by one of the participants in this book. The bureaucrats do most of the planning, draft most of the laws, and implement them when they are passed. The politicians elected to the Diet represent the voters and pass those laws that their constituents will support. They legitimate the system and act as both a prod and a check on the bureaucrats. Private businessmen play a major role in creating the wealth of Japan. They contribute funds to the political parties and use their influence to maintain a political climate that is supportive of private enterprise. As Tokio Kanoh put it, "No one sector steers everything or is in charge. The system requires that we work with each other."

INTERNATIONALIZATION: WHAT DOES IT MEAN?

Internationalization is the English translation of the Japanese word *kokusaika*. In Japan, it usually refers to the broadening and strengthening of Japan's connections with the outside world, which can be done in many ways and for many different reasons.[6] On the national level, it means improving Japan's ability to participate in the world economic and political order, opening up the Japanese economy, and becoming more like the other advanced industrial societies. For individuals, including the leaders in this book, internationalization means mastering foreign languages and culture in order that they can deal effectively with foreigners, and in so doing promote the security and prosperity of Japan, their party, ministry or firm, and themselves and their family. For the most part, they are not interested in spinning elaborate, systematic

---

6. One of the best books on this subject is Hiroshi Mannari and Harumi Befu, eds., *The Challenge of Japan's Internationalization* (Tokyo: Kwansei Gakuin University and Kodansha International Ltd., 1983). Herbert Passin's article, "Overview: The Internationalization of Japan," is an excellent introduction to this subject.

theories about internationalization.

There is, however, an interesting divergence of opinion among them about the pace and form of future internationalization. On the national level, Japan appears to rank fairly high as an internationalized country. It is extensively involved in the world. Its international trade is very large, its overseas capital investment has been expanding rapidly, and Toyota, Sony, and Matsushita have become household words all over the world. More than four million Japanese go abroad each year for business or tourism, and two million foreigners visit Japan. Several hundred thousand Japanese live abroad, and each year about fifteen thousand go abroad to study. English is a required subject for every Japanese student in junior high school and language education is a large industry in Japan.

Nevertheless, only a tiny percentage of the 120 million Japanese have become internationalized in the sense of mastering a foreign language and culture. There are no precise figures available, but the number is probably between one and two million, less than 2 percent. This relatively small group has helped to lead Japan into the world, kept their countrymen informed about international matters, and acted as translators and interpreters. The question is whether Japan will be able to handle the press of future international business, technology transfers, and political interaction with its existing small, steadily growing cadre of internationalized individuals, or whether many more, perhaps five or ten times the present number of Japanese, will have to learn how to deal directly on a regular basis with foreigners.

If a quantum jump in internationalization does become necessary, it will raise issues for Japan that go far beyond language training. Up to now, Japan has been able to interact effectively with the outside world without changing the basic structure and values of its society. That may not be possible in the future. Toyoo Gyohten explained that traditionally the "Japanese are a tribal, island people. We have always believed that to be safe . . . and to be effective, it is better to assimilate with our group--our tribe. Yet, the Japanese as a group have been amazingly flexible, versatile and quick to respond to outside influences.

"In the 7th century, we imported Buddhism and much of Chinese culture. In the 16th century, we responded quickly to the first, small wave of European culture. In the 19th century, we had a massive encounter with Western culture and absorbed enormous changes. After our defeat in 1945, we again responded effectively to major outside influences. In these four cases, we responded as a group. Our leaders, our elite, saw the need for change, assimilated what they thought was necessary to adapt effectively, and transmitted it. The group below remained intact. That was true even after 1945.

"Now, because of the way business, banking, and communications work, our interactions with the outside world are becoming so widespread, so diversified, that I don't think the process can be controlled and directed from above, the way it used to be. Maybe now, for the first time, in order for us to adapt successfully, we may have to change the nature of our society. We may have to loosen the group somewhat. We may have to learn how to respond in a more individualized way."

POLITICIANS

Under the 1947 Constitution, the Lower House elects the prime minister of Japan, who in turn appoints the cabinet. Since 1947, every prime minister and virtually all cabinet ministers have been members of the Lower House. Moreover, since 1948, every prime minister has been a leader of one of the conservative factions that in 1955 organized themselves into the Liberal Democratic Party (LDP). In Japan, the route to political power runs through the LDP and the Lower House, up through the cabinet, and reaches its pinnacle in the prime ministership. With few exceptions, the cabinet ministers have also been members of the LDP.

Wataru Hiraizumi

WATARU HIRAIZUMI represents the district of Fukui Prefecture in the House of Representatives of the National Diet, as a member of the ruling Liberal Democratic Party (LDP). Fukui is a mountainous, snowy, farming district on the Sea of Japan, facing Asia, almost due west from Tokyo across the main island of Honshu. Rice subsidies and improved roads and housing have greatly improved the lot of the farmers, but the Japan Sea coast, including Fukui, is still called *Ura Nihon,* Japan's Backcountry. It has been a stronghold of conservative politics.

Mr. Hiraizumi's background, his career, and his personality dramatically exemplify the complexities and contradictions of internationalization. Wataru Hiraizumi is a descendant of a family of priests who have had charge of the Heisenji Temple in Fukui for many centuries. In fact, Heisen and Hiraizumi are written with the same Chinese characters. The Hiraizumis were probably among the ancient settlers who came to Fukui from Asia. The Heisenji Temple guards a sacred, snow-capped mountain that archeologists believe served as a landmark to early mariners crossing the stormy Sea of Japan.

Wataru Hiraizumi was born on November 26, 1929, the third son of Kiyoshi and Hayako Hiraizumi. Although he frequently visited Fukui, he grew up in Tokyo, where his father was a professor of Medieval Japanese History at Tokyo Imperial University. As a passionate believer in the uniqueness and spiritual superiority of traditional Japanese culture, Professor Kiyoshi Hiraizumi was a well-known nationalist author and lecturer before and during World War II. Yet, his son Wataru, who is an accomplished linguist, learned French, English, and German in his father's library.

Left: a diplomat in Paris, 1950s.

Above: a recent photo.

Below: with parents, 1930s.

When he completed his studies at the Law Faculty of Tokyo University in 1952, Mr. Hiraizumi entered the Ministry of Foreign Affairs. He served as a diplomat in Paris, Tokyo, New York, and Teheran until 1964. Then he entered politics--at the behest of his father-in-law, Mr. Morinosuke Kajima. Mr. Kajima was head of the Kajima Corporation, one of the largest construction firms in the world, and was also in politics, having been twice elected to the House of Councilors, the Upper House of the Diet. In 1965, Mr. Hiraizumi also ran for and won a seat in the House of Councilors. He represented the National Constituency[1] in the Upper House for eleven years, and in 1970-1971 he was a minister in the cabinet of Prime Minister Eisaku Sato, serving as director-general of the Science and Technology Agency.[2]

In Japan, although the Upper House is prestigious, real political power resides in the Lower House of the Diet. Consequently, after two terms as a councilor, Mr. Hiraizumi began to cultivate a Lower House constituency in Fukui. In the 1976 general election, he ran for the House of Representatives as an Independent, without LDP endorsement, won his seat at the expense of an incumbent LDP Representative, and was promptly readmitted to the party.[3] This is a highly risky but not unusual way for politicians to win admission to the Lower House.[4] Mr. Hiraizumi was reelected in the general elections of 1980, 1983, and 1986. In 1985, when we had these conversations, he was director-general of the International Bureau of the LDP. In December 1985, he once again became a minister, joining the Nakasone Cabinet as director-general of the Economic Planning Agency.

---

1. The House of Councilors consists of 252 elected members. One hundred and fifty-two are chosen from forty-seven local election districts that are coterminous with the Japanese prefectures. The remaining one hundred are chosen from the national constituency, in which all Japan is considered a single electoral district. Councilors serve for six years, with half the members standing for election in regularly scheduled elections every three years.
2. *Seikan Yoran, Showa 59 Shunkigo* (Political Directory, Spring 1984), (Tokyo: Seisaku Jihosha, 1984),121.
3. Ibid.
4. For an excellent, detailed explanation of how this method of electioneering works, please see Gerald L. Curtis, *Election Campaigning Japanese Style* (New York: Columbia University Press, 1971).

FAMILY AND EARLY EDUCATION

On a hot, muggy evening in June 1985, I met with Mr. Hiraizumi at his private office in the Kajima Institute for International Peace, on a quiet, residential street in Akasaka, not far from the Diet. Mr. Hiraizumi is also president of the Kajima Institute. His spacious, tastefully furnished, booklined office was an oasis of cool, dry comfort. He was in his shirtsleeves, relaxing after a long, hard day. Wataru Hiraizumi is of medium height, has unusually expressive eyes and mobile features, and a voice that many an actor might envy. It ranges from a purring stage whisper to a commanding roar, from gentle concern to biting sarcasm. His English is excellent, and it ranges from Oxford to West Side Manhattan. He is also fluent in French and has a good knowledge of German and Russian. After sipping green tea for several minutes, he began to discuss his family background.

"The exact origin of my family is not very clear, to some extent because it has not been a strict father-to-son succession. But we have been connected to the Heisenji (the Japanese word *ji*, means temple) for many centuries. Did you know that Heisenji had long been a holy place before it became a Buddhist temple? Even before Buddhism was introduced, there was a cult of the high, snow-capped mountains along the Japan Sea. There is still a chain of these very ancient shrines in Toyama, Ishikawa, and Fukui prefectures. The Heisenji was one of the major shrines.

"Then in the 7th and 8th centuries, Buddhism came over from Asia . . . was introduced by the court nobles. These old Shinto shrines were transformed into Buddhist temples, the way Celtic temples in Europe were transformed into Christian churches-- with a higher form of culture, a new way of thinking, new attire, a new system of priests . . . all that. A large Buddhist temple was built at Heisenji, and hundreds of smaller monasteries, all under the Heisenji jurisdiction. It was like . . . medieval Italy, where the church governed large tracts of land. My ancestors became a part of that Buddhist priesthood, but it is not clear exactly when."

Question: "Are any of your family still connected with the Heisenji?"

"Oh yes. My eldest brother, who is the head of our family, serves there. For many years, he also taught history at a local higher school, but now that he is getting older he spends most of his time at the shrine. My other brother is a writer. I am the youngest."

Question: "One thing I have heard repeatedly--from at least a dozen people--is that your father was an ultranationalist. I have no basis for judging, and I am hoping you can help me on this point. What is the basis for these statements, if any?"

(serious, severe tone) "It is too easy to toss around these labels. He is a famous man--and he was associated with nationalist trends. He was against . . . not so much the foreign cultures themselves . . . but the contamination of Japan by foreign cultures."

Question: "Hmm. I see. Were his ideas related to what is now called *Nihonjinron*, the theory of Japanese uniqueness?"

"Yes, his ideas were related to *Nihonjinron*. (pause) He was a very bright man, tremendously well read, and also a passionate man. He had a real influence in Japan before and during the war. Many of his students used to idolize him, and some of them became . . . well, disciples. After the war, when Japan was defeated, of course, he left official academia, which suddenly shifted to the left. He went back to the shrine in Fukui. But before and during the war, he was a great, official authority on the meaning of the ancient, holy Japanese writings.

"I can tell you, he was personally an extraordinary man-- much brighter than I am--and full of character and intellectual vigor, even to the end of his long life. Did you know that he was born in 1895, and lived until 1984--eighty-nine years?"

Question: "That is extraordinary. How did you get along, you and he? You are so cosmopolitan, so much at home in foreign languages and cultures?"

"Well, he had no prejudice against foreign languages. (smiling) He had no trouble getting along when he was in Europe. He read extensively in German, French, and English. He had many foreign books in his library. In his study at home, he was surrounded by photos and portraits of his famous friends from Oxford and Berlin. (laughing) Certainly, he was a worshipper of Japan-- but he was not at all disdainful of the world.

"For him, all of Japanese history . . . was still alive. I felt as a small child that people in old Japanese manuscripts from . . . oh, the 13th century, were his friends . . . as alive as his sons. He would argue with these historical characters and agree with them, as though they were there. He used to resuscitate these long dead people by his power and spirit. (pause) A fascinating education--just being near my father. "

Question: "How did he come to terms with the defeat in 1945?"

"Very tragically. It was terribly . . . personal for him . . . and not so much a military defeat . . . but a moral failure. (pause) He felt that Japanese culture and thinking were not Japanese enough. That is why we lost the war. We were not worthy of our ancestors."

Question: "What a harsh condemnation. It seems to me that that generation of Japanese made terrible mistakes, but they also sacrificed and suffered enormously. But he did not think it was enough?"

"For my father, the central question was . . . how to succeed in modernizing without losing our traditional culture . . . our sense of who we are . . . our belief in Japan. He saw a world in which modern, Western cultures clashed with and overwhelmed ancient, traditional cultures. To him, that was the greatest danger to Japan. (pause) As he saw it, some Asian nations had already succumbed, by going Communist. That was the worst possible outcome. They had confronted the West, which was so much more advanced and powerful . . . and had been attracted by it, and had lost their souls. Suddenly, all their rich traditions and values, thousands of years old, had lost their flavor and color. But they were also too proud to just imitate the West and join it or become copies of it. Their answer was to try to leap ahead of the West by adopting Communism, the ideology of the future . . . the next stage. Well, he was afraid that could happen to Japan.

"After the war, through the fifties and sixties and into the 1970s, he was very unhappy at the Americanization of Japan. It seemed to him that Japan was becoming like Weimar Germany of the 1920s, right after their defeat in the First World War, when they were so demoralized. But then, toward the end, he started to reconcile himself. He began to believe that perhaps the Japanese were going to keep their character and their soul . . . and perhaps become alive again."

Question: "Yes. I see. You know, this study of internationalization addresses the same question. What does it mean to internationalize? How does it relate to this issue of cultural identity?"

(laughing) "Aha, I should have realized you were leading me to that. Well, so far, Japan is a rare case. We seem to be modernizing, industrializing, and even learning how to deal with foreigners, without losing our traditions. Of course, geography counts. We are not a continental country. The oceans insulate us. (shaking his head, smiling) Nevertheless, it is a mystery to me. I think my father helped us to do what we have done . . . to build this prosperous, modern, international Japan--that still has its soul."

WAR, OCCUPATION, AND TOKYO UNIVERSITY

Question: "Perhaps we can discuss your schooling and formal education. Shall we?"

"Of course. I don't think there is too much to say. First, I went to a local primary school, near my father's home, in Tokyo. From there, I transferred to Seishi, a better quality school, with a good record of sending its pupils on to higher schools. After Seishi, in 1942, when I was thirteen, I went into the Tokyo Higher School, which was a seven year school--comparable to a European gymnasium. It combined four years of middle school and three years of higher school. Once admitted to the middle school, one entered the higher school without taking another entrance examination.

"Well, in 1942 and into 1943, it was still . . . alright. We could breathe some atmosphere of learning . . . of higher learning. But by the end of 1943, it was getting tough. Food started becoming scarce. Eventually, my class had to do factory work--defense work. Your planes began to bomb our city, to destroy it. There was a curfew. And people became . . . well . . . it was a harsh atmosphere. Lots of scolding and some bad temper.

"Our house was destroyed in an air raid in 1945, with about ten thousand of my father's books. We--my father, mother, two brothers, and our housemaid--moved into his office at the university. We lived there for awhile, slept and ate there. (laughing) You see, Todai was home to us. Then, we found other houses to live in. So many people had fled, that many of the remaining houses in Tokyo were vacant. It was like . . . Moscow, when Napoleon invaded Russia in 1812, and the Russians deserted the city. For us, the worst raids were in April 1945. They hit our section. The raids in March had wiped out downtown Tokyo. Horrible. Fires and dead people.

(long pause) "I had to realize . . . it was clear that we were losing the war . . . that the end was near.

(another pause) "You know, in those bad years, I immersed myself in books. I was surrounded by books. I was especially attracted to European culture, and I decided to really learn French. I still remember going to a back corner of Kanda (a student neighborhood in Tokyo) in the torrid summer days of 1945, to take private lessons from a strange, very old man. The streets were deserted, except for some soldiers and old people. Everybody had left, either to fight or to escape the city. I forget the old man's name, but he was so calm, so detached. (imitating an old man's voice, very slowly and calmly) 'Oh, you want to learn French. Very well. Now, I have two students.' "

Question: "What were your reactions in September of 1945, when the American Occupation forces arrived?"

"Hmm. No enormous reaction. I had seen many of these big, strangely colored, bold-featured foreigners in our house, before the war. The Americans looked like the German professors who had come to visit us. You know, in 1940, my father had been invited (switching to a German accent) to teach Japanese Kultur at the Berliner Universität. (laughing and switching back to English) He refused. It was a time of crisis. How could he leave his fatherland? He saw our alliance with Hitler's Germany as a . . . necessity . . . a marriage of convenience--to avoid complete isolation in our conflict with the Anglo-Saxons.

"I should also mention to you that my father was an only son, and even though his work kept him in Tokyo, at the university, he went to the shrine in Fukui as frequently as he could, and took us with him. So, I got to know my grandmother and my aunt in Fukui. As chief of his family, he also had to serve at Heisenji. He never missed an opportunity to tell us that the shrine is our home, and to be proud of it, proud of our past. So, I have always had two homes, here in Tokyo and in Fukui."

Question: "Did any of your teachers, or friends, or the books you were reading, leave a strong, memorable impression on you?"

(thoughtful pause) "I was more interested in my father than anything else. You see, when you have a father like him, everybody else looks so pale, so intellectually deficient. (pause) It is terrible . . . and it is so . . . fortunate.

"Even in the worst days of the war, our evenings were full of his brilliant talk. Whenever I could, I would spend the day reading some book, some deep, intellectual book . . . and in the evening, I would tell my father about it, how fascinating it was. My father would say (in a good natured, self-confident tone) 'Oh him. He doesn't know what he is writing about. He ignored this source, or that important book. Don't get too excited about such a book.' (much laughter) And he knew the subject and the authors and the important books. I would go and read them, to see . . . and my father was right. (shaking his head at the memory) He was amazing."

Question: "How did the Occupation education reforms affect you?"

(thoughtful pause) "Very little. I was sixteen at the end of the war--a young man. I stayed in Tokyo Higher School under the old system, finished in 1949, and entered Tokyo University, the Law Faculty."

Question: "You mentioned that your father went back to Fukui. Where did you live?"

"Oh, after the war, my brothers and I stayed in our school dormitories, here in Tokyo. You know, the Occupation seemed strange to me. I saw all these Occupation officials teaching democracy to the Japanese. But these American officials were mostly shopkeepers and salesmen trying to talk like professors. It was a crazy time . . . crazy. I took refuge in European cultures, in books.

I felt . . . attracted to that distant foreign culture. It was a . . . comfort . . . a refuge to me in those days.

"When I was at Todai, in 1950, I saw a notice in the Japanese papers announcing the entrance examination for the diplomatic service of our Foreign Ministry. It was considered extremely difficult. I did not expect to pass it. But I took it anyway . . . (laughing) as a practice test. I received the best score. The course at Todai Law Faculty in those days was still three years. In 1951, before I graduated, I joined the Foreign Ministry as a diplomat."

Question: "It seems too quick, to smooth, almost accidental. After all, wasn't your choice of a career more complicated than that? How did you decide?"

"Well, I took the most basic decision when I was getting ready to enter Todai. My father suggested that I should follow in his footsteps, become a professor of Japanese history, or perhaps European history. (pause) At that point I said, 'Well, perhaps we have been scholars for too long in our family. A different kind of life, a more normal life, would be better.' So, I decided to enter the Law Faculty at Todai, which meant a career in the Higher Civil Service. I was already attracted to things foreign--to the wide, wide, outside world. Before long, I said that I expected to go into diplomacy. My mother was not happy about that."

Question: "And your father?"

(laughing happily) "He was very happy. I would be defending Japan and Japanese values against foreigners. That was fine. But my mother . . . well, I would be away, far away, for a long time. She did not like that. Meanwhile, I concentrated on my French and English."

Question: "Did you give any thought to other powerful, prestigious ministries, such as Finance or MITI (Ministry of International Trade and Industry)?"

"No. Never. They did not appeal to me at all. Too bureaucratic. (much laughter, then in his seriocomic tone) Diplomats are different. They are gentlemen, not bureaucrats." (more laughter)

Question: "What effect, what influence do you think the war and the Occupation may have had on you . . . on shaping your values and thinking?"

(thoughtful pause) "You know, Japan is not the only country that has lost a war . . . has known defeat. In my readings on Europe, I could see that the French . . . oh, in 1870, the Germans in 1919, even the Americans in your South in 1865, had all tasted defeat, at one time or another. I could not keep count of how many times the Italian city-states or Chinese dynasties had been defeated. It is nothing new. Japan should not be oversensitive about it. The fact that it was happening to us . . . to me . . . did not make it remarkable. It was not the end. History keeps moving on . . . up and down. The most important thing is not to be defeated spiritually . . . to keep one's pride, one's self-respect."

EUROPE, TOKYO, AND MARRIAGE

"I flew to France from Haneda Airport in the spring of 1952, just a few weeks before the San Francisco Peace Treaty came into effect. Haneda was still under American military command. It . . . reminded me of the past. I flew off to France, to Paris. Our embassy left me on my own for two years to perfect my French, and then I served as an attaché in Paris for the third year.

"Suddenly, my life was rich . . . in a material way. Compared to most young Japanese in the 1950s, our allowances were good. (laughing) I had to live like a diplomat, not a student anymore. I had a car of my own. As I expected, I liked France. My French was good, so the French treated me well. The French like you . . . if you speak their language.

"At first, it felt strange to be always surrounded by people whose whole appearance, gestures, way of talking was so different. But these racial feelings were eventually overcome by time and frequent contact. I was free to travel--extensively--and I did. I had no duties. I went to Italy, Spain, Portugal, and England. I was in my early twenties, and I had a marvelous time. And my languages improved. It was especially hard, at first, to get used to the company of Western women. I was accustomed to Japanese girls and suddenly, here are these European women, talking out and boldly laughing. (both laughing) But, I even became accustomed to that. (more laughter) As it turned out, I married a Japanese. I did not suffer the sad destiny of some of our young diplomats, who fall prey to these luscious Western ladies." (more laughter)

Question: "How did you manage to be saved? Did you meet your wife, Mieko, in France?"

"No. But I met her mother and father there. In 1954, Dr. Kajima came over to Europe, to Vienna, with his wife, to attend a meeting of the Interparliamentary Union. They toured Europe. (pause) I was just thinking, he was in his mid-fifties then, about the same age I am now. Well, he was touring with his wife. He had three daughters and a son. He said, 'My son must continue our business, and at least one daughter must marry a diplomat.' (laughing) The older sisters were married. Dr. Kajima had been a diplomat, and he wanted Mieko to marry a diplomat. The Councilor of our embassy called me in and said, 'Senator and Mrs. Kajima are coming here. I want you to interpret for them, and help them out.' So, I did, and I found them charming, not as temperamental as they had been described. (both laughing) Dr. Kajima got to know me, and when I returned to Tokyo the next year, he invited me to their home . . . and arranged for me to meet Mieko, their daughter. We married in 1957, two years after my return to Tokyo.

"My father-in-law took a keen interest in my career, and he also put me into politics. So, that meeting in Paris was . . . fateful for me.

"All his life, my father-in-law was interested in foreign affairs and in politics. He had been a diplomat for ten years, you know, in the 1920s and 1930s, in Rome and in Berlin. Then, he took charge of the family's construction company. He also ran for the Lower House, in 1930, but he was not elected. (pause) He went to his rural constituency and talked about things they had never heard of, like the unification of Europe. Nobody understood what he had to say. (in a gentle tone) The old farmers shook their heads and said, 'What is this young man talking about?' (laughter) In 1953, he won a seat in the Upper House, in the National Constituency. He became chairman of the Foreign Relations Committee for some years.

"When I returned to Tokyo from Paris, in 1955, I joined the Treaty Bureau. I immersed myself in books on international law. Our work was mainly to supply official legal positions for the government on international problems. Very technical, very detailed. I spent a little over five years in the Treaty Bureau, until 1960. It was an unusually long assignment, because the revision of the 1951 (U.S.-Japan) Security Treaty came up, and I was kept on to work at that. My last two years in the Treaty Bureau were spent almost entirely in the Diet building.

"I also kept up my French and German. I was considered a Western European specialist in those days. In 1956 and 1957, I used to think to myself that I might be assigned back there after Tokyo. (smiling) But my father-in-law started his own campaign in the Foreign Ministry to have me assigned to our U.N. delegation in New York City. (laughing) He considered it a waste of time for me not to be in America while I was young. That is what he said. (raising his eyebrows expressively and shaking his head)

"In 1958, whilst I was still in the Treaty Bureau, I was sent to New York, on a mission for some international legal work. I stayed there for five weeks . . . and I enjoyed it enormously. (both laughing) You know, I first went to New York with a typical Continental attitude of . . . disdain for the Anglo-Saxons. (laughter and then continuing in a comic tone, with a French accent) These Americans are a young people . . . trop jeune. They are extremely well organized and practical . . . you know, but not yet entirely civilized. That sort of thing. (pause) But . . . my eyes were really opened . . . to a new dimension. New York astonished me in those five weeks. Your New Yorkers were . . . audacious people. If they wanted something . . . anything, they planned it and did it. Amazing energy and confidence. I was overwhelmed."

NEW YORK

"In August 1960, after the revised Security Treaty was finally approved in our Diet--after all the street demos and trouble for Prime Minister Kishi--I was appointed as a junior secretary to our Permanent U.N. Mission. I arrived in New York, and started hunting for an apartment for my wife and our two and one-half year old son. (laughing) That apartment hunt was exhausting, a day and night job. I negotiated and wheedled with those Jewish landlords, and finally found a place on the West Side, on Riverside Drive, not too far uptown. The East Side was too expensive. The West Side was reasonable, and still comfortable. You know, my wife had always had a comfortable life. I could not suddenly make her live like a student.

"My wife had never been abroad before. When Mieko arrived in New York . . . she was completely shocked. (laughing merrily) But even now, she says that New York is 'my hometown.' (pause) She loved it. After all, those were the years of our youth. Our second child, our daughter, was born there.

"Those years were the golden years of your American empire. The entire U.S. was shining with confidence, pride and . . . wealth. The greenbacks were shining like . . . the gold of Venice had shined. Nobody had a single doubt about the future. There was a serene confidence . . . a bottomless optimism, in the 1950s and early 1960s. When we lived in New York, it was the last of those glamorous, glowing years . . . and I was burned by that fire. (both laughing)

"It took us almost two years to really get attuned to the rhythm of life in New York. Very fast, impatient, but terribly exciting and interesting. Oh, it is extraordinary! It was a northern European, merchant culture, plus Jewish energy and eagerness. Very vital. Everything is possible in that city. Everything is tested there.

"Of course, I know that people say it is not typically American. And some Americans denounce New York--decadent, Sodom and Gomorrah. But I think they are secretly proud of that city. It is the heart of America. It could not be anyplace else but in America."

Question: "And your work at the U.N., on the Japanese delegation?"

"Not much to say, really. We had just been admitted to the U.N. several years before, you know, by grace of the great powers. We were still self-effacing . . . almost to the point of invisibility. (laughter)

"But, we had a marvelous life there. I was amazed at the way people accepted me. (laughing) Perhaps they thought I was . . . interesting. They are always looking for something a little different, you know. (both laughing) And also, I fell in easily with their style

. . . their argumentative style. (more laughter) Oh yes. France and New York brought out the argumentative streak in me. And we had many friends. We liked the scenery, too . . . the way New York looked and felt--the cold rains in autumn, and the Hudson in winter, with huge blocks of ice flowing out to the harbor. (pause) It was really our place.

"In a way, we had something of the immigrant experience, too. (laughing) When our daughter was born and I went to see her at New York Hospital the doctor told me so proudly, 'She is an American.' He did not know I was a diplomat. He just assumed that I would be so happy to know that my daughter had . . . made it . . . she had been born in America. (both laughing) And our son (shaking his head in mock horror) with pure Japanese blood in his veins, was turning into a little American--a New Yorker, right under my eyes. He had a horrible New York accent.

"Then, one beautiful morning in the spring of 1963, I was walking around in Manhattan with my son, trying to place him in a good summer school. I was feeling . . . good . . . and finally feeling affluent. I had paid off the loans for our Buick Wildcat. I was dressed and looked like a prosperous American salesman. (both laughing) I was trying to teach my son decent English, and to prepare him for a decent education. Of course, he thought that morning was tiresome. Several times he looked up at me and said, (mimicking a boy's voice in a strong New York accent) 'Daddy , I am just useless.' (both laughing long and hard) Yes, that is the way he talked."

Question: "Useless? What . . . did he mean?"

(astonished, laughing at me) "You don't know that slang? He meant he was bored . . . bored useless. (both laughing)

"Well, that same morning, a brief wire arrived from Tokyo. 'You have been appointed to embassy Teheran.' Just like that. I had to cancel everything and start packing immediately. My wife was at a concert in San Francisco. We went back briefly to Japan, and then I went on to Teheran, by myself, at first.

"Our last morning in New York, when the movers were finished and we were about to leave, my son was clinging to the bannister in our building, crying and saying, (again, in a little boy's voice and strong New York accent) 'I duwanna leave. Daddy, I duwanna leave.' (shaking his head at the memory) I had to pry him loose from that bannister."

Question: "Yes, I can picture it quite clearly. And how did you feel?"

(pause, smiling at me sadly) "Exactly the same as my son."

TEHERAN

"Well, I went to Teheran alone, because we did not know whether it was healthy for our children. Could we drink the water? Could we find a decent place to live? Where would they go to school? I spent about one year in Teheran, from June '63 to August '64. My wife joined me for the last six months. It was a year of changes. Your President Kennedy was shot during that year. And my work in Iran gave me a good look at a strange life, a kind of life that would soon disappear.

"If you were a foreigner, you had to shop at a special, imitation American supermarket, where the onions and potatoes cost three times as much--to make some bazaar merchant richer. The social life was unnatural. The Westernized Iranian ruling class, and the resident diplomats and business people--always thrown together for cocktails, dinners, receptions--over and over again.

"It was a strange life for me. I could not speak Persian, which left me in an unaccustomed, uncomfortable position. You know, I am used to knowing the language. I met only a few real Iranians. I could not go to theaters and restaurants. There were none to speak of. So, of course, I immersed myself in my books again . . . and I decided to bring my wife to Teheran.

"I spent two months hunting for a place for us. I became an expert on Teheran real estate. (laughter) I knew all the brokers and every available house and flat. I saw most of them two times. An agent would describe a newly available flat to me, tell me it was exactly what I wanted, perfect for me . . . in such glowing words, that I would go to see it. Of course, I had already seen it, weeks before. (more laughter) Finally, I found a very nice house, with an extraordinary garden. The garden had one-hundred different roses, blooming almost all year round. And the garden came with a gardener. I moved in and called Mieko to join me. We had an interesting, exile life in Teheran. Sometimes it was beautiful . . . in our fragrant rose garden, on a moonlit night. There were a thousand stars in the desert sky. It was so still. Such solitude."

Question: "Hmm. As a diplomat, what was your view then of Iran's stability--its future?"

(laughing) "Well, fifteen years before the revolution, I was reporting to Tokyo, time after time, about the revolution."

Comment: "Well, the Shah lasted longer than you expected. You were a bit . . . premature."

"Yes, yes. But I still boast about it. I was only in error by a few years. (laughter) I was always warning Tokyo about the instability. I described and analyzed each small riot, each little political incident . . . each quiver. I was absolutely certain it was about to collapse. I will tell you why.

"Iran, in many essential ways, was like India and Egypt before World War II. The social fabric was . . . terribly weak. The Shah and his ruling class were superficially Westernized and Americanized--imitations, most of them. They had lost touch with their own culture and traditions--with the powerful Islamic culture and with the soul of their own nation. They were part European, half American, part Russian . . . odd people. They looked so nice, but they were weak and . . . decadent. The Iranian ruling class wanted only . . . a dolce vita, a sweet, easy life. They had morally collapsed. They had not been able to withstand the onslaught of the Westerners. And the Iranian people--even some of those who were becoming more rich and comfortable from the Shah's Westernization--even they were seething with pent-up resentment and hatred for these infidel intrusions--onslaughts on their life. So, I wrote in my reports in '63 and '64, that the Shah's government could not last. It was disconnected . . . alien to its own people.

"Japan had had to deal with that danger. Perhaps, we were the most successful in withstanding it. (thoughtfully) I don't know why. (another thoughtful pause) We had . . . a kind of fighting spirit. We were willing to learn, but we would not really give in to anyone. We would compete with them . . . with anyone. Why not? (pause) I think that it is also the key to understanding and getting the best from your Western and American culture. Yes. The essence of your culture is--fighting guts."

Question: "Not democracy, or the rights and dignity of individuals?"

"Yes. But even those things rest on fighting guts.

"Well, I was living this exotic life in exile, admiring our roses and sending these . . . wild reports to Tokyo (laughter), when one summer morning in 1964, a telegram unexpectedly arrived from the Foreign Ministry. 'Your father-in-law says that you are going to stand in the next Upper House election. Are you leaving the ministry?' Well, my Tokyo ministry and the embassy were . . . very displeased. Can you imagine what it would be like if one of your junior diplomats, a first or second secretary in some small embassy, got such a cable from Washington, announcing that he is to become a senator?"

Question: "Yes, I can imagine it. You knew nothing-- nothing at all, beforehand?"

(In a quiet tone) "Absolutely nothing. The Upper House election was scheduled for the next summer. I would have to go back. "

THE HOUSE OF COUNCILORS

Question: "I can see how your political debut occurred and the role Dr. Kajima played. But, I wonder, had you given any thought to entering politics, perhaps at a later time? Or did you intend to stay in diplomacy, become an ambassador, a vice-minister?"

"I thought I would stay in the Foreign Ministry for another ten years or so. That is what I had in mind. My plan was to get another posting in Tokyo. Then, perhaps, councilor in Moscow, before returning to New York again as minister-councilor. At that point, when I would have been about forty-five, I thought I might leave diplomacy, and go into politics rather than become an ambassador. My father-in-law had different ideas. He told me that he had learned that if you want to be a successful politician, you have to start young. Otherwise, he said, you will become finance minister at the age of seventy, while your prime minister will be fifty-five. (pause, smiling) You know, he was not so far off the mark."

Question: "I see. But why run for the Upper House? The prime ministers and the top cabinet posts are chosen from the Lower House, aren't they?"

"Yes, they are. My father-in-law was ambivalent about this. He was confident that I could win a seat in the Upper House, and hold it. I could get into national politics that way. But he had mixed feelings about the Lower House. It is extremely hard to get a seat in the Commons, you know. And it is just as hard to keep. You have to gamble your life in each general election, whenever they may be called, and the competition is . . . fierce. It is a hard, insecure job. (pause) He was probably thinking of his daughter, my wife.

"Well, I resigned from the Foreign Ministry and jumped into politics, running for the House of Councilors in the National Constituency. My father-in-law's company, Kajima Corporation, is a national concern with business and local connections all over Japan. He mobilized his whole organization for the campaign, and paved the way for me. Suddenly, I was traveling around Japan, making speeches at political rallies, meetings and banquets. You know, it was an entirely new world for me--completely different than my recent diplomatic life. (smiling) Down-to-earth politicians. Tough construction people. It was fascinating.

"After all, I was born and grew up in the home of a scholar, who had a special, extraordinary way of thinking. From higher school, through Todai and in the diplomatic service, I spent my life in another special world--always with the same kind of people, educated the same way, all speaking the same Todai Law Faculty jargon. (laughing) Well, in 1964-1965, I found myself in another Japan . . . in real life, where all kinds of people exist. I am sure that many of them found me as odd as I found them. (both laughing) But I went everywhere, gave speeches, talked with all kinds of people, and in the July 1965, Upper House election, I won a seat."

Question: "You were thirty-five. Young for a councilor, weren't you?"

"Yes. I believe I was the youngest member of the Upper House. (pause) But not really so young, after all. I had thought about that when I switched over to politics. At thirty-four, I felt that my youth, my light-hearted youth, was behind me. I felt that I ought to have a more serious life--either as a serious bureaucrat, or as a serious politician. It seemed to me that a politician is more . . . free. In fact, it is not the case. As a politician, you have your constituency, your voters and supporters. (smiling) You are bound to them. Sometimes it is more difficult to know what they want."

Question: "Yes. But isn't that the way a parliamentary system should work?"

"Of course. A politician should be bound to his constituency, and he is also dependent, in a personal, intimate way on other politicians. (laughing) You have to always pay attention to other politicians, to understand them. Do you notice the way politicians greet each other, how courteously, how attentively?

"But the essence of parliamentary politics . . . and it is a good thing, mind you, is that people's opinions, even their whims, are dangerous and important. They must be courted. That is how one gets on in politics. A good politician knows this by instinct, and does it naturally, wants to do it, enjoys doing it."

Question: "While you were in the Upper House, didn't you serve on Prime Minister Sato's cabinet, as director-general of the Science and Technology Agency, in 1970-1971?"

"Yes. Prime Minister Sato was interested in me. He wanted to give me an opportunity, and he did. But, you know, I had to resign from that cabinet post to take responsibility for an incident at the agency."

Question: "I heard about that. What happened? What was the incident?"

(in a quiet, detached tone) "A landslide. Yes. The Science and Technology Agency authorized some experiments to measure the instability of land under varying conditions. The chief scientist in this project stood under one of his experimental slopes. The land on that slope proved so unstable that he, himself, was immersed, buried, and killed. So, I had to take responsibility and resign.

"Well, altogether, I spent eleven years in the Upper House, from 1965 to 1976. During the last four years in the Upper House, I decided that I must make a try for the Commons."

HOUSE OF REPRESENTATIVES

"Naturally, since my family has always been in Fukui, I went there, to my home district, to start building a constituency for the House of Representatives. I started working on that about . . . 1974."

Question: "Well, I believe there was a general election in 1972. So you started out soon after that election. Did one of the LDP incumbents from your district intend to retire, or did one of them die?"

"No. Nothing like that. I just came in, and started building a constituency. I hoped, for a time, that I might be able to get LDP endorsement, but . . . it was not to be, not that first time. In 1976, when the next general election was looming, I was asked to see the secretary-general of the party, who was Mr. Nakasone, our prime minister now. He told me I must wait for sometime, until there was an opening for me. He said, 'If you do not wait, if you force this thing, you will ruin your political future. So, be patient and wait. Otherwise, if you run against our wishes, your name will be eradicated from the list of party members.'

"If I had lost, his warning would probably have come true. Since I won, they accepted me right back into the party."

Question: "Was it a very hard fought, close election?"

(looking at me silently for some time, then in a quiet tone) "Yes. Tough. Very tough. We have a four-member district. In the election of 1976, two of the incumbents, both senior, long-standing Dietmen, were defeated and lost their seats. I defeated a senior LDP Dietman. The other loser was a Socialist, who lost to a younger Socialist. It was a hard battle. (smiling thinly) Before the election, our district was represented by three LDP and one Socialist. After the election, three LDP and one Socialist. So you see, nothing was changed."

Question: "Yes. I know how hard the party infighting is for your Lower House. How did you do it? How did you manage to get enough votes to pull that upset?"

"Door-to-door canvassing. I visited almost every single house in my hometown of Katsuyama, a town of thirty thousand people. Door to door. Those last two years before the election were especially intensive. I talked with thousands and thousands of my constituents, again and again, with their groups and their clubs. I kept shuttling back and forth from Tokyo. Hard work. A busy schedule--but always trying to appear rested and unhurried (laughing) or at least unhurried. (pause) That is it. If I tell you anymore . . . you will try to steal my seat from me." (laughter)

ROLE OF A POLITICIAN

Question: "Allright. You have told me everything you can about how a politician gets elected and gains power. But what are they supposed to do with it? Your bureaucrats seem to do most of the planning and policy formulation. Are the Dietmen there basically to legitimize the bureaucrats and, if necessary, to check them, when their policies will upset the voters?"

"Those are important tasks--to oversee and influence the civil service. But the political leadership has a task beyond that. That is to choose when the choices are not obvious, when the bureaucrats do not know or understand the choices. To create more choices. Your President Franklin Roosevelt did that when he was elected in 1932, in the worst time of your Great Depression. Churchill did that for England after Munich, in 1938. Hitler also did it for Germany, but in the most disastrous way. In Japan, Prime Minister Ikeda exercised this creative political leadership in 1960, when he made his decision to commit Japan to doubling its income within a decade. Not many people believed it was possible. He set the basic course for the next twenty years or more.

"Now, we are waiting for another course. We want economic growth to continue, but there is a sense that something else-- we don't know what it is yet or how to define it--but something more is needed. What will it be? That is the task of our political leadership?"

INTERNATIONALIZATION

Question: "Several of the people in this study have suggested that Japan's course in the coming decades will be an expanded,
intensified continuation of internationalization. They have said that
in order to continue its economic growth and to maintain its security,
Japan will engage in even more international finance and investment
as well as trade, and will take a more positive, active role in organizing the international political-economic system. Do you think that
this role will meet the need you have brought up--this somewhat
vague, undefined need?"

(long, thoughtful pause, and then in a serious, intense tone)
"I have mixed feelings about what you have said . . . on what you
have defined as internationalization, and this concept of Japan's future role. If it simply means playing the role of an expanded banker
and merchant in the world without contributing to the world anything constructive or new in the field of ideas and ways of thinking,
then, I doubt if it will work."

Comment: "I see your point. (pause) You are being critical, in a way, of the low posture, basically economic approach to
both domestic and foreign policy--if not the substance of this policy,
then its tone and goals. And since you are director-general of the
LDP International Bureau, I think your views must have support in
the party--although no one else has expressed them to me as clearly
as you have.

"Prime Minister Nakasone seems to be trying to move in the
direction you favor, and he is popular with the voters."

"Yes, he is. And he is popular for precisely this reason . . .
he has been telling things--giving his own point of view--to foreign
leaders instead of simply reacting to or answering to what they were
telling him.

"The Japanese have long had the impression that their leaders were either defending or explaining themselves without making
any noticeable impact on political leaders of other major nations.
Until quite recently international society has been built largely on
American and European leadership. The Japanese voice has been
necessarily the voice of an outsider. If the so-called internation-

ization of Japan actually means a sort of taming of Japan--a process of absorbing Japan and its culture into the established international order, it will not add anything truly valuable to the world of the future. It will just mean destroying one more old culture. I am certain that will not happen. Nobody in Japan wants that kind of internationalization, and I don't believe the rest of the world does either.

"The problem of Japan's internationalization is not, in reality, a problem solely for Japan. It is probably more a problem for America and Europe. For many Europeans their 'real world' has actually meant only an area between Berlin and Chicago or between Stockholm and Istanbul. For most Americans the world has consisted mainly of the Western Hemisphere and Western Europe. The coming of Japan as a truly major international power gives both the Japanese and other major powers an immense opportunity to rejuvenate their vision of the world. It is a challenge. Whether we like it or not, Americans and Japanese have already started taking up this challenge."

Question: "Yes, I can see that and I agree with you. We Americans talk too much about the need for Japan to internationalize but seldom think that the process applies to us as well.

"I would like to ask you about language training. Language training is not all there is to internationalization, but it is necessary, isn't it? Some time ago, I read an article of yours on language training. You were critical of the existing system in which all school children are required to study English for six years in middle and higher school. You wrote that only a pitifully small number of students actually learn English this way, because the whole system is compulsory. You proposed that a way to increase the number of Japanese really proficient in foreign languages is to have three years of voluntary language training in the higher schools where the better language teachers should devote themselves to teaching the really willing students, who are eager to learn languages, and not forced to do so."

(laughing) "Well, you certainly read it. (laughter) Yes, and if this kind of a plan is ever carried out, I think we will increase the number of people really competent in foreign languages from about 1 percent or 2 percent of our population to 5 percent or 10 percent."

Comment: "I was astonished by the article written against you by Shoichi Watanabe--a well known intellectual, isn't he? He denounced you in quite passionate language for having an 'Occupation mentality' and a 'colonial' view, because you are so eager to criticize the true Japanese way of teaching languages, and want more Japanese to really be able to speak foreign languages, rather than pass grammar tests."[5]

(In a thoughtful tone) "I certainly did not expect so much controversy over my proposal. Hmm . . . Language is a terribly important tool of international communication. At the same time, precisely for that reason, it can be a formidable barrier between peoples. I have long been advocating a complete reform of language training methods in schools around the world. For centuries, people have been wasting a vast amount of time trying to learn foreign languages. The French learning English, Germans studying French, Americans learning Spanish, and Japanese learning English. But very few people have been able to acquire enough of a foreign language to use it in a meaningful way, when they need it. But the problem is simple and can be easily corrected.

"First, languages must be taught by native speakers.

"Secondly, they must be taught intensively in a time span of less than two years.

"The people who have had experience effectively teaching and learning languages have known about these techniques for a long time. But we have done very little to change the centuries-old systems that don't work--partly because there are formidable interests involved, but also because most people have not been convinced that it is necessary to really learn foreign languages. Now, that is changing.

"Some of the ideas that I proposed are now being slowly incorporated, step by step--in a typically Japanese way--in the

---

5. Mr. Hiraizumi wrote his proposal, "Foreign Language Education in Japan--A Tentative Plan of Reforms," when he was a Councilor and Vice-Chairman of the LDP Special Committee on International Cultural Exchanges. It was published by the Government Printing Office in a pamphlet dated April 18, 1974, and sent to educational administrators. Mr. Watanabe's response, "Hiraizumi Proposal for Reform of English Education--A Plan to Invite National Decay," was published in *Shokun,* April 1975. Good translations of both articles are available in *Japan Echo,* II, 3, 1975.

Japanese education system. As a nation, Japanese are starting to become better linguists than Americans and Europeans. At least in the sense that very few Europeans and Americans can speak Japanese."

Motoo Shiina

MOTOO SHIINA represents the Second District of Iwate Prefecture in the House of Representatives--usually called the Lower House--in the National Diet. He first stood for and won his Diet seat as a Liberal Democrat in the general election of 1979, and then won reelection in the general elections of 1980, 1983, and 1986.

Since a Dietman usually has to survive at least five or six general elections before being considered for a cabinet post, Motoo Shiina is still in the intermediate stages of his political career. Nevertheless, political analysts and the media in Japan pay attention to Motoo Shiina and frequently allude to him as a future leader. He comes from a distinguished political family, with a solid base in Iwate Prefecture and with strong connections to the bureaucracy and the business world. Apart from these credentials, however, which he holds in common with a number of other Dietmen, Motoo Shiina is somewhat atypical for a conservative politician. Instead of studying law or economics, he majored in physics at Nagoya University. After working six years as a nuclear reactor physicist, he switched fields, starting and building up his own business, manufacturing precision measuring instruments for industrial machinery. Very few Diet members have backgrounds that combine science, technology, and practical business experience. Moreover, he is one of the handful (18 out of 258) LDP Dietmen who are not members of one of the party's factions.[1] Finally, although Motoo Shiina's traditional Japanese roots run deep, he is also internationalized. His English is fluent, and he communicates easily and effectively with foreigners.

---

1. See *Kokkai Binran, Showa 60 Nigatsu* (National Diet Compendium, February 1985), (Tokyo: Nihon Seikei Shimbunsha, 1985), 236.

Motoo Shiina and family.

Motoo Shiina is slim and intense. His features are sharp and clear and his hair jet black. He looks young for a man in his middle fifties. In a dark suit, he fits almost unnoticeably into any crowd of office workers on a Tokyo street. Nevertheless, at our first interview in his Diet offices, I was struck by his individuality. In conversation, he has a memorable keenness and independence of mind. In Japan, where even leaders usually fit in and go along with their group, Motoo Shiina is a bit of a maverick. He is not a rebel, but he likes to set his own course.

FAMILY BACKGROUND

Motoo Shiina, a second son, was born to Etsusaburo and Kimie Shiina, in Bunkyo-ku, Tokyo, on August 19th, 1931. Since there is a sizeable literature available in Japan on his father, Motoo was reluctant to talk about his family background. He felt that to do so would be unnecessarily repetitive. When I explained that I wanted to know about his own views on his family, he turned my request over in his mind for a long moment and then spoke out.

"My family has several well known names. Choei Takano is the first. Choei Takano (1804-1850) was a doctor and a scholar in the late Tokugawa period. He learned Dutch in order to study Western medicine.[2] He also became very interested in world politics and strategy. The more he studied these subjects the more he became concerned about Japan's future. In those years, in the 19th century, China was collapsing and Western powers were going into China and taking it over. Choei Takano was worried that the same fate might come to Japan--unless the proper steps were taken. So, he wrote books against the Tokugawa policy of keeping foreigners out of Japan, and forbidding Japanese from traveling abroad. He believed that we had to quickly learn everything we could about the foreigners, including their science and technology, in order to protect ourselves against them. The Tokugawa government did not like his criticism. They arrested Choei Takano and threw him into

---

2. The Dutch at Nagasaki were the only foreigners then permitted into Japan, and were the main source of knowledge about the West.

prison. (pausing, shaking his head) But there was a fire in Edo (the old name for Tokyo), and the prison caught fire. The police released the prisoners to escape from the fire, but ordered them to return in four days. (smiling at this thought) Almost all the prisoners returned. But Choei Takano did not. He fled from place to place, hiding from the police, and kept on writing and criticizing the government. Finally, the police found him and tried to arrest him. He resisted and was killed.[3]

(Motoo Shiina gave me a sharp, challenging look) "Did you know that my father had the same name as Choei Takano?"

Comment: "The same name? But your father's name was Etsusaburo Shiina . . . I don't understand."

(laughing merrily) "Well, in those times it was more common than now for children to be adopted and change their names. So, first they had a boyhood name, and then an adult name. Choei Takano was actually born in the family of Goto, in Iwate. In those days the place was known as Mutsu. His original name was Etsusaburo Goto. Later, he was adopted into the Takano family and his name was changed to Choei Takano. My father was also born into the Goto family in Iwate. When he was in the university, he was adopted by the Shiina family. So, you see, my father's boyhood name was also Etsusaburo Goto."

Question: "From what you have said of Choei Takano and the Goto family, I assume that they were samurai before the Meiji Restoration. Is that correct?"

"Well yes, but not at the top. They were, what do you call it? . . . retainers in a small feudal clan. Up in Sendai, there was the big Date clan. The Date daimyo (lord) lived in the great castle in Sendai. The Date clan had a cadet branch, a family connection, in Mizusawa. This branch was the Rusu clan. The Goto family was one of the samurai families in the Rusu clan. (Mizusawa is an old farming town in the narrow valley that bisects the mountains in what is now Iwate Prefecture.)

"By the way, many years after he died, Choei Takano was

3. A more dramatic account of Choei Takano's death may be found in E. Papinot, *Historical and Geographical Dictionary of Japan* (Tokyo: Charles E. Tuttle Company, Inc., 1984), 631. "Choei defended himself, killed two of his assailants, then killed himself."

honored by the Meiji government. He was given the rank of shoshii, the fourth rank in the peerage. That was in . . . let me think . . . about 1898.

"Another well known name in our family is Shimpei Goto. He was the uncle-in-law of my father. Originally a medical doctor, Shimpei Goto became the administrative chief in Taiwan, not long after Taiwan became a Japanese colony. (Japan acquired Taiwan in 1895, following a brief war with China, and lost it in 1945.) He was one of the men who founded the South Manchurian Railroad, and he became president of it. Some years later, Shimpei Goto became mayor of Tokyo. He played a big part in rebuilding the city after the Great Earthquake of 1923. He was also a cabinet minister afterward.

And then, there was my father. (long pause while he looked out the window and collected his thoughts) He was also born in Iwate. His father was mayor of that small town--Mizusawa. He was such a strict, honest mayor that he even spent his own money for the town. (smiling and shaking his head) So, naturally, he was poor--so poor that he could not afford to pay for his children's education. My father had to work as a helper in another family to earn money for school. He did house chores for them. In Japanese we call it a *shosei*. He wasn't a servant, but a kind of family helper. Still (laughing) he was very short of money.

"His older brother, who died years before my father, made it possible for him to attend the university. The older brother went into business, and did well enough to pay for my father's education. So, my father graduated from Todai (Tokyo University) in the early 1920s. He passed the Higher Civil Service examination, and went right into the Ministry of Agriculture and Industry. Almost immediately after he started, that ministry was split up into the Ministry of Agriculture and Forestry and the Ministry of Commerce and Industry (MCI). My father joined Commerce and Industry.[4]

---

4. The Ministry of Commerce and Industry was established in 1924. During World War II, it was renamed the Ministry of Munitions (MM). Following Japan's surrender in 1945, it was renamed the Ministry of International Trade and Industry (MITI). MITI is generally credited with a major role in Japan's phenomenal postwar economic growth. In his well known book, *MITI and the Japanese Miracle*, Chalmers Johnson includes Etsusaburo Shiina in that small group of economic bu-

"After working in Tokyo for about ten years, my father was sent to Manchuria in . . . 1934. Japan, you know, was sponsoring the new government in Manchukuo. Many Japanese officials were sent over to help. My father was put in charge of industrial development. There was hardly any industry there at all in 1934. So, he had the whole country surveyed . . . a geological survey . . . for minerals, coal, and iron and also for possible agricultural development. Then, he made the plans for the industrial development of Manchuria--where the mines and new railroads and factories would be.

"We stayed in Manchuria until 1939. I remember it well. It was so wide . . . vast, really, and flat. I was born here in Tokyo, you know, but I have no memory of Tokyo as a small child. My memory begins in Manchuria.

"We came back to Tokyo after the war with China had begun (1937), and my father became vice minister of the Ministry of Munitions. In 1945, after the defeat, he was purged by the Occupation. In 1953, after the Occupation was over, his purge was lifted and he ran for a seat in the House of Representatives, in our district, the Second District in Iwate. Well, he lost that election. But he ran again in 1955, and did better. He was elected eight times, the last time in . . . let me think . . . it must have been in the general election of 1976. You probably know his political career. He was Minister of MITI twice and also chief cabinet secretary twice. In the middle 1960s, he was foreign minister. He was also high in the LDP. He was Chairman of the Policy Planning Committee and lastly he was Vice President of the party.[5].

"You know, these famous people in my family are . . . a big asset to me. But there is also a danger. It is easy to become a sort of . . . family flag bearer, and not do anything serious or real. I

---

reaucrats who, using the economic and political lessons they had learned at MCI and MM, formulated and directed Japan's postwar industrial policy.
5. In addition to holding these senior and prestigious cabinet posts and party offices, Etsusaburo Shiina was an influential, behind-the-scenes party leader. For example, in 1974, when Prime Minister Kakuei Tanaka was forced by money scandals to resign, Mr. Shiina was asked to mediate the LDP factional dispute over the succession to the prime ministership, and it was he who arranged for the appointment of Takeo Miki as prime minister.

think there is some danger of that in Japanese politics now. We have a number of second-generation or third-generation Dietmen who know very little outside of election campaigns and party politics."

MANCHURIAN DAYS

Question: "Do you mind if we go back to your boyhood in Manchuria?"

"No. I like to remember Manchuria. We lived in Changchun, which means long spring. There is an old city there, but the Japanese built a new part, a modern part, with streets one hundred meters wide, long lines of trees, parks and government buildings. The Chinese are using it now, and like it very much. Around the city it is big, open country, like the American West. There was hardly any industry in the city. It was an administrative center.

"The country was big and open, and it was not such an orderly . . . established place. It was like the old American West in that way, too. When we were traveling by train in the early years of our stay, sometimes the train was stopped for two or three hours because there was an ambush down the line."

Question: "An ambush? Were they anti-Japanese guerillas, or bandits?"

"I don't know. People said that it was not easy to tell the difference.

"As a little boy there in Manchuria, I felt that the beginning period was very good. I still remember that almost every night the young men who worked for my father in the government used to get together in our house. They would talk until late about building industry . . . about building the country. Their idea was for the five races--Manchus, Chinese, Mongolians , Koreans and Japanese--to live and work together . . . in harmony. They were full of energy and hope . . . and ambitious plans for Manchukuo. I think that kind of life is good for people. Those young officials were big-hearted and cheerful. They were good to other people. I liked to be around them.

"After about three years, I felt a change in the mood. Maybe I was growing up and seeing more. But I think there was also a real change in the mood . More Japanese were coming into the country, and they were coming to make money . . . a quick profit. I began to see more of these people in Changchun. And I began to see changes . . . bad changes. For instance, there was a sort of taxi service in the town of rickshaw and horse carts. There were no meters, of course, and no rules about pricing. The rickshaw man and the passenger--most of the passengers were Japanese--would just agree on the price. At first, it went very well. The passengers were fair and generous, and the rickshaw men were satisfied. I remember how grateful they were for the generosity of the passengers. Then it changed. In the later period, there were quarrels. I saw some at the train station. In the discussions at my father's house, I heard that the Japanese passengers were underpaying and making unfair demands. These people who were flowing into Manchuria were money grabbers. They messed up the kind of society that those able, good-hearted young officials were working for. I have thought of that many times over the years. The way we deal with people is the most important question. More important than money.

SCHOOL DAYS IN WARTIME TOKYO

"I came back to Tokyo in 1939, when I was eight years old. For the first three or four months, I was sort of neurotic. Everything was too small. I was used to wide, open spaces--to a road one hundred meters wide. In Tokyo, the streets were so narrow that I thought the buildings on both sides were falling down on me. I was really . . . uncomfortable. I was put in one of the best elementary schools--Seinan Elementary School in Aoyama. That didn't help. It made it worse. The boys were all so clever, and they talked so fast. They liked to tease me because I was from Manchuria. Luckily, I was a bright student. In the first term, I got the best grades in my class. That stopped the teasing . . . and I became used to Japan.

"Then, I remember it was a few years later when Tojo made his declaration of war. I heard it on the radio. There were many victories . . . at first. I was about ten years old. It was all . . . very exciting.

"In 1943, when I was twelve, I went into the upper school. It was the Furitsu Kotogakko, the Metropolitan Higher School. It was an excellent school, with only a small number of students. The old middle school and higher school were combined into a single seven year school at that place. I think that was good for me. In the ordinary middle school in those days the oldest boys were only seventeen. But at our school, from the first year, when I was only twelve, I was thrown in with boys up to nineteen, almost adults. I learned a lot from those older boys.

"I think our school was unusual for Japan, in those wartime days. It kept a kind of liberal atmosphere. Very different from other schools where boys were strongly encouraged to prepare for the military service, and to get into special courses for becoming soldiers. But in my class, only one boy wanted to do this. The army officers who were stationed at our school resented this lack of military spirit.

"In those days, there was at least one army officer in every middle and higher school, to give military training. Ours was a strange . . . but sweet old man. A retired officer. (laughing) Do you know what he used to do? In the training class we had to crawl on the ground on our elbows and knees. If it was a nice day . . . and if the boys were tired . . . he ordered us to take a rest. He used to say, 'Stop. Listen to the beautiful song of the lark.' So we boys would lie there quietly on the ground . . . sometimes for twenty or thirty minutes. (laughing hard and shaking his head)

"Later, we had a strict officer, too. He was very cruel to my class. All the boys hated him. I was the class monitor, and we talked it over and decided to boycott one of his periods of military training."

Question: "But it was wartime. Wasn't that a serious matter?"

(smiling and speaking in a slow, careful tone) "Hmm. That was considered to be almost . . . treason. So we planned it very carefully. We boys all promised each other never to leak the plan. It was a simple plan. If anyone was absent for a day, or a period, they had to submit a written excuse, signed by their parents. So, each boy got an excuse from his parents. On that day none of us, not even one boy, appeared on the field for that officer's training class. He was on the training ground, waiting, and no one came. He was furious.

"So, this terrible officer rushed into the room of Mr. Matsuoka, the teacher in charge of my class. He told Mr. Matsuoka that we must have planned this boycott and that we must be punished. Well, Mr. Matsuoka was an artist, a painter. He understood how we felt about this officer. He managed, somehow, to protect us. He called me to his room first, and told me how angry the training officer was. He told me that our plan was a very bad, serious matter. I said, 'I know nothing about a plan. I was absent.' Then I gave Mr. Matsuoka my signed excuse. Mr. Matsuoka called the other boys to his room, one at a time. The other boys all said the same thing. (laughing merrily) What a coincidence. It went perfectly.

"Our absence also came up at the teacher's meeting. Mr. Matsuoka said the right things, and protected us. Maybe there was a serious side to this. But we boys enjoyed that incident . . . greatly.

"In the last year of the war, the boys in my class were telling each other that it would end in defeat. We saw the B-29s fly over Tokyo and drop their bombs, and there was no way to stop them. The city was being destroyed, and shortages became worse and worse. The radio news still reported victories, (smiling) but we fourteen year old boys were not fooled. Still, we wondered what adults . . . really thought. I think that war makes boys mature faster.

"There was a newspaper reporter of about twenty-eight or twenty-nine, Mr. Yoshimoto of the *Jiji Shimpo,* who was very close to my father. He used to come often to our house. One night, in autumn 1944, when my father wasn't home, Yoshimoto was chatting with me. He said, 'For Japan, it is over.' He quoted President Roosevelt's speech on war aims, and compared it to the speeches by our war leaders. He said, 'Roosevelt's speech is more concrete. It has a firm purpose. But we don't. Our aims are too abstract and vague.' He said, and I remember it clearly, ' You cannot win a war without a firm, clear purpose.' And he also predicted there would be a tremendous inflation soon after the war ended."

Question: "What effect did Mr. Yoshimoto's remarks have on you? Did they simply confirm your own ideas?"

"Yes . . . but it was different . . . and important, for an adult to say these things. I took it in a . . . cold hearted way. So, that was it. When my father came home he found out what Yoshimoto had said to me and he got angry. Not because he disagreed with Yoshimoto, but because he thought I was too young for such talk. He was worried that I would repeat what I had heard and people might think my father and our family shared these opinions."

Comment: "Hmm. Yes, I see. It was dangerous to say these things in 1944, especially in the government. People were put in jail and sometimes executed for such things."

"Yes, they were. In that last year of the war my father was always working. His job was difficult . . . no, impossible. He was trying somehow to keep up production of munitions. He went over the plans, and tried to make them as good as possible. But every day and every night some factories and materials were bombed and destroyed. So, he would work into the night to revise the plan, and again, it would be . . . destroyed. Not enough aluminum or steel. And I remember that he used to complain that despite these shortages, the army and navy refused to cooperate. Instead, they were wasting time quarreling over war materials. Also, my father used to say that the government's plan to control the whole wartime economy had turned into a mess. That it was creating shortages."

Question: "What do you recall of the air raids?"

"Well, the city was being destroyed. One raid after another. Terrible fires. Life was . . . very dangerous.

"The closest call I had was when I was traveling in July 1945, with my grandfather to Tsu City in Mie Prefecture. The house we stayed in was beside a canal. A bomb landed in the canal, close to us. The explosion was close enough to destroy the house and us, but the blast was deflected upward by the canal bank, so it just ripped off the roof and the upper part of the house. We were sitting there, and the house just blew away above our heads. We were lucky. We were not hurt. I realized . . . afterward . . . how good it was to be alive.

"I saw many dead bodies--bodies of people killed in the air raids. There was death around us after every bombing. It was common. That's the way life was. But, you know, it was not as grim as it sounds. I learned that people are very . . . resilient. I saw people who had lost everything--their homes and even their families --pull themselves together the next day, and go on living. If they were not injured, if they were alive and in one piece, they cheered up. They said a polite good morning. They found something to eat. There was very little food, but people shared whatever there was. If something funny happened, or someone told a joke, they laughed. Not a forced laugh, but real, healthy laughing. The environment was terrible . . . unnatural. But their laughter was natural."

Question: "Several other people in this study who are about your age were taken out of school toward the end of the war to work in factories, to dig ditches, or do other war work. Did that happen to you?"

"The class that was one year ahead of mine did that. I was only sent to a factory to work temporarily, for a short time. It was nothing."

Question: "How was the food situation?"

"Bad. We were hungry. (laughing) Teenage boys always seem hungry. But we were really hungry. Not to the point of . . . serious malnutrition, but to the point of discomfort.

"When I see friends from those days, we joke that our hunger then is bad for our health now. We got into the habit of finishing whatever was put before us. (laughing) So now, even when we are stuffed, we still eat whatever is on the table. (pause, then in a more serious tone) The deepest feeling that I have--and I share it with others my age--is that something like that could happen again. It is easy--easier than people who have not had the experience think --to go from a full stomach and peace to hunger and war. Life can quickly become . . . unpredictable.

"But, you know, my generation learned to survive, to be resilient. We learned to share when there was not enough for everyone--and to smile when times were hard. I don't know if the postwar generation has these qualities. There is so much wealth now, but people seem to be more selfish . . . more greedy. Well, I wonder if these people . . . if our whole society could survive hard times again . . . if it had to."

AFTERMATH OF DEFEAT

"In some ways, though, I think the year after the war was worse . . . for me. Suddenly, there were accusations about everything in the past, everything Japan had done . . . everywhere . . . for twenty, thirty, even forty years before the war. Occupation headquarters told NHK (the government radio station) to broadcast a program every night which was titled, "The Truth," or something like that. Our whole history, all the way back to the war with China in the 1890s, was denounced as evil . . . as aggression. There was nothing else to do in the evening, and nothing else on the radio, so everyone listened to this program. They pounded, and pounded, and pounded. It was too much. It went too far.

"In the schools, the students were accusing the teachers. 'Why did you tell us the emperor was a god? Why didn't you protest against the war? Why did you cooperate in Japan's aggression?' For one year, at least, school was very messy. The students had no respect for the teachers. Everyone was making wild accusations.

"The Communists took advantage of that atmosphere. There was a cell in each school. They were the leaders in accusing the teachers. They were always calling for democratization, but they really were trying to confuse and disrupt the school . . . and our whole society."

Question: "Did it seem to you that they were accusing your own family and your own father?"

"Yes. I *knew* that they were twisting things. What they said was not an accurate picture. But you know, I didn't argue with them. Somehow, I got along with those people, first in high school, and then later at Nagoya University. (smiling at the memory) The physics students at Nagoya University were bright, excellent students, but most of them were impressed by Communist ideas. Some were real party members, and others were pro-Communist."

NAGOYA UNIVERSITY

Question: "You entered Nagoya University in 1950, I believe. Was there any particular reason you chose Nagoya?"

"Nagoya was very good in physics, better than Todai (University of Tokyo), in more advanced fields such as elementary particle physics and nuclear physics."

Question: "How did you come to be interested in nuclear physics and elementary particles?"

"My high school physics teacher--Mr. Kusukawa--was excellent. He made physics . . . very imaginative. It was not a dry, technical subject. He taught us how physicists expound a hypothesis, check it with experiments, and then correct the hypothesis. It is imaginative . . . and yet logical. A good book on physics is like a well-written detective story. (pause, and then in a low, firm voice) That is how I was attracted to that subject.

"I knew that I would have to talk to my father about it. I was ready for his opposition. He was a graduate of Tokyo Law and a bureaucrat, and I thought he would not like my choice. So I expected trouble.

"But he told me it was a good idea to study science. (laughing) He really surprised me. And then he explained why he liked my plan. He said that when he was about to graduate from Todai, and had already passed the examination to become a bureaucrat, he felt very proud of himself and he visited Shimpei Goto, his important relative, to tell him he would become an official at the Ministry of Agriculture and Industry. But Shimpei Goto was not very impressed. He told my father that the study of jurisprudence and law is useful for settling problems between people. But in modern society, and especially in agriculture and industry, that is not enough. He said, 'You should learn about science and technology. In these days, officials should understand these subjects, too. I can talk to your ministry and get them to postpone your job for one year, and arrange for you to work in a research laboratory. Just for a year . . . to see what science is like.'

"My father was twenty-four or twenty-five years old then, and very proud that he had passed the government examination. Of course, he turned down Shimpei Goto's proposal. (chuckling) But later, when he was sent to Manchuria and given the job of building industry from scratch, he remembered Goto's advice. He told me that Goto had been right, after all. So, he was pleased that I wanted to study natural science.

"I am grateful to my father for that. I took the entrance examination for the Physics Faculty at Nagoya, and got in. That faculty was noted for having really outstanding physicists. They had a tradition going back to prewar days, to Dr. Nishina, who had been the head of the Institute of Science. Nishina had studied in Copenhagen under Dr. Niels Bohr. And he was noted as a physicist who had suggested the possibility of the atomic bomb.

"The academic atmosphere was excellent, and the boys-- there were eighteen of us in my class--were bright. So bright that at first I had a little bit of an inferiority complex. There are *must* books which must be read and mastered if you want to claim to be a physicist, and I discovered that the other boys had already read almost all of them. I had to work hard to catch up. The lectures were . . . fascinating . . . and stimulating. Those famous physicists would go to the blackboard empty-handed and write their equations and formulas and explain them. The students would listen and watch--never taking notes--in a relaxed manner. Sometimes a student would say, 'Sensei (teacher), I think what you just put on the board is wrong.' Then, the professor would check it, and if the student was right he would just say, 'Yes, you are right,' and correct his error and go on. It was an open, relaxed discussion--very different than most education in Japan.

"That was the Copenhagen spirit that Dr. Nishina established--very liberal, free, and flexible. The students were competitive, but the atmosphere was open and friendly. We would discuss some problem, take a walk over to the nearby zoo and maybe solve it there, and then go for a drink or two.

"But you know, I discovered that I was not bright enough to be in the top echelon in physics. I did not have the talent to . . . make a discovery or a breakthrough. I had enough talent to appreciate and enjoy the instruction at Nagoya, but I decided that I should not stay in theoretical physics. After graduation, I goofed around

for some time at Nagoya, and then I decided to go into nuclear reactor physics."

Question: "You mentioned that these bright students in your
class were almost all Communists or sympathizers. How did that
work out?"

(smiling) "There were no serious problems over that. But I
learned some things about these Communists. In my class of eighteen, two-thirds were party members or sympathizers. At that time,
Marxism and communism were . . . fashionable. We all lived
together, and they often talked about communism and tried to get me
to join them. I would discuss with them, but I would not accept
their views, and they knew it.

"I found . . . grave contradictions between their beliefs and
their . . . behavior. They used to preach the love of all human beings . . . in the vast sense, you know. But in practice, most of them
were not kind or helpful, in an everyday, practical way.

"They were also paranoid. They thought that the government, the Capitalists, and the police were hunting them, night and
day. They believed they were surrounded by plots and spies.
Sometimes, it was . . . absurd. In those days, the Communist Party
advocated violence, and there was a secret publication--a very secret
pamphlet on how to make and use bombs. On the cover, they enti-
tled it *Kyukon Saibai-Ho*, which means, how to raise a good bulb
or tuber. (smiling and shaking his head at the memory) Well, one
of those Communists was carrying this pamphlet in his school bag.
And he just left the bag somewhere. Of course, someone found his
bag and turned it in to the police box in our neighborhood.

"The Communists in the Science Faculty called an emergency meeting. About thirty members gathered, and severely questioned the man who lost his bag. They expected the police . . . to
swoop down on them. They felt their whole organization was in
great danger because of this one man. Some of them were really
accusing this student.

"So, I asked them what evidence they had that the police
knew about their bomb pamphlet--that the police knew it was in the
lost bag. They thought I was terribly simple-minded--that I did not
understand the police--or anything. I told them that if it was turned
in to the lost-and-found, the bag would be intact, unopened. I said

I would pick it up for them, if they would describe it to me. They were really surprised. They warned me of the great danger. They said that if I did not come out from the police station, they would attack it. (laughing)

"I went there, and said that I had lost my school bag. A woman police officer asked me to tell her the color and markings. I told her, and also I said there were three books, a pamphlet, and some pencils inside. She looked in the bag, counted, and said, 'Yes, this is the right one. Please be more careful next time.' " (much laughter)

Question: "So you were a hero?" (more laughter)

"Yes. A hero. And they were so grateful that they never again asked me to join the party. (laughter) But we remained friends. You know, most of them got out of the Communist Party after they left school. It was just a childhood disease."

REACTOR PHYSICS AND THE ARGONNE LABORATORY

Question: "Would you tell me about your work as a nuclear reactor physicist?"

"Well, I stayed at Nagoya for about a year after I took my degree in 1953--working in a kind of loosely structured graduate course. Then, in 1955, I got a job in the Nuclear Electric Power Development Company. (pausing and smiling at the memory) It was the very beginning of the nuclear power industry in Japan. They were still trying to decide what to do . . . what approach to take. My job was not a job . . . in the usual sense. I had no regular duties. They wanted me to keep studying . . . reading the books I enjoyed reading. (chuckling)

"In 1959, I was sent over to Argonne National Laboratory, near Chicago, for more study. At first, I spent my days working over equations and now and then going to a special lecture. One of the lectures was about nuclear reactor physics. The man who gave that lecture mentioned this book by Weinberg, head of Oak Ridge (walking over to the book shelf, finding the book and handing it to me) and said it is a must reading, and must be studied very careful-ly. Afterward, I chatted with him about this book, and he said,

'You know this book very well.' So I told him, 'Well, I spent some time on it in Japan.' He was a little surprised, but then he laughed and he said, 'In that case, there was no need for you to come here. You have already done the work.' I realized that he was serious, and I did not have to worry about my studies. I decided to bring my wife over, and to travel and learn about America . . . attending conferences and traveling on our own."

Question: "How long did you stay?"

"Just one year. But I was very lucky, and it was a . . . great year. When I first arrived at Argonne, all of us foreign physicists and engineers stayed in a college dormitory close by. Then we moved into a guest house on the Argonne compound. That was comfortable and convenient, but still . . . (shaking his head, smiling) too confining . . . like a school. So, I rented a small house for me and my wife. She joined me two months after I arrived. But you know, my pay was not very much and the rent was high. So, we asked our friend from Italy--Zizo Livolsi--to move into our house as a boarder, and to help pay the rent. He is . . . very friendly . . . a very good-natured man. Zizo married an American girl, and now he works in Connecticut. Well, we shared that little house together for about three months and then a surprising thing happened. (shaking his head and smiling at the memory)

"When I was still living in the dormitory, all of us foreign physicists and engineers from Argonne had been invited to a reception--in a town near Chicago--for the Pan American Games. I was asked to supply some background music on the piano, so I played a little."

Comment: "I heard that you also play the violin . . . fairly well."

"Not so well. But I enjoy it. So, I was playing the piano, and sipping my drink, and a couple struck up a conversation with me--Mr. and Mrs. Depner--Bill and Audrey Depner. He was the chief of one of the manufacturing divisions of Western Electric Telephone Company. He had come to America from Germany as a teenager, started as an errand boy of that company, and worked his way up. We got to be friends with the Depners, and they helped us when we moved into our little house. They used to invite us over, and we would go and see them. Then, one day, Mr. Depner said, 'I have been thinking about your house. For the rent you are paying, it is small and shabby. We know that you are only here for one year, and we feel guilty--as Americans--to see you spend so much money on that house. You should spend it more usefully. So, Audrey and I want to invite you to live in our house. No rent. We will just split the cost of groceries.'

"Well, my wife and I were . . . astonished. . . and we accepted . . . and we had a wonderful time. They had a big, beautiful house in a suburb west of Chicago. The Depners said that ever since the Pan American Games reception, they had been thinking that they didn't know any foreigners. They wanted to know people from all over the world. So, they asked us to invite our friends from Argonne to their house, almost every weekend, for drinks, for food, and for talk. Sometimes five or six friends came. Sometimes there were thirty. They continued doing that, after my wife and I came back to Japan. So, now the Depners have hundreds of friends all over the world. They keep in touch. Sometimes they visit, and they always send cards at Christmas."

Question: "Were their children all grown and on their own?"

"Mrs. Depner had a grown child, who lived somewhere else. Between them, they had no children. Some years after we lived with them, they moved to northern Michigan. That's where they live now. Whenever I am in the U.S. and I have the time, I go there and stay with them. I feel at home, like one of the family, when we are together. I help peel peaches and cut wood.

"They are beautiful people. Knowing the Depners is . . . one of the most precious things in my life. (long pause)

"Well . . . when I got back to Japan, I found that some decisions had been made about nuclear power development. Before I had left, there were plans for building our own reactor from scratch. That is what I hoped to work on. But the national policy decision was to buy shelf items. So, there was not much use for a reactor physicist. I decided that I had better move into some other work."

BECOMING A BUSINESSMAN

"I spent about two years deciding what to do, planning and making preparations. Then, in 1963, I started a small company for making measuring instruments for industrial use. The company is called Samtak Incorporated."

Question: "Yes. Several people have told me that you are a self-made businessman. What led you to choose measuring instruments?"

"I had a friend who had some good design ideas for this equipment. He is not formally educated--does not have a degree--but he is a very good engineer. We worked on it together, and decided to set up a company. We began on a small scale--renting the second floor of an old factory in West Chofu (Tokyo suburb), and employing seven workers. Our first product was a precision speedometer for machines, with a unique detecting mechanism. The feedback from this instrument could be used for numerically controlled machine tools--in the control system of a steel mill, for instance. After several years of life-or-death struggle, it worked out quite well, quite profitably.

"When our landlord company downstairs went bankrupt, we bought the property and now it is our headquarters. Recently, we also bought another factory in Kanagawa Prefecture (also next to Tokyo). So, we have two factories and a small subsidiary workshop here in Tokyo. We employ about 120 workers.

"We started out in 1963 with a simple transistor, and now we are using LSIs (large scale integrated circuits), and making components for automatic control systems and for robots. The LSIs have been bringing down our production costs, and keeping up profits."

Question: "Have you been giving your main attention to the manufacturing side of the business, or to the financial side?"

"Well, I have worked on both sides, and I have to know both. But I arranged for the financing--for the bank loans. I found that I was . . . (laughing) not too bad at that. I liked doing it. So, I became a businessman. Because of my experience in building a business from scratch, MITI asked me to sit on the board of directors of the World Economy Information Services. I was also invited to be on the board of the Asia Club. This foundation works at cultural and educational exchanges with countries in Asia that are trying to build up their industries . . . and they also support our economic and business activities in Asia. (pausing and smiling) When I talk with the economists at some of these board meetings, I realize that I am a businessman . . . that our minds work differently."

POLITICS

Question: "During the years when you were working in nuclear reactor physics and at building up Samtak, did you have any interest or experience in politics, or were you too busy for that?"

(long, thoughtful pause, looking out the window and then swinging around to face me) "I was not really interested in politics in those days, but I spent time--not much--working at it. I did it for my father's sake. I knew he was a good politician, and was doing useful work. So, I helped in his election campaigns . . . right from his first try in 1953. I took some days off from my own work and went to the Second District and made some speeches and helped out in any way he wanted. As soon as the election was over, I used to go straight back to my work.

"That was my political experience until 1979, when my father decided to retire. Then, his supporters talked it over--very thoroughly--and decided that I was the best choice to succeed him. They came to me and said, 'Please run for your father's seat. It is the easiest way. The voters know the Shiina name.' "

Comment: (both of us laughing) "Well, that is undeniable, and crucial in elections."

"Well, I made a small speech to them. I said, 'Being a Dietman is a very important job, but I am against the trend of having second generation Dietmen. The LDP is a good party and has done a good job governing this country, until now. The main reason is that the LDP was established in the 1950s and has been run by people who had experience in administration and decision making--national level bureaucrats, for example--who made national policy and administered it. They understand how the country works and its real, broad interests. Now--I said--the sons of these experienced, able men are taking their father's seats in the Diet. But they don't have their father's experience. They have only worked as secretaries for their fathers, or as junior executives. They have not made national policies, or been responsible for a bank note or run an entire company. If this trend goes on, the LDP will become a party of inexperienced people who just like being in politics. This trend should be stopped. It will be a good example for the party if I do not run for my father's seat. My father also believes that this trend should be stopped. That is why I decline your offer.'

"Then, one of them said that exactly because of my clear understanding of politics, he believed that their choice had been right. Most of the others nodded their heads in agreement."

Question: "How long did it take you to change your mind?"

"About three months. (very seriously) The final point . . . the reason I changed my mind was that I decided I *was* qualified for politics, and that this was my best and maybe my last chance to get into the Lower House. Even then, one side of me was against running--strongly against running. 'But', I thought, 'if there is a small chance that when I come to die I will regret not going into politics, I should go into it and know what it really is. I am always free to leave.' I suppose that is the final reason."

Question: "Well, that was six years and three general elections ago. How do you feel now about that decision?"

(pause) "I don't regret it. I have found that I can be useful. I can do some worthwhile, useful things. Then, there is a paradox. Since I feel this way, it is important for me to be in the Lower House. But that means I have to keep getting elected, hopefully with a safe margin. But this leads to a fundamental, difficult question."

Question: "I realize that this is a sensitive area, but could you explain what you mean . . . give me an example?"

(after a slight pause, in a level, clear tone) "I have to be very careful how I handle requests from my constituents in my district. Sometimes they insist that I support policies that . . . seem unreasonable to me. Then, I am tempted to give them a flat no. Of course, if I did, I would soon lose my seat. They want more railroad construction, and a bridge or two, and another recreation center and so on. (shaking head sadly) They do not understand the budget deficit and they are not worried about it."

Comment: "I imagine that the railroad building and the bridges and recreation centers are also attractive to the construction industry."

"Oh yes, very attractive. And they have lots of connections, and influence many votes. So, I have to find some middle ground. I try to find a good political argument for my position.

"But, this compromising is always . . . tricky. Once you start . . . it is easy to compromise away everything. I don't want to do that."

Comment: "Yes. I see your point. But I have been out in the countryside, and I can see why the voters keep pressing for rice subsidies and railroad trains, and more bridges and recreation centers. These have all made the countryside much richer than it was twenty-five years ago, when I first saw it. Along with the public improvements, they also have new houses, and fine pickup trucks, and good farm machinery."

"Yes. That is fine. Those are all good changes. But lately, many farmers are getting too deeply in debt, and are on the verge of bankruptcy--even if they live in a beautiful house. They borrowed too much from the Agricultural Cooperative. The coops don't want to foreclose . . . to take their land. But even so, there are more cases of bankruptcy.

"But, you know, there is a long-range shift going on in farming districts like mine. The number of farmers will decrease very rapidly in about ten years, and go on decreasing until about twenty-five years from now. The biggest reason for the farmers' improvement was the U.S. Occupation land reform. That made all the poor, tenant farmers into small landlords, and they loved their land. It was everything to them. Now, the sons of those small landlords are in their fifties and sixties, and they also have a strong feeling for their land. But in ten or fifteen years, most of them will be too old to work their farms. And most of their children are not so bound to the land. The third generation has no memory of being poor, landless farmers. They have more education, and have been well off. They think about farming as a job . . . or a business . . .

from the standpoint of profit and loss. This third generation will see
that the farm economy is tightening, becoming more risky and less
profitable, and many of them will want to leave their farms, if their
proprietary right to the land is firmly protected."

Question: "For Tokyo, or other big, over-crowded cities?
Won't that create economic and political problems? Aren't the
farming districts already too lightly populated?"

"No, no. They will stay in our prefecture. But they will
move to towns and take jobs in industry and services. Because of
the Bullet trains, more industry is coming to Iwate. Fujitsu and
Toshiba have opened chip plants, and Matsushita has a big factory
for communications equipment. These companies are moving into
towns like Hanamaki, Kitakami, Mizusawa, and Kanegasaki.

"So, I think this can work out very well, if we are patient
and if over time we gradually lower the rice subsidies. Even now,
many of our marginal farmers only get 20 percent of their income
from farming. As the number of industrial jobs increases in our
towns, it will not be such a hardship to leave farming. And the remaining, larger farms will be more efficient and cost everybody less
in taxes and food prices.

"Well, you can see that I favor this decentralized, local industrialization. That is one of the most important goals that I am
working for. So, (smiling) I also push for local pork barrel projects, but the ones I want are for infrastructure, to attract industry--
certain roads and schools and water-works . . . and some selected
stations on the Bullet train line. (in a serious tone) When these
projects are coming along, then I can persuade more companies to
do business in our district.

"The people in my constituency--the farmers and small busi-
nessmen--are sensitive to these trends, and are willing to adjust.
They are more willing to adjust than the city council members and
the prefectural council members and local bureaucrats. Those are
the people who are resisting change."

Question: "How do you gather your information or impressions of what the voters think?"

"When I go around my constituency, I don't like to give
speeches in auditoriums. My policy is to organize many small
meetings of . . . oh, twenty or thirty people, where we sit down

and talk together for about two hours, in an informal, direct way. In a setting like that, we can really have an exchange of views, and people tell me what they think."

Question: "Do you also discuss foreign policy and security issues at these meetings?"

"Oh yes. Many of the people in my district know that the Soviets are much stronger in Asia than they used to be, and that our American friends do not have the overwhelming advantage they had fifteen or twenty years ago. But they don't want to spend more money on defense--not yet. They feel that Japan is still . . . pretty safe, and that maybe a military buildup would increase tensions and danger. If it really becomes necessary to spend more and to make a greater defense effort, they . . . are prepared to do it.

"You know, at these meetings I tell them some of my own views--that we should spend our defense budget more efficiently. We should spend more for equipment and weapons and less for personnel--for salaries. We should have fewer people on active duty in the Self Defense Forces--especially in the ground forces-- and a larger, better-trained reserve that we can call up in an emergency. More like the Swiss. We need more helicopters. Our forces should be very mobile, on land and at sea.

"We have even discussed the relationship of nuclear weapons and conventional forces. My view is that the more destructive a weapon is the higher the threshold for its use--especially for our side, especially for the U.S. It is as simple as that. That means that unless it is the ultimate emergency, or crisis, we cannot count on U.S. nuclear weapons to defend us. Therefore, there must be adequate conventional forces. I developed this idea several years ago in an article I wrote for a meeting at Stanford."

Question: "How do your constituents react to that?"

"Well, the younger ones see my point, and they agree with it. (smiling) But still, they don't think we need a bigger defense budget--not now."

MARRIAGE AND FAMILY

Question: "Do you mind if we change the subject and talk about your family? Was yours an arranged marriage?"

"My marriage was not arranged. I found my wife . . . (smiling) and she found me. We married just about two years before we went to the U.S.--in 1958."

Question: "How did you happen to meet?"

"Some friends of mine introduced us. It was not long after I came to Tokyo to work as a nuclear reactor physicist. When we had made up our minds to marry, I went and told my parents that I want to marry this girl. You know, I expected that they would want the usual investigation of her family--to see if there are any criminals or crazy people in her bloodline. That was the customary thing here in Japan. But they didn't ask for that. They listened to everything I wanted to tell them, and then they said, 'If you like her, then go ahead.' My father was . . . especially understanding. (smiling very deeply) We have been married for twenty-seven years--very, very happily.

"When we married, Kishi (Nobusuke) was prime minister. He and my father were good friends and Kishi has known me since I was a boy in Manchuria. So, he came to our wedding reception. It was a small, intimate reception--only about forty-five people. I appreciated that. Two years ago, when our daughter married, I asked Prime Minister Nakasone to attend her wedding . . . and he was there."

Question: "Is your daughter the oldest child?"

"Yes. We have three. A daughter and two boys. (laughing and shaking his head) We always joke that our daughter should have been a boy. She is very able . . . bright, quick, and talented. My wife and I are very glad that she married a wonderful man. He is an official at MITI, exceptionally bright--(laughing) not one of these bureaucratic cart horses. Also, he is an exceptionally loving husband. Now, we have a small grandchild . . . (smiling very deeply) two months old."

Comment: "Congratulations."

"Our older boy has a liking for music. He is pretty good at the violin, and plays in a youth orchestra. He also helps to manage the orchestra--which is a difficult job. They are a big group. He is doing allright.

"With our third child, we have a very grave problem. He is autistic."

Question: (pause) "He does not talk? He does not respond?"

"It is not that way, with him. He is much better than the average autistic boy. He responds. He is understandable . . . in his way. But still, it is our life long problem. He is twenty years old now, and in a way, a charming boy. He talks . . . when he wants to. It is very selective. In some ways, his brain is exceptional. I have gotten to know many autistic boys and girls, and some of them are able to do . . . special things. My child has memorized all the calendars from at least 1850 to 2100. He knows the day of the week for every date. When he meets someone, he asks their birthday, and then instantly tells them what day of the week they were born, or will celebrate their birthday. He knows hundreds of people's birth dates, and asks me to call them on their birthdays."

Question: "Do you think he will be able to put this to use for himself in some way?"

"No. That is the problem. He will never be able to hold a job. This has been very hard for my wife . . . and for me. (pause, looking out the window, speaking slowly) We came to the conclusion--some years ago--that even though this is bad, it is not totally bad. Because of our child, we know many handicapped people, and we know their hardship and the hardships of their families. This has opened our eyes. It has made us more understanding about . . . other disadvantaged people in our society. (swinging around to face me, smiling slightly, in a brighter voice) So, it is not totally bad. That's it. And when I step back and look at it, well, we are a happy family and a lucky family."

JAPAN AND THE WORLD

Question: "There is a lot of writing and talk in Japan these days about *kokusaika*, internationalization. What does internationalization mean to you? How do you think it is working for Japan?"

"Hmm. Internationalization. (thoughtful pause) I am not sure I know what it means. It includes, well, so many possibilities. In practical terms, for the future, it means that we Japanese have to learn to think and work together with the other advanced, industrialized countries--with you Americans and with the West Europeans. I think we are just beginning to learn how to do that.

"Up to now, we selected and took the best things from Western civilization--in science, technology, and art--and used them for ourselves. But we changed ourselves as little as possible. We had to change in some ways, you know (smiling), but usually it was unintentional or against our will. Now, we can't keep skimming off the cream anymore. In order to keep developing we have to learn to really interact--to think and work together, in science and technology and in politics and economics.

"To some extent, our education system and our universities have to change. The teachers say they favor internationalization, but many of them are really uncomfortable with foreigners and foreign ideas. Especially the older ones. I think that some of the young teachers and university faculty are much more open and ready for what I am talking about, and I hope that they will get a chance to do it.

"But this internationalization is one aspect--or one way of approaching a whole set of global problems and policies. Shall I?"

Comment: "Why yes, of course."

"We, in the First World, have to work out some basis upon which we will build our future cooperation. I see a number of problems here. There is the problem of what Herman Kahn called 'educated incapacity'--a kind of hyper-conservatism with a high level of education and a 'sophisticated' way of thinking that masquerades as humanitarian and idealistic. This educated incapacity is most common in Western Europe, but it also exists in Japan and in the U.S. It is the attitude of rich, comfortable people, who while calling for various public causes, more than anything else want to be comfortable and hang on to what they have. They are afraid of any real change, technological, economic, or social. We cannot be static. We have to move forward and continue our own scientific and industrial development. But in order to do it, we must have a firm belief in a better world and the spirit to work towards it. That is the necessary basis for helping the Third World, and that is the necessary basis for keeping ourselves secure against the Soviets.

"I think that waves of important technological and industrial innovation come along about every thirty years. Another wave is just beginning to build up. I think the Americans and Japanese are confident enough and energetic enough to catch it, surf on it. I hope the Western Europeans will do it, too.

"We should not try to organize or program scientific and technological progress. There is too much of a tendency to do that in Japan--as we see in the fifth-generation computer project. The best way is to encourage a free, open, creative environment in the universities and in industry. Let intelligent people, people with ideas, try them out--even if they seem to duplicate each other or propose silly schemes. I really believe that the most creativity and progress come out of that kind of free, unprogrammed, somewhat disorganized environment.

(smiling) "The Soviet Union demonstrates my point--in a negative way. They are always organizing their scientific, industrial, and military research--deciding we will not do B and C--we will work only on A. Then, after a few years, they realize that in the confused West, which is full of irrational contradictions, B and C led to important breakthroughs. (laughing) So, they are always behind . . . always sending spies to learn what they decided was not going to be important. No one, no government or committee, is smart enough to really organize research.

"Another important issue is that we must find a way to coordinate our defense policies and strategies with our civilian, peacetime economies. The military strategists are focusing on war and deterrence, but they tend to ignore the economy--except at budget time. The economists tend to see the military budget almost entirely in economic terms. They like to avoid politics and strategy. This is a real danger for our countries. The strategists could bankrupt us, or the economists could get us killed. We have to find some intelligent way to coordinate them--to get them to share resources instead of always competing for them.

"It is going to take time, a lot more time than we used to think, for the poor countries to start curing their poverty. We have to keep working with them, helping them . . . and not getting too impatient when they blame us for all their problems or make unrealistic demands. The important things are to build roads, and power plants, and factories, and schools--together. Doing practical, useful things together is the best way for them to develop, and the best way to break down bitterness and misunderstanding between us."

Question: "How do you propose to deal with the Soviets?"

"I think it is a battle of patience and endurance. If the West stays reasonably strong economically and militarily, I don't think it will come to a war. I believe that our system is better--much better than theirs. It is not perfect, but it is much freer and better for people, and much more productive and powerful. So, the most important point is to keep our system going and working well. If we do that, we will naturally stay ahead of them and we will be safe. Maybe in one hundred years or two hundred years they will realize that their system is bad and change it by themselves."

Question: "That is the most long-range and patient version of containment that I have heard. You are really serious about this?"

"Yes. (smiling) I am completely serious about this. We don't have to always be looking for agreements and compromises with the Soviets. We can avoid war, and we should keep our countries healthy and strong, and let the future work for us."

Kazuo Aichi

KAZUO AICHI represents the First District of Miyagi Prefecture in the House of Representatives of the National Diet. Miyagi is a prosperous farming district on the Pacific coast of northern Honshu. It is blessed with a large, fertile coastal plain flanked by the rugged, beautiful mountains that have made most of northern Honshu an economic backwater. Although he is now in his early fifties, young for a Japanese politician, Kazuo Aichi has weathered five general elections. He first stood for and won his Diet seat as a Liberal Democrat in 1976.

Kazuo Aichi is in the intermediate stages of his political career, and he too, is frequently mentioned in the media as a promising future leader. His constituency in Miyagi is considered solid. Beginning with his first election victory in 1976, he has been one of the leading vote gatherers among the five Lower House members representing the First District.[1] He has strong ties with the bureaucracy and the business world. Mr. Aichi has shown considerable skill in harmonizing the conflicting interests and values in the conservative LDP. In many respects, he is a model of the "new" LDP politician, clean-cut, cosmopolitan, and an advocate of tax and education reform. At the same time, however, he is a member of the faction of the party that was headed by Kakuei Tanaka before the faction was taken over by the current prime minister, Noboru Takeshita. Kakuei Tanaka is a self-made construction millionaire. A former prime minister who was forced out of office in 1974, he was arrested and spent several weeks in jail because of his involvement in the Lockheed bribery scandal. With his gravelly voice, his

---

1. *Seikan Yoran, Showa 59 Shunkigo* (Political Directory, Spring 1984), (Tokyo: Seisaku Jihosha, 1984), 39.

Graduation day at Tokyo University, 1961: directing the chorus club and with his mother, Chiyo Nakada.

A recent photo, with family.

folksy Niigata style, and his aura of scandal, Tanaka is the epitome of an old-guard politician. Although advised to cut his ties with Tanaka during the 1976 election, Kazuo Aichi remained loyal to the old man, and has never spoken out against him.[2]

Mr. Aichi is a second-generation politician and the scion of a distinguished political family. Kiichi Aichi, his namesake, began his career in the Ministry of Finance, entered politics in 1950, and rose very quickly to cabinet rank. He held nine cabinet posts during his political career, and served in every administration until his death in 1973. He was twice appointed to the influential position of chief cabinet secretary, and also served as minister of foreign affairs and minister of finance, two senior cabinet appointments.[3] Although the Aichi name has certainly helped Kazuo, he had to work unusually hard to convince the politicians and voters in Miyagi that he was a worthy heir to the Aichi family. Kazuo is an adopted son-in-law, whose family is from Toyama Prefecture, and he had no local ties in Miyagi until he moved there in 1974.

I met Mr. Aichi in April 1985, at his offices in the the Second Diet office building on the park-like grounds of the National Diet in Nagata-cho, Tokyo. When I entered, he was in the reception alcove, busy dictating a note to his stenographer. He is tall for a Japanese of his generation, slim and fit. He has a broad brow, strong but neat features, and a firm chin. When he is being serious or attentive, he conveys a strong sense of maturity and responsibility. When he grins, he is boyish. He quickly finished his note, informally introduced himself, and led me into his office. It is a modest room, somewhat crowded with a large desk set in a corner, and a group of old couches and armchairs surrounding a glass-covered coffee table. One wall is covered with photos, mostly of Mr. Aichi and his family and political friends, including several of him in action on the ski slopes in Miyagi--which explained his unusually fresh color and his springy step. On another wall is a very large, detailed map of the First District, stuck full of colored pins. An old

---

2. See *Kokkai Binran, Showa 60 Nigatsu* (National Diet Compendium, February 1985), (Tokyo: Nihon Seikei Shimbunsha, 1985), 334.

3. *Showashi Jiten* (Historical Dictionary of the Showa Era), (Tokyo: Showashi Kenkyukai, 1984). Also see *Jinjikoshinroku* (Personnel Directory) 24th Edition, (Tokyo: Jinjikoshinjo, 1984).

pendulum wall clock, and an elegant *bonsai* make the room cozy.
The large picture-window looks out over the Diet grounds, which
were lush and green on that rainy spring morning.

We sipped coffee and exchanged pleasantries. Mr. Aichi's
English was slow, punctuated with pauses but correct and relaxed.
Following one of his longer pauses, Mr. Aichi told me that his English was rusty and asked if we could continue in Japanese. He
explained that he would be willing to participate in this study on internationalization, but did not feel confident about being interviewed
in English--at least not in the first stages. Instead, he proposed to
respond to written questions by preparing a taped interview of his
life in Japanese, which would be translated into English by his
young American aide, Mr. David Hirsch. I explained to Mr. Aichi
that in terms of this study, an internationalized Japanese means a
Japanese who is comfortable in a foreign language. Did he feel that
he fit that definition? He smilingly took up the challenge, switched
back to English, and choosing his words carefully, assured me that
he would meet with me again after I had listened to the tapes he
would make, and discuss any questions I might have, all in English.
Feeling that this was a fair and generous approach, I agreed. When
I listened to the tapes, I could not help but notice that Mr. Aichi is
almost as deliberate and leisurely in choosing his words in Japanese
as in English. At our second meeting, a two hour session in July,
during which we clarified his tapes and discussed several additional
topics, Mr. Aichi was indeed comfortable and at ease in English.

Early in our first meeting, Mr. Aichi spoke of his family
background.

FAMILY

"You probably know that I am a second generation politician, following in the footsteps of my father. That is not unusual in
Japan. But my situation is . . . somewhat special. My father, Kiichi Aichi, had no children, and was anxious to carry on his family
name. So, he adopted my wife as his daughter. He expected that
when she married, her husband would take the Aichi name. I want
you to know that my original family--and also my wife's original

family--still exist. We are very close to them, as well as to the Aichi family."

Kazuo Aichi was born in Nagoya, where his father was then working, on July 20, 1937, to Ryokichi and Chiyo Nakada, but his birth was registered in Toyama Prefecture, the family seat on the Japan Sea coast. When he was two months old his family moved to Tokyo, and that is where he spent his childhood. Mr. Aichi felt that his family background and ties were extremely important factors in his life, and helped to explain his career in the steel business as well as his entrance into politics.

"My former name is Nakada. My original father is an engineer, who studied in the Department of Architecture at Todai. He made his career in telecommunications and construction. After graduation, he entered what used to be called the Telecommunications Agency. It was later reorganized into the Ministry of Post and Telecommunications and then into Nippon Telephone and Telegraph (NTT). At NTT, my father was responsible for construction projects, mostly constructing telephone company offices around Japan. He ended his career at NTT as the director-general of the Construction Bureau. After he retired from NTT in April 1965, he opened a private architectural firm. He is still running that firm today.

"Although he was educated as an architect, and his work may sound like engineering work, he is not . . . a technical, engineering type. By nature and family background, he is more of a manager. And in his career, he spent most of his time in management--managing construction projects.

"My father's family are basically an old, regional manufacturing family, who branched out into local business and banking, and also into local politics. Their original factory made medicines and pharmaceuticals for quite a few generations. Then they started a number of other enterprises, including banks. At one point, the Hokuriku Bank in Toyama City was owned by the Nakada family. They also went into prefectural politics. The most recent example is my father's younger brother, Kokichi Nakada, who was governor of Toyama Prefecture. He became ill and died in office, several years ago, in 1980. He was very energetic and able, and since his death, the Nakada family businesses and their political influence in Toyama have . . . unfortunately . . . declined somewhat.

"My father was, in some ways, an exception in his family, since he studied architecture, and then left Toyama for Tokyo and entered the national bureaucracy.

"My mother's family is from Yamagata Prefecture in *Tohoku* (northeastern Honshu). Her grandfather, Toshiki Sano, had to struggle . . . struggle very hard to get through school, but he finally graduated from the Department of Architecture at Todai, and he became a professor there. He did important work. He helped to found the field of anti-earthquake structural mechanics. (laughing) Pronouncing that is a test of English. Since we have so many earthquakes here in Japan, it is extremely important to know how to construct buildings that will endure these quakes. My mother's father, Kiyoshi Muto, who was the son of this pioneer, succeeded him at Todai and further developed this field. Professor Muto left Todai in 1977 and joined the Kajima Construction Company, one of the biggest in the world, where he helped to develop the field of earthquake-resistant high-rise architecture. That made all these new Tokyo skyscrapers possible. Professor Kiyoshi Muto's contribution was recognized last year (1984), when he received our country's highest honor, the Cultural Award. But it is important to remember that it was his father who laid the foundation for this achievement.

(smiling) "Well, as you may have noticed, the Todai architecture department was the--what shall I call it--connecting place for my mother and father. My mother's family are almost all in architecture or engineering, in one way or another. Even though my father is the managerial type, he also was in architecture and construction. So, the atmosphere in my family . . . was almost a pressure pushing me into these fields. I was expected, as a small boy, to be good at math and the hard sciences, and I did get good grades at these subjects. I did poorly at the humanities, at Japanese studies and at foreign languages, because they seemed unimportant to my future. I am also the eldest child--I have a younger brother and younger sister--and even as a boy, I felt a responsibility to carry on the family tradition in science and technology.

(pausing, shaking his head and smiling at the memory) "One other point I should mention. As a child, I suffered from bronchial asthma and I was very weak, nervous, and high-strung. Because of asthma attacks, I often missed school and I was home in bed or recovering. I had few friends and I used to worry about small, unimportant things. My relatives--uncles and aunts--got used to seeing me as a sickly, nervous, lonely boy who was good at science and wanted to be a scientist. (laughing) Now, they always tell me how surprised they are that I look healthy and that I am in politics, in the Diet." (both laughing)

WAR AND OCCUPATION

"I was born in 1937, the year that the China War began, and by the time I started elementary school in 1943, the Pacific War had become . . . very fierce. My clearest memory of my early school years is that I often changed schools. I started school here in Tokyo, in Omori School in Ota-ku. But before too long, Tokyo was being bombed and we moved to Kamakura, not far from Tokyo, where my mother's parents--the Muto family--had a house. Kamakura was not bombed as heavily as Tokyo, but even Kamakura gradually began to seem dangerous. Some bombs dropped there. Several times when I was in the street, going or coming home from school, there were explosions and pieces of bombs fell near me. We began to have air raid warnings and we had to take sudden shelter. It was a long train ride to my school in Kamakura, and several times we had air raid warnings while I was on the train. We had to flee to the nearby hills and take shelter there for the whole night, and I was unable to get home on those nights. There was probably no great danger (pause) but I remember that I was . . . very worried.

"So, in 1945, we moved again to the Muto family place in Yamagata Prefecture, in Kamiya City. We were in Kamiya City when the war ended. Then, shortly after the Surrender, we returned to Kamakura, where we stayed for about two or three years. In 1948, as things improved, we came back to Tokyo. I took my last year of elementary school and graduated from Omori School in Ota-ku . . . where I began.

"Looking back, I have . . . hmmm . . . no fond memories of those years. The result of my asthma and of changing schools all the time was that I made very few friends as a young boy. We were always newcomers and outsiders. People were . . . not friendly to us. We were not accepted and I did not fit in well, especially in Yamagata."

Question: "Did you get enough to eat at the end of the war?"

"I don't remember being so hungry during the war. But when we returned to Kamakura right after the war, there was no food. I have a very intense memory of that. We had a good-size garden in Kamakura, and we raised pumpkins and some potatoes. Pumpkin was the staple food in our family. Everyday, almost every meal was pumpkin--sometimes with potato leaves or other strange plants. (grimacing in distaste at the memory) It seems to me that I was always hungry for about two years. I was always dreaming of good things to eat.

"Because of that experience, I am not finicky about my food. I eat almost any kind of food. But . . . I hate pumpkin. I never eat it."

Question: "How do you think your experiences in the war and right after the war affected your values, your way of looking at the world?"

"Hmmm. It is hard to say. It was a sad . . . an unpleasant time for me. I like to think that I . . . overcame that experience, and that it did not affect me too much."

MIDDLE AND HIGHER SCHOOL

"Well, after graduating from Omori, I wanted to enter a good, private middle school. I applied and took the entrance examination, but I failed to pass. It was another bad shock for me, and it seemed like a terrible . . . setback in my life. So, I had to attend an ordinary, public school--Number 3 Junior High School in Ota-ku, here in Tokyo. Looking back now, that school was good for me. I stayed in that school for the whole three years. The students were the children of regular, ordinary people--fishsellers, greengrocers, clerks, everybody in the neighborhood. (smiling) With them, I began to come out of my shell. I made all sorts of friends. I began to have some fun. I did well at my math and science courses, and for the first time in my life, I participated in sports. I was in track, and I found that I was a fast sprinter. (laughing) I became so enthusiastic about running that I overdid my training in my last year, when I was fourteen or fifteen, and I injured both knees. (shaking his head at his foolishness) That was also a terrible setback for me. I had to have several knee operations. Afterward, I could walk normally, but I had to give up running and track."

Question: "Do those knee injuries bother you when you ski?"

(laughing) "No, no. I was lucky. My knees are allright for skiing now. Let me tell you more about my school years. In 1952, I entered Hibiya Higher School. I would call that a . . . turning point in my life. Nowadays, the reputation of Hibiya has declined. But in 1952, it was famous for sending many of its graduates to Todai. I can tell you, I was very worried about that entrance examination . . . but somehow (laughing) I managed to pass it.

"During my three years at Hibiya, I concentrated on my class work and studies . . . and to some extent, I went back into my shell again. I became very quiet and serious. Even so, I did only so-so work, and my grades were not especially good. I did not participate much in the school clubs and other activities. (pause) Looking back, I really wonder why I lived that way. I should have met more people and made more friends. (pause) Anyway, I did make a few good friends at Hibiya, and one of them, Uta Masanaga, had a great influence on my life. Our families got to know each other, and later I met his younger sister . . . and she and I ended up getting married. (laughing) So you see how important Hibiya has been to me."

TOKYO UNIVERSITY

"When I graduated from Hibiya, in 1955, I applied for Todai. The first time I took the examination I failed, and for one year after that I was a *ronin*.[4] Then, I took the test again in 1956, and that time I passed and entered Todai.

"As you know, ever since I was a child, math and science had always been my strong subjects. However, when I went to Todai I studied in the Law Faculty. I did that on my father's advice. He told me that when he looked back on his own career, it seemed to him that those who reached the top positions, such as company presidents and vice-presidents, had all graduated in law. He said that the men who graduated in architecture, or engineering, or economics all wound up in the middle. Therefore, he advised me to enter the Law Faculty at Todai, and to study the humanities.

(thoughtful pause) "Hmm. Maybe it was not such good advice. I was so badly prepared in the humanities that I hardly did any work in my courses. I just did enough to get by. That is not a good way. I think I would have gotten more from my years at Todai if I had taken science or engineering. And nowadays, as it turns out, quite a few of the top positions, including company presidents, are filled by engineering graduates. Well, in 1956 no one knew that would happen. My father was doing his best to help me, so . . . .

"My main activity at college was an all male, all university choral group called the *Dansei Shibugasho* (literally, the male quartet). A cousin of mine who was a year ahead of me was in that chorus, and he asked me to join. (pause, smiling and looking at me questioningly) Does it seem strange to you that I could learn more from a choral group than from my law courses? Well, I think I did. There were about one hundred students in that singing club, from all the different faculties--medicine, economics, engineering and so on, as well as from law. Many of these singers came from different parts of Japan, some of them from small towns where only one student every few years--the very best one--could ever hope to enter Todai. They were used to being, what do you call it, yes (smiling at the term and making a face) the big man on campus. (both laughing) They were . . . confident and strong-minded. In my sophomore year, one of the officer positions on the chorus became vacant, and I was selected to fill it. Well, I was very enthusiastic

---

4. Literally, a masterless samurai; slang for a student who has failed the university entrance test and is studying to take it again.

and I worked hard at it, and in the next year, my junior year, I became the leader of the *Dansei Shibugasho*. I was responsible for organizing the group activities and leading them.

"That was the most valuable experience I had at Todai. It is something I will never forget. I still continue the friendships I made in that chorus. Even now, twenty-five years after graduating, every two or three months at least ten or so of us get together for an evening of drinking and singing. They are my closest friends--all working in different professions, and some in important positions now. But we get together to drink and sing." (smiling warmly)

Comment: "Yes. I see. So your closest ties at Todai were formed in this choral group."

"Yes. That is true. But there is . . . more to it than that. Hmm. How can I explain it? (knitting his brow) Well, in order to sing together . . . in good harmony . . . the hearts have to blend together. There must be good feelings among all the members of the chorus. Human relations--*ningen kankei*--is the most important thing. (laughing) Often those strong-minded, big men on campus were ready to quarrel with each other or even to split up the group. As the leader, I had to find a way to settle their differences. I was friends with all of them. They knew I was not against them. They helped me to settle their differences, and so we all stuck together. We had to stick together to sing well. (nodding his head for emphasis) That was the most important lesson I learned at Todai."

INTRODUCTION TO POLITICS

"Actually, as important as the choral group was to me, maybe it was not as important as the political campaign experience of my senior year. I did not have to write a thesis to graduate, and it was already decided that I would go to work at the Nippon Kokkan (NKK) steel company after Todai. So, I expected to do very little school work and fully enjoy my last year of student life before starting to work. That was in 1960, you know, and there was an especially important general election that fall.[5] Just by chance, my

---

5. This was the general election following the June 1960 demonstrations and riots against the revised U.S.-Japan Security Treaty, which led to Prime Minister

wife's older brother, my old friend from Hibiya, asked me if I would like to come help with Kiichi Aichi's election campaign . . . to do something a little different. Well. . . why not? (laughing) I had the time. I had met Mr. Aichi several times in Tokyo, and even though I did not know him very well, I had a good feeling toward him. So, I went up to Sendai (largest city in Miyagi Prefecture), for the first time in my life, to help in his campaign.

"I knew nothing about elections. The campaign is limited by law to twenty days, and I spent about a month working in Sendai. My job was (laughing) to help out in any way that I could. From early in the morning until late at night, I was with Mr. Aichi. I acted as a sort of personal secretary. Sometimes I drove his car. I ran errands, and did whatever little things had to be done. I went everywhere with him--to meetings, to speeches. It was a . . . very intense experience. I got to know Mr. Aichi and to know his family, too. We became close friends in that election campaign.

"I also had my first lessons in politics--practical lessons. I realized that our election struggles are much more in our party, among the different factions of the LDP, than with the other parties. In Mr. Aichi's campaign, we were fighting for our share of the LDP votes.[6] I learned how a Japanese politician meets with his constituents, and his *koenkai* (support groups), and what he says to them."

Question: "Since you were at Todai during the anti-U.S.-Japan Treaty demonstrations in the spring of 1960, what were you doing or thinking at that time? Did you join the demonstrations against the treaty?"

(thoughtful pause) "Hmm. I pretty much . . . stayed out of it. I had some doubts about the way Prime Minister Kishi handled the treaty. But I didn't like the anti-treaty meetings and demonstrations. They were too . . . noisy . . . and too radical."

Nobusuke Kishi's resignation and raised serious doubts about the continuation of the political dominance of the LDP.
6. One of the best accounts of how a candidate for the Diet gathers votes in a general election is Gerald L. Curtis, *Election Campaigning Japanese Style* (New York: Columbia University Press, 1971).

GOING TO WORK FOR NIPPON KOKKAN

"Well, when the election campaign was over, I returned to Todai, graduated, and joined Nippon Kokkan--as I had planned to do."

Question: "Were you giving any thought to getting into politics . . . in the future? It sounds as though your experience in the 1960 election caught your imagination."

(thoughtful pause) "Yes . . . it did. But at that time I had no . . . intention . . . no serious thought of entering politics. The 1960 campaign work was a good experience. That is what I thought. My ambition was to rise to the top of NKK--to try to become president of that company.

"So, I joined the company and threw myself into my work. (grinning) It was a big change from college life. (laughing) But I was ready to do some real work. The first two years, from 1961 to 1963, I was assigned to the plant in Kawasaki, near Tokyo, to the Production Evaluation Section. That was an unusual job for a Law Faculty graduate, but my earlier math and science training helped me and made it possible. We did time and efficiency studies. I studied more statistics . . . and I got very interested in the work. I spent my days roaming through the factory, mostly on the production line, wearing a company suit--just as the workers did. This gave me a chance to know many people on the production line . . . who are quite different than the white collar, salary men in the offices. We got to be friends. We went out drinking in the evenings and took some ski trips together. (reminiscent smile) That was a good time. It was good, useful work, and they were good people.

"In 1963, I was transferred to NKK headquarters in Tokyo, in the Marunouchi district, to the Business Operations Division. That was also a valuable, four-year assignment. My job was to sell our steel products. I soon learned that it was basically a matter of human relations--*ningen kankei* again. Of course, technology and efficiency are . . . essential. Without them, a company cannot even compete. But if you look at the steel products manufactured by NKK, or New Japan Steel, or Sumitomo, these products are all . . . very close in quality and cost. The buyers know that. So, in the end, it is usually personal relationships that decide what company gets the contract. You have to get to the point where the buyer will say, 'I am going to buy your company's product because I want to deal with you. I know that you are good and reliable.'

"The best men in Business Operations were expert at *ningen kankei*. I don't mean that in a deceptive, hypocritical way. No. They were really good and reliable men. They knew what the buyers were looking for, and how to make the buyers trust them. I watched them, and tried to learn from them. Of course, politics is almost entirely a matter of human relations--of knowing how to deal with people, how to win their trust. I think I learned most of what I know about human relations in those four years in the Business Operations Division.

MARRIAGE

Question: "Didn't you also get married during this time?"

"Yes. My wife and I were married on (smiling) you know, that is one date I don't forget--December 10, 1964. (in a serious tone) That is the most important event of my life. (pause) Mr. Aichi played a key role in our marriage.

"As I said, my wife Ayako is the younger sister of my friend Uta Masanaga from our school days at Hibiya. However, she was adopted into the Aichi family when she was a little girl. This meant that legally she had the Aichi name, but she was brought up and raised in her own home, by her real parents. I had known Ayako ever since my Hibiya days. While at Todai, I started dating her . . . now and then . . . and kept on seeing her after I graduated. But I did not think of her as a special girlfriend. I don't think she considered me as her boyfriend, either. We . . . just got along very well. We were pleasant company for each other. She was a student at *Nihon Joshidai* --Japan Women's College.

"Meanwhile, I had become friendly with Kiichi Aichi, after the 1960 campaign. Well, when Ayako was getting ready to graduate from Japan Women's College, Mr. Aichi first mentioned marriage. He asked me about his adopted daughter. He thought we would be a good husband and wife. Once he raised this idea, it seemed . . . natural. Ayako and I started thinking seriously about it, and before long . . . we decided yes . . . we should certainly be married.

"Well, it was not as easy as we thought. The problem was what our family name would be. (noticing my slightly surprised expression) It was . . . quite serious. In my family, I am the eldest son, and I was supposed to carry on the Nakada name. My younger brother had been adopted into my mother's family, the Muto family, since their only son had died in the war, and they wanted him to carry on their name. My wife's family, which is related to the Aichi family, had agreed to her adoption by the Aichi family. Kiichi Aichi had adopted her on the understanding that when she married, her husband would take the Aichi name. So, you see, it was a kind of a . . . deadlock.

(shaking his head and smiling) "At that time, my wife and I wanted very much to get married . . . and we really didn't care about what our name would be. We decided to leave it up to our parents, to choose any name they wanted, so long as we could be married. I told this to my mother and father, and Ayako talked with her parents and with Mr. and Mrs. Aichi. It ended with all three sets of parents having many discussions together--time after time--to settle this question.

"Kiichi Aichi showed his real political skills--as you can tell from my name. (smiling, then in a serious tone) It was not at all easy for him to do it, but he managed to persuade them."

Question: (long pause) "Is it possible. . . can you tell me how he did it?"

"Hmm. Yes. I can. Basically, he said that for him it was crucial to have me as his legal son--through marriage--only until he retired from politics, which he would do in 1977, when he became seventy years old. He said that after he retired from politics, my wife and I could take the Nakada family name, or any name we wanted.

"This was his reasoning. If he had a son who looked like a potential politician, who would probably succeed him in his Diet seat, that would help to keep peace among his *koenkai* . But if he did *not* have a political heir, some city councilman or prefectural assemblyman would say, 'Aichi has no heir. I will succeed him when he retires.' They would squabble among themselves, and he would lose votes . . . and maybe even his Diet seat. This has really happened to a number of senior politicians. That is what he said to our parents. Finally, they accepted his case. My younger brother was returned to our family and became a Nakada again, and I was allowed to join the Aichi family and to get married."

Question: "Yes. I see. Mr. Aichi did not pledge you to be his political heir--but just to take his name until he retired in 1977. Is that it?"

"Exactly. I liked Mr. Aichi . . . very much . . . but I had no plan to enter politics as his successor. I wanted to become president of my company, NKK (laughing) and most of all, I wanted to marry my wife."

NEW YORK

"While I was working at sales in Tokyo, a cousin of mine suggested to me that I should get a transfer to the NKK office in New York. NKK has several overseas offices. New York is the biggest. My cousin also worked for NKK, and he had served in New York. He said it would make me a broader, better trained man. I discussed this with my father, and also with Kiichi Aichi, and they both liked the idea. Then, I let the NKK management know what I had in mind, and they were kind enough to assign me to New York.

(long pause) "It may sound simple enough, but it was a big decision for me . . . and sometimes I wondered . . . I was married, and by 1967, when all this was going on, we had two children, a one year old and a three year old. Well, NKK was very generous and arranged for my wife and children to accompany me to New York. That was very important.

"Another question was . . . language. . . and culture. Like all Japanese, I had studied English in middle school and higher school. The courses were not very practical, and I was not a conscientious student at languages. I had never studied English conversation. I had never been outside Japan. (pause) The truth is, before I went to New York, I had an allergy for Westerners and

Americans. If I saw one, a part of me wanted to keep as far away as possible. That was the easiest thing to do. There were so many problems of language . . . and manners. (shrugging his shoulders and frowning to convey the anxiety he had felt) Well, going to live in New York meant that I would have to cure my allergy. (both laughing)

"At the end of 1967, I went over by myself for two months or so to arrange for our housing. Then, early in 1968, I went to the United States with my wife and children. We flew from Haneda to Los Angeles, and then on to New York. (smiling at the memory) It is hard to explain how exciting that was for us. All of a sudden . . . the whole world expanded. (laughing). I remember vividly how everything looked--the airports, the city streets, the people. (pause) My allergy disappeared. (both laughing)

"Frankly, my work in New York was most of the time . . . pretty boring. There were ten people in our office, and I was the youngest man. My job was to be a guide and look after the NKK people and our customers from Japan who were in New York on business trips. I was supposed to help them out with everything. I met them at the airport, helped them to check into their hotel, go sightseeing, or eating and drinking. Well, the work was not exciting, but it made me practice English conversation.

"I became fascinated with American politics in the 1968 Nixon-Humphrey presidential election. It was extraordinary for me. The Vietnam War debate was . . . raging on, and also racial problems. I saw President Johnson on TV announcing that he would not run in 1968. Then, Robert Kennedy was shot in Los Angeles . . . and afterward Martin Luther King was also assassinated. It was such a . . . turbulent time. (pause) I wondered what was going to happen to your country. But somehow you came through allright.

"During the first Nixon administration, the reversion of Okinawa to Japan was negotiated. My father, Kiichi Aichi, was foreign minister to Prime Minister Sato, and he became responsible for those negotiations. He traveled to Washington, countless times. He always wanted to see us, and we wanted to see him. Whenever he had the time, he visited with us in New York, and played with his grandchildren. Or, sometimes, we went to see him in Washington. I had nothing to do with the negotiations, but I followed them with great interest. When they were concluded successfully, the signing ceremony was held simultaneously in Tokyo and Washington, and broadcast on American TV. That was in . . . June 1971. We were very proud and happy to see Kiichi Aichi taking his Japanese brush pen and putting his name on the document.[7]

"Although American politics was . . . so turbulent, I learned something important from it. Even in the midst of all your problems, your politicians were talking not only about what is good for the U.S., but they were talking about America's responsibilities in the world . . . what the impact would be of staying in Vietnam or getting out. Well, that opened my eyes. Japanese politicians were thinking only about what was good for Japan. I began to wonder, to doubt . . . if we Japanese could go on being so narrow. I wrote letters to Kiichi Aichi about this. Of course, Japan has changed since the early 1970s, and accepts more international responsibility now. It must go on doing that.

"Well, that assignment lasted until late in 1972. Living in New York for those four years had a great influence on my life. It changed my perspective on many things--especially about how Japan looks in the eyes of foreigners. I think I also learned something about U.S.-Japan relations--how important they are for both our countries, and also how much careful attention and work they need."

TRANSITION

"Our years in New York, so rich and full of good memories, came to an end in late 1972. I returned to the NKK head office in Tokyo, and was assigned to the Export Division. Well, (shaking his head and smiling) it was a most unusual situation. Usually, the people in exports work very hard and rack their brains for new ways to increase sales. However, when I was assigned to exports, the Japanese and U.S. governments and steel industries had reached an agreement on voluntary export restraints by Japan. It was . . .

---

7. For a carefully written, detailed account of the Okinawa reversion negotiations, please see Destler, et. al., *Managing an Alliance: The Politics of U.S.-Japanese Relations* (Washington, D.C.: The Brookings Institution, 1976), 23-34.

strange. Some Americans were asking us to sell our products to them . . . and we had to refuse. As you can imagine, our office was quiet and relaxed.

"By this time, in 1972, Kiichi Aichi had resigned as foreign minister. The Tanaka cabinet was in Office, and was facing a big diplomatic and political problem in trying to normalize relations with China. The governments of the other Asian countries, especially the ASEAN governments (Indonesia, Malaysia, Philippines, Singapore, and Thailand) needed to be informed and reassured that Japan and China were not doing anything behind their backs. So, the Tanaka cabinet asked Kiichi Aichi to become a special ambassador and to visit all these countries and explain Japan's policy. Kiichi Aichi knew that my office was very quiet, and asked me to request a short leave and accompany him as his private secretary. I did so. It was in October 1972.

"Oh yes, before that ASEAN trip, there was an UNCTAD Conference in Santiago, Chile. I think that it was in April 1972. Kiichi Aichi was dispatched to represent Japan, and I also went as his private secretary. During these trips we became even closer, and my interest in international affairs and in politics began to grow more active. I began to think about what it might be like to enter politics.

"At the end of December 1972, the Tanaka Cabinet was reshuffled and Kiichi Aichi was appointed finance minister. He had been a cabinet minister many times, as you know, but never finance minister. He began his career in the Finance Ministry, and it was his dream to someday be head of that ministry. He was . . . extremely happy, and eager to get to work. Again, he asked me to accept an appointment in the Finance Ministry as his private secretary. Well, this appointment would not be as brief as the ASEAN and UNCTAD missions. Kiichi Aichi expected to be finance minister for about one or two years. I did not want to quit NKK in exchange for a one or two-year job, so I worked hard to arrange a special, extended leave. I talked with the NKK president and a number of senior officers. Kiichi Aichi helped. The NKK people realized that I could be more useful to them as a company executive if I had good contacts and knew many people in the Finance Ministry and in politics. So, they granted me an extended leave to help Minister Aichi.

"I worked in the finance minister's office, from morning to night, for most of 1973. It was a busy, busy job. (pause) That was . . . an invaluable education. I was worried at first that I might not do well. The bureaucrats are extremely able, and I wondered how they would accept me. But it went well. I became friends with many of them, and that has been a great help to me as a Dietman. I can talk to them about budget matters."

Question: "Had you decided to enter politics by then--or even half decided?"

(laughing) "Not yet. I still expected to return to NKK. It is true that my interest in politics was growing. But as a practical matter, I had no chance to run for any office.

"As the minister's secretary, I did have a chance to meet many, many Dietmen and to see them negotiating and haggling with the minister over budget items. That is an important part of a Diet-man's job. In those days, the last two to three days of the budget process was called *daijin sessho*, ministerial negotiations. It was very dramatic and even . . . fierce. The cabinet ministers would meet with the finance minister, day and night, for a final battle over their budget requests. It was fascinating to be with Minister Aichi during his *daijin sessho*. Recently, it has become more formalized and calm, and it is finished now in about half a day.

"In the summer of 1973, while I was in the Finance Ministry, the LDP in Miyagi had to decide on a candidate to run for mayor of Sendai. The incumbent, Mayor Takeshi Shimano, was a very popular independent politician, somewhat progressive and to the left, who had announced that he was going to run for reelection. There was not much chance that the LDP candidate would win. Ki-ichi Aichi was the chairman of the Miyagi prefectural LDP, but he had not backed any candidate. The politicians in the prefecture were having difficulty picking someone to run. Then, my name came up. Some politicians said, 'Let's run Kazuo Aichi.' They wanted a fresh, young LDP candidate to run against old Mayor Shimano. This would help to dispel the LDP image as an old man's party. They wanted an energetic candidate, who would campaign hard, even though he was a sacrifice. That was important to LDP votes and morale. Hmm. For some of them, including the incumbent LDP Dietmen from Miyagi, there was also a complicated reason.

They knew that running a strong campaign for mayor of Sendai--
even a strong losing campaign--could be a good way to build a voting base for a Diet seat. In the previous mayoral election, Hiroshi
Mitsuka had run a strong but losing campaign against Mayor Shimano, and in the next general election he had been elected to the
Diet. He is still serving in the House of Representatives. Well, they
knew that no matter what happened in the mayoral election, so long
as Kiichi Aichi was in the Diet, I would not run for the Diet. So,
they would not have worry about competition from me.   Some
people thought of me as Kiichi Aichi's eventual successor to his Diet
seat, and they felt that the mayoral campaign would be a good way
for me to begin in politics, even if it led nowhere in the short run.
Finally, there were a few people who thought I might even win the
election and become mayor of Sendai, and then I would use my
relationship with my father, Kiichi Aichi, to help the Sendai budget.
So, you see, there were all kinds of thinking, some contradictory.

"When Kiichi Aichi heard about this talk of running me, he
was not pleased. He said, 'No. Forget it.' He said I was too
young and inexperienced, and that I was not from Sendai. Moreover, as LDP prefectural chairman, he did not like the idea of nam-
ing a relative as a candidate. So, he refused, and when they came to
me, I refused too. So, the idea disappeared, for a time.

"However, they could not seem to agree on anyone else as a
candidate, and eventually my name came up again, and most of the
local LDP politicians agreed on it and began to put pressure on my
father, Kiichi Aichi, to let me run."

Question: "What was your own view of all this?"

(laughing merrily) "I was lighthearted about it. Maybe I did
not realize completely what a serious choice it was. I was ready to
run--to give it a good, hard try and see what would happen. So,
under strong local pressure, Kiichi Aichi reluctantly gave in. At the
end of September 1973, I left the Finance Ministry and prepared to
begin campaigning for the mayoral election scheduled in Sendai for
January 1974.

"Kiichi Aichi suggested that we travel to Sendai together, but
I wanted to make my political debut there alone. So, on October
1st, 1973, I took the train to Sendai. That was a turning point for
me. I remember that day and the next day clearly. When I arrived

in Sendai, I went to an LDP rally and made my first political speech. Afterward, I held my first press conference, and answered many questions about my plans for Sendai's future. (smiling) I was . . . deeply surprised and pleased at the number of people at the rally . . . and at their interest and support. It was a very fine feeling to be there with them. (pause) I think that day marked the beginning of a new life for me.

"You probably know that even though the official, legal campaign for a mayoral election is only seven days before the election, there is a lot of political activity before then--an unofficial campaign. The unofficial campaign is more informal. There are no posters, or sound trucks, or TV. Well, I threw myself into this informal campaigning. I met with local political leaders and with business and social clubs. I visited many private homes and went to many, many small meetings where I made speeches and talked with people. It was very busy, and I was completely absorbed in the mayoral race.

"November 23d is Labor Day in Japan. On that day in 1973 I went to several meetings around Sendai. In the early evening, after the last meeting, somebody handed me a brief memo. It said, 'Kiichi Aichi has a cold and has been hospitalized in Tokyo. Please give him a call.' It did not seem serious. When I got home between eight and nine o'clock, I called the hospital--to say hello and cheer up my father. On the phone, I realized it was much more serious. Someone at the hospital told me I should come immediately to Tokyo. (pause) Well . . . I reserved a ticket for the next train that night--an 11:30 sleeping train. Then, since there were several hours to wait, I stayed at home to watch television. At ten o'clock, there was a news bulletin. Kiichi Aichi, minister of finance, had died. (pause) Well . . . I was completely unprepared for that. Within a few minutes, the house was flooded with people, all shocked and stunned by this sudden death. It turned into an uproar.

"I could not stay in the house--in that noise and confusion--but there was still time before the train. I went out to my car and drove around, wondering what it meant and what I should do . . . and then I stopped by a friend's house--a lawyer--and waited there until my train left.

"The next few weeks were full of . . . grief and . . . indecision. Kiichi Aichi was my father and my political sponsor. Without him . . . I would never have been in politics. Also, his death changed the political environment in Miyagi and in Sendai. I had three choices. One choice was to stay in the mayoral race. The second was to drop out of the mayoral race and to start campaigning to fill Kiichi Aichi's Diet seat. (pause) The last choice was not to run for anything . . . to leave politics. (pause) After all, I was unknown. I hardly existed in the political world. Well, that last choice soon faded, but for awhile I thought about it.

"Most of my advisers in Miyagi urged me to quit the mayoral election and immediately start working on the House of Representatives. They strongly urged me . . . but I held back. Somehow, I did not think it would be a good idea to quit the mayoral race. I was not sure who to talk to . . . to ask advice. So, I went to Kiichi Aichi's political friends. I asked to see Prime Minister Tanaka, and the LDP secretary general, Tomisaburo Hashimoto, and his deputy, Noboru Takeshita. (Mr. Takeshita became prime minister in December 1987). They all talked with me and advised me to stay in the mayoral race. They said that with only a month and half before the Sendai election, it would be too late to find another LDP candidate. They said, ' If you quit the mayoral race and then come to us later and say that you want to run for your father's Diet seat, it might be difficult. You should run in the mayoral election and see how you do. That is also the best thing for you. Then, we will see.'

"Well, many local people were not pleased with this. My mother, Mrs. Aichi, was not pleased. But they gave in to my wishes. In the Sendai election in January 1974, I did surprisingly well. That election was reported all over Japan. For awhile, it was famous. Of course, I did not win . . . and I think some of the votes for me were . . . sympathy votes. But my total vote was unexpectedly high.

"That mayoral election--even though it was a defeat--made it possible for me to run for the Diet. If I had quit or done poorly, that would have been the end of me in politics. It also gave me some confidence in my political judgment. I learned that sometimes it is better to follow my own ideas, even against the advice of my closest friends and supporters."

Question: "Was there a special election scheduled to fill Kiichi Aichi's seat, or would it remain vacant until the next general
election?"

"His seat would remain vacant until the next general election.
But the last general election had been in 1972, so some people
thought that the next General Election would be soon. As it turned
out, it was not until 1976.[8] (pause) In the Miyagi First District we
have five seats in the Lower House. If one seat becomes vacant,
there is no special election. If two seats become vacant, we must
immediately call a special election."

RUNNING FOR THE DIET

"Soon after the Sendai election, I made up my mind to run
for Kiichi Aichi's vacant seat--to become his successor. I sent in
my resignation to NKK, and I . . . committed myself to a life in
politics.

"The first thing I had to do was to plant roots in Sendai.
You know, neither I nor my wife were born in Sendai, or had gone
to school there. It is true that Kiichi Aichi and his wife had not lived
in Sendai and usually only went there for elections. But I did not
think I could continue to do that. There were skillful local politicians coming up in the First District. So, we moved our whole
family to Sendai, and started a new life there. My oldest son was a
third grader in elementary school. My second child, a daughter,
was in the first grade and our youngest was not yet in school.

"Hmm. (long, unusually thoughtful, sober pause) Building
political support was . . . much more difficult that I had expected.
Of course, I knew that I would have to work very hard and spend
long hours going all over the district to talk with people and get to
know them, and also to solicit campaign contributions. The difficulty that I did not expect was . . . Mr. Tanaka's troubles. Even in
the summer of 1974, there were newspaper reports of money prob-

---

8. The Constitution requires that there be a general election at least every four
years. The prime minister may dissolve the House of Representatives at any time
short of the four-year term and call a general election at what appears to be an
opportune time. In practice, general elections have seldom been four years apart.

lems and scandals. They got worse and worse, until Prime Minister Tanaka and his cabinet were forced to resign in December 1974. Mr. Takeo Miki then became prime minister . . . which was . . . most unforeseen."[9]

"As you know, Prime Minister Miki pursued the Tanaka case . . . vigorously. In the summer of 1975, everyone was astounded when the police arrested Mr. Tanaka and put him in jail for some days for his alleged part in the Lockheed scandal. (pause, then in a very serious tone) Well, when Tanaka was arrested, I thought it was all over with me. I was wondering if I could become a salary man in some company again, or how I could make a living. (pause) I was so shocked . . . that I went to bed . . . and stayed in bed for a whole week.

"My father, Kiichi Aichi, had helped Mr. Tanaka become prime minister in 1972, and he had become finance minister in the Tanaka cabinet. As Kiichi Aichi's successor, I felt close ties with Mr. Tanaka. As I told you, Prime Minister Tanaka met with me at a difficult time after Kiichi Aichi's death, and gave me good advice. When I moved to Sendai and started running for the Diet, I told everyone that if they supported me as Kiichi Aichi's successor in the Diet, and I won the seat, Mr. Tanaka would take care of our district. That is what I was saying in 1974. Prime Minister Tanaka was my strongest selling point. Then, in the summer of 1975, he became my . . . weakest point. Some politicians told me to just quit the Diet race--that Tanaka's arrest had finished me. Others said my only hope was to cut my ties with Tanaka completely. That was the majority view.

"Well, I went over these views again and again as I lay in

---

9. Please see footnote 5, in chapter on Motoo Shiina for the role of Etsusaburo Shiina in the selection of Prime Minister Miki. In 1974, Mr. Miki was a senior LDP Dietman with a reputation for independence and honesty, and the leader of a small LDP faction. He was not considered a likely successor to Mr. Tanaka. The leading candidates for the prime ministership were the leaders of two large LDP factions, Mr. Takeo Fukuda and Mr. Masayoshi Ohira. In December 1974, in the confusion and quarreling that followed the fall of the Tanaka Cabinet, neither Mr. Fukuda nor Mr. Ohira had sufficient factional support in the LDP to win the prime ministership, and neither man would step aside for the other. Both preferred to see Mr. Miki become prime minister, probably thinking that his term in office would be very brief. As it turned out, Prime Minister Miki remained in office until December 1976, and he was unexpectedly energetic and authoritative.

bed, and they depressed me. But other ideas also went through my mind. There was the good relationship between Kiichi Aichi and Tanaka. I also had to think of all the help Mr. Tanaka had given to me after my father's death. Even though he had been forced to resign from office and had been arrested, there was no court judgment against him--not yet. That came later.

"I began to feel that I could not stay in bed forever, that I must do something. I finally decided that I knew what to do, and I got up. No matter how painful my position might become, I could not cut my relationship with Mr. Tanaka. As a human being, it would not be right. I gathered my supporters and told them that I understood their feelings and I appreciated their worries about my future. 'However', I said, 'Mr. Tanaka has helped me and there is no judgment against him. I cannot cut my ties with him. It would be too disloyal. If you cannot agree with me on this, I am sorry but I will not be able to accept your support, and we will have to part here.'

"Looking back, I think that what I said then was too . . . severe. I was too defiant. That was my tone. A few people left who would have stayed with me if I had been more reasonable. But, basically I did the right thing. There was . . . no easy way. I have had many bitter moments since then, even after my election to the Diet, because of the Tanaka problem. On the other hand, I believe I have also benefited both personally and politically from my loyalty to Mr. Tanaka. It was the right decision."

Question: "How did your relationship with Mr. Tanaka help you in winning your Diet seat in 1976?"

"Well . . . running for the Diet seat meant spending lots of money . . . constantly . . . every month. I had to hire secretaries and pay their salaries, and travel, and entertain people, and so on. I had no money of my own, worth mentioning. I calculated that my savings from all the salaries and bonuses I earned at NKK would hardly cover one month of political campaign expenses. I also decided that I could not accept any money from the Aichi family. (pause) I was determined to resolve this on my own. So, I had to get political donations from companies. I was trying to do that, but several times during those first two years we ran out of money and it seemed as though we were . . . finished. Somehow, each time we were saved by a contribution at the last minute.

"I went to see Mr. Tanaka about this problem. This was after he had resigned as prime minister and had his hands full with his own troubles. He told me that my father had gotten contributions from many companies with offices in Tokyo. He advised me who to see . . . and said that I should avoid taking contributions from just a few sources, because I would become indebted to them and it could hurt me later. I think he helped me with these men. I took his advice and started visiting many companies in the city, at the same time keeping my campaign organization running in Miyagi, and often getting back to my district and visiting every neighborhood, every support group. My campaign finances finally began to improve, and I could see my political support becoming . . . more firm.

"Including the 1976 election, I have been elected five times. But the first election was certainly the most trying . . . most difficult and also, in many ways, the most satisfying. I spent almost three years, from early 1974 to late 1976, of hard work, uncertainty . . . often without enough money . . . working to gather votes. (long pause, very seriously) It is true that I am a second generation politician. But no one can say that this Diet seat was given to me. I had to shed a lot of my own sweat and tears to get it. I had to earn it."

Question: "From what you have said, it sounds as though the scandal surrounding Prime Minister Tanaka was by far your biggest problem--much more important than any other candidate in the First District, or any other issue. Was that the case?"

"Yes. Yes it was. You know, Kiichi Aichi had already built a strong constituency. That was the constituency that I was trying to hold together. But the Lockheed scandal was tearing it apart. So yes, my biggest problem was to try to somehow overcome the effect of the scandal."

ROLE OF A POLITICIAN

Question: "Would you care to comment on your experience in the Diet or in politics since 1976?"

"Well . . . this could get us into current issues (laughing) and then I would give you a press conference. (both laughing) But there are a number of items I might mention. After my first election, I was appointed to the House Finance Committee. My work under Kiichi Aichi in the Finance Ministry helped me on this committee-- which is an important one, similar to your House Ways and Means Committee. After my second election, I was promoted to the Steering Group of the Finance Committee, where I had to work with the Opposition parties as well, since they are represented on the Steering Group.

"Then, following my third election, I had the chance to become parliamentary vice-minister in the Foreign Ministry . . . and I took it. I held that job for more than a year in 1981 and 1982, under the Suzuki cabinet. I took several trips to Washington, and I was also the first Japanese official to visit West Africa--Zambia, Zimbabwe, Ghana, and the Ivory Coast. Sometimes we joke that I was the vice-minister for two foreign ministers--for Minister Ito and Minister Sonoda. You may remember that after the summit meeting between President Reagan and Prime Minister Suzuki in May 1981, our prime minister said in a news conference that there was no military relationship or alliance between Japan and the United States, even though these words were used in the joint communique he had just agreed to. Well, there was a . . . storm in our newspapers, and then the Prime Minister said that Foreign Minister Ito had not properly briefed him, and Foreign Minister Ito resigned."

Question: "Yes, I remember that incident. Why was there such a mix-up? Whose mistake was it?"

"Well . . . Foreign Minister Ito resigned because he was . . . angry that Prime Minister Suzuki had criticized him . . . and actually, Mr. Ito had not made a mistake. Prime Minister Suzuki was not familiar with the Security Treaty or security relations with the United States . . . and he made some . . . incorrect statements in his press conference. That was all."

Question: "Is it unusual for a three-time winner in the Diet to become a parliamentary vice-minister?"

"No, not really. But to take the post of parliamentary vice-minister for foreign affairs is . . . (smiling) not such good politics. It does nothing to help win votes or to increase political contributions. But my experience in New York, and working for Mr. Aichi on his ASEAN and UNCTAD missions, convinced me that diplomatic relations and foreign affairs are . . . of critical importance to Japan. Of course, we politicians must look after the needs of our constituents . . . each in our our own voting district . . . but we should also take more responsibility in larger policy questions, including foreign policy. (pause) I know that is not easy to do in Japanese politics. The competition for votes in the local constituency is so fierce.

(all in a quiet, calm, thoughtful tone) "Hmm. My feeling is that there are a number of basic, long-term issues facing Japan--including foreign policy--and that our politicians--our Diet members--should tackle these issues. We do not finance our government properly. I do not favor a giant government . . . or a giant bureaucracy. But it is not reasonable for us to have a big government deficit and to finance our government on borrowed money--on bonds. We should reform our tax laws to raise more revenues. Bureaucrats have many ideas and plans about this--some of them are good--but tax reform is basically a job for the Diet. It can only be done . . . if we do it. I favor more sales taxes and consumption taxes. I think if we do this carefully, we can reduce the present high taxes on the small taxpayer and small businessman, and have a fair method of taxation without . . . stifling business.

"We should also shift to economic and tax policies that will improve the quality of life in Japan. Housing and education are two promising areas for improvements. The voters have had this goal for many years. They wanted to improve the quality of life for some time . . . before we politicians started talking about it as a national goal. Of course, this also means some basic changes in tax and finance policies . . . in the basic framework. The Diet should take responsibility for helping to initiate these changes."

Question: "Yes. I see your point. Yet many people think that the Diet is not well organized or prepared to make policy, and that is why it usually seems to follow the lead of the bureaucrats on major policy issues."

"Well, on day-to-day matters, or even on policies that are for one or two years, that is the way it should be. But on long term issues, I think the Diet must take more responsibility. We should work together with the bureaucrats, but we should . . . not hesitate to take the initiative sometimes . . . especially in setting national goals. Then, the bureaucrats will help us to make plans to reach the goals.

(continuing in a very calm, quiet, almost gentle voice) "Another example of what I have in mind is defense policy. The bureaucrats can do very little about this. Our basic defense policy is a budget issue, and a Diet issue. The idea that our defense budget must be limited to 1 percent of our GNP seems . . . very strange to me. The size of our defense forces should be related to the international security environment. Maybe it should be less than 1 percent, maybe more. But this 1 percent figure . . . is arbitrary . . . and it shows a lack of faith in the voters and in democracy. (pause) It seems to say that if we do not have some arbitrary figure like 1 percent . . . the country will go . . . wild. (smiling) That is not the case. Our voters and our politicians are more cautious and responsible.

"Well . . . I feel that the Diet is the place to discuss and decide on long range defense policy. By the way, I also favor sending units of the Japanese Self Defense Forces to help out in U.N. peace-keeping operations. I think this is . . . long overdue. We should do this as part of accepting more international responsibility.

"Hmm. You raised an important question when you asked about relations between bureaucrats and Dietmen. (pause) Sometimes bureaucrats are . . . high-handed in their attitude toward Diet members--as if they always know best. This makes many Diet members irritated . . . and the result is a kind of tension between them. Because of this tension, politicians sometimes meddle too much in policy details that bureaucrats know more about. Or politicians sometimes . . . wash their hands of policy matters. That is not responsible. My experience has been that politicians and bureaucrats work well together and get good results if they . . . show respect for each other."

INTERNATIONALIZATION

Question: "How do you define internationalization? Do you think that the internationalization of Japan is going as it should--and that it will meet Japan's future needs?"

(smiling) "I have a neat, simple definition ready for you. I think there are three requirements for internationalization. First, we have to know and understand our own country--Japan--our own culture and heritage. Then we have to understand foreign cultures and values--including some foreign language. Lastly, we must know how to communicate, how to use this knowledge to really exchange ideas and get along.

"That is a neat definition . . . (laughing) but it is very tough. Only a small number of Japanese can fit that definition. (pause) Even by a much easier definition--most Japanese . . . are not internationalized. I think that is why the bureaucrats and the businessmen are more internationalized than the politicians. For most of us in the Diet, being internationalized does not count for much in our voting district. It helps here in Tokyo. In the voting districts, most ordinary Japanese still have the allergy for foreigners that I had before I went to New York. Foreigners--not movies or TV shows--but real foreigners, make them uncomfortable, and they prefer to avoid them.

"Well, I believe that we should cure this allergy. It is important for our future. We will have to deal more and more with foreigners if we are to have healthy international trade and finance and also political relations. The politicians must understand and participate in these policies . . . but how can they do it if most of their constituents are uncomfortable with the idea of foreign things?

(pause) "Last month, I published a proposal in the newspapers on how to deal with this. It is being discussed in the Diet, and maybe something will come of it. This proposal should improve our English language training and also help cure our allergy.

"Ever since 1978, we have had a program with Britain. In this program, forty to fifty British teachers have been teaching English in our middle and higher schools each year. In the schools that have had these British teachers, the results have been very good.

The students learned much more English, and also they learned to feel more comfortable around foreigners. This is what we need, but the existing program is not big enough. So, I have proposed that we establish a program like this on a much bigger scale between Japan and the United States. There are about fifteen thousand middle and higher schools in Japan. I think that we should arrange to have at least one American teacher of English in each of these schools. This would really improve our English language training, and help to cure our allergy for foreigners. I think the American teachers should come to Japan for a two year stay. After ten years or so, there would also be more than one hundred thousand Americans who would know Japan at first hand--from living here in our country.[10]

"I think this program, or one like it, is needed if we are to go on having fruitful, good relations. The trade and financial relations and also the security relations between our countries is very big and important . . . for both of us . . . and even for other people in the world. But I am concerned . . . that there is some misunderstanding and bad feeling in recent years. This program will help us to promote better understanding and better human feelings for each other."

---

10. A modified, smaller version of Mr. Aichi's proposal became law and went into effect in 1987. In 1988, 1,350 English speaking teachers, most from the United States, were invited to Japan, and this number is expected to increase to 3,000 per year in the next four years.

Koichi Kato

KOICHI KATO represents the Second District in Yamagata Prefecture in the the Lower House of the National Diet. Although he is the youngest politician in this book, Koichi Kato has weathered six general elections. He first stood for and won his seat as a Liberal-Democrat in 1972. In the July 1986 general election, Koichi Kato was the most successful vote gatherer among the three Dietmen elected in his constituency.

He is the scion of a samurai family. His grandfather was a locally prominent lawyer, and his father also represented the Second District in the Diet. Although he is still in the intermediate stages of his political career, from November 1, 1984, to July 22, 1986, Koichi Kato served in Prime Minister Nakasone's cabinet as director-general of the National Defense Agency, the Japanese equivalent of the minister of defense. Given his age, political background and experience, and the national prominence he has established as a cabinet minister, it is not surprising that political analysts in Japan frequently allude to Koichi Kato as a future leader.

Koichi Kato's constituency in Yamagata Prefecture is in the region known as the *Yukiguni* (Snow Country), in northwestern Honshu, facing the Sea of Japan. In winter, the wind blows from Asia, picking up moisture as it sweeps across the stormy Sea of Japan. When this moist air strikes the rugged mountains in Yamagata, it precipitates into heavy snow falls, frequently accumulating to a depth in excess of ten feet. The two-story houses of the *Yukiguni* villagers are half-buried in snow from December to April. In spring, the snow melt gushes and roars off the steep slopes, irrigating the rice paddies in the narrow valleys. Until recent decades, Yamagata was isolated and poor, part of *Ura Nihon*, Japan's Outback. Now, as a result of the postwar land reform, government rice subsidies, and the extension of the Bullet train lines into this region,

During high school.

Director-General and Minister of National Defense Agency, with Secretary of State Caspar Weinberger, June 1985.

the prefecture is relatively prosperous and solidly conservative in its politics. Nevertheless, the voters in Yamagata have strong memories of their harsh past, very deep local roots, and they tend to be a trifle suspicious of city people and outsiders.

Koichi Kato knows and understands his constituents and identifies with them. Although he is a graduate of Tokyo University, has studied at Harvard, and has served as a diplomat, he retains a certain rural earthiness in his manner. He is a stocky, bespectacled man of medium height, smooth faced, dark haired, and younger looking than his years would suggest. His eyes are unusually large and lively, and frequently full of good humor. His English is carefully chosen, stilted at times, but very expressive.

I first met Koichi Kato at a small, Japanese-style dinner in early February 1985, shortly after he was appointed minister of defense. In early May, after he had settled into his new job, he agreed to meet with me at his office in the Defense Agency to discuss this book. Later in May, and then again in July, we had lengthy dinner meetings at a quiet, elegant Buddhist-style restaurant that is a favorite of his, the *Daigo*.

CHILDHOOD AND FAMILY

Koichi Kato was born in Tsuruoka City in Yamagata Prefecture on June 17, 1939, to Seizoh and Nobu Kato, the fifth of their six children. He has four older brothers and a younger sister. When I asked him about his childhood and family background, he sat thoughtfully for a long moment and then turned to me and said:

"My family used to be of the samurai, warrior class. Not at all high ranking. We were lower-echelon retainers in the Sakai clan. The Sakai were a good, popular *daimyo* (feudal lord) family, and there is still a lot of respect for them in Tsuruoka City, which was their castle town. Every year on January 1st, there is a ceremony at the city hall to greet the new year. It is a local event. I go to that ceremony, and afterward I go to the Sakai home to pay my respects and write my name in their book. So you see, the old traditions and values are still pretty strong in my district. It is important to know that.

"My grandfather was not a politician, but he was a well-known lawyer in Tsuruoka. He worked for the local people--sometimes without charging a fee--so he was well liked. I have also heard that he was a skillful lawyer, well respected. He went to Todai, which was very unusual in those days, and graduated before the First World War, early in this century."

Comment: "I see. Well then, he was among the earlier Todai graduates. I think the university began around the turn of the century."

"Yes, and he influenced my father to also attend Todai."

Question: "So, you are a third-generation Todai graduate as well as a second-generation Diet Member?"

"Yes. And going to Todai is very prestigious in our district. Only one student every two or three years manages to pass the entrance test. So, if you are a Todai graduate, you can be accepted into the local elite.

"When my father graduated, he took the Higher Civil Service examination and went into the Ministry of Interior. In prewar Japan, you know, that was probably the most powerful ministry--maybe more powerful than the Finance Ministry is nowadays. (laughter) They were in charge of local government and the police. Toward the end of the war, when he was a fairly high-ranking bureaucrat, my father was drafted into the army. That was . . . an unusual thing to happen. I don't know any of the details. But I think he had some trouble with his seniors in the ministry.

"After the Surrender in September of 1945, my father came back home to Tsuruoka. He expected to return to Tokyo and the Civil Service, but the elders of the town asked him to become the mayor in that difficult time. There were no elections in those days. The elders held a kind of caucus, and they picked him as mayor. He accepted the job. Of course, as soon as the Occupation arrived in Yamagata they organized elections, but the local elders had a pretty good sense of what the people wanted. My father was elected several times, and stayed on as mayor for seven years. When he was mayor, he built a strong electoral base. Then, in the general election of 1952, he ran for the Lower House and won a seat."

Question: "Since you were born in 1939, you were very young during the war and Occupation, but do you remember those times? Were you living in Yamagata? Were there any air raids or other war experiences that you recall?"

"I lived in Yamagata, with my mother and brothers and sister, while my father worked at his ministry in Tokyo and then went into the army. There was no bombing in Tsuruoka. We had no factories worth bombing. Just a few silk mills. It was a market town for the local farmers, a quiet castle town in the Shohnai Plain. It has a population now of close to one hundred thousand, but in those days it was only about forty thousand. So, there were no American air raids, but there was one kind of crazy air attack. An American plane flew over one day and dropped a hand grenade. Just one grenade, one explosion. No one was hurt. (shaking his head) I wonder why they did it? Anyway, I have no terrible memories of air raids and bombing."

Question: "Were you short of food?"

"We did not have much food, but it was not so bad for us in our town. And, you know, I was so young that eating just rice and vegetables seemed normal to me. I don't remember any real hunger during the war, any real lack of food. Just a very simple diet."

Question: "Do you have any memory of the Surrender in 1945? You were about six years old then. Did it have any meaning to you?"

(thoughtful pause, thinking back) "Yes . . . I remember the Surrender, at the end of the summer of 1945. I remember my mother and my uncles and aunts talking for some days about a radio broadcast to be given by the emperor. They thought that was . . . really extraordinary. Then, I remember that we all listened to the radio--everyone very serious--and how astonished my family was. I did not understand what the emperor had announced. I didn't know it was the Surrender. But I could see that my family was astonished and . . . deeply moved. Later, I understood what happened.

"After the Surrender, especially in that year of 1945-1946, we had a more serious food problem than we had during the war. I remember that very clearly . . . because we seemed to be living on American grain . . . mostly crushed corn kernel. It was very tough corn, and hard to cook. I think it was feed grain for cattle. You had to boil it and boil it. And then (grimacing at the memory) it was not very tasty. But you know, we didn't know how to cook any good dishes with corn. And it kept us alive and fairly healthy. So we were lucky to get that corn from you.

"I also remember that when my father was mayor of Tsuruoka, every month or two an Occupation officer would pay him a short visit at the city hall. The officer would be driven up in a jeep, stay with my father about twenty or thirty minutes, and then drive away. We boys used to run down to see the jeep, to admire it. (laughter)

Comment: "Yes. All the men I have spoken with who were boys during the Occupation remember those GI jeeps. Those jeeps were irresistible to little boys."

"I also remember my first taste of Coca-Cola. (smiling) Once, a special train with some high Occupation officers came to Tsuruoka, and my father, as mayor, went to the station to meet them. I don't know why, but he took me along. Anyway, one of these officers gave me some delicious chocolates to eat and a bottle of Coca-Cola. I really liked sweets, and for me that chocolate and Coke was . . . like a gift from heaven. I just enjoyed every bite and every sip. The bottle seemed so beautiful and precious that when I finished drinking the Coke, I tried to return it to the officer who gave it to me. (much laughter) He also thought that was funny, and that I was a funny kid. Anyway, he told me to keep it, that I could keep it.

"Well, I took it home and showed it off to my older brothers. We all thought it was a very heavy, strong bottle and would not break easily. So, we tested it. We went out in our yard and I dropped it on the ground. It didn't break. Then we dropped it from the porch. Still OK. Then my brother dropped it from the second story, and it still didn't break. We were astonished at the strength of that American Coke bottle. (laughter) No wonder the Americans won the war. To us young boys, it was clear. Jeeps and Coca-Cola. (much laughter)

"I also remember a morning late in the autumn, I think it was in . . . 1948, when I picked up the newspaper at our front gate, to take it to my father. I used to do that every morning. I was nine years old, so I could read some of the characters in the headline and on the front page. It said something about a court sentencing thirteen war criminals, including General Hideki Tojo, to death by hanging. But there were many characters I still could not read, so when I got in the house I asked my mother what it was about. Just then my father came into the room, took the paper, and said to my mother, 'Don't let the child see this kind of news.' So, I knew it was something very special . . . and bad. But it was years before I found out what had happened."

Question: "What effect or influence do you think the war, the Surrender and the American Occupation had on your values and perspective?"

(thoughtful pause)"Hmmm. It is hard . . . very difficult to say . . . because it seemed normal to me. Well, the very simple, frugal life that we had then made me think that it was a normal way to live . . . maybe as normal as the rich life we have now. Otherwise, there was . . . how can I explain it . . . no break in the flow, at least for me. In Tsuruoka, life just seemed to go on, just kept flowing on. No break or sudden change. It was not like Tokyo, or some big city that was bombed."

Question: "I think that you started primary school just after the end of the war, so you probably were not conscious of any educational changes or reforms, were you?"

"Well, no . . . not really. I was too young. The democratic ideas in school seemed normal to me. I didn't know anything else. I was in the Tsuruoka Second Elementary School. But I have no special memories of my school days. I did my school work and lived in my family. You know, with four big brothers to keep me busy . . . .(some laughter) There were the winters, long winters with deep, deep snow. Then the warm, rainy rice planting season, the hot summers, and then the rice harvest. (reminiscent pause and a warm smile) I do have a strong, vivid memory of the Obon Festival (a memorial festival held in mid-August) the summer after the war, in 1946. Somehow, the people in our town sang and danced that year with . . . so much happiness and energy . . . and hit the drum so hard. Probably because it was peace again. I remember the noise, and how happy and beaming their faces were. That was a liberation festival, that Obon."

Question: "Yes, I can imagine how that was, especially that wild beating on the ceremonial drum. I have heard that, and you can feel it right in your stomach. (laughter) You mentioned your four older brothers keeping you busy. Did they give you a bad time, as the youngest boy in the family?"

(laughing) "Well, sometimes they did. But they were not especially hard or cruel. No. Just older brothers, and I was the youngest. (more laughter and then after a thoughtful pause) Probably the most important thing was that being the youngest brother, I could never--as a boy--be the leader in my family. So, it made it more difficult for me to have confidence . . . confidence that I could make decisions and be a leader."

EDUCATION IN TOKYO

Question: "When your father won his Diet seat in 1952, did you move to Tokyo or stay in Yamagata?"

"My older brothers were already at school, at the university in Tokyo. My father said that since he would have to be in Tokyo so much of the time, my mother, and I, and my younger sister should move there too. So we all moved, and that was a turning point in my life. That year, I was in the second year of middle school, and in Tokyo I entered the Kojimachi Middle School. It was a good school, the start of the education escalator for me, the escalator to Todai. After two years at Kojimachi, I took the difficult entrance examination for Hibiya High School, and I passed it and got into that good school. In those days, Hibiya High School used to send many of its graduates to Todai, so it was a big step. In . . . let me see . . . 1958, I graduated from Hibiya and I took the entrance test for Todai, and I failed it. So, I became a *ronin* for one year. The second time, I passed, and I entered Todai in the spring of 1959."

Question: "Had your older brothers attended Todai, too?"

(looking at me keenly) "No. They went to other universities. (pause) Somehow, although my father never said it to me, I felt that he expected me to enter Todai. That he was counting on me to do it . . . to follow in his footsteps. (very serious look and tone of voice) It was a . . . heavy obligation for me."

TODAI AND THE
ANTI-U.S.-JAPAN SECURITY TREATY MOVEMENT

Question: "Almost all the Todai people I have spoken with have said that the entrance test was the biggest hurdle, the most difficult part, and that they had a relaxed life at Todai at least for the first two years. Was that true for you, too?"

"Well, I was so relieved to enter Todai, that I was relatively more relaxed, but only for a few months. (smiling at me) You know, you are asking me a lot of personal questions, and it is not so easy to answer them. (pausing to consider and then speaking seriously) I don't think back on those school days that often now, but they were not always so happy and easygoing. The Ampo Movement (Anti-U.S.-Japan Security Treaty Movement) was already starting at Todai in 1959, when I went there.[1] Unless you joined that movement and were pro-socialist, you were labeled as a . . . reactionary . . . not intellectual . . . a bad person. That was the atmosphere. So, I was caught in the middle. My father, the LDP Dietman, supported the U.S.-Japan Security Treaty and the 1960 revision. But all my classmates kept saying that the Ampo (Security Treaty) was bad--fundamentally wrong, because it was against Communist China and the Soviet Union. In those days, we had a utopian vision, especially of China. In Peking, the streets were spotless, there were no flies, and all the people were working unselfishly for the public good and for world peace. In the eyes of the students, the U.S. was an aggressive, Imperialist country . . . very warlike and dangerous . . . ready to drag Japan into a war. So, it was wrong for Japan to cooperate with the U.S. against these good, peace-loving Socialist countries.

"I was pulled back and forth. In my mind, I mostly agreed with my classmates. But here (pointing at his stomach) in my guts, I had a loyalty for my father. It was not such an easy time. I was never sure what to do."

Question: "Did you participate in the Ampo demonstrations

---

1. For a detailed, vivid account of the student movement against the revised Security Treaty, please see George R. Packard III, *Protest in Tokyo*, (Princeton, N.J.: Princetion University Press, 1966).

against the treaty and Prime Minister Kishi (Nobusuke Kishi) in the spring of 1960, as so many other students did?"

"At the final stage, I at last went into one demo (demonstration). Even then, I was half-hearted about it. It was in June of 1960. I felt that Kishi was . . . really undemocratic. That his maneuvers in the Diet were almost illegal. So, I had to resist his policies. (shaking his head in some dismay) But even then, I wasn't really confident what to do."

Question: "Did it cause you much trouble at home?"

"Not so much. My father did not take the student movement . . . very seriously. He probably saw it as a passing stage. His idea, even then, was that I would succeed him in his Diet seat. He planned to retire after a few more years in the Diet and become mayor of Tsuruoka again. As mayor, he would hold the constituency together, and then some years after I graduated from college, he thought I would become a young Dietman and take his seat."

Comment: "Well, it sounds from your tone as though you may not have agreed with all of his ideas."

"It was a . . . messy time for me. All through high school I was under my father's . . . invisible guidance. He did not tell me what to do, or order me. But I had enormous respect for him. I wanted to please him, and I knew what he wanted me to do. To get into Todai. So I worked very hard . . . for his sake. Then, when I entered Todai in 1959 during the Ampo Movement, my feelings about my father began to change . . . gradually change. Because I was not sure which side was right, the Ampo students or my father. You know, in the summer of 1960, after Kishi forced the revised Security Treaty through the Diet, he was forced to step down and Ikeda (Hayato Ikeda) became prime minister. In the fall, several months later, Ikeda called a general election. I worked in my father's election campaign. (pause, looking at me seriously and picking his words slowly and carefully) During that election campaign, I lost my respect for my father. Maybe I had too much respect before then. Maybe this . . . breaking away . . . came too late. Maybe . . . I should have had a more independent mind by the time I entered the university. Anyway, after that election campaign, I psychologically . . . left my father.

"I decided I wanted to become a journalist, to join the Asahi Newspaper (at that time, Japan's largest and most influential national daily, known for its outspoken criticism of government policy and its sympathy for the Socialist Opposition). I wanted people all over the country to read my articles in the Asahi. That was my ambition in those days. (smiling reminiscently) You know, for our Ampo generation, joining the Asahi was a beautiful idea. (chuckling) If we went into the Civil Service, or joined a big company like steel or a trading company, we would make a good salary, but we would have to become a running dog for the Capitalist-Imperialists. If we joined the Asahi, we could also make a good salary and have a good life, and at the same time, we could attack the Capitalist-Imperialists every day in the newspaper. (both laughing) Beautiful, eh?"

CHOOSING A CAREER

"During my last year or two at Todai, my mind began to change. I got a new ambition. I decided that I wanted to enter the Foreign Ministry and become a diplomat."

Question: "A diplomat? I thought that working for the government was unacceptable . . . too Capitalist."

(nodding his head and smiling) "I found a way around that. I wanted to be a specialist in China--Communist China. I wanted to go there and really learn how their system worked, and also to improve Japan-China ties. So, in a way, I became interested in the Foreign Service because of my interest in China."

Question: "Why did you become interested in Communist China? Wasn't the Soviet Union the leader of the Socialist camp?"

(with a twinkle in his eye) "Oh yes. It was. But China was more . . . like home to me. More like Yamagata. Even though I had broken away from my father, I still felt a . . . strong tie to our home country, to Yamagata. It is the soil . . . the old fashioned farmers who came to drink tea and to chat in my father's house in Tsuruoka. Asian people. Farmers. I believed that China would be something like that.

"I remember when I went to the Foreign Ministry building in Kasumigaseki for the first time to get the application forms for the

Foreign Service. The building was very new then in the early sixties. The marble floor was so highly polished, you could slip on it
very easily. The people there were so well dressed, sophisticated,
and had an elegant way of walking. (pause) So, I asked myself,
'Can I live here with these beautiful city people?' (pause) I was not
comfortable with that question. But then I persuaded myself that it
would be OK. I was not going to study French, or go to Paris or
Washington. I am going to China. No marble floors there. More
of old Asia, you see?"

Comment: "Yes. I can see how it worked in your mind."

"Well, in my last year at Todai, I took the examinations for
the Foreign Ministry and for the Asahi. I failed the ministry examination that time and was accepted by Asahi. But by then, my dream
of becoming a famous journalist had . . . faded. I couldn't revive it,
even when Asahi recruited me. My mind was set on China and the
Foreign Service. So, I studied more for the Foreign Ministry, took
the test again, passed it and joined the ministry in April of 1964."

TAIWAN AND HARVARD

"A few months after I entered the Foreign Service, on August 1st, I was sent as a trainee to Taiwan, to study Mandarin Chinese. It was a two year course. Well, after twelve months I got a
call on the phone from home telling me of my father's sudden death.
I came back to Japan to attend his funeral, and then returned to my
language study in Taiwan. Soon after I got back to work on Taiwan, my older brother Jiro, who was the closest to my father's political organization, also came to Taipei. My father's political supporters in Tsuruoka had sent him to persuade me to leave the Foreign Ministry and to run in the election to fill my father's Diet seat.
Well, I couldn't do it. Not then.

"I told my brother that my mind was not . . . settled enough
and firm enough to be a good politician. I didn't know what I really
believed yet. A politician has to have solid, clear ideas about domestic policy, foreign policy, and defense. Unless you know what
you want to do, you should not get into politics. My ideas were still
. . . mixed up. I had a kind of half-hearted respect for socialism--

for a kind of Maoist, Chinese, utopian vision of socialism. But I had no clear ideas, and I felt I could not run for the Diet. So, I stayed in Taipei and finished my language training.

"Then, after language training, the ministry assigned me to Harvard for one year, in 1966-1967. They wanted me to study Chinese politics and socialism with the China experts in your country--men like John Fairbanks and Ezra Vogel. Hmm. You know, Harvard was . . . very important to me . . . in a way that I never expected. The teachers there made me think . . . think on my own. I wanted to get good marks. At first, I couldn't do it, no matter how hard I worked. I read so many books and quoted from them, but it wasn't enough. The teachers told me that to get an A, I had to have my own ideas. I had to reach my own conclusions in my paper and explain what my logic and evidence was. (shaking his head at the memory) That was hard work! I lost about fifteen pounds that year. (laughing) But it was really interesting . . . and challenging. I enjoyed it, and later I found that it could be useful, too."

Question: "This is an unexpected twist. When you joined the Foreign Ministry, you seemed uncomfortable with Western culture--even with the idea of Paris or Washington. Now, I find you studying China at Harvard, writing papers in English, and living in Cambridge, Massachusetts--close to the cradle of American Independence. (both laughing) Were you as uncomfortable as you expected to be?"

(smiling) "I felt more at home in New York than at Cambridge. Cambridge was so . . . Caucasian . . . almost pure white. It had a kind of chilly, snobbish atmosphere. A good place to study, but not comfortable . . . not for me. (both laughing) In New York, the people were rougher and louder, but I could see all types of people, all colors and races--Latinos, Asians, Blacks, Eastern Europeans, everything. It was a warmer atmosphere in New York, more relaxing for me. (laughing) And it was easier to meet girls there. So, when I could take some time from my studies, I used to go to New York to relax.

"Anyway, even though I studied at Harvard for only one year, it was important for me. It changed my ideas about education. If I ever become minister of education, my experience at Harvard will influence my education policy."

HONG KONG AND DECIDING TO ENTER POLITICS

"After three years of training, I finally got my first posting in June of 1967. I was assigned to our consulate-general in Hong Kong. We didn't have any diplomatic mission in China yet, so the consulate-general in Hong Kong was like our embassy to China. And in many ways, it was easier to find out what was happening in China at Hong Kong, than if you were actually inside China . . . because the controls and censorship were so strong in China. My job was . . . just what I hoped. I was in charge of writing our reports on what was going on in the Great Cultural Revolution. I met a lot of Chinese people who were coming from the Mainland, and talked with them in their own language. Sometimes they let me read letters from their relatives at home, describing what was happening in their factory, or village, or office. I was also in charge of the Japanese expatriates who were coming out of the mainland from up in Manchuria, as refugees. They had left their farming communes because of the chaotic situation, and wanted to return to Japan after thirty years in China. They had forgotten most of their Japanese, and I spoke to them in Chinese, too, in a difficult Manchu dialect. At first, they were very hesitant to talk about their experiences. So, I would make reservations for them on a ship going to Japan, and find them a hotel to live in while they waited for their ship. I tried to see them every day, and sometimes have a meal with them in a Japanese restaurant. After a week or so, they usually became less worried and careful, and told me about their communes and the Cultural Revolution.

"So, from all these people that I talked with, I was able to get some realistic reports about China. (pause) Hmm. Before very long, my utopian vision of China . . . was gone . . . finished."

Question: "Yes, I see. And with your utopian vision of Chinese socialism gone, one of the important reasons that kept you from entering politics was also . . . gone. Am I guessing correctly?"

"That's right. That was an important reason why I changed my mind and eventually ran for the Diet. You know, after my father died, and my brother came to Taipei and tried to persuade me to run for my father's seat, I asked some advice from a senior diplomat--my boss. He said to me, 'You are only twenty-six years old, so it is natural that you don't have strong ideas and enough confidence in yourself to run for the Diet. Stay in the Foreign Ministry for at least ten years and then you will find your own values, your own ideology, and you will have enough self-confidence.'

"His advice seemed sensible to me. But I only stayed in the ministry seven years, until 1971 . . . not ten years. There were two general elections while I was in the Foreign Service--in 1967 and then in 1969. I could not help but notice what happened in our constituency in those elections. The core of my father's *jiban* (territorial base) was in Tsuruoka City. In the 1967 election, Mr. Masaki Tanaka tried to get the support of my father's *jiban*, and he couldn't quite do it. He lost. In 1969, another candidate, Mr. Reizoh Yaguchi, also tried to get my father's core constituency, and did not make it and lost. In both elections, the political leaders in my father's *jiban*, after some reluctance, agreed to support Mr. Tanaka and Mr. Yaguchi. During the campaign, they seemed to be in full, 100 percent support of these men, hot and enthusiastic, you know. But suddenly, just as election day approached, some group in my father's *jiban* got cool. They backed off, and Mr. Tanaka and Mr. Yaguchi didn't get quite enough votes to win a Diet seat. They came . . . so close. But both times, that small shift at the end . . . defeated them.[2]

"I'll tell you why they got cool and backed off. It was not an accident. They said, 'If we elect Mr. Tanaka or Mr. Yaguchi to the Diet, what will become of Mr. Kato's son, the youngest boy in the Foreign Ministry? He is the one we want.' For these loyal supporters, Mr. Tanaka and Mr. Yaguchi were outsiders trying to get into the *jiban*.

(smiling) "That constituency is like . . . your Monroe Doc-

---

2. The Lower House of the Diet has 512 seats. The Representatives are elected in multi-member, single vote election districts. Each district (except the special district of the Amami Islands) sends three to five Representatives to the Lower House. In the general election each voter in the district casts a single vote for one of the candidates. The candidates with the highest number of votes fill the available seats. For example, if it is a three-member district like Mr. Kato's, the three candidates with the most votes win the three seats. For a more detailed explanation, please see Robert E. Ward, *Japan's Political System* (Englewood Cliffs, N.J.: Prentice Hall, Inc., 1978), Ch. 8, "Elections."

trine in Latin America. (both laughing) They have a doctrine of no outside interference. Yes, that's the way it works.

"Another factor is that while I was serving in Hong Kong, I met lots of Dietmen. During the Diet recess, many of them take trips to different countries in Asia. On their way back to Japan, they often stopped in Hong Kong and stayed for a few days, to shop, to buy gifts, and to relax. One of my jobs as a young diplomat was to help these Dietmen, take them shopping and sightseeing, make them comfortable. So, I had a good chance to talk with them and to get to know them better . . . as human beings . . . their strong points and weaknesses. Well, that made me more realistic about politics and politicians. You know, after awhile, I felt that I was . . . not unqualified . . . that I could do the job, too.

"Well, sometime after the 1969 election--I am not sure when--but when I saw that even Mr. Yaguchi could not get the full support of my father's constituency, I decided that in the next election, I would run. I felt that with the full support of our *jiban,* I could win."

MARRIAGE AND FAMILY

Question: "Before we talk about your first election in 1972, do you mind if we shift the subject and look at your marriage and family? Did you marry before you entered politics, or afterward?"

"I married when I was in the Foreign Service. It was on July 8th, 1967, during the time I was serving in Hong Kong. I took two weeks off and went to Japan. That was when I got married."

Question: (pause) "Hmm. Yes. I see. Well, that sounds so . . . abrupt. (both laughing) Can you tell me how you met your wife, and a bit about her? What was her name before she married you? (pause, no response) Did you have a traditional, arranged marriage?

(chuckling) "No, no. I met my wife through a friend from Hibiya High School. We picked each other. Then I went into the Foreign Service. After three years, I came back to Japan, from Hong Kong, so that we could get married."

Question: "Is your wife from Yamagata? Did she also have a special interest in China?"

"No, no. (laughing) She is from Takasaki. She had no special interest in China. She studied Japanese literature at Japan Women's University. (pause) OK. I'll tell you how we met. My friend from Hibiya, Hideki Ebihara, had a *miai* (a traditional, arranged meeting between a prospective bride and groom, usually with the families present), and he and the girl he met this way were going to get married. During their engagement they sometimes went skiing, and sometimes these ski trips were overnight. So, they had to have chaperons. I went along as my friend's chaperon. My wife was the younger sister of my friend's fiancée, and so she was her sister's chaperon. That is how we met.

"My wife's name, by the way, is Aiko. We have four children, three daughters and a son. Our oldest daughter was born in 1969, so she is eighteen now. Her name is Ariko. In 1971, our second daughter, Aoi, was born. Then, in 1975, we had our son, Ryohsuke. And in 1979, our youngest girl, Ayuko, was born. Our second daughter, Aoi, went over to California to take her junior year at Santa Catalina High School, in Monterey."

GETTING ELECTED

Question: "I know that you first ran and won your Diet seat in the 1972 general election. Could you please tell me when you resigned from the Foreign Ministry? How long before the election was it?"

"I put in my resignation in 1971. It was pretty clear that there would be another general election within a year or two, and I knew I needed some time to prepare for the campaign."

Question: "Most of the politicians I have talked with have said that their first election was the toughest. Usually they had to run that first time without party endorsement and they had to unseat an established incumbent from their own party. Was that true for you, too?"

"Hmm. That first election was not the toughest for me. If you were reading the newspapers, it sounded very tough. But it went fairly . . . smoothly. I ran with my party's endorsement in that first election, but so did my main rival, Mr. Masanosuke Ikeda, who was the incumbent. My second election, four years later, in 1976 was a tougher fight. The tough part in 1976, was getting the LDP endorsement, not the election itself. You see, Mr. Ikeda, the man whose seat I took in 1972, was also an LDP politician. He did not give up after he lost his seat. No. He worked very hard within the local party organization, using all his contacts, to get the party endorsement and win back his seat in the next election. So, I had to compete with him.

"The seat that I hold has its voter support in Tsuruoka City and the surrounding area. Masanosuke Ikeda is from Akumi-gun, which borders on Tsuruoka City. So, we had to compete for the same voters."[3]

Question: "I see. How did the local party leaders decide whom to endorse. On what did they base their endorsement?"

"They had to decide which of us had the strongest voter support in Tsuruoka. You know, they are always meeting and talking with leaders of the neighborhood associations and the local clubs and so on. That is how they decided. They felt that I had more support . . . and a more promising chance to be elected. So, even though I was the incumbent, I had to work very hard in my district for that election. But once I began to do that, I was . . . fairly confident of the result."

PENSION POLICY AND THE HARVARD EFFECT

Question: "Would you care to tell me about your experiences in the Diet, including your work on the Diet committees?"

"When you are elected from Yamagata, an agricultural district, the most advantageous committees are Agriculture and Construction. Those help to win votes. But these committees are so popular that it is very hard for a freshman in the Diet to get on them. So, in my first year in the Diet, I asked to be put on the Social and

---

3. For a well informed discussion of how Japanese Diet candidates deal with the question of party endorsement, please see Gerald L. Curtis, *Election Campaigning: Japanese Style*, (New York: Columbia University Press, 1971).

Labor Affairs Committee, to work on social welfare--old age pensions and medical benefits. There were no openings on Agriculture
or Construction, and I wanted to . . . balance my experience in foreign policy with experience in domestic policy. That was my reason."

Question: "Did your constituents think this was a good assignment? What was their reaction?"

"They . . . didn't have much interest in that committee, but it
was OK. (some laughter) I also had another reason . . . a personal
reason. In 1971, about one year before I joined the Diet, we had
our second daughter. She was very premature, very small and
could only live . . . only survive in an incubator. In the end, she
came out healthy. When she was born, and her life was in danger, I
felt that I would give anything, even one hundred million yen, to
save her. So, I could understand parents . . . poor parents, who
have sick children. I thought that if I had a chance, I should do
something for them."

Question: "That makes sense to me. But isn't the public
welfare system in Japan, including medical benefits, very limited?
Aren't personal savings, company medical plans, and the family, the
extended family, the main resources for medical care, in most cases?"

"Yes. The public system is limited, as you say. But I
stayed on this committee for five years. I specialized on medical
benefits, including benefits for the handicapped, and also old age
pensions. I was able to do some good. And I learned something
about how our government works. Near the end of this assignment,
I got into a debate on old age pensions. That debate made me use
my Harvard training in independent thinking. And it was a . . . political debut for me. It made an impact on the pension system--
helped to change it.

"I had learned that the pension system for our government
employees is much better and more complete than for our private
sector employees. Yet the government employees and the private
sector employees were paying about the same amount into their
pension systems. So, at the committee session, I asked the high
civil servant in charge of the pension policy to explain this.
(chuckling) Well you know how the civil servant took care of me.

He said, (putting on a pompous tone) 'Mr. Kato, your question is very good. I will get the answer for you.' Some days later, he came to the committee and said, 'I have prepared a report for you. This is a complicated matter, but I will give you all the facts.' (both laughing) Then he gave a thirty minute lecture, very difficult to follow . . . but full of facts. Of course, we did not really understand his explanation, but most Dietmen are so busy that they nod their heads and say, 'Yes. I understand now. Thanks vice-minister for your good explanation.' (more laughter) That is the way the bureaucrats handle politicians.

"Well, I was not satisfied. So, I went on my own to find and study the facts of these pension systems. I studied for several months, and I reached the conclusion that the government was quietly putting a lot of funds into the government employees' pension. That was not secret or illegal, but nobody seems to have paid attention to it before I prepared this report. So, I wrote my report and recommended that government expenditures on pensions be cut . . . by changing the government employees retirement age from fifty-five to sixty. That got quite a bit of attention . . . even in the media. That was in 1977. In 1984, the government pension system was revised. The retirement age was changed to sixty. So, I felt that the report I wrote was useful, after all."

DEPUTY CHIEF CABINET SECRETARY AND MINISTER FOR DEFENSE

"In 1977, I finally was appointed to the Agriculture Committee. I was on it for close to seven years. But during the period of the Ohira cabinet, I was not able to attend committee meetings, because I was the deputy chief cabinet secretary. (Masayoshi Ohira was prime minister from December 1978 until his sudden death in June 1980.) There were two chief cabinet secretaries under Ohira. First, there was Mr. Rokusuke Tanaka. Then, in the second Ohira cabinet, Mr. Masayoshi Ito. I stayed as their deputy for the whole Ohira administration."

Question: "Doesn't the deputy chief cabinet secretary preside over the parliamentary vice-ministers? Isn't he generally senior to them, a former parliamentary vice-minister himself . . . and a senior Dietman?"

"Yes. You are right. (laughing) And I was only in my second term when Prime Minister Ohira appointed me . . . and he kept me on in that post."

Question: "Why do you think he did that?"

(Thoughtful pause and then in a matter-of-fact tone) "Loyalty. Loyalty to him and to his faction. I was one of the first of the six or seven Dietmen who joined the Ohira faction when he became the faction leader in 1971. That is important in Japanese politics--to pick the right faction . . . at the right time."[4]

Question: "Yes, I can see how that worked in the case of your appointment by Prime Minister Ohira as deputy chief cabinet secretary. But now you are defense minister in the Nakasone cabinet, and you are not in the Nakasone faction . . . and the newspapers say that your faction is not that friendly to the prime minister. When we met last winter, shortly after your appointment, I remember that you said that being selected to head the Defense Agency was a shock. Were you really surprised? How did it happen?"

"Oh yes. I had never even considered the possibility of heading the Defense Agency. Because of my committee experience and my policy interests, I think of myself as a possible labor minister, or welfare minister, or even agriculture minister. But not for defense. (some laughter) Most people think of me as more a domestic policy type . . . and they also think that my generation is . . . still too young for a ministerial appointment. As to why . . . why

---

4. The Liberal Democratic Party (LDP) is composed of six factions, each so well defined in terms of leadership and membership that some analysts refer to the factions as parties within the party. Until recently, the faction leaders competed for the presidency of the LDP, which is tantamount to the prime ministership as long as the LDP controls a majority in the Lower House. In this decade, since several of the faction leaders have had their turn at the prime ministership (Fukuda, Miki, Suzuki), their lieutenants are now the main contenders for this office. The faction leaders must be successful political fund raisers. Faction members depend on their faction leader for an important part of their campaign funding. Faction members also expect that in return for their loyalty, the faction leader will use his patronage to gain political appointments for them, hopefully to a cabinet post. For a detailed and realistic description of the LDP factions, please see Nathaniel Thayer, *How the Conservatives Rule Japan* (Princeton, N.J.: Princeton University Press, 1969), Ch. II. "The Factions". That Thayer's work continues to be relevant almost twenty years after he wrote it, attests to the stability of Japanese politics.

Prime Minister Nakasone appointed me . . . hmm . . . I am still . . . not sure. He did not consult with Mr. Suzuki. (Zenko Suzuki was prime minister from June 1980 until October 1982. When Prime Minister Ohira suddenly died in June 1980, Mr. Suzuki succeeded him as faction leader.) Mr. Suzuki was also surprised when I was given this appointment."[5]

RICE SUBSIDY, INDUSTRIAL
DEVELOPMENT, AND TRANSPORTATION

Question: "I have seen a number of studies that show that many rice farmers in rural prefectures like Yamagata are marginal farmers, that they get most of their income from nonagricultural work and only stay on the farms because of the government subsidy. The city people in Japan complain that the price of rice is too high because of the rice subsidy, and some foreign rice producers also say that they could sell rice in Japan for much less than the presently protected, subsidized Japanese rice. What is your view on the future of the rice subsidy?"

"Hmmm. I think it can be worked out. As a practical matter, reducing the rice subsidy is only possible if we create more jobs, good jobs, in rural areas like Yamagata. We must encourage the new industries, high-tech industries, to start up in the rural areas. And that depends very much on transportation--more and faster transportation so we can be connected with the rest of the Japanese and world economy. The Shinkansen (Bullet train) is good, it helps, but it is not enough. We also need high-speed highways and better roads. And in my district, we need an airport. Of course, air transportation is expensive. I want to see very high-tech industries grow in my district--industries that will produce very expensive, lightweight products. Products that are economical to transport by air.

---

5. Japanese political analysts speculated that Prime Minister Nakasone appointed Mr. Kato to the Defense Agency to soften the Suzuki faction's opposition to the prime minister's efforts to increase the defense budget and to pursue a policy of more active security cooperation with the United States.

"In practical, realistic terms, these are the requirements of reducing the rice subsidy. (thoughtful pause) This kind of local economic development is connected to the . . . bigger issue . . . of the future of Japan and the future of our party--the LDP."

THE FUTURE OF THE LDP
AND THE TASK OF THE POLITICIAN

"You probably know that many critics in the Opposition parties and in the media say that the LDP has been able to control the Diet and to control the cabinet for the past forty years because we have money--money to spend in election campaigns. That is too simple. There is more to it. The Japanese people are well educated and very keen. They pay attention to what is going on. I don't think anyone can buy their vote just with campaign money or advertising. No. The voters must see some attractive, worthwhile, and practical policies before they support a politician . . . or his party.

"So what do the voters see in the LDP politicians? Our most attractive point has been economic development and growth--especially the growth of income, personal income. Our second most attractive point has been a successful diplomatic and defense policy, a policy based on solid ties and cooperation with your country. There has always been a lot of discussion and disagreement about what is the best foreign policy for Japan. (Noticing an amused expression on my face) You are thinking of the 1960 Ampo Movement, and the young student, Kato. (laughter) But in the end, most Japanese think that close ties with the U.S. makes sense. Not perfect, but it is practical. Before 1971-1972, when your government improved its relations with China, there were many more doubts in Japan. But since China and America ended their hostility and moved closer, it is much easier for Japanese to support U.S.-Japan ties. So, most of the voters support the LDP foreign policy.

"The problem is that in the last ten years or so, more and more of our voters say that economic development is not enough. We must have it, but it is not enough. They say that we must also protect our environment--and improve it. That we must educate ourselves better--improve people's minds. They want to improve the quality of life. Nowadays, making more money and buying more manufactured goods cannot absorb all the energy of the Japanese people.

"What we need now in Japan is a concept like Mr. (Kiichi) Miyazawa's infrastructure doubling plan. (Mr. Miyazawa succeeded to the leadership of the Suzuki faction in 1986, and became the faction's candidate for prime minister.) You remember that after the Ampo Crisis of 1960, when Mr. Ikeda became prime minister, he got the country's mind off foreign policy by setting up the goal of income doubling. That policy was good for Japan, and it was the secret of the LDP's strength after the 1960 crisis. Now, we should shift our attention from income doubling to doubling the value and quality of our basic economic infrastructure--housing, schools, hospitals, parks, highways. That is what most Japanese want. That will make Japan a better-quality country to live in. It is good for Japan and good for the LDP."

Comment: "Yes. I have seen a number of articles on Miyazawa's plan. This policy could also help with your trade imbalance, your trade surplus with the United States and the rest of the world. It could move your economy away from its heavy reliance on exports to spur economic growth."

"Yes, it will help there too. But it must be changed from a plan into a real, working policy. (thoughtful pause) The first and most important thing is that this infrastructure doubling must become the new goal of Japan, the new basis of our concensus. That is the job for us, for politicians. After Ikeda set up the income doubling goal, we politicians . . . didn't have so much to do. We could respond to complaints about policy, and try to adjust it, but the basic policies were set. (laughing) In a way, our job was to avoid disturbing the efficiency of the bureaucrats and the private sector. But now there is growing dissatisfaction with the goal of just building our income. We are losing our social and political concensus. So now we politicians have creative work to do again . . . as Prime Minister Yoshida did in the 1950s and as Prime Minister Ikeda did in the 1960s.

(pause and then in a serious tone) "Unfortunately, many of our Diet members are not working at this basic work--not yet. Times have been so good, so easy, for such a long time, that many politicians have gotten used to . . . not thinking about basic policy. They are not so eager to change. It is hard work . . . and risky to set up new goals and build a new concensus. But that is what we need to do."

INTERNATIONALIZATION AND
JAPAN'S FUTURE IN THE WORLD

Question: "Japan has been internationalizing--learning to do business and get along with foreign countries and cultures--for more than a century. The process seems to have accelerated since 1945, and your country is now one of the world's major exporters of manufactured products, the largest importer of petroleum in the world, and you are rapidly becoming the number one creditor in the world. Do you think that there are now, and will be in the future, for the next ten to twenty years, sufficient numbers of Japanese who can use foreign languages and deal knowledgeably with foreigners to keep the internationalization process moving ahead successfully?"

"I think the answer is yes. We have enough internationally trained people now, and I think we are training enough young people for the future. I read somewhere that we send about fifteen thousand young Japanese overseas for training each year.

(thoughtful pause) "The more important question is whether these internationally trained people will be in the main stream--in the inside, policy-making groups in the organizations, companies, and banks where they work. Twenty years ago, I think the answer was . . . doubtful . . . and often it was no. But it is getting better. I think the government ministries, such as Finance and MITI, led the way. And more recently, big companies and banks are also starting to put internationally trained people in key management, decision-making jobs.

(smiling) "The Diet is the least internationalized, compared to the bureaucracy and the business world. I think that about 10 percent of the Diet members can use foreign languages and have experience living and working outside Japan. And that is a big increase over thirty years ago. The reason for the increase is the number of Dietmen who are former bureaucrats. (laughter) These internationalized bureaucrats, who used to have to retire when they were fifty-five, have been . . . infiltrating into our Diet."

Question: "Like you?" (both laughing)

"Yes. I am an infiltrator. So, you see I am optimistic on this aspect of internationalization. I think that there will be enough internationally trained Japanese, and that they will have enough influence and control over policy."

Question: "What about trade frictions with the U.S. and Europe? Will protectionism bring about a sharp reduction in world trade, a world depression, and force Japan to turn in on itself again?"

(pause and then in an especially thoughtful tone) "I wish I could be more certain of my answer. I hope not. I don't think so. There is lots of pushing and pressure in this direction, and we already have some protectionism--your quotas on the import of our cars, our restrictions on your agricultural products--but I don't think it will get . . . out of control. Too many people realize how dangerous this could be. So, I think we will . . . not repeat the 1930s."

Question: "What do you think of *Nihonjin Ron*, of the articles and books that have been coming out in recent years that say that Japan is getting to be too much like America or Europe--is in danger of losing its unique Japanese identity? Do you think these ideas and these writings indicate a turning away from internationalization?"

"I am not too worried about these writings . . . these ideas and criticisms. What is really going on is that we Japanese are starting to realize that we can't keep improving our country by following foreign models. You know, for the last one hundred years, whenever we wanted to improve something, we tried to imitate a foreign model. If we wanted to be culturally sophisticated and fashionable, France was our model--Christian Dior and Cardin were our models. When we wanted to be rich . . . affluent, your country was our model. When we thought of how a social welfare system should work, we studied the Scandinavian model. For discipline and social justice, we admired Socialist countries, like China and the U.S.S.R. You know, no dirt in the streets, no flies, all people working together for world peace. (laughter)

"So, you see my point. The foreign models were all, to some extent, illusions. The more we go to these foreign countries, the more we realize that they are not as perfect as we used to believe they were. We cannot find the magical bluebird in a foreign country. So now, we are like a . . . traveler who has taken a long journey to foreign places looking for the ideal society, and is coming home. We have learned that we must create our own bluebird, our own model. We are just starting to realize that we have to do that, that we cannot just keep on imitating, keep on catching up. Some of those writings about *Nihonjin Ron* are excessive . . . too emotional. But that is what I think is going on.

"We are not going to turn away from internationalization. We will go on interacting, more and more, with foreign countries. But we will not be able to see foreign cultures in . . . such an idealistic light. I think that we will build our own future society on many traditional Japanese values. Not all, but many. We will keep our strong family and our seniority system--our way of respecting elders. These are not perfect either. But they work. They help to keep people decent . . . respectable."

BUREAUCRATS

Ryohei Murata

A PROFESSIONAL diplomat, by definition, is internationalized. He is competent in foreign languages, deeply versed in foreign cultures and values, and at the same time is a trusted, responsible, and in some cases an influential official within his own government. In 1895, when the Ministry of Foreign Affairs began to use an examination that was designed to select applicants who could meet all these requirements, it moved to the forefront of the internationalization process in Japan.[1] Before 1895, Japan's foreign relations had been largely conducted through interpreters, some of them extraordinarily talented and respected, but there had been no official institution designed to recruit and train an elite of insiders capable of operating comfortably and effectively with foreigners (*gaijin,* literally, outside people). The Foreign Ministry's special needs, its methods, and its success eventually made it the model for the subsequent internationalization of other ministries, as well as banks and corporations.

The Foreign Ministry's method of recruiting and training has been quite simple, and has not changed much over the decades. With few exceptions, only the more successful graduates of the most demanding and prestigious universities have taken the Foreign Ministry diplomatic examination. In 1895, only three applicants were accepted. In 1920 and 1921, the number rose as high as thirty-seven.[2] In the postwar period, about twenty to thirty diplomatic applicants a year have entered the ministry. This means that the dip-

---

1. Usui Katsumi, "The Role of the Foreign Ministry", in *Pearl Harbor as History: Japanese-American Relations, 1931-1941*, eds. D. Borg and S. Okamoto, (New York: Columbia University Press, 1973), 129-30.
2. Katsumi, "The Role of the Foreign Ministry," 129-30.

A recent photo.

Wedding day.

lomatic service has been staffed by the same educational elite who preside over the other ministries in Tokyo, as well as the political and business worlds. This elite has been open to all classes of Japanese, from rich to poor, who have been able to pass the rigorous examinations. The basic distinction for Foreign Ministry applicants is that they have also been tested on their foreign language skills. Those who have passed in both the general subjects and the foreign language, and who have shown a high degree of poise and maturity in their interview, have been taken into the ministry and then sent abroad for several more years of full immersion in a foreign culture, usually including study at the best foreign universities. Only after completing intensive training abroad has the young diplomat been considered ready to take up his official duties.

Every member of this select diplomatic service has been able to look forward to serving as an ambassador, usually in several foreign capitols. The best of each class also serve as director-generals of the ministry's bureaus and as vice-minister for foreign affairs. These senior diplomatic officials are usually influential in shaping Japanese foreign policy. Their powers are closer to those of their counterparts in the British and French Foreign ministries and generally greater than those of career diplomats in the State Department.[3] Since 1945, three of Japan's prime ministers have been diplomats-- Prime Ministers Kijuro Shidehara, Shigeru Yoshida, and Hitoshi Ashida. As one would expect, the result of this selection and training has been a Japanese who can stand on equal footing with any politician, official or businessman in Tokyo, and who is also at home in Paris, New York, Vienna, Moscow, or Beijing.

Ryohei Murata, who joined the Foreign Ministry in 1952, is a trim, graying, quietly thoughtful man in his middle fifties. Working in shirtsleeves in his office on Tokyo's Kasumigaseki, he has the look of a college professor grading papers. His eyeglasses, and his quiet, careworn face convey an academic, studious impression. At a diplomatic conference or a cocktail party, a metamorphosis oc-

---

3. Haruhiro Fukui, "Policy-Making in the Japanese Foreign Ministry", in *The Foreign Policy of Modern Japan*, ed. Robert A. Scalapino (Berkeley, Calif: University of California Press, 1977), 3-35. See also, Misawa Shigeo, "Seisaku Kettei Katei no Gaikan," in *Gendai Nihon no Seito to Kanryo*, (Tokyo: Iwanami Shoten, 1967), 14-18.

curs. Ryohei Murata becomes a smooth-faced, quietly confident, impeccably tailored diplomat. The quiet, sober expression gives way now and then to a warm, engaging smile. His remarks, whether delivered in German, English, or Japanese are clear, to the point, and occasionally edged with a playful wit.

When I interviewed him in the winter and spring of 1985, Mr. Murata was director-general for inspection in the Ministry of Foreign Affairs. This was a relatively brief (October 1985-May 1985), quiet, administrative post between more demanding, policy oriented assignments. His previous position was director-general of the important and prestigious Economic Affairs Bureau, from 1982 to 1984. In May 1985 I wished him farewell and good luck at the ministry reception marking his appointment as Japan's ambassador to Austria. In the spring of 1987, he was called back to Tokyo to become vice-minister of foreign affairs.

Vienna was Ryohei Murata's second ambassadorial post. From 1978 to 1980 he was Ambassador to the United Arab Emirates--and also the youngest Japanese ambassador at that time. When he returned to Tokyo from Abu Dhabi he became director-general of the Middle Eastern and African Affairs Bureau. Ambassador Murata's posting in Vienna was probably related to his fluent German and his expertise on Central Europe as well as both the Middle East and economics. OPEC headquarters is in Vienna, and Arab oil ministers and their staffs are frequent visitors to that city. Despite efforts to diversify Japan's energy sources, OPEC still furnishes 70 percent of Japan's oil and 40 percent of its total energy.

FAMILY

Our first session was on a wet, chilly January day. It began over a steaming, fragrant Chinese lunch at the Okura Hotel, not far from the Foreign Ministry, and continued afterward at Mr. Murata's office. Mr. Murata, in his clipped, careful English with a tinge of a German accent, told me that his family came from the outskirts of Kyoto. He was born in Kyoto, the third of four sons, on November 2, 1929, to Tahei and Yoshiko Murata.

"Tanabe is the place of my ancestors. It is about ten miles outside of Kyoto, between Kyoto and Nara, the two ancient capitals. When I was a boy, Tanabe was a farming village. Now, it has grown to a town . . . and in due course it will become a city. My forefathers served as the heads of a small rural community. In Japanese we call it an *aza*. Tanabe was made up of about a half dozen *aza*. They were not the mayors of Tanabe, but just the heads of an *aza*. They were not really peasants because they did not till most of the land they owned themselves, but rented it to tenant farmers. But they were not samurai either--even though the feudal lord allowed my great grandfather to carry a sword. They were commoners. By the time of my great grandfather and my grandfather, I would call them rural officials . . . and small landowners. They were able to live off the income of their small landholding because in those days the landlords took about 30 to 40 percent of the peasant's crop."

Question: "Would you say that your father's family was fairly well-to-do?"

"Fairly . . . yes . . . but certainly not rich. They could live in a decent, comfortable house, and they could afford to give their children some sort of schooling. (quietly but firmly, wanting to be accurate and precise) They were better off than the average Japanese, who were very poor in those days, but there was nothing unusual . . . nothing illustrious about them."

Question: "You mentioned that your father was the first in the family to attend a university?"

"Yes. He was born in 1888. The first Western style universities in Japan were being built around 1880. (smiling) So, it was not possible for anyone to enter a university in Japan before that time. My grandfather sent him to a school for teachers--a normal school--so that he could become a primary school teacher, which he did. Somehow, my father aspired to become something more . . . more important. He worked and studied very hard on his own, and after several years as a teacher, when he was in his middle twenties, he got into Kyoto Imperial University. That was around the time of the First World War. In those days, just a small percentage of people went on to a college or university education. Only well-to-do old samurai families, landowners, and the new class of rich people were sending their children to universities. Anyway, my grandfather thought that was too high for my father. At first he objected and would not pay for him, until his friends changed his mind and he gave his grudging consent.

"There were no organized scholarships then, but there were people who provided funds for able students who could not pay their tuition. They helped my father. He studied in the Faculty of Literature. His subject was sociology--a new subject in those days. He wrote his thesis on the evolution of marriage. (smiling) He compared the evolution of marriage in Japan and in the West."

Comment: "Well, that is fascinating . . . and perhaps a somewhat unusual subject for a university thesis in the first years of this century."

"Yes, it may have been. He saw marriage as an evolutionary development . . . everywhere. First, men just took women by force. Then, they bought them, like property, like livestock. As people became more civilized--that was a very gradual, long process--(smiling) they tried to improve on these primitive arrangements."

Question: "Did your father use foreign languages for his research? Was he a linguist?"

"His command of foreign languages was not particularly good. He could read foreign books . . . a bit in German . . . somewhat better in English. He could not converse."

"His real interest was something close to what you might call social work, or social education. He wanted to improve Japanese society by enlightening more people, by reviving some traditional virtues and bringing in some new Western ideas. After he finished at the university, he created a small organization for this purpose and set up an office in the city of Kyoto. That is why I was born there. He wrote quite a lot of books and articles and made a lot of lecture tours throughout Japan. He tried to help unfortunate people, too-- such as rehabilitating former criminals who had been in prison. Between the First and Second World Wars, especially in the 1920s, when Japanese businesses were growing and there was a strong liberal current in Japan, there were people who would support and contribute to his work, by subscribing to the periodicals he issued, for example. Anyway, he kept at this kind of work until the outbreak of the Pacific War. Then there were various restrictions . . . and, eventually, there was not even any paper to write or print on. Finally, in March 1945, he closed his office and moved back to Tanabe. He was neutral in politics, and stayed away from political parties.

"After the war--and I think as a consequence of the war--he had long talks with an American priest who established a church in Tanabe, and he converted to Catholicism. I did not convert. By tradition, our family is Buddhist. Then, the Kyoto prefectural government hired him to do public relations and research work. After he retired, he wrote several books on the archeology and history of the southern part of Kyoto Prefecture, and was honored for this in Tanabe."

Comment: "Your father seems to have been a scholarly man, and a bit individualistic and out of the ordinary in his . . . idealism and in his broad interests."

"Yes, he was. And he was a good teacher for his children. My three brothers and I had an ordinary education at school. But at home, our father used to tell us about the classical Japanese and Chinese literature, and such things--that were most interesting. My mother did, too. My father owned a library of several thousand books, mostly on social science, philosophy, and Japanese, Chinese, and European literature. Even when I was in primary school, my mother encouraged me to read those books"

Question: "Yes. I wanted to ask you about your mother's family and her role in your early education. Could we do that?"

"My grandfather on my mother's side was a textile merchant. My mother always spoke of him as a very intelligent and cultured man who had wanted to get a higher education for himself, but had not been able to. So, he wanted his children to be well-educated. In those days, when my mother was a girl, there were no colleges or universities in Japan for women. Instead, he sent her to a special women's higher school in Tokyo, and when she graduated she became a teacher at the normal school--the school for teachers in Kyoto.

"You can see that my father and mother were both well educated and I would say intellectual--interested in learning and ideas. That was the atmosphere in our home. We were not rich. In fact, after the war . . . we lost most of what we had. But we were encouraged to study."

Question: "Did your parents have any ideas or advice for you on what kind of work or profession you should enter?"

"Not in any specific sense, no. My brothers and I all felt that our parents wanted us to graduate from the university and go into some honorable vocation--some respectable work. But my parents never gave me detailed advice on my future. When I was a boy, I sometimes talked to my father about my ideas for the future and he would listen. He did not say much. He was a good listener.

"Well, as it turned out, we four brothers graduated from Kyoto University. My oldest brother has a law office in Osaka. The second brother is now a high school teacher in Fukuchiyama in Kyoto Prefecture. My younger brother went into the Sanwa Bank and is now the manager of a branch office in Osaka.

"For some reason--I really cannot remember why--when I was very young, my mother told me that one day she would like to see me off at the port of Kobe--to see me go abroad. That stuck in my mind. (thoughtful pause) She never said what I was supposed to do when I got there, but she thought it would be nice if I went. (both laughing)

"The only international connection in my family was the husband of my mother's younger sister--Morisawa was his name. As a young man, he went to the U.S. and worked his way through a small college in Illinois, washing dishes in the evening to pay his tuition. Later, they went to China. By the end of the Pacific War, my uncle was a sort of mayor to the Japanese community in Tsingtao. There were a couple of million Japanese living in China then, so it was not so unusual for my aunt and uncle to be there. Now and then, when I was still a young boy, they came back from China and visited with us. I remember that my aunt and uncle both had a pretty good command of English. I got some ideas from them about the U.S. and China. But apart from them, my family had no international connections."

Question: "Has coming from the region around Kyoto and Nara had any particular meaning for you? After all, these are the ancient seats of the imperial family--very rich in history and art?"

(with modesty verging on diffidence) "It is not . . . a bad place to be from. My mother and father were . . . steeped in Japanese history and literature. We went often to the temples and shrines and famous gardens--not only on school excursions--but on family outings on Sundays. They also took us children often to the Kabuki theater, as well as to modern plays. Just as a matter of course, my father and mother would tell us about the history and the people associated with all these places and events. It was a natural part of our life."

THE WAR

Comment: "At lunch, when we talked about your memories of the war, I realized that for you those memories reach back before Pearl Harbor and the Pacific War, to the war in China in the late 1930s."

"Yes. That is probably true for most of my generation. I remember clearly going to kindergarten and primary school in the late 1930s, when the war in China was going on. In school we learned how glorious Japan's history was, and at the same time the newspapers and the radio were announcing great Japanese victories at Nanking and at Beijing and such places. All the people celebrated those victories. We small school children marched in the streets with lanterns to celebrate the Imperial Army.

"Our conditions in Japan were not too uncomfortable in those days, in 1937 to 1941. There were no serious shortages yet, and our life was not so militaristic . . . or totalitarian as it became after the outbreak of the Pacific War. By the time I was in second and third grade I was reading the newspapers, following our government's negotiations with Great Britain. (seeing a look of surprise and doubt on my face, and laughing) Yes. I was . . . a precocious reader, and my parents used to answer my questions and try to explain to me what was going on. I read about Foreign Minister Arita and his negotiations with the British Ambassador Craige in 1939, and two years later about your Secretary of State Cordell Hull and his talks in Washington with Admiral Nomura. I saw all their faces in the newspapers. Of course, I had no idea what was really going on. I was just a boy.

"I was twelve years old when the Pacific War began. I was at school, in the last year--the sixth grade--of primary school, on Monday morning, December 8, 1941. The headmaster called for us to assemble in the schoolyard and gave us a long speech, telling us we were engaged in a patriotic war and that we all had to dedicate ourselves to serve the state. I was . . . deeply moved. I was ready to serve.

"In the spring of 1942, when I began middle school, I remember that we were still winning victories. Middle school was normally a five year course, but the good students were permitted to take the higher school entrance examination after only four years. In 1942 and 1943, we had a normal life and a normal education--except that we had to help planting and harvesting rice--there were no longer enough farmers to do it--and do military drills for three to four hours a week. We learned how to handle a gun and a bayonet--to make fast marches--to become soldiers. I expected to become a soldier and to fight for Japan.

"By 1944, the war in the Pacific was not . . . going well. I remember the shock I got when Saipan fell in the summer of 1944. I felt that was a turning point for us. Around that time, we middle school boys were ordered to work for the munitions industry. Our classes at school almost stopped. Every two weeks or so we would have a day of classes. My class worked in a factory that produced parts--screws and rivets--for war planes. Kyoto was not being bombed, but some people realized that the city might be bombed. So, in March 1945, the factory was moved to Shiga Prefecture and I went with the factory. In Shiga, the food became so scarce that . . . my health deteriorated. (pausing) The doctors declared me unfit for work and told me to go home. (long, uncomfortable pause) I was-- hmm--very embarrassed to be unfit for my . . . duty. But I had no strength, and I went home, as they told me."

Question: "I see. You were sixteen years old in 1945. A sixteen-year-old boy needs a lot of calories just to grow. What kind of meals did you have at the factory?"

"Usually rice and sweet potatoes--or some vegetables or soybeans. There was no meat or fish. Our official ration was supposed to be 330 grams of rice a day and a fixed amount of sugar and other food, such as meat or fish. Vegetables were not rationed. But in 1945 . . . the food for this official ration . . . was not there. I did not get enough to eat. I was emaciated. I went back to my home in Tanabe in June of 1945 and I could do nothing. I had no strength.

"Then, in August, I heard the recording of the emperor on the radio. It was a very noisy broadcast, full of static . . . and I could not really understand most of what he said. But we understood that we had lost the war, and that the war was . . . over.

"My feelings then, and for some weeks, were . . . very mixed. I was, in a way, relieved. But I was also . . . anxious . . . about the Occupation . . . about the Americans. All during the war, we had very bad propaganda about the cruelty and barbarity of the Americans, and now they were coming . . . to rule over us."

Question: "How long did this anxious period last? Do you remember?"

"Yes. Quite well. I encountered the first Occupation troops in September. Some were riding along in jeeps, some were traveling in the Japanese trains. They were tall . . . and very well fed. They were not cruel . . . or barbaric. (both laughing)

(thoughtful pause) "They had so much equipment . . . tanks, trucks, and jeeps, not mention all their weapons. So, I thought, no matter how much courage and tenacity our Japanese soldiers have, it would not be enough to defeat this kind of an army."

THE OCCUPATION AND HIGHER SCHOOL

"Although my anxiety about the American soldiers disappeared, the early years of the Occupation, in a material sense, were even worse than the end of the war--at least for our family. I felt that there was no help for it. It was the price of losing the war. The emperor had said in his Surrender speech that we would have to . . . bear the unbearable.

"Almost immediately after the Surrender, I went back to school, together with the rest of my class. In September, we returned to our studies--with very empty stomachs. The harvest of

1945 was the worst since the Meiji Restoration of 1868. There was a lack of fertilizer. There were not enough farm workers. On top of everything else, the weather was bad. Then the winter was unusually cold. Millions of Japanese would have starved, I think, if General MacArthur had not provided us with food.

"The next few years were not as bad, but they were very . . . grim. Conditions were very poor. Food was still scarce. Buildings, railways, even our clothing was in poor repair. There did not seem to be much hope for the future. It seemed to me that conditions did not begin to really improve until 1949. By then, you wanted us to recover economically. You began to see Japan as a possible future ally. In 1949, China was taken over by the Communists, and then in 1950, the Korean War broke out and you began to place large orders in Japan. Then, our factories and shops began . . . to hum again.

(thoughtful pause, slowly wiping his glasses) "For our family . . . those were . . . hard years. The land reform and the property taxes hurt us badly, and also my father lost his occupation. So, for several years after the Surrender we had no income worth mentioning . . . and there were still the four of us children to be raised and educated. Our parents could not afford it. (pause) Somehow, we all got through. I had scholarships all through higher school and university, and in the university, I worked as a tutor."

Question: "Yes. I can understand that your family did not benefit from the Occupation reforms. (pause) You were in higher school, *koto gakko* , from 1946 to 1949. Did any of your teachers in that school--or in your earlier schools--make a strong, memorable impression on you?"

"Hmmm. (thoughtful pause) There was Mr. Nishida, a teacher of the Chinese classics at Sanko, my high school. (shaking his head at the memory, and smiling inwardly) Mr. Nishida had very strong, clear ideas--based on the Chinese classics--of how an individual should act, and what a society should be, or strive to be. (looking at me intently, for emphasis) His way of thinking was very open, reasonable, and tolerant--what I would call liberal. Even without the Occupation education reforms, Mr. Nishida knew what liberalism--in a broad, philosophical sense--was, and he was an excellent teacher.

"The other teacher I remember well was Mr. Uchiyama, who taught German--not just the language, but also the German classical poets, Goethe, Kleist, and Schiller. Not the Germany of Hitler, but a very . . . civilized, humanitarian, artistic Germany. That was my image of Germany. (pause) Partly by family education and because of Mr. Nishida and Mr. Uchiyama, the two countries whose culture I was closest to in those days were China and Germany."

Comment: "So, that is why your German is so good. It was Mr. Uchiyama at Sanko."

"Yes. In the old higher school system, the students had to specialize in either English, German, or French. I selected German. Prime Minister Nakasone studied French at Shizuoka Higher School. That is why he can still converse to some extent in French with President Mitterrand. But German was my choice, and later, I passed my Foreign Service language examination in German."

Question: "Why was your higher school called Sanko, and not Kyoto Koto Gakko (higher school)?"

"In the Meiji period (1868-1912), when the first eight higher schools were established, they were . . . just numbered. The first was in Tokyo. Ichiko, it is called. The second was in Sendai, and the third in Kyoto. Sanko is the abbreviation for *Dai San Koto Gakko*, Number Three Higher School. Afterward, in the Taisho period (1912-1926), the government built about twenty more higher schools, and named them after the locality--such as Shizuoka Higher School."

Question: "Hmm. I see. I have heard that Sanko was one the best higher schools in Japan, but I did not know how it got its name. Was it difficult to enter?"

(laughing) "Difficult? Yes. I suppose so. The examination was considered to be so difficult that not many students took it, because they knew that they would not pass. Of the ones who took the examination, perhaps one out of six or eight passed. My whole class had about two hundred young men in it--all very bright, hard working young men. We all knew each other, and the teachers knew the students well. Even when we were sixteen, seventeen, eighteen years old, we felt like an . . . elite. With that feeling was also a sense of duty . . . a duty to serve society--to do something useful."

Question: "Well, it sounds as though you were a small, tightly knit group. How do your Sanko school ties compare with your Kyoto University ties?"

"The Sanko ties are stronger and deeper. We still get together . . . and we have a special bond. Mr. Ro Watanabe, the Democratic Socialist Party (DSP) Dietman whose name I gave to you recently, is a classmate from Sanko. When I have to answer his questions at the Foreign Affairs Committee, I use polite and even honorific expressions. (both laughing). But when we drink sake together, we use more familiar language because we are Sanko friends, not a civil servant and a Dietman drinking together. There are a number of Sanko people in the Foreign Ministry, and in all the ministries, as well as in the Diet and in business. It is a fairly influential group . . . and we keep in touch.

"My class from Kyoto University are friends, but our ties are not like these Sanko ties. You might not want to generalize too much from my personal experience. I think that the graduates from some of the better private universities, such as Keio, Waseda or Sofia in Tokyo, or Doshisha in Kyoto, have very strong school ties."

Question: "Why did you decide to go to Kyoto University?"

"Well, all the people in my Sanko class expected to enter one of the better national universities. Tokyo University was regarded as the best--especially its Law Faculty. I thought of going there. I wanted to, but I had to consider . . . my family's finances. So, I entered Kyoto University, which is also quite good and was close to home."

Question: "Did you take the entrance examination for Todai?"

"No. (laughing) But if I had . . . I probably would have passed it."

KYOTO UNIVERSITY AND CHOOSING A CAREER

"Before I entered Kyoto University, I had to decide on a course of study. I was . . . pulled in two directions. Because of Mr. Nishida and Mr. Uchiyama, I had a strong attachment to Chinese and to German--to their literature and culture. The obvious way to pursue that attachment was going into the Faculty of Literature. But somehow, to study languages and literature in this way was . . . to indulge myself. They were almost . . . like a hobby, and in the conditions of 1949, I felt I should do something which would be of use to the state and to society. I had no idea yet of going into diplomacy, but I believed that the Faculty of Law would prepare me for a more . . . responsible, useful life. So, I entered the Law Faculty. It was still a three year course in 1949, under the old system.

"In my second year, I started to think seriously about applying for the Foreign Ministry."

Question: "Did you talk over these decisions with your family, or teachers, or your friends?"

(thoughtful pause) "Not very much. I told my parents what I wanted to do, and they did not object. I think, as I recall it, the strongest factor in my thinking was . . . the defeat of Japan. I wanted to do something . . . to help Japan to recover from the defeat. (pause) I was not the only one who felt this way. Many of my classmates from Sanko thought the same way.

"I knew, relatively speaking, that I had a talent for languages, and I had an interest in things international. So, in my second year at Kyoto, I began to study international law, economics, diplomatic history, and so forth, to prepare for the diplomatic examination. I knew that the higher-level Foreign Ministry examination was not easy to pass, but I decided to try it. I took it in 1951, in my third year. About one thousand applicants signed up for the examination, but only about five hundred to six hundred actually attended and completed the written examination. That covered a variety of subjects, such as the Constitution, administrative laws, economics, diplomatic history, international law, and so on. I managed to pass that. I also passed the language examination in German, which included translation and composition. I was the only one who passed in German. Then, about forty of us were selected for the oral examination, which included in my case a dictation test and conversation in German. Of that forty, eighteen of us were finally accepted by the ministry. (pause) That is how I chose my career.

(smiling) Or perhaps I should say that is how I was chosen for my career.

"While we are talking about universities, there is something I wanted to mention to you. You know that about 70 percent of the diplomatic officers are from Todai. The next largest group--which is not very large--is from Kyoto, and the third is from Hitotsubashi. If you want, we can get the exact numbers. However, there is no university clique in this ministry. When the question of assignments and promotions comes up, the ministry officials judge by the capabilities of the individual. There is a certain camaraderie among the graduates of particular schools. That is true. But the university from which one graduated has no particular bearing on one's career."

EARLY YEARS IN THE FOREIGN MINISTRY

"In the spring of 1952, soon after I graduated from Kyoto University, I entered the ministry. In those days, we had one year of training and apprenticeship here in Tokyo, and then two years of study abroad before our first assignment. We went to our Foreign Service Training Institute for three months, to study such things as manners, protocol, Japanese art and culture--which a good Japanese diplomat should know well--and of course more language training, in my case English as well as German.

"We were lucky at that time. The prime minister was Shigeru Yoshida, himself a diplomat. He lived in a house here in Tokyo, near Shirogane, that belonged to the imperial family, and was being used temporarily as the residence for the prime minister. Mr. Yoshida arranged for us to live in what had formerly been the servant quarters of that house. They were fine rooms, and two of us young attachés shared a room. Our class of eighteen was divided in two, and each group lived at the prime minister's residence for one and a half months.

"On two occasions Yoshida invited us to dinner. (shaking his head, smiling at the memory) There was the prime minister, and we were just out of school, very young (laughing) and some of us did not even know how to use a knife and fork properly. He seemed to enjoy those dinners--so much that we relaxed and enjoyed them too. He talked informally about his experiences in England and Italy, and in Japan. He was a master at telling jokes. He had us all laughing. He was . . . short and thickset, and always smoking on a cigar, which is unusual for a Japanese. His jokes and stories were often ironic and even sarcastic, but we could sense his good intentions behind his harsh words. (pause) I would recount some of them for you (laughing) but I cannot tell them the way he did. They lose too much of their flavor.

"After the three months at the institute, we were taken on a trip to Kyoto and Nara, to visit all the important historical and cultural places. Of course, I knew them from childhood, but most of my class had never been to these places, and had only read about them. Then we spent about eight months as apprentices here in the ministry--doing odd jobs and watching and learning how the others do their work. Finally, in April 1953, each of us was sent to a foreign university.

"I went to the University of Freiburg in Breisgau, not far from Strasburg and Basel. When I arrived in Germany, I reported to our embassy in Bonn, with the idea in my head that I would go to the University of Heidelberg, which I thought was the most famous. (pause, smiling at the memory) There was a first secretary in our embassy, Mr. Suga, who was my . . . adviser. He urged me to go to Freiburg instead of Heidelberg because, he said, there would be no Japanese at Freiburg, and I would have only Germans and other foreigners to talk to. That would be very good for my language training. So, I gave up my dreams of Heidelberg and went to Freiburg. Of course, there were two Japanese waiting to greet me at Freiburg, one in music and the other in botany. (both laughing) Anyway, it was allright. He was trying to do the best thing for me. I enrolled in the German literature course . . . and I avoided the other Japanese." (more laughing)

Question: "Did you have any problems adjusting? Was there any culture shock?"

(thinking back carefully) "None. None at all. I had a fair command of German when I arrived, and I had read so much about Germany . . . that it was already familiar to me. (thoughtful pause) It was also easier for me because Germany was . . . another defeated country. Some of my colleagues who went to Cambridge and Oxford, often felt the resentment that the British still harbored against Japan. I don't think that the young diplomats who studied in the U.S., at Amherst and Williams, had that trouble. The war was much harder on the British than on your country, and their feeling was . . . only natural. But Germany was a defeated country--much of it still in ruins--and I was a young Japanese, whose country had suffered the same fate. I knew something of their language and culture. So, the professors at Freiburg received me warmly, and my German landlady, who was a very good, helpful woman, was also friendly and kind to me.

"I spent a year studying at Freiburg, and then, since it was very easy to change universities in Germany, I spent a semester at Innsbruck in Austria, and then my final semester at the Free University in Berlin. I was in Austria in the summer of 1954. Of course, I wanted to learn about Austria, (laughing very merrily, eyes twinkling) *and* I also wanted to climb their mountains. (both laughing) I haven't mentioned it to you, but when I was at Sanko and at Kyoto University I used to save up a little money from my scholarship and from my tutoring job, and on the school vacations I went to the Japan Alps and climbed and backpacked. I liked it . . . very much. I climbed all the important peaks in the Japan Alps. My ambition was to climb the Alps in the Tyrol and in Switzerland--and that summer I did it. (smiling contentedly) I did not study very much at Innsbruck. (both laughing)

"At the Free University in Berlin, that winter, I took more German studies, and I also worked for Professor Eckhardt, who taught Japanology. I was made a *Lehrbeauftrager*--a sort of lecturer without pay. (laughing) That gave me a chance to brush up on my Japanese grammar twice a week. I enjoyed the people I met there, but in 1954, (pause) Berlin was a dim, shabby place.

"Then I was assigned to our Bonn embassy for a year and a half, doing odd jobs--sometimes decoding cables, sometimes acting as an interpreter for high level Japanese. That was interesting work. It gave me the chance to be at some important meetings between Japanese cabinet ministers and people like Chancellor Conrad Adenauer and his economic minister, Ludwig Erhard.

"In the summer of 1956, I came back to Tokyo, to the Economic Affairs Bureau, and I stayed here for about five years. I worked that whole time on our trade problems with Europe. With the partial exception of the Germans--and perhaps I should include Switzerland and one or two Scandinavian countries--the European countries had severe restrictions on Japanese imports. (shaking his head in dismay at the memory) Perhaps the word severe is an . . . understatement. In the case of the French and Italians, the restrictions were really awful. Japan had just become a member of the GATT (General Agreement on Tariffs and Trade) in 1955, but many European countries refused to enter into a GATT relationship with Japan by invoking the famous Article 35, and we could not get most-favored-nation treatment in those countries. So, we had to negotiate with each European government over many, many different categories of trade. The negotiations were . . . complex and detailed . . . and the results not very satisfying. But it had to be done. Japan had to export to live, and we had to do our best, everywhere. Fortunately, your country had accorded us most-favored-nation treatment in the Treaty of Commerce and Navigation of 1953, and our trade with you was able to expand and prosper. That was critical for Japan's economy."

Question: "When my younger Japanese diplomat friends are working here at the Foreign Ministry in Tokyo, they seem to be in the office frequently until late into the night, or the early hours of the morning. Were those the hours you kept, too?"

(matter-of-factly) "Yes. Not all the time, but such hours were not unusual, and if necessary, we spent the night at the ministry. The biggest difference then was that we did not have to spend much time dealing with the Diet. Now and then, the foreign minister or a director-general was called over to the Diet to answer questions, but it took much less of our time than it does now."

Question: "Did you spend much time ironing out differences with other ministries, such as MITI (Ministry of International Trade and Industry), or among the different bureaus in the Foreign Ministry?"

(laughing) "Sometimes, yes. But in my office, it was usually the details and facts needed for those trade negotiations with the British, or the French, or the Germans, that took so much work and time. In those days, in the late 1950s, we did not have to negotiate so much with MITI or other ministries because there were only a few people in those ministries who knew foreign languages or what was going on in foreign economies or governments. For example, Mr. Nobuhiko Ushiba, the diplomat who later became our vice-minister and then ambassador to Washington, was on loan to MITI in the 1950s as the director-general of their International Trade Bureau. MITI had no one of their own yet who could do that job. Soon after I came back from Germany in 1956, Mr. Ushiba came back to this ministry and became director-general of the Economic Affairs Bureau."

Question: "Wasn't Ambassador Ushiba also a German language officer, and a specialist on Germany?"

"Yes, he was . . . and because of that he had some special, personal feelings for me--and I was always happy to help him. Whenever he needed a German article, or he had to give a speech in German, he would ask me to draft it for him. He was a most . . . impressive man . . . and a very careful, skillful negotiator. He taught me a great deal."

Question: "How did he go about training you?"

"At first, he would just allow me to attend a negotiation and work on the preparation. Then, after some time, when I knew the facts and figures well, I was allowed to suggest that we should go for a certain import quota--that sort of thing. Mr. Ushiba always trained the junior diplomats who worked under him, preparing them for more responsibility . . . and we are still doing that today. You know, each division of each bureau in our ministry has between ten and thirty people in it--including clerks, Foreign Ministry specialists (who have to pass a specialist test), and usually three or four diplomatic officers, who passed the higher level test, the one I took. Well, the division chief, who is a diplomatic officer himself, gives special attention to training these young diplomatic officers--holding them to the most severe standards. They must work the hardest. They are the ones who are most frequently here until after midnight. *That* is their privilege." (both laughing)

MARRIAGE

(in a dry tone) "I cannot recall anything else worth mentioning during those five years in Tokyo, (pause) except, perhaps, my marriage." (grinning)

Question: "You are incorrigible. (both laughing) Please tell me about it. Was yours a traditional, arranged marriage?"

"Hmm. It was not exactly a traditional, arranged marriage, but there were some traditional elements in it. In the old style arranged marriages there was a formal meeting--called a *miai*--between the young man and woman, with their families present. A go-between made the arrangements. Before the *miai* , the families used to check each other, in fact, investigate very carefully to make sure about the health of the prospective spouse, the condition of the family's finances, and so on.

"Well, my wife and I had a more informal *miai*. By the late 1950s, these things were changing. My Sanko school ties led to our *miai*. In those days, the Sanko club at our ministry--about thirty or so--used to get together two or three times a year. The highest ranking man was the then vice-minister, and I was the youngest. Mr. Yasusuke Katsuno, who was then the director of our ministry's Liaison Office in Osaka--he later became ambassador to Sri Lanka, Norway, and Portugal--came to one of these meetings and got to talking with me. He asked me if I was single or married. I told him I was a bachelor. Then, he said that he knew a fine young lady and that I ought to meet her. He gave me a photo of her. Well, she looked nice . . . and since Mr. Katsuno was a good man and was being kind to me . . . well . . . I agreed to meet her. So, one summer day in 1957, my wife and I, and Ambassador Katsuno, met at the Shiseido coffee shop on the Ginza. You know the place. We talked over coffee and cakes for awhile, and then Ambassador Katsuno made some excuse and disappeared. My wife and I chatted on for awhile longer (pause) and that was that." (long pause)

Question: (confused, at a loss) "You mean . . . you only met once and . . . ."

"No, no. I mean, I did not propose another date. I had . . . a good impression of her . . . but . . . perhaps I was too shy. About

two weeks later, Ambassador Katsuno saw me and told me that the
ceiling of her home had collapsed and had landed on her head.
(seeing a look of alarm on my face) Not a heavy beam or anything
like that. Probably some plaster. But she was slightly injured, and
he suggested that I should go see her and console her. So, I called
her up and we met again . . . and then several more times . . . and
somehow . . . ." (throwing up his hands and laughing)

Question: "How did Ambassador Katsuno come to be your
go-between? What was his connection with the Akama family and
with their daughter, Reiko?"

"As I said, he was the director of the Foreign Ministry Liaison Office in Osaka. My wife's father was the governor of Osaka,
and whenever foreign dignitaries visited Osaka, the governor enter-
tained them and Ambassador Katsuno was supposed to be with
them. Ambassador Katsuno had his office in the prefectural government building, and he and my father-in-law used to meet there
too. My father-in-law had been a MITI official before the war when
it was called the Ministry of Commerce and Industry, and also during the war, when it was known as the Ministry of Munitions. In
1944, he became the head of their office in the Kansai region, where
Osaka is. After the Surrender, he decided to enter politics and he
ran for the governorship of Osaka City. He knew Prime Minister
Yoshida rather well, and with Yoshida's support, he won the election in 1948.

"He had three daughters. The eldest is my wife. At first, he
wanted her to marry a MITI man, but he could not . . . succeed.
(laughing) So, he asked Ambassador Katsuno if there was a good
man in the Foreign Ministry." (both laughing)

Question: "Did your wife live in Osaka or in Tokyo?"

"My father-in-law had a house in Tokyo, as well as his official residence in Osaka. He was often in Tokyo on business. She
was living in Tokyo, attending the *Gakushuin*, the old Peer's
School." (This was one of the best and most exclusive schools in
Japan.)

Question: "Did your two families come together at some
point soon after you met at the Shiseido?"

"Hmm. Not as soon as my wife would have liked. She is
still somewhat irritated at me about that. Her parents knew that she

was dating me, and after we had met two or three times they wanted to meet me, and my family. She told me so . . . but I was rather shy and slow to do . . . anything about it. After putting it off for awhile, I agreed to these meetings. Then, about six months after our *miai* at the Shiseido, we had our wedding."

Comment: "So, it was not a completely traditional, arranged marriage, but it was not entirely modern, either."

"That is true. My wife and I had to decide. Yet Ambassador Katsuno was like a traditional go-between, and my father-in-law must have checked me and my family before he agreed to our marriage."

Comment: "I suppose your parents were pleased, too. After all, this marriage could not do you any harm."

"Yes. They were quite pleased. (pause) After my wife's father served as governor for twelve years, he was elected to the Upper House of the Diet, and he served there until his death. He was a distinguished man. Yet the fact that I married his daughter did not bring any particular advantage to me--except perhaps in a vague way that I will explain. It has certainly not been a factor affecting my assignments and promotions. (noticing a questioning expression on my face) In this ministry, we have so many men who married daughters from very distinguished, influential families that it is nothing special. It does not count for much."

Question: "I see your point about distinguished marriages and careers. My impression is that in Japan, being well connected by birth or marriage can give one access to opportunities and responsibility, but it does not guarantee success or promotion. If a well-connected person makes mistakes or shows that he lacks ability, he is usually quietly eased off to the side. If someone without connections shows real ability, he acquires connections and gets chances to move ahead. Is that generally correct?"

(thoughtfully, pursing his lips) "Hmm. Very often that is the way it works. I mentioned the indirect advantages of my wife's family connections, and you may want to keep them in mind. It is this. It can make it easier for me to talk to some people, and that is helpful in my work. For example, my father-in-law was once commissioner of the MITI Examination Board. The MITI people who entered in his time and are now senior officials know that I am

Governor Akama's son-in-law. So, some personal feelings exist between us, and we can talk less formally, even on serious, official subjects. My wife also has lots of cousins, and many of them were in government or married to government officials. Several years ago, the vice-minister for international finance in the Finance Ministry was Mr. Takehiro Sagami, my wife's cousin. That helped me occasionally when I had to talk to officials in his ministry. That sort of thing may be counted as a small advantage of family ties. But there are no special favors, no breaking of rules for relatives . . . nepotism, as you call it. I have seen that kind of nepotism in the Middle East. In some places there, family relations are almost the only thing that counts. But not here--not in my experience.

"One other point. My wife has good ability at foreign languages. In January of 1961, I was assigned to Vienna, and we went there to enjoy our married life properly, since I was too busy at the ministry for the two years after our wedding. (smiling warmly at the memory of Vienna) It was a very nice place. My wife learned German very quickly and still speaks with a Viennese accent. Her spoken French is better than mine, and beside English and German, she also knows some Italian. Of course, that helps me very much. She is good at meeting with foreigners, and knows how to conduct our social life. In this sense--apart from her family--my wife plays an important part in my work, more so than most Japanese wives."

Question: "There is a very low divorce rate in Japan compared to the U.S., and family life here seems much more stable, and I think it is also more supportive for a husband in his work. Do you think so?"

"Hmm. This may be changing somewhat, but family life for most Japanese men probably takes less of their time and attention. The wives run the families. They are good mothers and decent wives . . . and they send their husbands off to work for long hours. They don't expect to see them too much. (laughing) But of course, most Japanese wives do not have to plan dinners for foreign guests, as mine does, or even plan dinners or parties for their husband's colleagues, as many American wives do. So, most Japanese wives are less involved in their husband's career but they are supportive by taking care of the family and not interfering with their husband's work.

"On the other hand, if a Japanese man who works in a ministry or a big company has affairs with other women and it becomes known so that his colleagues talk about it, it will hurt his career, much more seriously than I think it would hurt an American in such a case. Of course, Japanese men are . . . human . . . and have such affairs, but not so frequently, and when they do, I think they are more secret. (with exaggerated solemnity) That is all I will say." (both laughing)

VIENNA AND TOKYO

Question: "In that case, perhaps we should return to your career. Since you have mentioned that you were assigned to the embassy in Vienna in January 1961, why don't we pick up at that point?"

"I remained in Vienna until June 1964. Our embassy was small, so that I had to do many other jobs apart from the economic field, which was my main assignment. That was good. It made my work more varied and interesting.

"In June 1964, I was suddenly called back to Tokyo, again the Economic Affairs Bureau, this time to follow up on Japan's entry into OECD (Organization of Economic Cooperation and Development) in April of that year. At first, I was the assistant director of the newly established OECD division, and then in 1966, I became the director. Of course, becoming a full-fledged member of OECD was an important step for Japan. It meant we were being admitted to membership in the small club of the advanced, industrialized nations. (pause) However, even though the work was important, I was getting . . . a little fed up with economic affairs. For fifteen years, since I joined this ministry, I had worked almost exclusively on economics, and I felt I should . . . do other things. I let my boss know, in a rather discreet manner, and with the help of Vice-Minister Ushiba and Mr. Takashi Suzuki, director-general of the Research and Analysis Department, I was able to join Mr. Suzuki as director of the Research Division. That was in April 1968.

"Not long after I took this new job, Mr. Suzuki asked me to organize a new Division for Policy Planning, somewhat along the lines of your State Department Policy Planning Council. I did that job, and then I became the first director of that division. Our first important task was to help Prime Minister Sato to prepare for 1970. In 1970, the fixed ten year term of the 1960 Japan-U.S. Security Treaty would end, and either party could abrogate the treaty or request negotiations to revise it. In those days, all the Opposition parties used to say that because of this treaty Japan would be dragged into a war in the Far East--probably over Korea. They said that we would then become a target for Soviet missiles, and Chinese hostility too. So, they demanded the abrogation of the treaty, or at least revising it so Japan would have no military involvement.

"I worked on this with Hisahiko Okazaki, who was then director of the Analysis Division of the same department. We put together a small team of very bright, young officers, and then we armed ourselves with all the facts and arguments--on all sides. Of course, we got help from the Soviet Division and the China Division and so on. We studied the materials and had lengthy discussions-- sometimes including certain academic experts--and finally we decided on our approach and our arguments. We wrote them up in a set of basic documents, which were then used not only by our ministry, but by the whole government, including the prime minister's office. Everybody was churning out pamphlets on 1970. We explained how the Security Treaty served Japan, why it was so important, and that it was nonsense to say that Japan would be dragged into a nuclear war. As it turned out, 1970 was handled . . . rather smoothly.

(smiling) "Of course, such work was not the original meaning of policy planning, which was supposed to be more on the future and the long term. But we did some of that as well, on future relations with China and also the long term implications of the Vietnam War. Establishing this new division, and also some of its work, meant taking trips to Washington, and meeting your policy planning people --Mr. Henry Owen and Mr. Joe Yaeger. I liked this new work, and so I was pleased when I was told in late 1969 that I would be assigned to our Washington embassy in April 1970. Mr. Shimoda was our ambassador when I arrived, but several months later Mr. Ushiba became ambassador, and I mostly worked for him."

WASHINGTON 1970-1974

"Had Mr. Ushiba's ambassadorship been decided when you were assigned to Washington?"

"Yes. Everybody knew he was going there. He never said anything to me about it, but I assumed that he had asked for me. I worked closely with him.

"My first job was in the Economic Section of the embassy. That is where we handled the very serious negotiation over Japanese exports of wool and synthetic textiles--an extremely sensitive negotiation.

"In your 1968 election, President Nixon had promised Senator Strom Thurmond (Democrat, North Carolina; he supported Nixon in the 1968 election) to help the textile industry in the Carolinas by somehow restraining the import of Japanese goods. Prime Minister Sato wanted very much to arrange for the reversion to Japan of the island of Okinawa . . . nuclear free. He wanted your bases to remain on Okinawa, but without nuclear weapons, since it is our policy not to introduce such weapons on Japanese territory.

"So, after President Nixon took office these two issues became . . . in a way . . . linked. Prime Minister Sato promised to help on textiles, while President Nixon arranged for Prime Minister Sato to have the honor and to get the credit for Okinawa's reversion, nuclear free. That was, perhaps, a sort of deal. The diplomatic documents have not been made public yet.

"Well, when I arrived in Washington, the Okinawa issue was basically settled, and we had to resolve the textile issue. Your secretary of commerce, Maurice Stans, and our MITI minister, Kiichi Miyazawa, had negotiated but had been unable to settle it. The textile industries in both our countries were very emotional about this. So, Ambassador Ushiba was directed to resume the talks, in a calm, quiet manner. President Nixon appointed Peter Flannigan to negotiate for your side. The talks were held in the room of Flannigan, in the West Wing of the White House. Usually, Mr. Ushiba just took me as a note-taker, and sometimes also Mr. Bunroku Yoshino, who was the minister of our embassy. Mr. Fred Bergsten helped Mr. Flannigan. Henry Kissinger sometimes stopped by for five minutes or so--to see how it was going. However, even that quiet negotiation did not seem to be resolving the issue.

"Meanwhile, in February 1971, the Japanese textile industry, in a very complicated move, approached Congressman Wilbur Mills, (Democrat, Arkansas) chairman of the House Ways and Means Committee--thinking this might help to settle matters, and on March 8, they announced a plan of unilateral export restraints based on their dealing with Mills. This angered President Nixon very much. He refused to accept this plan on the grounds that it was worked out, so to speak, behind his back. There was . . . much resentment against Japan in the White House.

"Then, in July and August, President Nixon hit us with those two shocks. First that he was going to visit China--which he had not discussed with us in advance, even though we had always cooperated with you on China, at the U.N. and elsewhere. Then, the 10 percent import surcharge and the unilateral floating of the dollar, which forced us to revalue the yen. It was . . . unfortunately . . . a period of strain. I think that President Nixon's irritation at Japan over the textile issue was an . . . element in your government's decisions to hit us with these shocks. [4]

"On the day of the China shock--July 15, 1971--your secretary of state, (William) Rogers, wanted to inform Mr. Ushiba before the public announcement. But they could not reach him--could not find him. I had a dinner in a restaurant in downtown Washington, and when I came home that evening after nine o'clock, my wife told me that the White House had been calling--asking for me--thinking I would know where to reach Ambassador Ushiba, since I was close to him. My wife told me that the lady who had called had said that the matter was President Nixon's trip to Communist China. It was incredible to me. I decided immediately to call the ambassador's residence, but before I could lift the phone, I got a call from Mr.

---

4. For a detailed, carefully researched account of the textile dispute, see I. M. Destler, et. al., *Managing An Alliance*, (Washington, D.C: The Brookings Institution, 1976) 35-45. In late August 1971, the Nixon administration indicated that it would impose textile quotas on Japan by executive order pursuant to the 1917 Trading with the Enemy Act, if an agreement were not reached by October 15. A U.S.-Japan Memorandum of Agreement on textiles was initialed on October 15, in which Japan agreed to the administration's textile quotas.

Matano of our Political Section. He exclaimed something like, 'Blast it! Mr. Murata, the Americans got in touch with the ambassador. Do you know, Nixon is going to visit China . . . Communist China!' I told him that I already knew."

Question: "That is a very helpful, balanced, first-hand account of the textile dispute and the two Nixon shocks. 1971 was a rough period in U.S.-Japanese relations. Overall, what impressions of the United States did you carry away with you after your four years in Washington? After all, that was your first extended experience in the U.S., and it was the ending of the Vietnam War and also the time of the Watergate scandals, which led President Nixon to resign in the summer of 1974."

"Well, everything was new and fresh. I had no preconceived ideas about your country. I was deeply impressed with the process you followed in the Watergate affair--especially the resignations of Attorney General Elliot Richardson and his deputy (William) Ruckelshaus, when they believed that Nixon was not acting properly. The whole matter was conducted in a lawful, proper way.

"I was also impressed by the process of . . . extricating from Vietnam. It seemed to me that your government is truly responsive to public opinion, and your public wanted to . . . get out of Vietnam.

"I never spoke with President Nixon. I was in the room with him several times with visitors from Japan, and of course, I saw a lot of him on TV. I read the Watergate books by White and Ehrlichman.[5] I had a positive impression about him. You may not agree, but I thought he was a good president for foreign policy. That was how I saw him. The rapprochement with China--even though it was an unpleasant shock to us--was a master stroke. I think that the Ford administration and the Carter administration tried to make too much of the China opening and partly as a result made naive mistakes with the Soviet Union. But the opening to China in 1971 and 1972 was an intelligent policy, and I think it was Nixon's

5. Mr. Murata is referring to Theodore White, *Breach of Faith: The Fall of Richard Nixon* (New York: Atheneum Publishers, 1975), and John Ehrlichman, *Witness to Power: The Nixon Years* (New York: Simon and Schuster, 1982).

policy. Kissinger was his helper.

"Anyway, those are my impressions and views. Then, in August or September of 1973, Ambassador Yasukawa--who had just replaced Ushiba--told me that I would return to Tokyo in the coming spring to head the Western European Division. That sounded very good. However, in October, war broke out in the Middle East between Israel and Egypt and Syria. A couple of weeks later, Ambassador Yasukawa told me that my assignment had been changed. When I returned to Tokyo, I would take over the Middle East Division. So, I spent the rest of the winter learning what I could of the Middle East. I do not speak Arabic, but my other languages helped me, especially English. (smiling) Of course, I read the book that you gave me on oil and Middle East politics.

"From the spring of 1974 until 1982, I worked on the Middle East, except for the two years from 1976 to 1978, when I was deputy director-general of the Treaty Bureau. In November 1974, I was promoted from director of Middle East Division to become deputy director-general of the Middle Eastern and African Affairs Bureau. From 1978 to 1980, I was our ambassador to the United Arab Emirates, in Abu Dhabi. And from 1980 to 1982, I was director-general of the Middle East and African Affairs Bureau."

MIDDLE EAST 1974-1982

Question: "I realize that your Middle East work may be too recent and too sensitive to discuss in detail, but there is one episode I would like to ask you about. Weren't you a hostage in 1975, when a group of terrorists from the Japan Red Army took over some embassies in Malaysia?"

"Yes. That was in August 1975, when I was deputy director-general of the Middle East and African Affairs Bureau. Five Japan Red Army members attacked and captured part of the U.S. and Swedish embassies--they are in the same office building--in Kuala Lumpur. The Japanese embassy was also in this building, but for some reason they did not attack it. Anyway, they took about sixty people--some American and Swedish diplomats and mostly Malaysians who were there to apply for visas--as hostages. Then they demanded that some Red Army comrades in prison in Tokyo be released and sent by plane to Kuala Lumpur, and they would fly on from there to another country they would designate. The Japanese government was to release the prisoners and furnish them a JAL plane. That was their demand.

"Since many human lives were at stake, our government had to comply with their demand. I was called back to the office that night of August 4th. We were told that some high-ranking officials from the Transportation Ministry and from the Foreign Ministry should fly to Kuala Lumpur in the JAL plane when the prisoners were flown there. We assumed that the terrorists would demand further guarantees, possibly in the form of new hostages, and that there would be more negotiations. In the early hours of August 5th, Mr. Keisuke Ochi, who was director-general for Consular and Emigration Affairs, and I got the order, and we flew to Kuala Lumpur.

"The Malaysian interior minister negotiated with the Red Army on the telephone. After much talking, he arranged for the Red Army to give up the original hostages and most of their explosives. In return, they demanded that we supply two replacement hostages from the Malaysian government and two from the Japanese. They wanted fairly high ranking officials. We four officials would fly to Tripoli, on the JAL plane, together with the released prisoners and the Red Army people to guarantee their safe flight. The Red Army kept their firearms and hand grenades."

Question: "The newspapers said that you replacement hostages had volunteered. Did you volunteer?"

(pause, somewhat taken aback) "Not in the sense that I put myself forward to do this thing. No, no. I assumed when we left Tokyo for Kuala Lumpur that whatever situation develops, I would have to do my duty as a civil servant. (in a quiet, sober tone) I am not a courageous man. But I was the appropriate official--especially since the destination was an Arab country--and if I did not go, some other official would have to do it. Mr. Ochi had the same opinion. So, we said we would do it.

Question: "Did the trip to Libya go smoothly? Were you released promptly in Tripoli?"

"Yes. They frisked me and questioned me very thoroughly when I boarded the plane. They did not seem to believe that I was just Mr. Murata from the Foreign Office. (laughing) We replacement hostages sat in the First Class compartment. They kept us under guard but allowed us to read. I spent most of the flight doing crossword puzzles in German. That is my hobby. (both laughing)

"We refueled in Sri Lanka. Otherwise we would not have been able to reach Libya. The Malaysian interior minister had a difficult time finding a country that would let our plane refuel. After we reached Tripoli, the five Red Army members and the five prisoners left the plane first. The Libyans treated us correctly. On that same day, we flew back to Cairo, and I had my first decent sleep in four days. From the time I hurried from my home to the ministry on August 4th until we reached Cairo on August 8th, I had no real sleep, only a nap for an hour or so now and then.

"Another item I might mention is my two years as ambassador in Abu Dhabi. 1978 to 1980 was a turbulent time. The Iranian Revolution took place, and I had to keep watch on that. Then, as a result of that revolution, oil prices went up again. In those days, Japan depended on the United Arab Emirates (UAE) for about 14 percent of our oil. Before the revolution, Iran had been our second largest supplier after Saudi Arabia. The revolution stopped the Iranian oil for a time, and made us all the more dependent on suppliers like the UAE. Now, in 1985, we can buy oil easily again. But in 1979, we had to beg them to sell oil to us at their prices. My job in Abu Dhabi was to develop the best possible relations with their leaders to protect our oil supply. I think I formed a good, personal relationship with Dr. Mana al-Otaiba, their oil minister.

"I also got a very special assignment to initiate our first high level official contact with the PLO. I met secretly with the PLO people, like Farouk Khadoumi, in the private residence of Minister Otaiba for some time--until it was leaked in the Abu Dhabi press. So, it is no longer a secret that I met with them, but I cannot disclose what I discussed. These PLO contacts proved useful when I went back to Tokyo in 1980, to become director-general of the Middle East and African Affairs Bureau. While I had that job, Yasir Arafat visited Tokyo. He was not, technically speaking, invited by the Japanese government, but by the Japan-Palestinian Friendship Group in the Diet. Well, I was able to help make those arrangements."

PREPARING FOR THE SUMMITS

"In 1982, I went back to my old place in the Economic Affairs Bureau, as director-general. One of the most important jobs I had was to help prepare the Japanese position for the summit meetings in Williamsburg in 1983 and in London in 1984. You know, the foreign ministers and finance ministers also participate in the summits, and many economic issues are involved. (laughing) In fact, the summits were originally intended to deal with economic issues. The Foreign Ministry is responsible for . . . hmmm . . . coordinating the Japanese position, which meant that my job was to form the Japanese position internally--or hammer it out, as you might say.

"I was lucky to have Prime Minister Nakasone and Foreign Minister Abe. The foreign minister, of course, gave me good access and let me explain our position as well as my personal views on the issues. But Prime Minister Nakasone was also rather generous with his time, and gave me all I needed to express my views. Sometimes I would meet with him. Or, if it was more appropriate, I would send him a paper on the subject, which I drew up myself, and I could tell from what he said later that he knew the contents of that paper very well. Once, he asked me in for a long session, over an hour, to explain the GATT--how it works and what the New Round is about. He listened very attentively. Another time, he wanted to know about changing economic and social conditions in your country--the shift to the Sunbelt, the development of the service industries, the changing mood in congress--and why Americans are so angry with Japan."[6]

INTERNATIONALIZATION

Question: "What does the internationalization of Japan

---

6. Mr. Murata did not develop his views on U.S.-Japan relations in our meetings. However, his views as well as those of two other senior Japanese diplomats have been set forth at length in Hiroshi Kitamura, Ryohei Murata, and Hisahiko Okazaki, *Between Friends* (New York and Tokyo: John Weatherhill, Inc., 1985).

mean?"

(laughing) "I cannot give you a crisp, short answer to that. (pause) I don't like the word internationalization. It is too . . . abstract and pretentious, in English as well as in Japanese. But there is no other word, and it is in common use, so . . . .(shaking his head in good-natured disapproval)

"For my grandfather and my father, internationalization just meant Westernization. If Japan was not to become a colony of the strong Western powers, it was necessary for us to become strong, economically and militarily. To do that we had to learn and absorb Western technology, railroads and shipbuilding, and Western institutions, and even social and political ideas. In the time of my grandfather and father, we established a constitutional monarchy, and we created an elected Diet and a relatively free press, and we gave the vote to all men over twenty-five. We absorbed all these Western ideas late in the last century and early in the 20th century. The process was similar to our absorption of Chinese culture from the 6th to the 8th century--except for one crucial difference. This time we could not absorb what we wanted and make it our own and then turn away. Nor could we isolate ourselves from the world as we did between 1639 and 1854, except for a limited trade with China, Korea, and Holland.

"In this century, we had to deal with other countries--especially your country and the European powers. Not just in trade. We had to understand the interests, the point of view, and the power of these foreign countries. Before the Pacific War, we were not able to do that sufficiently. Our perception of the world based on our culture was perhaps too narrow, too one-sided. Perhaps the influence of our past isolation was too deep. That made us unrealistic. We were so unrealistic that we declared war on the United States and took on almost the whole world. (pause) Something was seriously wrong with us, or we could not have done that. So . . . we were defeated and humiliated in the war.

"For my generation, our task has been and still is to recover from that defeat and to make Japan an accepted country in the international community. (pause, very thoughtfully) Perhaps the underlying task is still to correct the cultural and psychological narrowness that led us to war and defeat. Of course, we basically succeeded in our economic recovery some time ago. Now and for some time in the future, we must define a useful and positive role for Japan in the international community.

"These economic, political, and cultural processes are all . . . connected . . . and they reinforce each other. After the war, since we lost all our colonies, one hundred million Japanese had to learn to live on these four small islands. We had to develop new technological and industrial abilities. The U.S. helped us greatly in that. Your technology and your open market were essential for our economic recovery. So one aspect of our internationalization after the war was learning even more from the West--especially from your country--and becoming much more involved in international trade and finance than ever before.

"At the same time, because of the development of world trade and finance, and because modern communications have made the world so small, we Japanese realized that we could not go on living on our islands as though we are on another planet. We know that culturally and psychologically we have to become . . . less insular. That has been happening. For example, partly because our standard of living is so much improved, last year--in 1984--4.5 million Japanese visited abroad. Foreign films, TV shows, and books are everywhere. Japanese now have a much better awareness of other countries and cultures than thirty or fifty years ago. Deep in their minds, some very Japanese elements persist, which is fine. Every country should keep its essential character. But Japanese are now more aware of foreign cultures and are more influenced by them. I think that this broad cultural internationalization will go on. Japan cannot isolate itself again."

Question: "To what extent are Japan's leaders internationalized--not just in this broad cultural sense--but in being able to understand and deal with the outside world in practical terms, to speak foreign languages and work and live comfortably with foreigners? Do you think they are sufficiently internationalized to meet Japan's future needs?"

"The bureaucracy is a part of our leadership, and it has become much more internationalized since I joined the Foreign Ministry in 1952. (laughing) In a sense, the Foreign Ministry has helped the process. Many Finance Ministry and MITI officials have served abroad in our embassies or consulate-generals dealing with finance and trade. In the 1950s, very few of them knew English or some other language, or had experience abroad. Now, in the case of MITI, almost all their younger officials know a foreign language fairly well, and I would say that at least 80 percent of their higher civil servants are capable of looking at things from a broad, international perspective. The other ministries have less, but the number is growing.

"There is a similar development in the Diet. A great number of the Diet members who are under fifty can speak English and have experience abroad. Quite a few of the senior Dietmen, too. You will have no trouble finding internationalized Dietmen for your study. (both laughing) These politicians are more . . . broadminded and more aware of international reality than their fathers and grandfathers. And, of course, a large number of our businessmen do business abroad and they are internationalized as well, and becoming more so. In fact, these three leadership groups--businessmen, Diet members, and our bureaucrats--are the most internationalized Japanese.

"However, I know from personal experience that our internationalization is still incomplete . . . even for those of us in the Foreign Ministry. We can understand and work easily with Americans and Europeans, and also with Chinese and Koreans. However, in the Middle East and Africa we still are not at ease and have difficulties. It was very hard even for me, and it still is, to really understand the Arab people and the Persians. Their use of language is . . . so different. Sometimes, they seem to be too assertive (pause) and perhaps . . . too eloquent. (in a serious tone) It is hard for us to grasp what is really going on in the depth of their mind.[7] (changing tone and smiling) Also, they know almost nothing about us Japanese--except that we make good cars and televisions." (both laughing)

---

7. Mr. Murata wrote a book in Japanese on the Middle East that is being used in Japanese universities, *Chuto-to-yu-Sekai* (The Middle East: Portrait of a World) (Tokyo: Sekaino Ugokisha, 1981).

THE FUTURE OF U.S.-SOVIET RELATIONS

Question: "How do you think Japan will do as the world moves into the 21st century? Do you think it will continue to prosper and to internationalize successfully?"

(pause, speaking slowly and thoughtfully) "Hmm. Unless the world falls to pieces economically . . . or tears itself apart in wars, Japan should do well . . . and as I have said, our internationalization will go on. I am confident of that.

"There are a number of dangers--including trade wars and U.S.-Soviet war--that must be prevented. When we spoke about my four years in Washington and your opening to China, I mentioned naive American thinking about the Soviet Union. If I may, let me explain what I meant. I said that Nixon's rapprochement with China in 1972 was a master stroke. However, the idea of using the China rapprochement to create a real détente with the Soviet Union-- which existed in Washington when I was working there--and was developed further by the Carter administration, was a bit . . . unrealistic. Not only did I think so, but also many of my colleagues.

"There are two false assumptions about the Soviet Union which are very prevalent in your country. Most people seem to make either one or the other. Sometimes, both. The first is that if one is nice to the Soviets, and reaches agreements on trade and arms control with them, then the Russians will start to behave. That is an incorrect assumption. In the 1970s, when the U.S. was practicing détente, the Russians invaded Afghanistan and before that they had their hand in Ethiopia, Angola, the Middle East, and Vietnam. So this assumption that détente will improve Soviet behavior does not work.

"Secondly, some of your people, especially in the Pentagon, think that if you squeeze the Russians hard enough, show them that they can never compete with America because you are too superior in wealth, in arms, in technology, then they will be forced to make concessions, that is, to behave as you would like. That is also an incorrect assumption. It was unrealistic to believe that somehow the China card would keep the Russians in line. The Russians can endure all your pressures. And if you get too carried away with this tough-line policy . . . well . . . it could lead to unnecessary risks.

"I think that President Reagan has been right to rebuild your military strength and to tighten your alliances. Your country's position was too weak in the 1970s. And now, it is possible to have some limited but practical negotiations again with the Soviets. I am not suggesting another illusory détente. I am talking about maintaining a reasonably stable coexistence. That is all that can be realistically achieved."

Toyoo Gyohten

WHEN I met with him in the summer of 1985, Mr. Toyoo Gyohten was the director-general of the International Finance Bureau in the Ministry of Finance (MOF). For most Japanese, who are highly conscious of organizational status, the MOF is the elite of the elite, the most prestigious of the government ministries. The MOF oversees and regulates much of the Japanese economy, and is primarily responsible for Japan's financial solvency. The wide range of its authority can be seen by listing its main bureaus: Budget, Tax, Customs and Tariff, Financial, Securities, International Finance, and Banking. Ever since they have been old enough to read the popular national newspapers, such as the *Yomiuri Shimbun* or the *Asahi Shimbun,* most Japanese, and most, especially businessmen, have known that MOF's control over the government's annual budget, and its influence in setting interest rates and the availability of credit have had a powerful impact on their daily lives.[1] In recent years, as Japanese finance and banking have become increasingly internationalized, and as shifts in currency exchange rates have grown in magnitude, Japanese businessmen, both big and small, as well as Japanese workers and consumers, have become increasingly aware of the impact of the ministry's international finance and banking policies. So have the non-Japanese who do business with Japan.

Between the fall of 1985 and the summer of 1987, for instance, the yen increased in value by 50 percent against the U.S. dollar. The price of Japanese exports was pushed up and many exporters and workers in export industries felt the pinch. The price of

---

1. John C. Campbell, *Contemporary Japanese Budget Politics* (Berkeley, Calif: University of California Press, 1977), 43.

With wife, Reiko, at the World Economic Forum; Davos, Switzerland, January 1988.

Yokohama, July 1951: Toyoo Gyohten; Yoshio (elder brother); Kimpei Itoh (brother-in-law); Ryoichi (father); Toshiko (mother); Fumiko Itoh (elder sister).

Japan's huge oil imports, which are paid for in dollars, went down, and energy prices declined across the board. Japanese banks and investment firms found that their already sizeable capital and clout had rapidly appreciated in the New York and London financial markets. The currency float that led to this dramatic rise of the yen and devaluation of the dollar was the result of a series of meetings, among the central bankers and finance ministries of the leading industrialized countries, including the MOF and its Bureau of International Finance.

Mr. Gyohten's office, where we met, was a spacious, high-ceilinged, old fashioned room on the fourth floor of the ministry, looking out on Tokyo's wide, tree-lined, traffic-clogged Kasumigaseki. High on one wall was a large electronic, digital board that displayed the exact and fluctuating value of the yen against the dollar. Dominating the room was a massive, old wooden conference table with chairs for twenty or thirty people. Beside the large, wood-framed old sash windows, in the corner where we sat and talked, Mr. Gyohten had his desk, and nearby, several upholstered chairs and a couch, arranged around a coffee table. He had added a personal touch to this otherwise impersonal room by hanging several tasteful prints and photos of ballet dancers on the walls. Although they were meticulously polished and dusted, the worn, old furnishings in Mr. Gyohten's office were a silent rebuke against ostentation and waste. The MOF is a model of frugality.

The Finance Ministry building is notable for its darkened, stained, stone walls and its ancient, slow elevators. It is also famous for the aloofness and ability of its higher civil servants--who are chosen from the pick of the yearly crop of university graduates, most of them from the Faculty of Law at Tokyo University.[2] Colorful individualists may occasionally take and pass the highly competitive written examination, but they rarely get past the interview conducted by a committee of senior MOF officials, who are looking for self-effacing, organizationally minded, ambitious recruits, who are willing to devote themselves to the ministry and to the nation. John C. Campbell illustrates this point in his account of a somewhat unconventional applicant who showed up for the writ-

2. Akira Kubota, *Higher Civil Servants in Japan*, (Princeton, N.J.: Princeton University Press, 1969), 109.

ten examination one year without a coat and tie, but posted a high score. For the interview, he borrowed a coat from another applicant and performed reasonably well. Nevertheless, this unusual applicant was rejected. An official explained to Campbell that, "he is too individualistic and might have an influence on others."[3]

Mr. Gyohten joined the Finance Ministry in 1955, one of the twenty-two young officials chosen that year. In the summer of 1985, as director-general of a bureau, he was two steps below the MOF administrative vice-minister, who is the most powerful civil servant in the ministry and an influential person in the Japanese government, comparable to a permanent under-secretary in Great Britain. Most of the members of Toyoo Gyohten's class of 1955 are no longer in MOF. After serving for twenty years or more and having reached the rank of division chief, they were not chosen for the few remaining senior positions. Instead, they resigned from the ministry, most of them to high positions in banking, business, or a public corporation. Some went into politics.

Although he is a Todai Law Faculty graduate who was recruited by this same rigorous process and was screened by these same supposedly unbending senior officials, Toyoo Gyohten does not fit the stereotype of the gray, aloof MOF bureaucrat. He has an easy-going warmth and charm. He is a short, slim, carefully but casually dressed man, with a shock of dark hair and a smooth, small featured face that belies his fifty odd years. Behind his wide, heavily framed glasses, his eyes frequently have a good-natured, humorous twinkle. Toyoo Gyohten's English is very natural and relaxed, although tinged with a slight Japanese accent and cadence. His voice is low, expressive, and carefully modulated.

FAMILY AND CHILDHOOD

Toyoo Gyohten was born on January 2, 1931, in Yokohama, to Ryoichi and Toshiko Gyohten, the youngest of their three children.

---

3. Campbell, *Contemporary Japanese Budget Politics,* 45.

"My father was born in a small farming village in Shikoku. The village is called Awai and is in Kagawa Prefecture. I think that at some time we may have been a family of Shinto priests. I make that speculation because our family name has an unusual, Chinese sound to it. It sounds like a Shinto priest's name. Anyway, my father's family were farmers, not very rich but not terribly poor either. In those days, as you probably know, only the eldest son could inherit the family assets. Since my father was a second son, he could not expect anything. So, when he was quite young--about twelve or thirteen--he decided to leave that small village in Shikoku and make his own way in the world. Let me see. My father is now ninety years old, so it was about 1907 or 1908, toward the end of the Meiji period, when he left his village.

"At that time, one of his uncles was in Tokyo working as the postmaster of a small, third-class post office. That uncle was considered a very successful man among his relatives. He must have made some money, because in those days people used to buy the postmaster positions. My father went up to Tokyo and stayed with his uncle the postmaster. During the daytime, he worked in the post office, and in the evenings he went to school. I am sure he worked very hard, because somehow he managed to graduate from the Waseda University Law Faculty. And he was ambitious, but he had no family connections, no influential relatives, and no money. So, in order to get on in life, he became the friend of one of the very successful financiers of that time--Mr. Shinbei Inui. Mr. Inui was a private banker who made loans to companies at rather high rates of interest. When the borrowers could not pay back, he took over their companies. That way he established a conglomerate--a fair sized business empire that included a shipping company, a warehouse company, and a variety of other firms.

"My father got to know Mr. Inui, and Mr. Inui liked him. Hmm. How shall I explain this? My father was not a typical businessman type, but he was smart and he had a personal charm and style about him that Inui liked. So, Mr. Inui took my father into his company, and my father eventually became a board member and served there until he retired."

Question: "I am a bit puzzled when you say that your father was not a typical businessman. Could you . . . ?"

"Yes. I will explain that. He spent much more time on the golf course than most young businessmen. (both laughing) And the reason why he started to play golf is interesting. When he was in his twenties, about the time of the First World War, he saw that golf was being imported from England into Japan, and that it was a very exclusive sport. At that time it was not as popular as it is now. Only the richest, highest class people played it. So my father thought that if he could learn to play golf it would give him a chance to mix with these people. That is what he did, and . . . well, he succeeded a bit.

"He was a poor, young man so he could not spend much money on golf. He used to take the train out to a golf course very early in the morning and play as much as he could. Sometimes he spent the whole day out there, playing three or four rounds, from sunrise to sunset. Well, he became a very good amateur, a zero handicapper. And while he was doing this he *did* get to know influential people--businessmen and politicians. (smiling slowly and nodding his head) So, you see, it worked out somewhat as he planned. He was aspiring and ambitious to get into those circles, and he did it .

"He married my mother when he was about thirty or so. My mother's father was a schoolteacher in a small place on the outskirts of Tokyo. Her mother, my grandmother, was a very . . . energetic, enterprising woman. She could not be content as a schoolteacher's wife. So, she persuaded my grandfather to move to Yokohama, where they started a small pawnshop. My grandfather was not very good at business, but my grandmother was very skillful, and she ran the pawnshop so well that before very long they made a small fortune.

"Then, in 1923, a huge earthquake hit Tokyo and Yokohama, and everything they had built was lost--burned to the ground. My grandmother told me that after the Kanto earthquake, my grandfather was so disappointed that he tried to persuade her to go back to the countryside, where they were born, and he could get a job as a schoolteacher. (an expressive lift of the eyebrows) But she refused to obey him. She dug around in the ashes of the pawnshop and found some gems and gold that had not been burned, and with that as her capital, she started all over again."

Comment: "Hmmm. She was . . . tenacious."

(chuckling softly) "Yes, and she had a head for business. In a few years she was prospering again. They had a rather large pawn-shop and they owned some houses that they rented. They were a fairly well-to-do family in Yokohama when my father married their daughter--my mother. She had seven or eight brothers and sisters, and she was somewhere in the middle. Their family name is Shimura. So, my father married this young daughter of the Shimura family.

"I remember as a young child that we did not see much of my father. He was so busy with his business life, and playing golf, and meeting people that he did not have much time for us--for my mother and my older brother and sister. (pausing reflectively) But when he was with us, it was very nice. (happy laughter) He was a dandy dresser, and he had a good smell--of good cigars and expensive whiskey. He used to like to take us out to fine dinners. Or, he would take us to watch Sumo wrestling in Tokyo. Or, occasionally, he took us on a trip to his family in Shikoku. That was a long trip in those days--a long train ride and then over to Shikoku on the ferry. Well, you can see that my childhood was rather quiet and comfortable.

"My mother was very good and very close to us. She cared for us, and nurtured us and educated us. In the evenings, after I got home from grammar school, she would teach me more arithmetic and languages. She was a good tutor. Firm and patient. (pausing and smiling quietly) Since my father was away so much she could spend a lot of time on us. And she wanted to. So, you see, I was fortunate. I had a good childhood.

"I was very small . . . short and small, a somewhat frail child. Not at all strong. So my parents put me into a special school, the Makado Elementary School, where there was more care for the children. It was by the sea, in Yokohama. I did pretty well in my studies. The teachers mostly liked me, and I was well treated there.

"That school was a small school, and there were only twenty students in my class. But in that class there were an unusual number of foreign children. Well, Yokohama was a busy seaport. We had a British boy, and a German, and an Indian girl, and several others. Some were of mixed blood, like the Indian girl, who had an

Indian mother and a Japanese father. Many of the children came from families that were in overseas trade or shipping. So, I was exposed to foreigners and foreign things in that class, and got somewhat used to them."

Question: "Was the Makado School a boarding school? Did you live at school?"

"No. Our family had a small house in the compound of my mother's parents, near the pawnshop. That is where I lived. At certain times of the year, such as the end of the year, when the poor people needed money to buy gifts or pay debts, the pawnshop would be hectic, and even I was asked to come in the shop and help out. That was a fascinating experience. (pause) I think I learned something about people there--all kinds of people. Some good, honest people down on their luck, some others who were lazy and heavy drinkers. I learned that human beings can be . . . so weak.

"There was one woman I especially remember. She was the wife of a gambler. When her husband lost all his money, she would come and pawn her jewelry and even her kimonos, and walk home in an old dress or a *yukata* (a simple cotton robe). When her husband got lucky, she would pull up in a cab, in a beautiful kimono, take back all her things, and chat with us while the taxi waited, and then she would be driven home in style. (smiling) She must have had a strong loyalty for that gambler husband."

THE WAR

"The Pacific War broke out when I was in fifth grade. Our schoolmaster, who was an old teacher, gathered all of us in the playground and delivered . . . a very emotional speech. I don't remember what he said, but he shed tears and we were all overwhelmed by his emotions.

(gazing thoughtfully across the room, as though searching into the past) "After that speech, I went back home. I was surprised to find my mother busy packing . . . packing a small knapsack with canned goods, medicines, things for an emergency. I didn't say anything then, but years later she told me that when she heard we were at war, her first thought was that the country will be attacked. (pause) She had a good intuition."

Question: "Did you live in Yokohama throughout the war and the air raids, or did you move away?"

"We stayed until our house was burned, in May 1945. Of course, we had air raids before that, many of them, and people were moving out of town. We knew that Tokyo was bombed nearly every day, and we heard about the terrible incendiary raid on Tokyo, in March, the one that started an enormous firestorm. But we were still in Yokohama, because of my grandmother. She refused to move. My grandfather had died a few years before, and she insisted that since her husband had died in Yokohama, how could she leave? We could not convince her. She had a strong will. She was like the captain of a sinking ship, staying at her post.

"We had relatives near Odawara, which we thought was a safe place, and we moved many of our things there. (shaking his head and smiling slightly) Actually, Odawara was not a safe place at all. If the war had continued another six months, the Americans would have landed there, in their invasion. Anyway, although I sometimes went to Odawara for a weekend, I spent most of my days in Yokohama, where I went to school. On that day, on May 5th, 1945, I was at school when the air raid warning sounded. It was a beautiful, clear day. We were sent home, and then the bombing began.

(pause) "Five hundred B-29s flew over and bombed us. The sky was filled with them. The entire city was burned in a single day. Incendiary bombs fell in our house and it started to burn. We got out, with my grandmother. We carried her. It was a Western-style house, two stories with glass windows. The pressure from the fires inside blew out the glass and then the flames burst out the windows. That was the last I saw of it. We fled to a nearby park with a small pond in it and stayed there. The raid did not last very long, but the fires kept burning. The sky was so dark from smoke and fire, we could not tell what time of day it was. We stayed in the park all night.

"The next morning was (shaking his head in dismay) . . . something. Ashes and dead bodies . . . everywhere. Our home was ashes. In those days, every house had one or two oil drums filled with water, to put out fires. I still remember that near our house, a mother with a little baby tried to take shelter in one of those drums, thinking she would be safe in the water. But they were dead, from the fire and heat, and their bodies were all puffed up-- like balloons. That was . . . . (shaking his head, silently)

(pause) "Well, our house in Yokohama was gone, so we took my grandmother with us and went to Odawara and stayed there until the end of the war."

Question: "Was your father in the military, or was he too old for that?"

"He was almost fifty, but he was a lieutenant in the reserves. Toward the end of the war even older reserve officers like him were called up, and he went into the army for awhile. He was supposed to be sent overseas, and got orders to board a certain ship. But the order was canceled. (chuckling) I think he arranged the cancellation. He convinced an army doctor that his eyes were poor--too weak for military service--and this doctor thought, 'Here is a man close to fifty, with weak eyes,' and he had my father discharged. So, he was with us when the war ended.

"The school in Yokohama was also burned down in an air raid, so our school moved to Zushi. That was a two hour train ride each way, and the trains were poor and crowded in those days."

Question: "Were you also short of food?"

(thoughtfully) "A bit short, but I did not suffer much from hunger. We had no sugar and other things that I liked, but we lived on the waterfront, and we could catch fish. So, we had fish to eat and there was farmland behind us, and we traded clothes and other things for rice. It was a very tough time for my mother--to feed all her family. But we did not suffer from hunger."

Question: "You were fourteen years old in 1945, a student in middle school. Was your class drafted for factory work?"

"We were given a different job. This was in Yokohama, before the May 5th raid. The government expected incendiary raids and decided to make firebreaks--open, empty lanes in the city--to keep the fires from spreading. So, we were mobilized to do that job, to demolish all the houses in the firebreaks. On certain days, instead of going to school, we demolished houses. We used to pull the houses down with ropes--all pulling on the rope together. By noontime, we were hungry and exhausted, and we took a long break. We just stretched out on the ground and rested.

"That was the time when I began reading . . . devouring literature. My young uncle, who was a student, had a good collection of books and I used to borrow them. I read on the train and during our long lunch breaks. I still remember vividly the shock I felt when I read *War and Peace* by Tolstoy, in Japanese translation. It was in thirteen volumes. It was a revelation to me. You know, for a young boy growing up during the war, education was confined, distorted. We were taught that Japan is a country ruled by the gods, invincible and unchanging. But I could see that we were being destroyed and everything was changing. Well, when I read Tolstoy, I immediately understood and believed him. He wrote that society keeps changing and nothing is permanent. Men are born and die. Wars are won and lost. Governments rise and fall. (looking at me keenly) You know, Tolstoy was right.

"Another book that deeply impressed me was a French one, *Les Thibaults*, by Roger Martin Du Gard. It is the story of a French family between the wars, and the personal history of a boy, Jacques was his name. It is a story of friendship, family troubles, study, and young love. This Jacques was a boy of my own age, and he fell in love with a charming girl. I could understand him . . . his life and his feelings . . . completely.

"Well, during those days, when I was fourteen or so, toward the end of the war, without much to eat, and reading these books, I became antiwar . . . very strongly antiwar. I did not say anything about it, or show it, but within myself, that was the way I felt.

"Toward the very end, we expected the worst. They started to dig foxholes and trenches near the beach to defend the shore . . . with spears. I met soldiers who were working with us and also doing that. They were . . . demoralized . . . badly demoralized. Then, the end came and it was finally over."

Question: "This is not a flippant question, but did your mother use that knapsack, the one she packed in 1941?"

(Giving me a quick, sharp glance and then laughing heartily) "Yes. She did. We ate the canned food."

EARLY OCCUPATION DAYS AND JUNIOR HIGH SCHOOL

Question: "How did the Surrender and the Occupation affect your life?"

"Well . . . my first reaction was . . . a feeling of relief--of great relief. That was quickly followed by fear, fear of what your Occupation troops would be like. We had been told that American soldiers were like demons, so we were genuinely afraid. But that fear was quickly dispelled. Of course, there were incidents, here and there, robberies and rapes, but not very many. On the whole, your troops were well disciplined.

"The most serious problem was economic--for our family and most families. We were even worse off in the early Occupation years, in 1946 and 1947, then during the war. My father's company had lost so much business that they could not pay him a regular salary. Instead, he became . . . a kind of trader, a middleman. In those days, the distribution system was working so poorly that if you kept your ears open, and were smart enough, you could buy some goods in one place and get on a train and travel a few hours and sell them at a higher price and make some profit. I think he was doing that to support our family. I was just fourteen or fifteen years old then, still in junior high school. (pause) I am very grateful to my father . . . that he was able to support us, and I didn't have to work to support us. (looking at me very seriously) You probably cannot imagine how poor we were--how poor most Japanese were in those days--just at the bare subsistence level. But somehow we were able to survive, thanks to my father.

"We were living in a small town on the beach, called Kozu, on the shore of Sagami Bay. My junior high school was in Yokohama again, more than an hour away on the train. During the first winter after the war, life was hard--very hard. Almost every morning there were dead people on the ground near Yokohama station--people who had died during the night from starvation and cold. That's how it was.

"My fear of the American Occupation troops didn't last long, because I soon got to know some of them. Yokohama was still burned out from the air raids, but the American army set up a camp right in front of the train station. It was fenced in with a metal fence and barbed wire. It was a camp for black soldiers. I think your army was still segregated in those days. Well, I was studying English in school, and since I walked by that camp every morning and afternoon, I and some of my school friends started chatting with these black soldiers, trying out our English. First, we talked through the fence, and then they invited us in to their living quarters. They were probably very bored, not much to do. They told the military police we were just harmless kids, and we were allowed in.

"Their living quarters were just huge tents on the ground, with rows of bunk beds. They had a portable shower in their tent, and it was a typical barracks atmosphere, so when they wanted a shower they just peeled off their clothes and took one. That was my first encounter with black people, and at first they looked very different and a bit frightening to me--very big and strong. But soon I became used to them, and some were very friendly and good.

"There were also . . . some humiliating experiences at the camp. In one corner, near the fence, there were garbage cans. After each meal, the soldiers who didn't finish their food threw the food into those cans. Hmm. (pause) There were dozens, sometimes hundreds of Japanese trying to get at that food, sticking their arms through the fence. Not a pleasant sight. Also, there were Japanese women who were working as laundry women, or pretending to be laundry women in that camp . . . who were also doing a side business with the soldiers. Well, the bunk beds were not very private, and the soldiers were . . . rather uninhibited. (pause) That was . . . shocking to me.

"But, in a way, I learned some important things in that camp. My English improved rapidly, and as it improved I got to meet some American families. The army camp helped to break down cultural barriers--to give me a more open, flexible way of thinking, especially about foreigners. The average Japanese, especially my generation, who learned about Japanese history and the emperor during the war, are very inhibited toward foreigners--uncertain how to act with them. I was lucky in this respect. First, growing up in Yokohama with foreigners around helped. Then, after the war, for several years, the strict Japanese values and standards--well, they just collapsed. And just at that time, I encountered these American soldiers and some American families, and just chatting with them, getting to know them in an informal, casual way really helped to overcome these cultural barriers and inhibitions.

"You know, these events and accidents, the war and defeat, the collapse of traditional values, the things I saw in the army camp, the soldiers I talked with, also gave me a sense that--what shall I say?--that *everything* is relative. There is no absolute value or virtue in this world. Everything ends or changes so quickly. So, I do not believe in any religion, neither Buddhism nor Shinto. (laughing) But I am not an atheist either.

"One other thing about that camp. There was one special black soldier--a serious, polite young man--who actually took the train to Kozu to visit my family. (shaking his head at the memory and smiling) That was a . . . most unusual thing to do. I'm sure there were more fascinating things for a young soldier to do than to visit the family of a small Japanese kid. But he did it. I got a very strong, good impression from that black soldier--a confidence that despite differences in nationality and color, people can communicate, respect each other, and get along."

HIGH SCHOOL

"My school days were not special or remarkable in any way. I went through the usual ordeal of working hard to pass the high school entrance examination, which was very tough if you wanted to get into the good schools. I failed at my first try, but succeeded the second time and got into one of the best schools."

Question: "Which one?"

"The Tokyo First High School. It was a national school, with students competing for admission from all over Japan. That school was the elite of the elite. So, my parents were very proud (pausing and smiling ruefully) and so was I. That was in the spring of 1948, when I was seventeen years old. My father was back in his firm by then, and times were not as bad as in 1946, but still very poor.

"As it turned out, I went to this school for only one year. That was because our whole education system was changed by the

Occupation reforms. Under the old system we went to elementary school for six years, then middle school for five years, high school for three years, and a university or college for three or four years. During my first year in high school it was changed to a six-three-three system for elementary, middle, and high school. So, since I already had twelve years of schooling, I was considered to be finished with high school.

"I lived in a dormitory at high school. (shaking his head in dismay) The way we lived there was terrible. We did not have enough food, but that was not the worst of it. Those youngsters had . . . a strange psychology. They despised order and discipline and respected negligence and filth. Six of us boys lived in one big room. We never cleaned that room, and it was so dirty . . . it stank, really stank. (wrinkling his nose) We studied or slept at any and all hours, night or day. We despised the idea of a regular, decent life--of getting up early, cleaning the room, working and sleeping on some kind of reasonable schedule. But I will say this, we did study very hard.

"The foreign language training--written not spoken--was demanding and good. German was my first language--fifteen hours a week. I took English as my second language--ten hours a week. We also had philosophy, history, and some math. It was foreign languages and liberal arts--not practical, vocational training, but interesting and valuable. In German, I read Goethe and Schiller on through to Herman Hesse, and Marx and Hegel, too, although I could not really grasp the philosophical works very well. But I still remember passages of poetry, such as the verses Goethe wrote when he first visited Italy. Beautiful poetry! In English, Robert Browning was my favorite. I do not regret that year. I still enjoy the things I learned--even now. My classmates were very bright and intellectual."

RONIN AND WASEDA

Question: "I suppose that the students in your first year high school class, along with those who had completed the second and third years, all competed to enter the university in the spring of 1949. Was that the case?"

"Yes. That was the way it worked. I took the examination for Todai in March 1949, and I failed it. (thoughtful pause) That was a big blow to me. I felt as though I had fallen from the heavens and had hit the ground--hard. As a student at Ichiko, the best high school in the country, I was very proud of myself. People looked at me with respect and awe when they saw my school badge and my school cap. Now, I had lost all that. I had become a *ronin* That was my first serious setback . . . a period of . . . hmm . . . discouragement.

"I signed up for a day school that was supposed to help me study, but I did most of my work at home. When I was not studying, I got together with other *ronin*, and we talked. During those *ronin* days I began to get suspicious about the whole, rigid idea of going to a public university, like Todai. Instead, I developed a strong interest in journalism. The book that aroused my interest is John Reed's *Ten Days that Shook the World*. [4] I read it in Japanese translation, and I was fascinated by it. I also ran across a translation of Edgar Snow's book, *Red Star Over China*. That also stirred up my interest in journalism, and in leftist ideas. In those days, Todai had no journalism course, but Waseda, a private college, did. So, in the spring of 1950, I entered the journalism course at Waseda.

"Waseda was . . . a good experience for me. It is a good school, but the students were very different from my high school classmates and from Todai people. They did not have . . . hmm . . . the strong sense of being 'chosen ones.' They were not as bright on the academic side . . . and they were less constrained by the old Japanese values . . . more open to the leftist movement, which was very, very popular when I entered Waseda in 1950. I was attracted by all that, and I joined some radical groups and many demonstrations.

"I was caught up by the student movement and the demos, but the journalism classes at Waseda disappointed me. They were much too vocational. We had to read things like the *New York*

---

4. John Reed was an American journalist who was in Russia when the Bolsheviks took over in November 1918. His book is a dramatic, first-hand, sympathetic account of the revolution.

Times and *Photography Magazine*, and some printing periodicals. Well, I became uneasy. I started to wonder how I could become a good journalist just from these vocational classes. I had read enough history, economics, philosophy and such basic subjects at Ichiko to realize that I knew very little about these . . . really important subjects. So, that is why I changed my mind about staying at Waseda and applied for Todai again in early 1951. That time, I managed to make it.

"I used to think that I had wasted those two years being a *ronin* and going to Waseda. But in retrospect, it was a . . . fruitful time for me . . . as a human being. I widened my circle of friends. (thoughtful pause and then looking at me very seriously) And I learned to suffer humiliation . . . and how to be patient and resilient."

TOKYO UNIVERSITY

"In the spring of 1951, I entered Todai. I joined the Faculty of Economics . . . not Law . . . and I was enrolled there for the next four years. I still aspired to become a journalist, in spite of my disillusionment at Waseda. Hmm. (thoughtful pause) I was not . . . a very good student. I am afraid I did not attend classes very often-- although I read a lot of economics and other books as well. In classes . . . well, I was doing the minimum necessary.

"The student movement was important to me in those days, first at Waseda and then at Todai. The Korean War was going on, and in the spring of 1952, you may remember, Japan regained its independence under the San Francisco Peace Treaty and the (U.S.-Japan) Security Treaty. Well, the Security Treaty was very unpopular among the radicals, and when it came into force there was a big riot here in Tokyo, in front of the Imperial Palace. There were Molotov cocktails and fighting with the police. I think one man was killed, shot dead. I was there, at Bloody May Day. That's what it was called. I was one of the student rioters, one of the followers.

"We had so little experience of life . . . and so we were easily attracted to seemingly reasonable arguments against social injustice, against the vices of big business, and against imperialism. The

ideas of communism seemed so clear. And there was a sense of excitement and of participating in a group . . . in a movement that was
supposed to change the whole world. We were . . . a bunch of
young boys and girls . . . organizing, getting into heated arguments,
carrying big banners and shouting. I was part of it.

(pause and then smiling at the memory) I went to factories
and out to the farms . . . to educate those workers and farmers. We
went as a group, boys and girls together. We were naive . . . and
childish. We had a chance to meet girls and to talk with them and be
close to them. That was exciting. And . . . we were sincere in our
ideology too, in our sense of mission. (shaking his head at the
memory) But those poor workers and farmers didn't want to listen
to us. They were mostly indifferent. The farmers were happy to
take us in, because we worked for them without pay. They just had
to give us something to eat and a place to sleep and we worked hard
for them. But when we tried to tell them our ideas, they were not
interested.

"I have many friends from those days. Almost all of them
gave up their radical ideas. It was a kind of childhood illness.
Some are now rich businessmen, and some are politicians in the
Conservative Party. We still have . . . share a special nostalgia for
those radical student days.

"My father was back at work and was earning enough to
support us, but we were still . . . quite poor, so I also did different
kinds of part-time work. Sometimes I took manual jobs, like handing out advertising for a company. I also did some tutoring in English and math. (mischievous twinkle) At one time, I was a tutor in
a brothel. (noticing a question in my eyes and laughing) No, no. I
was not tutoring the girls. One middle-aged woman who was a
brothel owner had two young children in elementary school. They
were not bright students, and the mother was worried about them
and wanted to improve their grades. She asked her dentist if he
could help her find a tutor. Well, one of my good friends at Todai
was tutoring at that dentist's house, and he asked me if I was prepared to teach at a brothel, and I took the job."

JOINING THE MINISTRY OF FINANCE

Question: "Well, your career at Todai does not seem to me to be . . . hmm . . . typical for an MOF official. (both laughing) You were not in the Law Faculty. You wanted to be a journalist. You don't seem to have been pointing toward the Higher Civil Service examination. How did you join this ministry?"

"I really wanted to become a journalist. In fact, when I was a senior at Todai, I applied to several newspaper companies . . . but it didn't work out. There were two factors.

"First, I graduated from Todai in April 1955, and the employment examinations and interviews were in September and October 1954. Well, the Korean War economic boom ended soon after the armistice in 1953, and in 1954 we had a serious recession. Many companies decided to hold down their costs by not hiring any new college graduates that year. The job market was tight--very tight. We seniors were afraid that we would be unemployed after graduation. (looking intently at me to see if I understood how serious this was) So, deep down, I had the feeling that . . . I have to get a job . . . any job . . . otherwise . . . well, the idea of not getting a job was very scary.

"Secondly, there was my father--born in a small village as the second son of a poor farmer. He had done pretty well in the business world, but for him the highest aspiration . . . his real dream in life, was to become a civil servant or a politician. He couldn't fulfill that dream, but he wanted me to do it, and he used to encourage me to try for the Civil Service--especially the Ministry of Finance, which was considered the highest ranking ministry. He knew that I had . . . liberal ideas . . . and wanted to enter journalism. So, he didn't order me. He used to say that a Civil Service job was not really so bad. He said it was up to me what job I wanted to take, but it would not do any harm to at least take the Civil Service examination. Then, if I passed, I could decide what to do. Well, I thought it over. I couldn't help but think it over. The job market was so tight, and my mother and father were getting older. And I thought, 'Why not take that examination . . . give it a try?'"

Question: "Yes, I see. And what about the newspaper jobs. What was going on there?"

"My first choice, the *Asahi* (at that time the largest, most prestigious national daily newspaper, with a liberal, progressive political complexion) did not hire any new staff that year. That was a . . . disappointment. So, I applied to *Nihon Keizai* (Japan's *Wall Street Journal*). There were several stages in their testing and screening. It was spread out over a few months. I did well in their examinations and interviews, but they still had not made a decision on me when the Civil Service examination came up, and then I discovered that I had passed the government examination. To please my father, I applied for the Finance Ministry . . . which seemed . . . well, unrealistic. But I did it for him. In those days only the top 5 percent of the Todai graduates applied to the Ministry of Finance, and I was in the top 30 percent or 35 percent.

"Well, I went to an interview with the senior ministry officials . . . and I must have done fairly well. I learned later that the interviewers had a small disagreement over me. Some of them said, 'This young boy's school record is not good enough.' The others held out for me. They said, 'He will be allright.' In that year, in 1955, the ministry took in twenty-two young officers. (smiling) I am quite sure that I was number twenty-two on their list. (both laughing)

"It was a difficult position for me. I still had no word from *Nihon Keizai*, and I had to decide whether to take the ministry job or whether to let it go and gamble that *Nihon Keizai* would give me a job. I was not courageous enough to take that chance. So . . . ." (shrugging his shoulders and spreading his hands)

Question: "I think . . . you are joking me. Do you mean that you would have turned down the Finance Ministry position if the newspaper job had been open to you?"

(seriously) "Yes. I would have taken the newspaper job."

Comment: "That is surprising . . . at least to me. But your father must have been happy with the way things had worked out."

(laughing) "Oh yes. He was very delighted. He and my mother came to attend the commencement ceremony at Todai, which took place just a short time after I decided to enter the ministry, and he was so happy with me that on the way home he bought me a fine pair of new shoes--quite an investment in those days. Those shoes cost about ¥3,500, which was about $10. My starting salary at the ministry was about ¥7,000 a month, about $20."

CUSTOMS BUREAU,
COURTSHIP AND FULBRIGHT SCHOLARSHIP

"So, I started my career. I was assigned to the Customs Bureau--not the most prestigious position. In 1955, this building was still being used by your military as a PX (post exchange). We didn't get it back until 1956."

Question: "How did you find the work? Did you like it?"

(Nodding affirmatively and speaking in a very incisive tone) "Yes. Very much. Much more than I had expected to. I was . . . just a small cog in the government apparatus, but I got . . . a certain sense of satisfaction . . . because the work I was doing led to some real results. Nothing big, but some small economic results.

"I was in the Legal Division. In those days we had many tariffs. For instance, there was a 20 percent across-the-board tariff on machinery imports. But since there were some important sectors in our economy that needed to import machinery, there had to be a way to make exemptions to this tariff. These exemptions were usually arranged here in the Finance Ministry, on a case-by-case basis. For these exemptions to be official and legal there had to be a decree for each one issued by the Cabinet Legal Office, which in those days was located in the Akasaka Detached Palace, (part of the Imperial Palace complex located in Tokyo, designed and built to closely resemble some of the buildings at Versailles). I was sent over there often to get the decrees through, especially when we had to meet a deadline. Many nights I worked there until very late. In the winter, those offices in the palace were terribly chilly. There was barely any heat. There was no place to eat in that building . . . and the only toilets were way down in the basement. But I enjoyed that work. (smiling at the memory)

"I was also sent around to visit the Customs Houses all over Japan. And I liked those trips. That was the kind of work I did that first year, before I left to study in the States."

Question: "Did the ministry send you abroad to study?"

"They gave me permission to go, but I went on a Fulbright Scholarship. When I took the interview at the ministry, in Spring '55, I told them that I was applying for this scholarship, and that I wanted to study abroad, in the United States. For someone like me, in those days, practically the only way to study abroad was on a Fulbright. Hmmm. It was tough and competitive to get an all expenses paid scholarship, because there were only about a dozen a year for Japan. Of course, spoken English was most important in that competition.

"So, in my senior year I had enrolled in the Japan-American Conversation Institute, one of the oldest language schools in Japan, founded by a very international gentleman named Itabashi. He really believed in building cultural bridges with language training. Of course, during the war Itabashi's school had been closed, but early in the Occupation he reopened and he had many students. When I joined the school in 1954, it was still in an old, burned out building in the Kanda neighborhood. The walls were still black from the air raid fires, and there was no glass in some of the windows, so it was freezing cold in the winter. But the instruction was intensive and good quality. Three hours a day from Monday through Saturday, from six to nine in the evening. Our teachers were mostly Japanese who had lived in the States, and a few retired American servicemen. The tuition was pretty expensive. That is why I took the tutoring job in the brothel.

"Well, Itabashi's Japan-American Conversation Institute was one of the most important places in my life. I met my wife there. She was also studying English there in the evenings. During the day she worked for an American trading firm in Yokohama. Her father had been a promising, talented painter--in the traditional Japanese style. He had been making his way up as an artist . . . but as sometimes happens, after he married and had children . . . he had somehow lost confidence in himself . . . and he died very young. My wife's mother was left with three children to raise, and she brought them up to become independent and self-supporting. As soon as my wife finished high school, she found a job and went to work.

"Her name before we married was Reiko Tauchi. Her father's family was samurai, and their social status was much higher than my family. Her great grandfather was a cabinet minister in the Meiji period, and many of her relatives were senior civil servants. So, if her father had not died, her life would have been much more comfortable . . . and different."

Question: "Perhaps you would not have met?"

"Hmm. Maybe not . . . or at least not in the same way. She would not have been working and studying English in the evening. (laughing) I was very lucky.

"Well, Reiko was not very happy when I passed the government examination and joined the Ministry of Finance. She had nothing against the ministry . . . but in her eyes, the Finance Ministry officials were so remote, so cool and proud . . . that she didn't know whether we could still be close to each other. She was afraid that I would move away from her . . . emotionally.

"She may also have thought that I would start looking for status, for promotions . . . and for a more advantageous marriage. That is just what my father wanted me to do after I joined the ministry. He wanted me to marry into a rich, socially influential family.

"You probably know that young, bachelor officials in the ministry are considered a good catch for the daughters of rich, good families. I was asked to quite a few *miai* . I refused them . . . because I had decided to marry Reiko. My father did not like what I was doing . . . at all . . . and he made that very clear. It was . . . hard on us . . . and on my mother, too.

"Meanwhile, I had taken all the tests and interviews for the Fulbright, and I learned that I was going to the States in June of 1956. The Fulbright Committee asked me which school I wanted to attend (laughing) and at first I had no idea which was which. I met someone who had studied at Princeton, and he told me it was a good college. So I told the committee that Princeton was my choice. I also found out that Jacob Viner, who was famous in international trade theory, was at Princeton, and I said that would improve my understanding of tariffs and customs.

"Well, in the spring of 1956, when I knew I was to going to Princeton, I thought of marrying Reiko . . . without my father's consent. That's what I wanted to do. My mother was sympathetic and had tried to help and bring my father around, but she could not stand up against her husband. She worried about us . . . very much. It was miserable for her, too."

Question: "But you didn't marry that spring, did you?"

"No. Reiko said no. She was just a young girl, but unusually reasonable and level-headed. I told her I wanted to marry her before I left for the States, and she said, 'Look, you say you love me, and I love you. I have no objection to marrying you. But now you are going abroad and nobody knows what will happen and how we will feel when we are separated for more than a year. I think we should wait. Why don't we just wait?'

"So, instead of marrying, we were engaged . . . very privately. I gave her a small, opal ring as a token of my love, because she was born in October.

"Even then, my father refused to acknowledge her as my fiancée. When I sailed from Yokohama, my family and relatives all came to see the ship off, but he wouldn't let Reiko join us. So, the day before I left we had lunch together. Reiko said she would come to the docks and wave goodbye to me from someplace where my father couldn't see her.

"The next morning, when my ship began to leave its berth, I couldn't see Reiko in the big crowd on the dock. I knew she must be there, but I couldn't pick her out . . . and I became afraid that she wouldn't be able to see me either on the crowded deck. So, I ran up to the higher decks, all the way up to the top deck where I was all alone and I waved my handkerchief toward the place she said she would be. I still couldn't see her, but she told me later that she had seen me--waving on that top deck and searching for her."

PRINCETON

"We took three weeks to sail to Seattle. We stopped in Hawaii, went on to Vancouver, and then down to Seattle. The ship was the old *Hikamaru* of the Nihon Yusen (Japan Freight lines). It was the only passenger ship that had survived the war. It is anchored now in Yokohama Harbor. Well, nowadays with jet travel there is no time to prepare for culture shock. Suddenly you are there. But those three weeks on the *Hikamaru* were . . . special. I was full of anticipation . . . of hopes and dreams . . . wondering what America would be like. Every now and then, I would remind myself to be realistic. A Japanese friend who had just returned from studying in the States had warned me that when I was traveling away from the campus and on my own I would have very little money to spend. The Fulbright scholarships were very generous and luxurious in some ways, but the stipends were limited. According to this friend, the best way to get enough food was to eat ham sandwiches and drink chocolate malts."

Question: "Didn't you have your salary from the ministry?"

"Yes, but they couldn't remit it to me because of the exchange controls. Anyway, in your currency my salary then--even after my first increase--was only about $25 or $30 a month.

"Well, as soon we landed at Seattle, I tried my friend's advice. (laughing at himself) I went right into a drugstore and sat at the counter and a black waitress took my order. The first thing I noticed was that she treated me like any other customer--not like a foreigner. That was much different than Japan. So, I ordered a ham sandwich and a chocolate malt, and she very casually asked me, 'White or dark?'. I was stunned by this question. (both laughing) I had no idea that you could have dark or white bread. I thought it over very carefully and asked her, 'What did you say?' I could see in her eyes that she was getting a little irritated and impatient. She repeated, 'White or dark?'. Then I had a flash of understanding. She wanted to know whether I was a white man or a black man. (more laughter) Well, I had heard about segregation in America . . . So, I answered, 'Yellow'. (long laughter) That black woman shook her head and looked at me as if I was hopelessly dumb, and then she brought me a slice of white bread and a slice of dark and said, 'Which one you want?' That was my first encounter in America.

"Then, I joined up with a group of about a dozen other scholarship students, and we all crossed the country by train. We rode on the Great Northern Railway, over the Rockies and on through Chicago, all First Class thanks to the Fulbright grant. We were going to several different places for our orientation, and when we reached Albany, we broke up. I was in a group of five that went to Bennington, Vermont.

"I spent the summer there, before going to Princeton. Bennington was an exclusive college for rich girls in those days--but none of them were around, because it was vacation time. We used their dorms. The idea was to mix foreign students from various countries in this orientation, and for all of us to get used to being in America.

"Well, again, I was very lucky. Vermont is a . . . beautiful place . . . especially in July and August, and in some ways it was very . . . traditionally American. Not big city America, but village America . . . town hall democracy. We had some courses to take, but for me, meeting the local people left a stronger impression. A surprising number of the Bennington village people were active in our program--all volunteers. They gave picnics for us, invited us into their homes, and were very active in our orientation classes. We seemed to meet some of them everyday. (thoughtful pause) They were so open and friendly to us foreigners--and so affluent and so generous. That was the middle of the Eisenhower era. Your country was definitely the strongest and richest in the world and your people had . . . an enormous sense of well-being and confidence. It is hard to describe it now. That made them benevolent-- really open and kind to foreigners. The outside world was not at all threatening to them. Of course, you had just come out of the Korean War, but that was nothing like Vietnam. It didn't leave any serious scars . . . no sourness or bitterness.

(speaking very slowly and thoughtfully) "You know, the good people in Bennington, deep in their hearts, looked down a bit on us foreign students. We were all from Asia, Latin America or Southern Europe. No Anglo-Saxons. Sometimes, I felt that . . . but it was not so bad. In those days, we completely accepted the supremacy of the U.S.A. It was . . . unchallengeable. You were the big brother and we *wanted* to be the little brother. It seemed natural. We were eager to learn, to follow. It was a simple, easy relationship. So, even though the Bennington volunteers might have been . . . a bit condescending now and then . . . it was natural, and I was much more impressed by how sociable and generous they were to us--to me.

"At the end of the orientation I made a homestay with an awfully nice couple. They lived on a nearby farm. Their name is McCabe. The husband, Jim, was a retired company executive and their children were all grown up and on their own. I still send Christmas greetings to Mrs. McCabe, since Jim died. They had a big, comfortable house, some cows, and a vegetable garden. They have a brook in their back yard, and there were beavers in it. And the yard was full of chipmunks when I was there, and there were hummingbirds, too. Several years later, I visited with them during the winter, and the deer came down from the mountain into their yard.

"Some years after that, I took my parents and family to meet the McCabes, in Vermont. The McCabes were . . . wonderful to me, and I wanted my family to know them.

"In September, we finished at Bennington. I took a bus down the Hudson River Valley and spent a couple of weeks in New York before classes started at Princeton. (nodding for emphasis) That was a fascinating, exciting time for me. I stayed uptown at the International House, near Columbia University. It was hot September weather, but the heat didn't bother me. I spent my days wandering around midtown and downtown. At night, I hunted for good jazz places, and stayed up to all hours, listening, drinking in that music. That was the heyday of the old jazz in Harlem--Lena Horne singing and Louis Armstrong on the trumpet. Harlem was not so dangerous then. I remember walking across Harlem toward International House at four in the morning, after a night of jazz. It was terrific!

"Well, you must be wondering if I ever reached Princeton. (both laughing) Yes. I settled into my dorm and started studying. My adviser was Professor William Baumol, one of the youngest and brightest professors in econometrics. The graduate curriculum I was in was a combination of economics and sociology. We had a mix of students. Some regular Princeton undergrads, some G.I. Bill students, and some from the State Department and other government agencies, as well as a few other foreign students. They were all bright, and even though we had very different backgrounds and preparation, I was astonished by how quickly we progressed in our courses, and how quickly people who were weak in math or some other subject managed to catch up.

"One memory I have is of a Filipino friend who really impressed me one evening. Do you remember in 1956 the Egyptians suddenly nationalized the Suez Canal, and Britain and France invaded the canal zone in the fall and tried to take it back? Well, a high British diplomat came to Princeton one evening and tried to justify the invasion. This diplomat and the reasons he gave . . . irritated me . . . very much. But I didn't say anything. I didn't have the courage to speak against him. My Filipino friend, José Encarnacion, raised his hand and politely challenged this diplomat and ended by saying, 'Sir, why don't you stop this unreasonable folly?' The Englishman didn't know what to say. Some people in the audience were embarrassed, but they also respected the courage and firm style of this Filipino boy. José went on to become dean of the Economics Faculty at the University of the Philippines, and we got together later when I worked in Manila, and became very good friends. His question that evening was a shock to me . . . an enlightening shock.

"I was from Japan--a defeated country, and still very poor, and I felt that it was natural to silently accept what this British diplomat said--even though it irritated me. But this little Filipino, from a country ever poorer and weaker than Japan, he stood up and firmly denounced this . . . imperialism."

Question: "Your Filipino friend was probably educated in an American school, don't you think?"

(laughing) "Yes, he probably was."

Question: "Did you take a degree at Princeton?"

"No. There was no master's degree program, and I was not in the Ph.D. program. (laughing and wagging his finger at me) But I studied pretty hard--harder than when I was at Todai. (both laughing) Life at Princeton then was much different than it is now. We dressed for all meals, and we were served by black maids. At dinner you had to wear a big, black gown. Nobody could tell if you had anything on underneath. We all went to chapel for prayers, and we had to pray in Latin."

Comment: "Well, you were being taught to be an English or perhaps a southern gentleman." (laughter)

"Yes, we were. But I also experienced other kinds of life, too. When I finished at Princeton in the spring of 1957, I was given another First Class train ticket to Seattle to catch my boat home, but I changed the ticket so that I took a swing south to Florida, over to El Paso, Texas, and then on to San Francisco and Seattle. I also volunteered to help build a schoolhouse for black kids down in Georgia, in Keysville, a small farming village. That was an ecumenical church activity. I saw it on the bulletin board, and since I was interested in the segregation issue, I signed up for it.

"I took a train to Augusta, and then a long, hot bus ride to Keysville. Some of the volunteer students--mostly whites, including a Dutch girl--had already arrived and started the work with some local blacks. The leaders were a young white clergyman and his wife. They had a small baby. They had cleared away some trees and stumps, made a concrete floor, and started laying bricks."

Question: "Were the local white people antagonistic?"

"No, not at all. It was not like that at all. But in Georgia, I sometimes got confused on the racial business. At Princeton, I was a member of the ruling class, you know, and I knew my place and kept to it. (more laughter) When I got to Augusta, I had to take a taxi from the train station to the bus station, and I discovered that there were two cab stands--one for whites and another for blacks. Well, I didn't know what to do. I stood there . . . somewhere between them, trying to decide, when a black taxi pulled up, and I took it. When I got to the school building project, they told me that I was considered a white. That was my official status in Keysville. (both laughing)

"Even though I was officially white, I tried to get as tanned as I could on that construction job. So, I got out there in the hot, Georgia sun without a hat and barechested. I worked that way for a couple of weeks . . . and then I got sunstroke. (I looked at him questioningly and smiled) It was kind of ridiculous . . . but not at all funny. I had a very high fever, terrible dizziness, and I was urinating blood. It knocked me flat on my back in bed for almost a week. There was no doctor around, and when the dizziness hit me, I thought I was going to die, there in Keysville. While I was laid up like this, some black kids would come and visit with me, and gather around my bed, all friendly and smiling. I thought the faces of

those happy, smiling black kids were the last human faces I would
see in this world. I liked those kids--a lot. When I got better, they
chipped in their pennies and nickles and bought me a Zippo lighter.
I still have it, even though I don't smoke anymore.

"There was also a young, black woman working at that project. Her name was Corrine, and we liked each other and talked a
lot. She was studying to become a schoolteacher, and later she
married a black minister. We exchanged Christmas cards for some
years and then lost contact. Well, when I got over the sunstroke, I
had to get going to the West Coast. The group leader and his wife
took me to the bus station in Keysville in their car, and Corrine came
too, to say goodbye. Segregation was pretty strict in that town, so
the clergyman had the black girl sit up in the front seat with him, so
people would think she was the maid, while the clergyman's wife
and I sat in the back. We got to the bus station and talked and waited for that Greyhound. I remember that there was a beautiful mag-
nolia tree in bloom next to that dusty bus station . . . and how sad I
felt. Then, when I got on the bus and put my head out the window
to say goodbye, that young black woman looked in my eyes and
said, 'Toyoo, I'm goin' to miss you most of all.' (with a sad smile)
I still remember her voice. She was a very . . . good, warm-hearted
girl."

MARRIAGE

"When I got back to Japan . . . my fiancée and I still wanted
to marry and my father was still completely against it. My mother
was still sympathetic with us. So, we met and talked . . . many,
many times about what to do. For a while we hoped we could convince my father . . . if we were patient enough. Finally, we decided
that the situation wouldn't improve no matter how long we waited.
So we decided to go ahead and get married.

"It was . . . awkward . . . with my father openly opposing
our marriage. We couldn't have the wedding ceremony and reception we wanted to have, with all of our relatives and friends and the
senior people from the ministry and Reiko's company. We couldn't
do that because the senior people and many relatives would not

come if my father refused to be there. Also, since we two would have to pay for everything, we couldn't afford that kind of a wedding. So, instead, we each took some of our savings and arranged for the wedding ceremony in the old school building where we had met and studied English together. We were married in our classroom. It was April of 1958. The principal of the school, Mr. and Mrs. Itabashi, presided. (smiling at the memory) It was very simple . . . but it was allright. I was in the business suit I usually wore to the office and Reiko borrowed a wedding dress. Afterward, we had a reception in a Chinese restaurant close by in Yuraku-cho--because Chinese restaurants were reasonable. We invited our close friends. My mother came, and so did my brother and sister. But not my father. Since I couldn't invite the senior people at the ministry, I sent them wedding announcements.

"We took our honeymoon trip to the Izu Peninsula--on a sort of discount ticket from a travel agency, which included hotel and train fare. (again smiling warmly) It doesn't sound like much, but we were happy.

"We got a small apartment in a municipal building on the outskirts of Yokohama and moved in. It took me about an hour and a half to get to the office. We were both working. (laughing) My wife, working as a secretary in an import-export company, was earning almost twice as much as I was--because junior officials had such meager salaries. So, we were getting on comfortably . . . until my wife became pregnant. There was no union or leave policy . . . or anything like that in her company. They just fired her. Our income was cut by about two-thirds. We got by . . . but it was a difficult time financially."

Question: "Did your father show any sign of relenting?"

"Yes, gradually. At first, he was very hard. But after Reiko had our son . . . well, that softened my father, but only gradually. There was no dramatic reconciliation. It was step-by-step."

Question: "Did getting married without your father's consent cause any problems in the ministry?"

"Hmmm. I don't think so. It was a little embarrassing for me not to be able to invite my superiors to the wedding, but I don't think it influenced my career, one way or the other. For one thing, having such a modest wedding, with so few guests, was more common those days than it is now, when weddings are (laughing) stupendous. The whole country was pretty poor, and our wedding was more or less ordinary. (smiling and shaking his head) So, it didn't make any difference."

TAX COLLECTING IN MORIOKA

"When I returned to the ministry from Princeton, they assigned me to the International Finance Bureau. By 1958, our government was gradually deregulating our strict exchange controls, and each of the changes they made generated new problems for us or for some industry or business . . . which we had to clear up.

"Well, my year at Princeton had clearly tagged me as one of the international people. There were just a few of us in those days. But my superiors did not want me to be too narrow. They wanted to make sure that I learned how things work here in Japan--who pays the taxes and how we collect them. So, in 1962, they made me director of the local tax office in Iwate Prefecture in northern Honshu.

"So, in 1962, I took my wife and our little two-year old son and moved up to Morioka. Morioka is the prefectural capital. It had about 120,000 inhabitants. Iwate was one of the poorest agricultural prefectures, very mountainous and backward, and some people used to call it Tibet. (both laughing)

"Directing that office was good leadership training . . . not very easy . . . sometimes exciting and satisfying. And I learned a lot about Japan up there. (noticing my quizzical glance) Morioka is a different Japan than Yokohama and Tokyo, where I grew up . . . much different.

"I had one hundred and twenty people working under me. In order to run that tax office, you first had to deal with the Government Worker's Union in the office. They were under strong Communist influence and . . . very unfriendly to management . . . meaning me. There were also several militant local groups who were against all taxation. And every now and then local politicians would try to meddle in some tax matter.

"While I was serving in Morioka, the Government Worker's Union split. One group was less militant, and I and the other managers in our office supported it, of course. The more militant group, which was more popular and had more supporters, denounced me--charged that I had conspired to split the union. They had some nasty tactics. They kept making threatening telephone calls to my house and sending telegrams to the office. When I came to work in the morning, they would surround me outside the office and yell at me."

Question: "Did they hit you or attack you physically?"

"No. They just harassed me. It went on for two or three weeks . . . and then gradually subsided."

Question: "Well, there you were, a former radical student, the target of the militant union?"

(smiling and shaking his head) "Yes. I saw . . . the irony of it. Well, that's the way it was. I didn't mind it very much. On the whole, we enjoyed our life up there.

"The farmers and fishermen worked very hard . . . but they were still poor--although not as poor as they had been early in this century. In the old days, if the weather was bad and the crop was poor, they had nothing to sell but their daughters. Before the Pacific War, the prostitutes in Tokyo and Osaka were mostly from *Tohoku* (northeast Japan). By 1962, with the agricultural reforms and rice subsidy, things were much better. I made many friends up in Morioka . . . good, personal friends. (smiling warmly) Some of the staff in the tax office still work there, and when I visit Morioka, we all get together for lunch or dinner."

TOKYO AND THE INTERNATIONAL MONETARY FUND

"Well, one summer evening in 1963, Tokyo called and told me that I was being transferred back to the ministry, to the International Finance Bureau, again. That was at the time that President Kennedy announced measures to protect your balance of payments--including control of capital, interest equalization taxes, and import surcharges. The most serious measure for us was the interest equalization tax. We were heavily dependent on the New York market for borrowing, and this tax virtually closed the door to Japanese borrowers.

"Foreign Minister Ohira (Masayoshi Ohira, prime minister 1978-1980) led a mission to Washington to ask for a partial relaxation of the capital control on Japanese borrowing. I was sent along as a very junior member, to take notes and to carry my boss's briefcase. He was Mr. Makoto Watanabe, our director-general. That gave me my first glimpse of international dealings."

Question: "How did it go?"

(in a quiet, flat tone) "It was . . . not successful. We met with your State Department people and trade union leaders, and they turned us down. There was no give at all. (thoughtful pause) I got an unpleasant impression. Your side had all the power and we had none. It was not a negotiation at all. All we could do was . . . plead timidly for some help. Your side was not rude. But there was no real discussion. Just a firm 'No'. Well, I was impressed by what a tough task we had ahead of us.

"Not long after that mission, in early 1964, I was asked to go to Washington, to join the staff of the IMF (International Monetary Fund). That was a big assignment for me. My predecessor, who is now president of the Asian Development Bank, was Mr. Masao Fujioka. He was seven years senior to me in the ministry, and had served for three years at the IMF. Normally, his successor would have been senior to me. So, I felt proud of that assignment.

"Off we went to Washington. Our son was then four years old, and we had our daughter, too, who was only six months old. The IMF is a generous institution. They paid us--the whole family-- to travel First Class and they gave us a huge allowance for shipping household goods. (chuckling) I could not even fill one-quarter of that household goods allowance, even though I shipped some soy sauce and rice with our furniture. (both laughing) The allowance was for an American family with furniture for a three-bedroom house and a car. But we had no beds, no sofas and arm chairs and not even a car.

"We came over on the *President Wilson*--a two week voyage, with an overnight stop in Honolulu. (smiling and shaking his head at the memory) It was . . . luxurious. Every night there were dinner parties, cocktails, and dancing parties. Reiko did not bring any . . . I don't think she had any dresses. Only some kimono. I didn't have a dinner jacket. (cheerfully) We were the poorest First Class passengers on that ship.

"From San Francisco, we flew to Washington and started our life there. We stayed until late 1966, almost three years. I was at the Japan Desk. My job was to collect information and make analyses of the Japanese economy. There were hardly any English language sources on Japan's economy in those days, so in a sense it was an easy job for me. I could do much of the job by telling them what was in the *Nihon Keizai Shimbun*. There was no English version then.

"I was also sent to Tokyo as a member of the IMF team, which was odd. (smiling gently) I had to sit across the table from my old friends and bosses, and to speak in English, because I was on the IMF team. That was . . . embarrassing. (both laughing) Well, that kind of work gave me a more objective view of the Japanese economy. I learned to see it from the foreigner's point of view."

ASIAN DEVELOPMENT BANK

"I expected to stay with the IMF at least four years, and they did too, but in late 1966, Tokyo called and asked me to fly home for a consultation. When I got to the ministry, they asked me whether I would like to work with Mr. Takeshi Watanabe, who was going to become the president of the Asian Development Bank (ADB). Mr. Watanabe was a former senior Finance Ministry official, and served as the financial minister at our Washington embassy and executive director of the IMF and the World Bank. He was an internationally known expert on development finance. The ADB was just then being formed by a joint sponsorship of the U.S.A. and Japan. Japan was the major contributor, so a Japanese was to become the president.

"The bank is in Manila, of course. I felt that I was ignorant of the Asian area, but I liked the idea of setting up a new bank in a foreign country. It would be a challenge. So, I took it. The IMF was not happy to see me leave without finishing four years with them, but the ministry persuaded them. We stopped off to look over Manila on our way home to Japan. We spent about three frantic, busy months in Tokyo, and then we moved to Manila.

"The early months with the bank were the most hectic. So much traveling that it is a . . . blur in my mind. We had the inaugural meeting of the bank in Tokyo. Then, I spent two months traveling all over the world with Mr. Watanabe, to America, Asia, and Europe. Traveling continued to be a big part of the job, even later. We kept on traveling about 100 to 150 days a year outside the Philippines, and quite a bit in the Philippines. Part of the traveling was to look over prospective projects, see if they were practical and financially sound. Then we had to raise money to finance them from bonds sold on the private market. We went to the capital markets in New York, Zurich, and Frankfurt. Not an easy job at all. The ADB was completely unknown, and to the Europeans especially it did not sound very credit-worthy. It took much time and work to get them to buy our bonds.

"I learned to respect . . . and to admire Mr. Watanabe. He was . . . very effective . . . in large part because he had a very firm philosophy. He refused to think about the ADB as an aid-giving institution. He insisted that it was a bank, and he was determined to run it like a bank. So, he took great care that our development projects were feasible and would pay off. He also thought of the ADB as a family doctor. He used to say that the World Bank, with its large funds, was like a big city hospital, full of modern equipment. The family doctor, the ADB, does not have as much money or equipment, but he knows the patients better. He knows their history and the condition of each family member, and he stays in steady contact with them. So, in many cases, his advice and care can be more timely and appropriate than the big hospital. That was his philosophy. The ADB, with its limited funds, would be the family doctor for the developing Asian countries. If the ADB's resources were not sufficient for a big, serious case, we would try to get help from the World Bank.

"When we got to Manila and set up shop in December 1966, we started . . . from scratch. We were in rented office space, and we had a total of seven officers--from Japan, the U.S., Korea, and

Ceylon. We used to call ourselves the Seven Samurai. (much laughter)

"For me, the ADB opened up . . . a new world . . . Asia. (noticing my quizzical smile) That may sound odd to you, but because of my experience at Princeton and then Washington, I had gotten accustomed to American things and American ways. So, I was shocked by the backwardness and the extreme poverty of some Asian countries. When I visited Hong Kong, Jakarta, Calcutta, I realized for the first time what 'teeming millions' means. (polishing his glasses and gathering his thoughts) I was fascinated by those Asian cities. In the U.S.A--in those days--everything was clean, well-organized, mechanized, and really worked. In these Asian cities, everything was dirty, crowded, disorganized. It was . . . chaos. But I could not help feeling an . . . unflinchable drive, a dynamism, tremendous human energy welling out from the millions of people crowding the streets. All the honking of cars, bicycle bells, shouting of people. All the smells--palm oil cooking, thick, humid monsoon air, smelling of trees . . . and the heat. (softly but with great conviction) I felt that all that human energy and force could somehow be . . . harnessed . . . made productive.

"But that was in the future. In Manila, in 1967, Marcos had recently become president, but not yet imposed martial law. The Philippines were economically and socially in poor shape--very disorderly. Every morning on the front page of the newspaper, there was a picture of another dead body, shot dead. If there wasn't a dead body on the front page, we felt that something was wrong. (laughter)

"Our family lived in a quiet, wealthy neighborhood. What a contrast to the teeming streets. We had many maids, gardeners, a chauffeur. My wife and I became worried about our children . . . the way they were learning to talk and behave. (pause) Our daughter was about four years old. She spoke to the maids in . . . an aloof, nasty way. A little princess--looking down on these . . . creatures. We had to talk to her . . . discipline her.

"Most of the time, I was so engrossed in my work and traveled so much that my wife began to complain . . . about being left too much alone. So, I started to take Reiko on some trips, and we traveled together, all over the Philippines. The Philippines is a sociable, friendly place. We made many good friends there, Filipinos of course, and also the people who worked with ADB--Koreans, Thais, Taiwanese, Indonesians, Pakistanis, and well as Americans and Europeans. It is surprising how we still stay in touch after all these years. You know, I finished my work at the ADB in 1969, after about three years. What is a bit unusual is that I have not been assigned abroad since then. I have been working out of this building since then. Of course, I travel a lot, but we haven't lived in a foreign country since 1969."

THE SECOND NIXON SHOCK

"When we returned to Japan, I worked in the Banking Administration Department as deputy director until 1971. Then, in 1971-1972, I served as special assistant to the vice-minister. So, I had a good chance to see what was going on at the time of the second Nixon shock--the monetary shock.[5] First, early in the summer, there was the China shock--the announcement of Dr. Kissinger's secret visit to China. Then, in August 1971, President Nixon discarded the gold standard and started pressing us . . . pressing us hard to revalue the yen. Our balance of payments were in pretty good shape in 1971, and the Western European governments also thought the yen should be up-valued--to cut Japan's price advantage in world export markets. So, everybody wanted us to up-value the yen, but we resisted . . . resisted very strongly, because we thought our economy would be hit too hard.

"The finance minister at the time was Mr. Mikio Mizuta, who died some years ago. I remember the squeeze he was in. Everybody in the Finance Ministry resisted revaluation. And interestingly, so did businessmen, journalists, and academics--the whole country. There were several international meetings that Mr. Mizuta had to attend on this currency issue between August and January, and the poor man had to go to them and fight the whole international community. The view in Japan was that our economy was not

---

5. For a detailed, carefully researched account of the U.S.-Japan monetary negotiations in 1971-72, see I. M. Destler, et. al., *Managing An Alliance* (Washington, D.C: The Brookings Institution, 1976).

strong enough to adjust to revaluation and that Mr. Mizuta must not give in . . . at all. If he held the line, that was allright. That was his duty. He was expected to do it. But, if he made any concessions, he would be a failure. He would fail the ministry . . . and the whole country.

"Even in 1971, there was a lot of talk here in Tokyo about how successful our economy was. The word 'internationalization' was already popular--in the sense that we Japanese were supposed to understand and meet international standards--American and European standards. But in fact, there was a huge gap in perception. I realized it at those monetary meetings that fall and winter. The rest of the world thought that our economy was strong and that we should up-value the yen by about 20 percent. In Japan, everyone believed that while we were doing OK, any revaluation would ruin us. There was no compromise at those meetings, no give and very little communication. Just confrontation. I was shocked and discouraged.

"The Japanese press was . . . full of its usual passion. They were exaggerating the international pressure on Japan and gloomily predicting our defeat, saying that our negotiators did not have enough backbone and would fail. So when we finally had to agree to up-value the yen by about 17 percent, the press announced the complete rout of Japanese diplomacy . . . and I think they were really glad.

"Actually, our economy did not collapse or suffer much damage at all. If we hadn't revaluated by 17 percent-- if we had held the line at say 10 percent--we just would have had to go back in a very short time and negotiate another revaluation. It did not ruin us at all. But in 1971, there was virtually nobody in Japan who realized that. So, despite the talk of internationalization, we were . . . too isolated. We were unable to see ourselves objectively and accurately."

Question: "How did you feel about revaluation in 1971?"

(smiling easily) "I opposed it. And I was surprised at how it worked."

Question: "I remember following the currency talks in the *New York Times*, and when I worked at Brookings in 1973, discussing those talks with several American negotiators. One senior

official felt that John Connally, the treasury secretary, was unnecessarily rough on Japan--that the same revaluation could have been
achieved more quietly and without so much Japan bashing. Is that a
correct view?"

(very thoughtful) "Hmmm. You know, the press exaggerated John Connally's toughness. At the bargaining table, he was a
hard fighter. But he was not crude or harsh. I met him at dinners
and receptions, and he was friendly . . . a charming man."

Question: "Well then, do you think that the Nixon shock
and Connally's tough tactics were necessary to achieve the revaluation?"

(thoughtful pause and then in a crisp tone) "Yes, I think so.
Yes, in that case. The Bretton Woods system, the whole postwar
economic system, was collapsing, and the Japanese yen was part of
the bigger problem. The yen was undervalued.

"But you know, it was not just between Japan and the U.S.
The Europeans were there. They were hard bargainers, too, and ar-
ticulate and forceful. Yet, at the same time, I thought their whole
attitude was completely different than our Japanese attitude. It was
more like a game--a poker game for them. We Japanese were . . .
dead serious . . . as if our country would collapse if we made one
wrong move. They were more . . . relaxed. Those Europeans had
a sense of history. They had survived centuries of fighting and
killing each other, cheating each other, invading and being invaded.
So, they knew that governments and states rise and fall, but people
persist. And they appreciated market forces. As they saw it, no
matter how hard we negotiated, if the results were out of line with
market forces . . . and reality . . . it wouldn't last.

"Well, I don't want to be too flippant, but it seemed to me
that in those currency talks, we Japanese were too serious and rigid,
not prepared to maneuver and bargain--as we should have been.
Also we took the setback too hard. I remember how badly we felt
and I felt. (shaking his head and laughing) It is . . . ironical. But
that currency revaluation in 1971 did us more good than harm."

BANKING

"Most of my jobs since 1969, have been on the international side, but occasionally I was assigned to a post on the domestic side so I could keep in touch with domestic issues. In 1972 and 1973, I was the customs commissioner at Tokyo International Airport. From '73 to '75, I was director of the International Organizations Department. In '77 and '78, director of our International Research Department. From '78 to '80, assistant vice-minister for International Affairs. From '80 to '83, I was deputy director-general of this International Finance Bureau, and then in '84, I became director-general.

"My assignments on the domestic side were from '69 to '71, when I was deputy director of the Banking Administration Department; '75 to '77, as director of the FILP (Fiscal Investment and Loan Program); and then in '83 and '84, as deputy director of the Banking Bureau.

"Those three jobs taught me something about business here in Japan. You know how FILP worked. We controlled the very sizeable funds deposited in our Postal Savings System, and channeled them to various government agencies--including the Export-Import Bank, Japan Development Bank, Housing Finance Corporation, Housing Construction Corporation, Highway Corporation and the JNR (Japan National Railway). So, FILP was called the world's largest bank.[6] In order to run FILP, I had to get to know the people in all these agencies, public corporations and businesses, and to learn what they do and how they operate. I traveled all over the country (smiling at himself) and became an instant expert on things like railroads, housing, agriculture and highways. By 1975-1977, the years of high-speed growth were over, the energy crunch was on, and I could see many of our current economic problems in their early stages.

"In a way, some of the most important and basic policies I have worked on have been in banking--in the jobs I did in 1969 to

---

6. For a detailed, lively description of the FILP, see Chalmers Johnson, *MITI and the Japanese Miracle* (Stanford, Calif: Stanford University Press, 1982), Chap. 6, "The Institutions of High Speed Growth."

1971, and then in '83 and '84, in our Banking Bureau. In those assignments, I got involved in the enormous changes in the financial and banking environment here in Japan and internationally. I could see those changes and feel them in my own skin.

"In the fifties, the task of our banking system was . . . hmmm . . . crucial but relatively simple. It was to encourage our household sector to deposit its savings, since capital was so scarce, and then to allocate the limited capital at low interest rates into the most promising enterprises . . . in a very capital-hungry market. We encouraged the small, private depositors by convincing them that their bank savings were secure. We did that by regulating the savings banks so that we have had no bank failures. That is what the depositors wanted the most--secure banks, even if their earnings were low. The way we kept interest rates low on loans was to organize the banks into specialized, compartmentalized groups-- such as financial institutions, city banks, long-term credit banks, trust banks, and so on. The banks in each group were sheltered--in a way--from competition, and were given a high level of security on the relatively modest earnings from their regulated low interest rate loans.

"Well, that was an effective and cozy system when our economy was small, capital-starved, and we had an insignificant impact on the international financial system. By 1970, when I first worked in the Banking Department, we could see that the old system was becoming . . . untenable. Our economy had become large and dynamic. We had become capital surplus. Foreign financiers wanted to do business in Japan, and Japanese wanted to lend and borrow in the international markets. So, we had to start deregulating, which means taking away the shelters and security of the old system. (shaking his head and smiling) Well, our smaller, local institutions are afraid to go up against the big banks and have strongly opposed deregulation. The local politicians naturally support them. Even the big banks are . . . ambivalent. They favor that part of deregulation that promises big profits. But if deregulation threatens them with . . . dangerous competition. Well, that's very different. (both laughing) So, to say the least, this deregulation is a gradual, difficult business.

"When I said I could see and feel the changes in my own skin, I was thinking of the international environment. I still remember how uncomfortable I felt when I first attended the meetings of OECD and the BIS (Bank for International Settlements) in Basel, Switzerland, twenty years ago. Our delegates were the only non-Caucasians. (pause) The European bankers were so polished. They did business at elegant luncheons, dinners, and cocktail parties. You know, they could switch easily from fluent English to fluent German and French. They were a real old-boy club . . . and we were a very new, very junior member. You can imagine how uncomfortable that was.

"I was kind of naive, but I used to think to myself, 'Look at these privileged European financiers, enjoying themselves while the Vietnam War deteriorates and the Great Cultural Revolution rages on in China. They know nothing. They don't hear the voices of the poor, under-privileged millions.' I had been to Manila, and I saw myself as the representative of the teeming billions in Asia. (some laughter)

(in a modest but matter-of-fact and pleased tone) "Well, since then the situation has changed . . . dramatically. Those international bankers have loosened up. They have a very different view of the economic importance of the Pacific Rim countries. It is amazing how the number of foreign bankers who visit my office has increased over the last few years. Now, not a single day passes without at least a couple of foreign visitors in this office. So, I have been able to personally see and feel the accomplishments of Japan."

INTERNATIONALIZATION AND THE FUTURE

Question: "Well, you have brought us right up to the question of internationalization. Please, tell me what it means to you? How do you use the word?"

(speaking very slowly and carefully) "Hmmm. I think the meaning of internationalization--the process of internationalization--is changing for us, in a basic way. We Japanese are traditionally tribal . . . a tribal, island people. We are very homogeneous compared with most other people. Not a hunting tribe, but a farming tribe. We have always believed that to be safe . . . and to be effective, it is better to assimilate with our group--our tribe. Avoid being independent and isolated from the tribe. Yet, the Japanese as a group have been amazingly flexible, versatile, and quick to respond to outside influences.

"In the 7th century, we imported Buddhism and much of Chinese culture. In the 16th century, we responded quickly to the first, small wave of European culture. In the 19th century, we had a massive encounter with Western culture and absorbed enormous changes. After our defeat in 1945, we again responded effectively to major outside influences. These four major encounters and adaptations to the outside world were our experiences in internationalization. (pause) But in these four cases, we responded as a group. Our leaders, our elite, saw the need for change, assimilated what they thought was necessary to adapt effectively, and transmitted it. The group below remained intact. That was largely true even after 1945. That was how internationalization worked up until recent years.

"Now, because of the way business, banking, communications work, our interaction with the outside world is becoming so widespread, so diversified, that I don't think the process can be controlled and directed from above, the way it used to be. Hmmm. Maybe now, for the first time, in order for us to adapt successfully, we may have to change the nature of our society. We may have to loosen the group somewhat. We may have to learn how to respond in a more individual way . . . in order for enough people to become internationalized in such diverse, complex ways."

Question: "Yes. I think I understand. But . . . is it happening? Is it going to work?"

"Well, it is necessary. But this new phase of internationalization poses problems. I am not sure whether we will be flexible and adaptable enough in this phase. I know we have thousands and thousands of our young people studying abroad, and there are some moves afoot to open our society more, but . . . sometimes I smell danger. Japan's dilemma, now, is that we seem to have gotten big enough and strong enough, so that most Japanese think we can deal with foreigners pretty much on our own terms. They know the outside world is important, but in their stomachs they don't feel that *they* have to learn foreign languages, or live abroad, or adapt to foreign ideas, unless they want to--on a voluntary basis, so to speak.

"So, I've noticed that because of our affluence and success in recent years, many Japanese are . . . moving away from internationalization. Some of our businessmen have become quite . . . arrogant, and less responsive to outside reality than they used to be. You know, they want to enjoy their wealth and success. Their attitude toward the outside world is, 'Leave us alone. Don't bother us with your complaints. Why are these lazy Americans and Europeans pestering us to bail them out from their own mistakes?' There is some truth to what they say about the weakness of some foreign competitors, but there is a . . . disturbing arrogance in their tone."

Comment: "Yes, I am afraid I have noticed it too, on occasion. And it just stirs up and adds to the protectionist feelings in the U.S."

"Our young people also seem to be getting less flexible and adaptable to foreign things. Life has become so comfortable here in Japan, that now it is getting to be difficult to get these young people to live and work abroad. You know, these young people have less inhibitions about foreigners. They are more easygoing and confident than my generation, and often they have more language skills, too. But they are less eager to interact with the world, in a continuous, serious way. They like to travel or stay abroad for a short stretch--when it is convenient for them.

"The slowing down of internationalization is also noticeable in the way we treat foreigners and foreign cultures here in Japan--especially in our schools. When we came back from serving in Manila, we put our children in Japanese schools. I was really disappointed at what happened. Not just the students, but even the teachers treated my son and daughter in a very strange, unfriendly way--as though they were somehow contaminated by living abroad, by foreign cultural traits. There was . . . no open-mindedness. Well, I don't know what that implies for our future internationalization."

Question: "Yes. I see your point. Over the last ten years or so, I have noticed the writings of some Japanese intellectuals on *Nihonjinron*. Does that tie in with what you are telling me?"

"Yes. *Nihonjinron* is another piece of evidence of these backward trends. (pause) You know, the *Nihonjinron* argument has a strange contradiction. First, they say that our traditional Japanese culture is unique--in its strength, in its persistence, in the way it permeates our whole behavior. Then, they seem to say that our culture is very fragile and weak--that if we don't protect it from foreign contamination, it will be quickly ruined. (laughing) It seems to me that our culture is at least as strong as the Western European national cultures. In those countries it is a normal, ordinary thing for people to learn foreign languages, to learn how to get along in foreign countries. And the Germans, the French, the Danes, and the Swiss have not lost their traditional culture. I don't think we would either.

(in a slow, serious tone) "So now, when it is more necessary than ever that we Japanese continue to adapt to the outside world, I see these . . . signs of withdrawal, of isolationism. Because of our affluence, because of our success.

"Hmmm. You know, there is another pattern of internationalization--the British or American model--but we cannot become big enough or strong enough to follow that model. That model is to become the number one nation--become so important and strong, that the rest of the world learns your language and culture so they can get along with you and do business with you. (smiling) Of course, that is an attractive model. But it is out of the question for Japan. Objectively, if we are going to continue to be prosperous and secure, we have to keep learning foreign languages and cultures. We have to keep adapting and responding to what is going on outside. And I think we have to let this process penetrate throughout our society, not just at the top. It is clear--clear to me anyway--that Japan cannot maintain the eminence we have achieved in the world economy and politics unless we are successful at expanding this process of internationalization.

(standing up, stretching his arms over his head, grinning and looking at me with a twinkle in his eye) "Sounds pretty bad, eh? (both laughing) It is not so impossible. But we should avoid

. . . complacency . . . and avoid this delusion that we are so big that we can deal with the world on our terms (in a satirical tone) on a voluntary basis (shaking his head for emphasis) when it is convenient for us." (more laughter)

Kosuke Nakahira

WHEN I met him, Kosuke Nakahira was director of the Small and Medium Banking Division of the Banking Bureau, in the Ministry of Finance (MOF). Japanese businessmen both big and small, who rely heavily on bank loans, are well aware that the MOF is very influential in setting interest rates and the availability of credit.

Banking in Japan is much more centrally controlled and regulated than in the United States.[1] The Banking Bureau of MOF supervises the entire system, from the Bank of Tokyo to the credit cooperatives in the countryside. Mr. Nakahira's Small and Medium Banking Division had the responsibility for overseeing the sixty-nine regional mutual loan and savings banks, as well as all of Japan's finance companies, credit associations, credit cooperatives and credit guarantee associations.

His office in the old, dark stone ministry building on the Kasumigaseki was a large, high-ceilinged room crowded with the worn, battered desks of the twenty or so officials who worked under him, as well several rows of old green and black filing cabinets and clothes lockers lined against the walls. It was usually bustling, and when we met at the ministry we retired to a small, quiet conference room, where we could talk more comfortably. A division director in the Finance Ministry does not have a private office. Mr. Nakahira worked alongside his men in a room that, except for the computer terminals, looked much as it did in the 1950s. If Toyoo Gyohten's office was a silent rebuke against ostentation and waste,

---

1. Yutaka Kosai and Yoshitaro Ogino, *The Contemporary Japanese Economy,* (London: MacMillan Press, Ltd., 1984), 93-105.

A recent photo.

University days:
above, with parents;
below, near home.

A picnic with friends (back left).

a visit with Kosuke Nakahira even more firmly underlined the Finance Ministry's credo: Japan's wealth is built on hard work and frugality--not on lavish spending.

Although Kosuke Nakahira is a more typical MOF type than Toyoo Gyohten--having graduated near the top of his class from the Todai Law Faculty--it would be inaccurate to picture him as an impersonal, gray bureaucrat. Our first meeting was a lunch arranged by a mutual banker friend at the Castle, an elegant, Victorian restaurant that is just a five minute walk from the ministry. In the sunny dining room, richly furnished in red velvet, dark wood paneling, and gleaming white tablecloths, and heavily populated by dark suited officials, Mr. Nakahira was noticeably fresh-faced, relaxed, and quietly good-humored. He crossed the room with a springy step, a trim man of medium height. Behind his glasses, his eyes were attentive, cheerful, and careful. He was energetic, but not at all tense or hurried.

As a division director, he was at that stage in his career at which the twenty higher civil servants with whom he joined the ministry in 1963 entered a process of selection which leads to promotion to the few bureau director-general positions, and ultimately to the powerful position of vice-minister. Those who are not selected for promotion are expected to resign from the ministry, and usually enter the business and banking world, take a position with a public corporation or a national trade association, or run for election to the National Diet.[2]

During our lunch at the Castle, since Mr. Nakahira's English was very natural, I asked him if he had spent much time in America or Britain.

"Not very much, and never for a long stretch. Just short visits. My overseas assignments have been in Bangkok, at the ECAFE (Economic Commission for Asia and the Far East), and in Manila, at the ADB (Asian Development Bank). Everyone at ECAFE and the ADB speaks English."

---

2. Chalmers Johnson, "The Reemployment of Retired Government Bureaucrats in Japanese Big Business," *Asian Survey*, XIV, no. 11 (November 1974), 953-65.

FAMILY

Kosuke Nakahira was born to Koshichi and Toshi Nakahira, in Yokohama, on January 30, 1939. When I asked about his origins and family, he said that local and family influences had been important in shaping his life.

"Both my parents and their ancestors are from Kohchi Prefecture, on the island of Shikoku. My father is from Susaki, in the western part of Kohchi, and my mother is from Kohchi City. Some of my relatives have come to work and live in the Tokyo area, as I have, but most of them live in Kohchi. Kohchi is our family home.

"My father's family were rice and grocery merchants. Now they are supermarket owners. We can trace the rice merchant and grocery business back to the middle of the Edo period (1603-1868), about two hundred years, or perhaps a little longer than that. My father's elder brother inherited the business, which is now two super markets.

"I think my father had a chance to run one of the stores, but he decided to work in Tokyo. He attended Kohchi Commercial College and then managed to go to Meiji University here in Tokyo. When he graduated from Meiji University, he went right into a petroleum company as a white collar, or a salary man, as we would say. During the war he was in the Petroleum Distribution Control Corporation, which was a government firm. After the war, he entered the Showa Oil Company, which was really Royal Dutch Shell. He spent his whole career in Tokyo, as a white collar worker in petroleum companies. Now, he is retired and does calligraphy.

"My father had an important influence on me, in several ways. As an oil company executive, he had quite a bit of contact with the Ministry of International Trade and Industry (MITI). During the war, MITI had been the Ministry of Munitions, and even after the war MITI carefully watched and regulated the oil refining companies. As a boy, I remember my father talking at home about MITI. His company always seemed to need their approval for this or that, and he went to MITI officials to get it. Even when I was too young to understand much of what he was talking about, I knew that the ministries were important and powerful. I don't think he ever said that I should try for the Higher Civil Service. But from the way he talked, it seemed like a good thing to do.

"My father had another influence that was also related to the petroleum business. He had to deal with English and Dutch people from Royal Dutch Shell. He did not know much English. He told me about the difficulty he had when he tried to make himself understood, and how useful English could be. He always encouraged me to study it.

"My father also gave me a strong feeling for traditional Japanese art and culture. When he was a student, he took up calligraphy--the art of drawing Chinese characters in brush and ink. He was good at it. Good enough so that he seriously considered becoming a professional calligrapher. But instead he went into the petroleum companies. I suppose they offered a more secure income. As a boy, I remember that when my father was at home, he was usually doing calligraphy--quietly facing a white paper, holding the writing brush. Since our house was not very big, we had to be quiet, not to disturb him. It was, somehow, more than a hobby. Perhaps he worked at the office so that he could do calligraphy. It was an important part of his life, and of our life.

"His work has been accepted at the Japan Art Exhibition a number of times, and he has been a member of the *Mainichi* Calligraphy Exhibition Committee. (The *Mainichi* is one of the four major national newspapers in Japan, all of which sponsor important cultural events.)

"At one stage, my father was also very much interested in Zen Buddhism, which is connected, in a way, with the art of calligraphy. Because of his interest in Zen, he named my younger sister--who is my only sister--Michiyo, after the famous Zen monk, Dohgen, since the character for Doh is also pronounced Michi in Japanese.

"My father took me to calligraphy exhibitions. He taught me calligraphy, and I practiced at it until I was in middle school. I don't do calligraphy now. But when I have time, when I am free, I visit old temples and shrines. They give me a feeling of great satisfaction . . . that is . . . ah . . . hard to explain."

Question: "I think that I have some idea of what you are driving at. But Zen is not verbal or intellectual, is it?"

(laughing) "That may be right. So I don't have to explain it, do I? There is a . . . certain balance . . . a sense of proportion. Anyway, (laughing again), even though this can't be explained, it has been important to me.

EARLY YEARS, WAR AND OCCUPATION

"We moved to Kohchi from Tokyo in early 1945 to get away from the bombings in Tokyo, and lived there until the winter of 1946, almost two years. I went to school in Kohchi, and I feel attached to the traditions of Kohchi. You probably know that what is now Kohchi Prefecture used to be Tosa, and that Tosa was one of the four clans that overthrew the Tokugawa and brought about the Imperial Restoration in 1868.

"My family is not connected with those famous Tosa samurai. But I have admired them for setting Japan on the way to modernization. The people of Kohchi are known for their particular character--stubborn but lovable. In Kohchi dialect we call them *igossoh*. Not just stubborn and obstinate, but a kind of cheerful persistence. In that sense, I would like to be a Kohchi type. (laughing) Oh yes, the men from Kohchi are also known as strong drinkers. My father told me not to smoke, but because we are from Kohchi, he never told me not to drink."

Question: "When you moved to Kohchi in 1945, you were six years old, and just starting school. Did your whole family move to Kohchi, or were just you and your sister sent there? Do you remember anything of the air raids in Tokyo?"

"I started kindergarten in Tokyo, in the spring of 1944, but that school was soon closed down because of the air raids, and then in spring 1945, we had to evacuate our house and move to Kohchi. Our house was being demolished to make a fire break, an open space that would prevent the fires that were started by the air raids from spreading. I recall that most of our household goods were packed and scheduled to be sent to Kohchi, but before they were loaded onto the train they were burned in an air raid. I don't remember very much of the air raids in Tokyo, but a few things still stick in my mind. I have a memory of B-29s moving through the sky, very high, and anti-aircraft fire on the ground trying to hit them. It was of no use. They were flying much too high for those anti-aircraft guns. And then there was the bombardment. The bombs fell and went off. I also have a clear memory of a bomb hanging in the ceiling of the house next to our house. It did not explode. It was just hanging there.

"When we left Tokyo for Kohchi, we all went except my father. My father had to stay and work in his company. When we first got to Kohchi, we lived for awhile in Susaki City. But then American fighter planes began to attack Susaki, perhaps because it is a good port. I remember the fighter planes coming in and strafing Susaki. There was one attack that seemed to go on for about two hours. There was a big hole in the wall of the house next door. We had to move again, to a very small village about 15 kilometers inland, away from the sea. I went to the elementary school in that village. I was the only city boy in that little school. Of course, the local boys did not let me forget that. " (laughing)

Question: "Do you remember anything of the post-surrender period, of the early days of the Occupation?"

"I don't remember a great many things, but I remember the American Occupation forces marching into Kohchi. I watched them marching in through a small eyehole in the sliding door of our house in Kohchi, because all the doors and shutters were closed. We were all afraid. First, I saw a few tanks roll in and then a huge number of soldiers on foot. I remember that first look at American soldiers because their faces were red or brown, while I had expected them to be all white. That surprised me. All those sunburned American faces.

"The fear we had for the soldiers did not last very long. They were good natured, and I remember that they gave little boys--but not me, I wasn't that lucky (smiling)--peanuts and candy. My friends and I liked their jeeps. Tokyo was full of their trucks and jeeps when we got back in 1946."

Question: "Do you recall anything about living conditions in those last days of the war and the early Occupation days?"

"Well, of course, everything was very poor. I and all the children I knew felt somewhat hungry most of the time. When we got back to Tokyo, there was no city waterworks and no city gas at my house. There was electricity and electric lights, but I remember that we had blackouts fairly often when the power failed. Everything was scarce. In my school in Tokyo, there was one textbook for five children."

Question: "I wonder what kind of an impact on your values and perspective these childhood experiences had? You were bombed and strafed, and you knew hunger and extreme scarcity. What effect do you think it had on you?"

(Mr. Nakahira knitted his brows thoughtfully and paused for a long moment before answering.) "It is not easy to say what the impact was. I am not really sure about it, especially the bombing and air attacks. I think the food shortage and the shortage of almost everything else had a stronger effect on me. Most Japanese are . . . fairly well off now. But Japanese of my age can never take this prosperity . . . this comfort . . . for granted. Perhaps that is the biggest difference between my generation and people who are younger. "

Question: "Will you elaborate just a bit more on your feelings about violence and war?"

"Well, my experiences during the war may not have had such a clear impact. Perhaps I was too young. I did not know anything else. Maybe the bombing and the air attacks seemed . . . well . . . not to be anything extraordinary. After the war, we learned at school that the war was bad and that militarism was very bad. We were still using the old textbooks, and we had to strike out every mention of the old army and navy. We were taught that Japan had been an aggressor nation and had caused the war. At the time, as a small boy, I believed that. It seemed very clear and simple. Later, as I studied more I learned that the history and politics of the war were more complicated than I had thought. It is difficult to remember how my ideas developed. But even when I learned that Japan had done terrible things in the war . . . atrocities . . . somehow I did not think that Japan was just bad. There was still something about Japan that we could be proud of."

SCHOOL YEARS IN TOKYO

Question: "The Occupation education reforms stressed the values of pacificism and democracy. What impact did the democratic ideas that were taught in the schools have on you? "

"Since the war ended only five months after I entered school, I naturally accepted the idea of democracy. It seemed natural and right to me."

Question: "Some of the people in this study who are a few years older than you are have mentioned that the defeat and the democratic reforms led them to question or doubt authority, the authority of their teachers or of their parent's generation? Did that happen to you?"

"No. I don't think so. Perhaps I was too young for that. By the time I came to understand such matters, the new ideas were all in place. I did not experience any big changes, as they did. Our relationship with our teachers was smooth and natural. We accepted their authority. Hmmm. (pausing thoughtfully and smiling) Perhaps the relationship between students and teachers is more important than what is in the textbooks."

Question: "Yes. I think there is something to that. Probably the persistence in Japan of the traditional parent-child, teacher-student, older-younger relationships account for much of the stability of Japanese society, despite very substantial changes in ideology or technology. Did any of your teachers in elementary school make a strong impression on you?"

"When I was in the fifth grade here in Tokyo, I had a teacher who had been in Burma during the war and had been repatriated. He was very young and had a strong personality. His name is Mr. Izumoji. From time to time I still write to Mr. Izumoji. Mr. Izumoji was an enthusiastic reader of Miyazawa Kenji, who was a famous writer of children's stories. Even now, Miyazawa's stories are included in the textbooks. He wrote a famous poem that was found after his death, in his notebook. In it Miyazawa said that for him the most important thing was to do something of value for other people, to be of some help to them. That was more important than what people thought of him. That made a very strong impression on me.

"Although they were not teachers in my school, there was an old Japanese couple living near my house whom I also remember well. The husband was an architect, and they had lived in New York for fifteen years. They returned to Tokyo after the war. The wife was a very sincere Christian, and since they wanted to do something helpful for children, she gave several of us English conversation lessons every week in their home. I was in fourth grade, nine years old then. She also took us to the Sunday school of her Christian church, the Nihon Kirisuto Kyohdan, a Protestant church in Kugahara. I think it is still there. Unfortunately, this kind woman died three years later. But the two things she did, the English conversation class and the Sunday school . . . made a big difference for me. I kept on going to that Sunday school almost every week for almost four years, until my second year in middle school. The Sunday school was basically Bible classes, taught in Japanese, not in English. "

Question: "Did that fit in easily with the values you were taught at home and in school, or did it create some conflict or clash? Did the individualism in Protestant Christianity conflict with the Japanese group ethic?"

"Well. . . I was not aware of any clash. My father used to ask me what I was learning at Sunday school, and I would tell him. I am not a Christian, you know, but it did affect my thinking. I think that our teacher gave more emphasis on Christian responsibility and duty--to help people.

"I also had two very good friends in my early school days, whom I remember very well. In elementary school there was Ichiro Ishikawa, a classmate of mine who loved nature, loved to catch fish and frogs, and hike in the hills and fields. I had a little training in catching eels and fish when I was in Kohchi, so we got on very well. Whenever we had time, we would go off together on our . . . adventures. In middle school, when I read *Tom Sawyer*, I thought that we two had been like Huckleberry Finn and Tom Sawyer.

"My other friend, Hiroaki Nakagawa, lived in a big, upper-class house close to where we used to live before we left for Kohchi. His father was also working in the Showa Petroleum Company. His grandfather had been a diplomat and had given him many books about foreign countries. His father had a stamp collection. Nakagawa got me interested in both those things. At first I had trouble even reading the names of the foreign countries on the stamps. But I was fascinated by geography, and when I was in fifth and sixth grade I used to go to the school library, even on Sundays, to study in the geographical encyclopedia. "

Question: "Since your education and the schools you attended prepared you for the Higher Civil Service examination, and for this ministry, perhaps we should focus on them. What kind of schools did you attend? How were your grades?"

"I went to a normal, ordinary public school in our neighborhood in Kugahara. That school is only three houses away from our home, and my son goes there now. I had good grades. My middle school was Omori Number 6, here in Tokyo. Again, a public school. It was badly overcrowded. We usually had seventy to seventy-five students in a class. But this school also had some strong points. It encouraged us to take the entrance examinations for the best high schools, and it was well known and even a bit famous for that. I also had some excellent teachers there, like Mr. Nomura, who taught Japanese history. He was eager to teach us and I learned a great deal from him. I still write to him.

"My high school actually had the greatest impact on my character and my education. I went to Hibiya High School, from 1954 to 1957. At that time, it was considered the best high school in Japan. I must have done well in the entrance examination, which was a difficult one, but in a way, it was just good luck that I went there. In the Occupation reform, Kugahara was placed in the same Tokyo First School District with Hibiya High School. Since I had good grades, my middle school teachers encouraged me to take their entrance examination."

Question: "Do you mean that only students from the Tokyo First School District could attend Hibiya?"

(laughing) "Well, legally speaking, yes. But this was such a good school--it was famous before the war as Furitsu Daiichi Chugakko (First Municipal Middle School)--that families from all over Japan, even from Kagoshima and Aomori, found ways to establish a legal residence in the First District, so that their children could attend. Before the Occupation reform, this school used to get good students from all over the country, (laughing) and in this way it kept doing that.

"The school is close to the Diet buildings, and we could see them from our classrooms. It was a very good atmosphere. When I went to Hibiya, it was very liberal. The students' personalities were respected. Most of our curriculum was set by the Ministry of Education, as it is in all the schools, but we formed our own classes. We students talked together for two days, and we divided ourselves into classes of about fifty for each subject--such as mathematics, Japanese, or music. The teachers were excellent.

"I think that the high standard of that school had a very strong influence on me . . . and on all the students there. Many of my classmates and friends from Hibiya are the same people I knew at Tokyo University and in the Civil Service. In 1982-1984, when I was in charge of the Foreign Ministry budget, the three most important division chiefs I had to work with in the Foreign Ministry were all from Hibiya High School--Mr. Matsuura, Mr. Hayashi and Mr. Fukuda.

Question: "Are there Hibiya graduates among the senior officials here in the Finance Ministry?"

"A few important officials are Hibiya graduates. Vice-Minister Yamaguchi, Director-General Yoshino of the Budget Bureau, Director-General Yoshida of the Banking Bureau, and Director-General Kishida of the Securities Bureau are from Hibiya."

Question: "Did you have any other experiences during those years--either in or outside of school--that helped to shape your values and character?"

"We had an active English speaking club at Hibiya, and a very good, kind teacher--a woman who was a devout Christian, named Ruth M. Elmer. She met with us once a week to teach us English conversation. My closest friends were also in that club. Mr. Hayashi was chairman of the club. Ruth Elmer was not a teacher at Hibiya, but she was a special . . . person. Some twenty years afterward, when she was about to return to the States, we old club members got together from all over Japan for a reunion, to honor her."

Question: "Did your parents give you much encouragement in your school work? Nowadays there is much talk about Japanese mothers who encourage their children so much at school that it becomes excessive. It becomes a problem."

(laughing) "Of course, my parents wanted me to do well at school, but there was no pressure on me. (laughing again) My mother was not a very enthusiastic *kyoiku mama* (education mother). She had just the right amount of interest . . . but not too much. My father did not talk to me about school very often. Now and then he said, 'Work hard,' but not much more than that. When he was at home, he was busy, working quietly at his calligraphy. There was no pressure on me. Just quiet encouragement."

KEIO AND TOKYO UNIVERSITIES

Question: "Since Hibiya High School had such a high reputation and high standards, and since you were in the same neighborhood with the National Diet and the ministries, did you make plans or think ahead much to your future, to the university and to a career?"

"Not much. I didn't think much about it. My friend Hayashi, whose grandfather had been a diplomat, used to talk about the Foreign Ministry, and I gave some thought to . . . perhaps . . . trying to become a diplomat. But not very much. I had no clear plans or ideas for the future."

Question: "That puzzles me. Many of the students at Hibiya went on to the best universities and then on to jobs in the Civil Service or with the big companies and banks."

(smiling) "Oh yes. That's true. But I did not really think about it or plan ahead carefully. I had good grades in my class at Hibiya, so it seemed natural for me to sit for the entrance examination for Todai. I took it in early 1957, and I failed it. About one hundred students from Hibiya passed the Todai examination that year--twenty-five or so from my class, and about seventy-five who were older, who had taken the examination before and failed it but managed to pass it that year."

Question: "Well, I suppose the competition was fierce. What percentage of the students who took the Todai entrance examination passed?"

"Between a third and a fourth passed. But only the top high school graduates sat for the examination. The others did not even try. So the competition was tough.

"Well, I entered the Economics Department at Keio University, when the school year began in April 1958. I had a very agreeable, useful time there. The Economics Department was good, and the English Society was active and good quality. They used to do even better than the Todai club at the speech contests.

"My economics course was taught by Professor Yanaihara, the younger brother of the famous Yanaihara, the former president of Todai. He was a fine teacher. We read and studied Paul Samuelson's textbook--in English."

Question: "Well, I have the impression that usually the first few years of university life--especially at private schools like Keio--were relaxed and easy going. A rest after the struggle to pass the entrance examination. But doing Samuelson in English . . . doesn't sound too easy going."

(laughing) "You are right. We had to do a lot of work for Yanaihara's course. But it was fascinating, and it turned out to be useful."

Question: "How did you come to sit for the Todai examination once again?"

"When I was at Keio, I did my assignments and went along in my courses from day to day. I was . . . fairly content. (laughing) I know that you find it hard to believe, but I was still vague about my future. I had the idea of the Civil Service in my mind, but not very clearly. I knew that if I continued at Keio and graduated from there, I would probably not go into the Civil Service. There were a few people then who graduated from the private universities and went into the ministries--but relatively few. (In 1960, close to ninety percent of the Higher Civil Service entrants were Tokyo University graduates. In 1980, the figure was closer to seventy percent.)

"Then, one day in November of 1958, it was a day of deep, rainy autumn, I was walking on the street and I happened to meet a teacher from Hibiya, Mr. Nakamura, and we had time to talk. Mr. Nakamura asked me whether I would try once again for Todai. I answered, 'Well . . . .'" (long, long pause)

Question: (laughing) "Yes, I can imagine that conversation in Japanese. (more seriously) And you really did not know?"

"Well . . . my mind was not set. Mr. Nakamura saw that. He said that it would be allright to give up my idea of going to Todai, if I was sure that I would not mind . . . would not regret it . . . in the future. That decided it for me. I began to study for the Todai examination that would be given in February 1959."

Question: "What was the test like? How long did it take? What kind of questions were they--essays, short answers? What subjects did you sit for?"

"I sat for the tests in mathematics, Japanese, English, chemistry, physics, and Japanese and world history. It took three days. There were no essay questions. The questions were short answers and multiple choice."

Question: "When did you learn that you had passed?"

"Nobody knows when the results will be announced. My aunt, who lived some distance away from us in Tokyo, happened to be up late, after midnight, listening to the radio. She heard the announcement, and she heard my name. She called up our house in the middle of the night, and woke us up to tell us. Well . . . we didn't mind her call. It was very good news."

TOKYO UNIVERSITY: 1960 TREATY

"I entered Todai in April 1959, as a freshman in what is called the Culture One course. That course gave me a wide choice of elective classes in my freshman and sophomore years. In the second semester of the sophomore year I had to decide on a major, either in jurisprudence or economics. The jurisprudence or Law Faculty at Todai was so strong that it was an easy choice for me. I expected to choose jurisprudence."

Question: "Well, was the schoolwork at Todai challenging and demanding?"

(smiling) "Not very much for the first year and a half. It became much more serious after I entered the jurisprudence course, and I knew I was preparing for the Higher Civil Service examination. But at first it was more relaxed, and I spent much of my time at the English Speaking Society."

"I was elected chairman of the society. That was during my sophomore year. We competed in speech contests and debating contests. One time, we competed against Keio, and I enjoyed seeing my old Keio teammates again. We also read and staged some good plays, by Oscar Wilde, Tennessee Williams and Eugene Ionesco. Several times during the year we took two or three day trips together to other universities in Kyoto, Osaka, and Sendai. It was very busy and enjoyable."

Question: "Did you get much teaching or tutoring in English at the society?"

"Very little. We had to teach ourselves. We listened to English records, and read people like Wilde and Tennessee Williams and then we discussed them (smiling) discussion after discussion. (laughing) Not everybody's English was fluent. We made many, many mistakes. But anyway, we tried, and we kept working on our English."

Question: "Your sophomore year, when you chaired the English Society, was also the year of the demonstrations and riots at Todai against the revised 1960 U.S.-Japan Security Treaty. Do you remember what you thought and did that spring of 1960, when the treaty and Prime Minister Kishi's actions were such stormy, emotional issues on the campus?"

"Yes. I remember May and June of 1960 very well. I thought that the issue had become very heated. (long pause, gathering his thoughts) I had my views, and I was . . . involved. I discussed the treaty . . . but I did not join the demonstrations.

"I felt that Prime Minister Kishi looked . . . somewhat defiant and that he had no ears to listen to his critics. I was doubtful at that time of some provisions of the treaty. (in a firm but cool tone) But I felt that the ratification should be decided by parliamentary procedures, according to the Constitution and the laws--not by demonstrations. If people really opposed the treaty, it would be an election issue and they could vote on it.[3]

---

3. As a result of nationwide demonstrations and riots against the treaty, which led President Eisenhower to cancel a scheduled visit to Japan in June 1960, Prime Minister Kishi resigned from office following ratification of the treaty in July.

"Many of the students in the English Society felt detached about the treaty. They were not very political and had no strong feelings for or against it. But some of our members felt very strongly against Kishi and the treaty, and they wanted the society to take a stand--a public stand--against the treaty. We had about two hundred members, one of the largest clubs on the campus, so I had to decide what to do.

"Well, the English Speaking Society was not formed as a political organization. That was not its purpose. I said that the club members could take any stand they wanted, as individuals, but we should not involve ourselves as a group, as the English Speaking Society. (pause as Mr. Nakahira thought back to 1960, then in a cool almost diffident tone) There was some . . . disagreement. I said that if the club did not like my way of thinking, they should get another chairman."

Question: "That sounds straightforward. How did it turn out?"

"They didn't throw me out. (slight smile, nodding his head) It turned out that most of the members did not want the society to be political."

AIMING FOR THE HIGHER CIVIL SERVICE AND STUDIES IN JURISPRUDENCE

Question: "In the second semester, the autumn semester of 1960, which was your sophomore year, you started courses in the Law Faculty. Was that related to your hopes or plans for your career after graduation?"

"Yes, it was. By that time I had decided to prepare for the Higher Civil Service examination, for one of the economic ministries, Finance or MITI, and not to aim for the Foreign Service.

"There was no dramatic decision. During my first two years I thought about this now and then, and talked about it with my fam-

---

He was replaced by another Liberal Democratic (LDP) faction leader, Hayato Ikeda. Prime Minister Ikeda called a general election in the fall of 1960, in which the treaty was a major issue. The LDP won that election, and the 1960 Security Treaty is still in force.

ily and friends. I knew that I would have to make a decision because in order to sit for the Foreign Ministry examination you have
to prepare for several special subjects, such as diplomatic history
and foreign languages. The work I did in the English Speaking Society would have helped me for the English examination. In fact, so
many of our members went to the Foreign Service that the English
Speaking Society was considered a training school for the Foreign
Ministry. I felt pulled to the Foreign Service myself, but I also began to feel that it is a special part of the government. Somehow, I
began to think I would be more suitable in one of the domestic ministries, one with wider coverage.

"When I was a freshman, one of my friends in the English
Society, Hiroshi Hirabayashi, used to tell me that he was thinking of
entering the Finance Ministry, that it was important and challenging
work. At that time, I was more inclined toward diplomacy and I
knew nothing about MOF. What he told me helped me to think
more about Finance and MITI. By coincidence, in my sophomore
year, about the same time I decided to aim for Finance, Hirabayashi
told me that he had decided to prepare for the Foreign Ministry.
This shows how vague our hopes or plans were then for our future
careers."

Question: "Do you recall the reasons that led you toward the
Ministry of Finance? For instance, did you believe that MOF was
very important in making the national budget and in guiding the
banks, and that it played an important role in shaping the present and
future prosperity of Japan? Did you consider that the Foreign Ministry diplomats have almost no domestic constituency, and that when
they retire from diplomacy it can be very difficult to start a good
second career? But MOF and MITI are closely connected with industry and banking, and there is a much better chance of a second
career. Did you have that in mind?"

"I knew nothing at all about second careers when I was at
Todai. (laughing) I was not even sure I would have a first career.
That was not a factor.

"I did begin to learn more about what MOF and MITI did--
from my friends, and from things my father said, and from what I
read and heard in discussions. I began to appreciate the importance
of finance and economics. My father's experiences inclined me

somewhat toward MITI, but he never told me what to do, at least in this matter. He said the choice was mine to make.

"So, it was, I think, a typically Japanese decision. I . . . gravitated toward MOF. I did not consider it a . . . difficult decision. It seemed to be a natural choice."

Question: "Do you feel that the Jurisprudence Course at Todai gave you useful training for the Finance Ministry?"

"Yes. Much of what we studied was useful--administrative law, civil law, constitutional law, as well as economics. In constitutional law I did both Japan and the U.S. So, this gave me some useful knowledge about how the Japanese government works.

"Our jurisprudence and law is basically patterned on the 19th century German system. We do not put as much importance as you do on cases and precedents. The way of thinking, the principle and the logic, are more important than precedents. That has not changed very much, but there have been important changes since the war from the older system. Before the war, our jurisprudence and laws gave much more importance to the state and society, and less to individual rights and the people's rights. Now there is more balance. In the jurisprudence courses at Todai and here in the government, you have to think how to adjust, to balance the people's rights and the interests of the state and society.

"Another useful part of my studies at Todai was just being exposed to many different ways of thinking. One of the economics professors whose lectures I attended was a Marxist, Tsutomu Ohuchi. He was a very intelligent teacher. So I had both Samuelson and Marx.

"I also have a clear memory of the seminar I took on American constitutional law, with Mr. Ben Bruce Blakeney. Do you know his name? He was the chief defense counsel at the Tokyo War Crimes Trial. Then he practiced law here in Japan. He had offices in Tokyo, in Okinawa, and on the West Coast. Many students signed up for his seminar, but after a few weeks only two of us were left--me and Akira Iida, who is also in MOF, now in Paris. Most of the students understood English, but we all found Blakeney's English was (shaking his head and smiling) not easy. Not only that, but the seminar was in a small room, and he used to pace and stalk around like a caged bear.

"When he saw that only Iida and I were left in the seminar, he told us that unless he had at least two students he would not be able to teach the seminar again. So . . . we had to stay. After we got used to his . . . style, we actually did learn some American constitutional law from him.

"Mr. Blakeney died one year after we studied with him, in an airplane crash. He was piloting his own small plane, and he crashed into Mt. Amagi, on the Izu Peninsula."

MINISTRY OF FINANCE

"I entered the Ministry of Finance in 1963, the same year I graduated from Todai. My first assignment was in the Foreign Exchange Bureau. That bureau doesn't exist anymore. It was changed into the International Finance Bureau. At that time, Japan was getting ready to move to Article 8 status in the International Monetary Fund (IMF). That really meant that in the international currency field, Japan was moving from the status of a developing country to the status of a developed country. That change took place in April 1964, and in that same month Japan also joined OECD. It was a busy time ."

Question: "That sounds like an important first assignment for a young, entering official. How did you get it?"

"Well, I was one of twenty new, entering higher civil servants in the ministry that year. We were . . . scattered among eight or nine bureaus, to some extent just scattered. You had to start somewhere. In my case, they knew that I had been active in the English Speaking Society at Todai. Perhaps that is why they assigned me to work on Article 8 status. It involved much work in English. In the same way, perhaps that is why I was sent to the International Organization Division in 1964 to help arrange the World Bank-IMF meeting in Tokyo that year. One of my jobs was to accompany the IMF and World Bank representatives around Tokyo to find suitable conference halls and hotels. That was the largest international meeting held in Tokyo up to that time."

Question: "Hmm. You had not yet been abroad to an English speaking country, had you? And suddenly, straight from the

English Speaking Society, you were in the thick of Article 8, and the IMF-World Bank annual meeting. Did you have to work primarily with English language documents and read and write in English on the Article 8 assignment?"

"Oh yes. That was the assignment. For the IMF-World Bank meeting I translated the prime minister's speech and the finance minister's speech into English."

Comment: "The ministry must have had great confidence in your English language skills."

(laughing) "There were just a few people in the ministry who could do it. There were not too many of us to choose from.

"Then, in June 1965, I was sent to join the secretariat of ECAFE headquarters in Bangkok. I packed one suitcase and stayed in Bangkok for a year and a half. (smiling at the memory) That was . . . exciting. All at once I was an international civil servant--a seconded official. My job was to help to set up the new Asian Development Bank (ADB).[4]   Also, I had to work on foreign aid issues. It was all new to me.

"My job was in the International Trade Division at ECAFE. The division chief was an Indian, Mr. Krishnamurti. The Deputy was a Filipino, and the other staff members were a Thai, another Filipino and a man from Nepal. (laughing) I had to become internationalized very quickly . . . to survive."

Question: "As a seconded official, working for ECAFE but knowing you would return to the Finance Ministry, how did you manage to balance your loyalties . . . between ECAFE and Tokyo?"

"It was no problem. There was no tension . . . or very little. I wanted to work for ECAFE and the ADB, to help them. My intentions and the intentions of the Japanese government were just about the same. There were only a few differences or disagreements. But most of the time they wanted me to do . . . just what I was doing.

"I came back to Japan for the inaugural meeting of the ADB in Tokyo in 1966, which was about the same time that my assignment to ECAFE expired. A week later the Finance Ministry sent me

---

4. For an account of this international enterprise, please see Po-Wen Huang, Jr., *The ADB* (New York, N.Y.: Vantage Press, 1975); and Dennis T. Yasutomo, *Japan and the Asian Development Bank* (Boulder, Col.: Praeger Publishers, 1983).

to Manila to work at the ADB for six months in the Administrative Department. I had to help write the rules and regulations of the bank. There were only about twenty people on the staff, and so we had to do whatever jobs came up. I was asked to attend the executive board meetings to take notes of their sessions.

"From 1967 to 1969, I returned to Japan to work in the International Finance Bureau, and then as chief of the Katsuragi Tax Office in Nara Prefecture. In 1969, I was sent back to Manila again to the ADB as personal assistant to President Takeshi Watanabe. That assignment continued until 1972. I spent about half that time away from Manila, traveling with President Watanabe. We did some work in the developing countries, but the main task at that time was to raise funds for the ADB. For the fund raising, we went to places like New York, Brussels, Vienna, Luxembourg, and Zurich.

"Mr. Watanabe was also from the MOF. He was quite famous because he had been liaison between the ministry and General MacArthur's headquarters during the Occupation. His grandfather had been a finance minister during the Meiji period (1868-1912), and his father had been minister of justice. He has also written a number of books. Most recently, he published his diaries.

"When we went to a developed country to raise funds, President Watanabe usually met with the finance minister or the development minister, and I accompanied him. That was good experience for me . . . to see how these matters are discussed and decided."

Question: "Looking at the ADB in 1985, it seems that the bank has done well--both in assisting development and in recovering its loans. Many--not all but many--of the developing countries in Asia have prospered . . . and done relatively well in paying their debts. Of course, it is easy to see this in 1985. But how did the prospects for this region look in 1969-1972? Was it difficult to raise funds for the ADB?"

"It was not easy, especially in the private sector. The governments that were members of the bank were helpful, but their contributions had to be supplemented by the sale of bonds to private investors. The ADB was brand new, and some bankers had never heard of us. Many of them knew very little about the Asian countries. We had to do much explaining, about the ADB and about the economies in this region. In New York, we had to go to the rating office and persuade them to give the ADB a triple A rating. It was not easy, even though the bonds we sold to private investors were substantially government-guaranteed.

"It worked like this. The U.S. and Japan each put up twenty percent of the bank's capital--forty percent between them. The remaining capital was contributed by the Asian and Western European governments. These contributions were partially in paid capital and partially in unpaid capital. Within the convertible currency portion of the unpaid capital, which was guaranteed by the governments, the ADB could issue bonds to private investors. The governments also contributed to the Special Fund, which they used to make soft loans--high risk, longer term, low interest loans. The money raised by selling bonds to private investors, mixed with the paid capital, was used to make hard loans--well secured, business-like loans.

"As you can see, much of my work has been in the financing field. In addition to serving in the International Finance Bureau, in the ADB, and in the Banking Bureau, I also worked in the Securities Bureau in 1972 and 1973. Since 1972, my assignments have all been in Japan. I worked in the Budget Bureau from 1975-1977, and again from 1982-1984. In 1980-1982, I went to the Mie prefectural government as director of administration, and had another good chance to see how local politics works."

Question: "I see on the record that you gave to me that in 1973-1974, you were a personal assistant to the then minister of finance, Mr. Takeo Fukuda. That was an extremely hectic, uncertain period in Japanese political and economic life, wasn't it? It was the period of the first oil shock, which triggered a twenty-five to thirty percent inflation in Japan in 1974. Would you mind reminiscing a bit about that assignment?"

(Pause, carefully arranging his thoughts) "That year of the oil shock and the inflation was the most unstable year since I joined the ministry. People were so worried about the future that they were hoarding. They were lined up outside the shops to buy all the kerosene and toilet paper they could. There was a rumor about a bank failure. It was a most . . . abnormal year.

"You may remember that Mr. Fukuda was widely expected to become prime minister in 1972, when Prime Minister Sato stepped down, but he was outmanuevered by his rival, Mr. Kakuei Tanaka. Prime Minister Tanaka appointed Mr. Kiichi Aichi as Finance Minister. But Minister Aichi died suddenly, in late 1973, at the beginning of the oil shock. Prime Minister Tanaka was being criticized for being a big spender, for encouraging inflation. Mr. Fukuda was a former MOF official who had already been finance minister three times. He was known as a hard money man, with the most solid financial credentials. So, it was logical and timely in a way for Prime Minister Tanaka to ask Mr. Fukuda to become minister of finance. Everyone expected Mr. Fukuda to curb the budget and to hold down prices. That is what he did. He requested the banks to sharply limit their loans. He persuaded enterprises to hold down salary increases, as much as possible. He even tried to set up voluntary price controls. In the earlier part of 1974, inflation was very bad. It did not seem to respond to these policies. Then, toward the end of the year the inflation eased. In the following year, 1975, I think the rate of inflation was down to about 11 percent.

"Minister Fukuda had two personal assistants. One of us had to accompany the minister all the time, from early morning until night. So there were two of us. We usually took turns at it, every other day. We were the contact point for Minister Fukuda. He was so busy, and so many people had to see him, and he needed so much information. I had to get the information, usually from the MOF bureau directors-general and division directors, and do whatever else was needed to help the minister. Of course, Mr. Fukuda was a Diet member, so I had a chance to see some political decision-making and electioneering. I accompanied him when he went out for election campaigns. If the MOF needed a decision from him on anything while he was on a campaign trip, it was my job to get it from him and tell MOF. I did that for almost nine months."

Question: "How did you happen to get this appointment? Did Mr. Fukuda ask for you?"

"No. He did not know me at all. The Personnel Division at MOF recommended us. I am not sure whether they gave Minister Fukuda a list of several possible assistants, or just recommended the two of us. Anyway, I had no personal or political connections with him. And I knew nothing about it in advance. I was in a meeting in the Securities Bureau when the director of the Personnel Division

gave me a ring and asked me over to his office. I walked right over
to see what it was, and he said, 'You have been appointed personal
assistant to the finance minister. You will want to go to the minister
right away.' That was all.

"Before I met and worked for Mr. Fukuda, I thought he
would be a . . . difficult man. He looked (smiling) . . . difficult.
But he was not . . . not at all. He never got angry or short-tem-
pered. He was quick when he was asked for a decision, but always
thoughtful. He was a good man to work for.

"After the House of Councilor's election in July 1974, Mr.
Fukuda resigned as minister, and I was sent to the finance minister's
secretariat, to the Research and Planning Bureau. My job there was
to draft speeches for the new finance minister, who was Mr. Ohira."[5]

Question: "Since you have joined the ministry in 1963, you
have had one challenging, important assignment after another. Did
the twenty officials who entered the ministry with you all have assignments like these?"

"My assignments were nothing special. We all have been
moved around every year or two to these kind of positions. Out of
the twenty people in my class, sixteen or seventeen have had extensive experience in foreign countries--not just short time visits. Everybody gets to run a local tax office, to see where the money really
comes from, and to get experience running an office and dealing
with people outside the ministry. Everybody gets challenging assignments here in Tokyo. For the first twenty-seven or twenty-eight
years we all get equal treatment. Then the head cutting or as we put
it in Japanese, the 'shoulder tapping' begins."

MARRIAGE AND FAMILY

Question: "We have looked at some length at your work in
the ministry. I suspect that you were married in the earlier stages of

---

5. Mr. Fukuda and Mr. Ohira both went on to become prime minister. Mr. Fukuda
held that office from December 1976 to December 1978, when he was succeeded by
Mr. Ohira who was prime minister until his death in June 1980.

your career. Could we go back and talk about that? Was yours a traditional, arranged marriage?"

"Well . . . not exactly. My wife and I met during the inaugural meeting of the Asian Development Bank, here in Tokyo in November 1966. She was assisting the Japanese preparatory committee, as an interpreter. She is an accomplished linguist. She does French and English, and is strongest at Spanish. We met at the office, and perhaps once or twice outside the office. While I was working in Manila at the ADB, and then while I was heading the Tax Office in Nara Prefecture, we wrote to each other . . . oh, about twice a year. When I came back to Tokyo, we met each other more often . . . and we decided to get married."

Question: "It was basically your own arrangement and your own decision?"

"Yes. But our families agreed with what we wanted to do. We visited each other's homes, and after the family meetings, we were engaged. I asked Mr. Matsukawa, who was then the deputy director of the Securities Bureau, to be our intermediary, our *nakohdo*. That was in . . . August 1969, just before I left for Manila to work for President Watanabe at the ADB. In November of that same year, I had a chance to come back to Tokyo. So, we set a date for the wedding in November. We got married, and then I took my wife to Manila and we had our first home there."

Comment: "I see. You and your wife were your own matchmakers, and the traditional customs, the intermediary and the family meetings, were added on, or perhaps I should say blended in."

(laughing) "Exactly."

Question: "Would you mind telling me how your wife became such an accomplished linguist?"

"Not at all. Her maiden name was Noriko Shibusawa. Her grandfather was a cousin of Eiichi Shibusawa, the Meiji industrialist . . . whose grandson later became finance minister. My wife's father was a diplomat. He took her to live in Madrid when she was a young girl, and she went to elementary school there. Later, she returned to Spain and studied at the University of Madrid. Now she teaches Spanish at Sophia University here in Tokyo, and she also lectures in the Spanish language course at the foreign ministry.

"My wife's Spanish helped our life in the Philippines. There were quite a few Spanish residents in Manila, and also Filipino nationals who were immigrants from Spain, many of them wealthy and upper class. Normally, we Japanese have no contact with these Spanish families. But because of my wife, we did.

"Spanish is also part of the Tagalog and other dialects in the Philippines. There are so many Spanish words that my wife was able to understand, and that was very helpful to us. It gave us a wider and fuller social life. We have many friends in the Philippines.

"We have three children, two daughters and our son. He is the youngest. Our two girls were born in Manila, and our son here in Tokyo."

Question: "Have your children been educated abroad?"

"No. So far, their schooling has been here in Japan. Our two girls are in Sacred Heart Middle School, and our son is going to the same public elementary school in Kugahara that I attended. The girls are starting to study English, and a bit of English conversation."

LANGUAGE TRAINING

Question: "Do you think that your children will get a good education in English or in other foreign languages in their schools here in Japan?"

"Hmmm. You know they will spend six years studying English in their middle school and high school, and many hours each week at their homework. So, they will have a good foundation. And our children will have more chances than most to hear or practice English conversation. As I did. So, for them, it may be allright."

Question: "But for most Japanese children, who do not have these opportunities outside of school? How does the foreign language training work for them?"

"Language training is being discussed and changed, you know, so I am not sure what it will be like in three or five or ten years. But up to now, the English courses in the middle schools and high schools have been very high quality in teaching grammar--formal grammar--and in making a very intense study of some literary classics in English. But the classes have mostly been taught in Japanese. The explanations have been in Japanese. So it was very difficult to learn English conversation--to learn practical English--in school. This is also true of the university entrance tests for English. They have been more of a grammar test, not a test of practical ability.

"Partly, this is because many of the people who have taught English have never had a chance to learn practical, everyday English themselves. And we also have the old tradition of studying the Chinese classics here in Japan--the study of *kanbun*. The traditional way to study *kanbun* is to spend two or three hours translating and analyzing one line of classical Chinese poetry--very slowly and carefully. No one is expected to learn to use Chinese in any practical way in *kanbun*. Well, I think that tradition has influenced the study of English."

Question: "Do you think this should be changed? How would you change it?"

"I think that the two ways of studying English--the classical and the practical--should be combined. Much more time should be used in practical language training. (thoughtful pause) Perhaps the students could begin by reading aloud, and then speaking aloud . . . easy, practical sentences . . . responding to questions. This would train their ears and give them practice speaking, and would develop into real English conversation. They should spend much more time this way. Once or twice a week they could make an intense study of some English language classic."

INTERNATIONALIZATION

Question: "That strikes me as a sensible, moderate way to reform the existing system. It seems to me that the question of language training relates directly to internationalization. What does internationalization mean to you? How would you define it?"

"Hmmmm. That is a powerful word. Since I entered the Finance Ministry in 1963, I have used the word *kokusaika*, internationalization, in Japanese or in English, almost every day, or at least once a week. In one sense, it is an objective, something we strive for, and so we often use the word . . . as a justification . . . as a reason for taking a certain action. We say we should do this or that because it contributes toward internationalization.

"But there is more to it than that. It has . . . a deeper meaning . . . on two levels. A personal level and a national level.

"I told you that when I was sent to Bangkok in 1965, to ECAFE, I had to work with men from India, the Philippines, Thailand, and other countries, and I had to internationalize to survive. (laughing) Well, what I meant was that being able to speak English was not enough. I had to learn to understand and get along with people who had completely different customs and manners. I was very shocked at first by some of the meetings. Everybody was quite aggressive. People spoke strongly . . . even emotionally. When an issue became heated, sometimes several people spoke at the same time, interrupting each other, even raising their voices.

"Well, we Japanese were not taught how to act in such a meeting. In a Japanese meeting things usually move quietly. Even if you have something important to say, you look around to see if someone else should speak first. You wait for your turn. Then you try to make your point as tactfully as possible--as quietly as you can.

"I had to learn . . . how to interpret the ECAFE meetings and staff members. At first I thought they were noisy and bad mannered. But usually that was my cultural ignorance. I had to learn these different ways of talking . . . of disagreeing. At first it was very difficult. I remember an Indian staff member who used to frequently visit our American administrative director's office to tell him how important and good his--the Indian man's--work was . . . in order to get himself promoted. I thought that was outrageous. That would be outrageous in Japan. I learned that this kind of forward, aggressive behavior is not so abnormal in India.

"After a few months I began learning how to adapt myself, how to realize what the real situation was . . . when there was a serious problem, and when the loud voices and aggressive speeches were maneuvers. I think I learned to sometimes . . . maneuver myself.

"The important point is that I had to develop several personalities. If I came back to Tokyo and used some aggressive ECAFE expressions, people would think I was crazy. So I had to learn to adapt to different cultural settings . . . and to use the appropriate expressions and tone. On the personal level, that is the meaning of internationalization. And this kind of internationalization is extremely difficult for Japanese.

"On the national level, Japan is a trading country. We cannot live alone. And now our economy has become so big that we cannot decide what our economic policies should be only by taking into consideration direct Japanese interests. We have to consider the impact of our policies--even of our domestic policies--on other countries, even on the United States and on the whole international economic system. We are not used to thinking that way.

"Now we are at that stage when people are saying Japan should take the initiative in international questions. In the 1920s and 1930s Japan tried to take the initiative . . . and it seemed natural then, but it turned out very badly. Now we must be much more careful . . . or we could get on the wrong road again.

"Maybe it is not necessary for one state or another to take the initiative, especially in economics. Japan has in many ways caught up with the Western countries, and we should interact more like equals. We should sit down and work things out. Perhaps joint policy-making or team policy-making would be better than deciding who should take the initiative."

Question: "Yes. I see. Do you think that a sufficient number of Japanese--individual Japanese--are becoming internationalized on the personal level so that Japan will be able to meet the requirements of internationalization on the national level, in the future?"

"Ha . . . that is hard to say, but I think so. Here in the ministry we have become more internationalized. When I entered in 1963, about 30 percent or so of the officers had extensive experience abroad and could do international work. Now, it is above 70 percent, for the whole group of about six hundred officers. For the younger officers, it is closer to 90 percent. I think MITI has changed in about the same way. In most of the other ministries, there may have been less immediate need for internationalization, and less change.

"I don't know any figures for bankers and businessmen. Most of them do business here in Japan. But more and more do business abroad and have to work with foreigners. They seem to be doing it.

"I think this trend will continue. It is hard to know how many internationalized Japanese we will have in the future. But the numbers are increasing."

THE FUTURE

Question: "What are your expectations for Japan, and Japan's place in the world for the next ten to twenty years?"

"Hmm. Of course, it is impossible to know, but I am optimistic.

"I think we will continue to have a moderate rate of economic growth--probably about 3 percent to 4 percent. Some years a little higher, some years a bit lower. Our growth rate will be closer to the other advanced industrial countries."

Question: "Do you expect any basic changes in the political party alignment in Japan during this period?"

"Probably no basic change. The Conservative Party, the LDP, may go on as it is, or some factions might shift and there could be a coalition with some of the moderate parties. But this would not be a radical, basic change."

Question: "What about the broader international environment, both economic and political? There are North-South issues, U.S.-Soviet relations, and relations between Japan and the U.S. How do you think they will develop, and how will they affect Japan?"

"In the 1950s and 1960s, many people were unrealistic about the developing economies. There was a feeling that with some economic help and technical help, and planning, they could quickly reach the take-off stage. Of course, some states have done well--such as South Korea, Taiwan and Singapore, and some of the oil producing countries. But in most cases, things are not moving so well. It is going to take a long time--many more decades of effort. I think that the developed countries should continue to give economic assistance, and at the same time many of these developing countries have to work harder, and give more attention to self-help. I don't expect any miraculous developments. Steady, patient efforts will . . . eventually bring results. I think Japan will continue to give economic assistance to the developing countries.

"The U.S.-Soviet relationship will not change so easily. Although I don't think the basic U.S.-Soviet tension will soon disappear, patient efforts for détente are required. Both sides know how dangerous it is, and I don't think they will go to war. But there is too much distrust, and it will take a long time to overcome. So, Japan will have to live in a dangerous world.

"The U.S.-Japan relationship has worked well in this kind of world. I think that we should continue it--that this part of the world will be . . . peaceful, if we do so."

Question: "Of course, you know that the Soviets have made an impressive, long term military build-up in Asia and the Pacific, and the U.S. no longer has the superiority in naval and air forces that used to guarantee Japan's defense in the 1950s and 1960s. Do you think that Japan should be making a bigger military effort for its own defense in order to compensate for this change in the military balance?"

"Hmm. (thoughtful pause) You know that we are making increases in our defense budget while we are cutting almost all the other items in our budget. But I know that these increases have . . . only a small effect on the military balance. I am not a military specialist, but I do not think that the Soviets will take any big risks around Japan. I think that we can have better chances of peace here if the United States and Japan have good economic and political relations . . . and if Japan stays economically sound and stable . . . and if we keep giving economic help to the developing countries in this region.

"We cannot take our relationship with your country for granted. We have to be very careful and work hard at it. But again, if we are patient and persistent, I don't think our relationship will break down. Japan's current account surplus is a political problem as well as an economic one. There were periods in the past when first Great Britain and then the United States had a large surplus for many years, and it was not necessarily bad for the world economy.

There seems to be a strong feeling in America that if only we Japanese would open our markets more, or make our banking system more like yours, the American trade deficit would go away."

Question: "You think that other factors are more important, such as the American budget deficit and the over-valued dollar and under-valued yen (in 1985)?"

"Yes. We ought to do something to stabilize the international currency situation. I don't think a single national currency can bear the burden of being the international currency anymore. This is one of the questions we should work out by team policy-making. Our governments and the Western European governments--the governments and the central banks--can do something about this. And you are exactly right about your budget deficit. It is critical that it be controlled . . . and reduced.

"I think we can make enough changes . . . enough improvements . . . to hold the system together. If we do that, and I think we will, then I believe Japan . . . will do allright for the years to come."

Yoriko Kawaguchi

WHEN I talked with her, Yoriko Kawaguchi was director of the International Business Affairs Division in the Ministry of International Trade and Industry (MITI). MITI makes industrial and international trade policy for Japan.[1] MITI guided Japanese industry into steel, chemicals, and heavy industry in the 1960s, and into electronics, computers, and semi-conductors in the 1970s. In the 1980s, Japan became one of the world's more important overseas investors, with large and growing investments in the United States, including the opening of several new factories by well known firms such as Nissan and Toyota. At the same time, foreign investments in Japan have also been increasing.

Ms. Kawaguchi's office, in conjunction with other ministries, administered the Foreign Exchange and Foreign Trade Control Laws, and played a role in both the outward and inward flow of direct investments. It drew up policies for overseas business activities for enterprises under MITI's jurisdiction. It examined contracts involving the introduction of foreign technology by foreign investors, and examined the acquisition by foreigners of stocks and other property in Japan--in those cases in which they were not approved by the Bank of Japan on the spot. In addition to these pressing daily operations, it also developed a sense of the future direction of Japan's international business activity and helped to formulate policies to guide it.[2] In her own words, "Our division's basic function is dealing with both outward and inward investment by creating an environment to facilitate them."

---

1. For a detailed account of MITI's leading role in the Japanese economy, see Chalmers Johnson, *MITI and the Japanese Miracle* (Palo Alto, Calif.: Stanford University Press, 1984).
2. Ministry of International Trade and Industry, *MITI Handbook, 1984* (Tokyo: Japan Trade and Industry Publicity, Inc., 1985), 47-48.

Recent photographs.

MITI has a sleek, solid looking seventeen-story office building on the Kasumigaseki, a broad avenue in the heart of Tokyo, just a few blocks from the Imperial Palace. All the major ministries are on the Kasumigaseki. The older, somewhat dowdy Finance Ministry is directly across the busy, traffic clogged street. The Foreign Ministry is on the next block. The National Diet buildings are a half mile away. When the Diet is in session and bureaucrats, including Yoriko Kawaguchi, are being called up to explain their budgets and policies, their dark limousines roll back and forth from their offices to the Diet chambers. This is the heart of official, governmental Tokyo.

There was, however, nothing pretentious or grand about Yoriko Kawaguchi. In part, this was because it would have been difficult to generate much pomp and circumstance in her office, which was a large, bright room jammed with desks, that she shared with the dozen or so men who worked under her. The International Business Affairs Division looked like a bustling, cluttered newsroom in a small town newspaper. In part, because Ms. Kawaguchi, a slim, graceful woman, is by nature unassuming and understated. It did not take long, however, for her leadership qualities to become evident. She knows what she wants to say, and she knows how to convey it to whomever she is talking to, in either Japanese or English. Her most compelling quality is the firmness and steadiness of her eyes, and the calmness of her face. When she is pleased, she emanates serenity. When she disagrees, she becomes very quiet and cool.

Ms. Kawaguchi began our first meeting by talking about her prospects as a future leader. She had doubts about whether she fitted into that category. As a division director, she was at just that level on the promotion ladder where she and the twenty other higher civil servants who joined MITI in 1965 began facing the prospect of either being promoted or taking up another career--usually an executive position in industry. This system is known as *ama kudari*, literally "descending from heaven." Ms. Kawaguchi told me that the number of MITI retirees who find good positions in industry is much smaller than it was ten or twenty years ago. The descent from heaven is no longer as secure and comfortable as it was.

Above the division director level, the MITI hierarchy tapers sharply to a small number of department and bureau chiefs, and councilors, and finally to the two posts of the administrative vice-minister and administrative vice-minister for international affairs. These are powerful officials in the Japanese government, more so than an assistant secretary in Washington, and roughly comparable to an English permanent under secretary. There are about one hundred and fifty divisions in MITI, but only eight internal bureaus and several related agencies. Ms. Kawaguchi wanted me to know that she had no idea how far she would go on this promotion ladder, and that she would not participate in the study if I was going to make a prediction about her future. She did agree that her background, education, and career experience were representative of her age group in MITI, which will be moving into these top positions during the next ten to fifteen years. She also acknowledged that MITI officials who go into industry or banking after having been bureau chiefs will be influential leaders in the business community.

FAMILY

Yoriko Kawaguchi was born to Toshikuma and Hisako Tsuchida, in Tokyo, on January 14, 1941, the year the Pacific War began. Most Japanese born at that time have a stronger sense of family history and regional loyalty than Americans of their age. Family and local traditions and ties have frequently shaped their careers and remain important throughout their lives. Yoriko Kawaguchi, however, did not fit into this mold. She was surprised and slightly amused when I asked her about her ancestors and regional ties. In a low, clear voice, speaking in excellent English tinged with a Japanese cadence, she said:

"I really know very little about my ancestors. I am surprised that you want to know about them. I was born in Tokyo, and so were my parents. I am almost but not quite a true child of Tokyo, an *Edokko*. To be a true *Edokko* takes at least three generations of pure Tokyo blood. My paternal grandmother was not born in Tokyo, so I did not make it. She moved to the city when she was a young girl. I hardly know anything else about them.

"There is a story in our family that my mother's ancestors were samurai or *bushi*, feudal knights, from the town of Iga in what is now Mie Prefecture. They were supposed to be in the service of Todo Takatora, who was a loyal supporter of the Shogun, Tokugawa Ieyasu. I don't know how authentic that is. There is no way to check out these stories.

"I do have a special memory of my mother's grandfather that I should tell you. He was rich and a very religious Nichiren Buddhist. Because he was so generous to them, the Nichiren Buddhists sent him to a religious conference in Chicago. I heard about this in my family, and I have seen pictures of it. That was just a few years after the Meiji Restoration of 1868. It was a rare thing at that time for a Japanese to travel abroad. Of course, he knew no foreign languages and I have no idea what he did in Chicago or what he thought about the trip. Hmm. That is about as much as I remember about my ancestors. (small laugh)

"My father, Toshikuma Tsuchida, graduated from the University of Tokyo, and my mother, Hisako, went to a college of education, where she earned a license to teach home economics. She married my father soon after she graduated, so she never taught. When she was young, the universities in Japan, with one or two exceptions, were not open to women, and most parents thought that a girl should not be very well educated. But she continued her education anyway, even after she finished middle school, which at that time went to the eleventh grade for girls. It was a long commute everyday from Kamakura to Tokyo. She told me how tiring it was sometimes.

"I think that I come from an intellectual family, probably an intellectual, upper-middle class family. My father was at the management level of a big petroleum refining company. When I think of my family, I usually think only of my immediate family--my mother and father and my older sister. We usually only have an extended family gathering with uncles, aunts, in-laws, and cousins once each year on New Year's Day at my grandmother's in Kamakura. That is probably why I think differently than people born in the countryside, who have stronger family and local ties, and a stronger sense of the past. There is an expression, *mukohsangen ryodonari*, which means three houses across the street and two next door neighbors.

In the countryside everybody knows everybody else. But in our neighborhood in Tokyo only your immediate family and your next door neighbors know you. I have been living in the Yamanote neighborhood since I was eleven, and that is the way it is there.

"I like it this way. It makes me feel more free. I do not have to worry about the prestige of my family or region. I can just be myself. If you are from a small town and you go to Tokyo University, as I did, you become a celebrity, and everyone expects great things from you. In Yamanote, nobody knew who I was. Even now, when I get into the newspaper now and then, our neighbors barely take notice of it. I prefer it this way.

"Of course, I have many friends from my school days, and this ties me into a sort of network--a school network. We meet sometimes at work, and in social life, and we know each other in a special way because we shared the same teachers and shared the same jokes. But that is not such a large or close network. We really don't see each other that often."

Ms. Kawaguchi seemed ready to move onto another subject when she suddenly laughed and added an afterthought:

"There may be one disadvantage for me in not having strong local and family ties. They are important in politics, and so I don't think I can ever become a politician."

Since many of the members of the Japanese National Diet are former bureaucrats, this comment was not entirely a joke.

EARLY YEARS, WAR AND OCCUPATION

Question: "It seems to me that one of the most important differences between Japanese and Americans of your age is their memories of World War II. Americans born in 1941 hardly remember the war at all. Japanese, who were bombed and went hungry, remember the war vividly, even though they were only four years old when it ended. Does that apply to you?"

"Yes. I think that what you say is true in my case, and also for other Japanese who lived in industrial centers and seaports. But I suspect that many of my generation who spent the war in the countryside have no strong memories of the war or even of the Occupation, except that they were very poor. My father was a high-ranking manager in an oil refining plant in Shimizu, a seaport in Shizuoka Prefecture. The Americans bombed Shimizu, and I remember those attacks clearly, even though I was only three or four years old. I remember going with my mother to air raid fire drills--training on how to put out house fires with buckets of water. Shimizu and nearby areas were bombed a number of times. There was a shelter in our garden, and we shared it with a number of other families. When there was an air raid, we took blankets and food into the shelter and we shared them. Most of the time the bombs fell some distance away. But I remember one night when they exploded very close to us, and houses were on fire, and we fled the bomb shelter and spent the night on the mountainside. When we came back in the morning, the houses around my house were burned to the ground. But our house was not burned. We were very lucky."

Question: "How do you think that experience affected your values? Did it give you a deep abhorrence of war? Did it incline you toward pacificism?"

"The bombings left a deep impression on me--but they did not affect my values--not in that way. When I began to go to school, right after the war, I was taught that everything that related to the war was bad--very bad. We still had old textbooks, and we used black ink to erase everything in those books that related to soldiers and the war. That taught us pacifism. At the same time, our teachers taught us to admire democracy and freedom, and that is still influencing us a great deal. And the U.N. We were taught that the U.N. was the hope for a peaceful and a better future, and so it is still natural for us to believe the U.N. is good, despite its weakness and inability. In some ways, I think our teachers gave us an excessively idealistic education. We were shown the picture of a very, very rosy world--a world which was never likely to exist.

"But the bombings did not teach me these things. The bombings taught me that war is very personal. It taught me to sympathize with people who are caught in a war--in Lebanon and other countries--because I know how they feel--especially mothers with young children. You have to do everything to protect your children. That's how I would feel, and I would be very afraid that I could not protect them. You try your best to find food and clothes, so that your family will survive. In this sense, I learned to respect my parents for having cared for me and my sister so well in the war.

"For me, I think that the scarcity--the material scarcity of the war and early postwar period, affected my values more than the bombing. My father was a fairly high ranking manager, and we were relatively well-off. I do not remember going hungry. The food was not abundant, and it was very simple and basic--rice, fish, and vegetables. Perhaps my parents took food from their own plates to feed me and my sister--but I do not remember real hunger. The little that we had seemed normal to me and enough. It was the only diet I knew. But for my parents, food must have seemed very scarce.

"I remember the scarcity of ordinary, everyday things. There was not enough paper in my elementary school for us to write on. Schools had been burned down, so we had to go to school in three shifts each day. Even though my family was better off than most Japanese, I had so few clothes to wear. When I started school, I could not buy a book bag--not even a cloth rucksack for my books. There were none in the stores. Now my children have leather book packs. And sometimes we had no shoes. That scarcity seemed normal to me at the time, but it still influences the way I act and feel.

"I remember how amazed I was when I went to the U.S. for the first time in 1957, to live with a family. Everything was so abundant. People wrapped presents in beautiful, heavy, brightly colored paper, and when they opened the gift they just tore away the wrapping paper and threw it in the fire. I was amazed! Really amazed! (very emphatically)

"I could never do that. I still open packages carefully, and fold the wrapping paper neatly and store it to use sometime."

Comment: "I think that your age group was the last to learn this lesson before the postwar economic miracle began. People born three or four years later--in the middle and late 1940s--seem to have no memory of wartime destruction, and little memory of material deprivation. For the most part, they have known only economic growth and prosperity."

SCHOOL IN THE PROVINCES AND TOKYO

Question: "In 1947, you began elementary school. Do you recall any of your teachers? Did any of your teachers, or class-mates, or school subjects have a strong or unusual influence on you"?

"I don't think that any of the subjects we studied in the lower grades had a special influence on me. In a way, I suppose they all influenced me. I do remember all my teachers. I was in grammar school mostly outside of Tokyo, first in Shimizu and then for a few years in Wakayama. We came back to Tokyo when I was in fifth grade. In Shimizu and in Wakayama, almost all the other students in my class came from farming families, and their parents were not as educated as mine. This gave me an advantage. It was not too difficult for me to be the best student in my class. My teachers liked me, and for my parents' sake, or perhaps for my sake, I can't be sure, they did extra things for me. Mr. Maeda taught me to swim during the summer holiday when I was a third grader. My house was only a one minute walk from the seashore. And another teach-er, Mr. Tanino, came to our house in the evening to teach me as-tronomy. (pausing and smiling warmly at these childhood memo-ries) Yes. They were very nice and kind, and I had the benefit of all this extra care and attention.

"It was also lucky for me that my family moved back to Tokyo when I was in the fifth grade, and moved into a neighbor-hood where there was a very good elementary school--Seishi. It was an excellent, special public school before the war--many fa-mous people and politicians had been there--and even though it had become more open, the teachers were still excellent. I remember that my homeroom classes had about seventy boys and girls, which was too big, but the teachers were really good.

"The junior and senior high schools I went to were attached to Tokyo Educational University, which is now known as Tsukuba University. That was the happiest time of my life. (again, pausing and smiling very warmly) The teachers were so good, and I had so many good, close friends. I still see my friends from those years. Many of them went to the university with me and are working in

Tokyo. Some in this ministry, and others in companies or academia.

"When I entered the Tokyo Educational University Junior High School, I stepped on to what in some ways was an educational escalator. It meant that unless I did very poorly, I would automatically get into their prestigious senior high school. And from that high school, about one fourth to one third of the graduating class of about two hundred students went on to Tokyo University.

"My classmates in that junior and senior high school were really impressive. Most of them had some special ability or talent in one field or another--in mathematics or music or astronomy. (laughing) I remember one boy who knew more astronomy than our teacher did. I learned a great deal from my classmates, and I had respect and admiration for them. There was not much open competition, but I worked hard just to be as good as my classmates, to earn their respect."

Question: "What subjects did you study?"

"English, Japanese, geography, world history and Japanese history, the natural sciences, mathematics, music, art, and gymnastics."

Question: "It is good to be reminded how broad and solid the curriculum is in the Japanese schools. You graduated from high school with a solid foundation in the liberal arts and sciences. Were the teachers as good as the ones at Seishi?"

"Oh yes. They were excellent. I remember my first day in junior high, when Mr. Sakakibara, our geography teacher, stunned me by pointing to the maps and announcing, 'These maps are not true. Everyone of them is distorted, in one way or another.' He really taught me to think, to be careful and critical of what is put before me. And my biology teacher also made sure we learned that biology is not just what was in our books. It meant observing nature. In the autumn, for example, he surprised us by adding a test question asking which trees had changed color, and what colors? That wasn't in our book. You had to look at the trees to know.

"I especially remember Mr. Hasegawa who was my teacher when I was thirteen or so--in the eighth grade. He knew my personality very well, and taught me an important lesson. My friends and I were waiting in line one day, teasing and playing. The girl behind me called my name, then held her finger here, just where she expected my cheek to be when I swung around. I was supposed to hit her finger and be surprised or yelp, and then everybody would laugh. But I was so serious, and not stupid, so I turned the other way and avoided her finger. Mr. Hasegawa took me aside, and told me that what I had done was not very clever. He said I should have turned my cheek into that girl's finger, even though it was stupid, because that is what the others hoped I would do to amuse them, and it would not harm anyone. Sometimes, he was saying, it is important to relax and behave a little foolishly to have fun with others."

A YEAR OF HIGH SCHOOL IN SWARTHMORE

Question: "You mentioned that you went to the U.S. in 1957, when you were sixteen, to live with a family. How did you happen to do that?"

"I was an American Field Service exchange student. A girl in my high school had gone to the States in this program in 1955, so I knew about it and I applied."

Question: "Well, that must have been an important, unusual decision. Did your parents suggest it or encourage it?"

"They did not suggest it. I took the initiative. But they encouraged me when they knew I wanted to go. I had to be tested for my English ability, and many of the students with whom I would compete were going to missionary schools or private schools where they had English instruction with native English speakers. But I was not going to such a school, so my parents said that I could take lessons in English conversation to prepare for the examination. That was a great help, and I passed the test and was accepted for the exchange program."

Question: "Can you tell me a bit more about why you wanted to leave your family and friends and fine teachers, and go off to the States? What put this idea into your head?"

After thinking this over, Ms. Kawaguchi shrugged her shoulders, smiled mischievously, and firmly announced, "I just wanted to go. I was so curious to visit foreign countries. I remember as a little child being fascinated by a travel book in our house, about a boat trip from Japan to Europe, stopping at ports like Hong Kong, Singapore, Suez, and then on to Europe.

(in a more serious tone) "There were other considerations as well. Because of the war and the American Occupation, America seemed closer and more accessible to me. Otherwise I might just as well have gone to Europe. I thought America was a more natural place to go. During the Occupation, and afterward, there were Americans living in our neighborhood, in Yamanote. My father's company was affiliated with Standard Vacuum Oil Company, and he took Americans to the old capitol at Nara to see the *Daibutsu* (Great Buddha statue). And when I was seven or eight years old, he took me on one of his trips to Nara, with some Americans. Going to America seemed to be my best--maybe my only opportunity to travel overseas. (again, very firmly) And I *was* just curious, and I wanted to travel.

"I went to Swarthmore, Pennsylvania, and the American Field Service arranged for me to live with the Van Urk family. Swarthmore is a college town, many Quaker people, very intellectual. The Van Urks were very warm and well-to-do. Mr. Van Urk's father or grandfather came from Holland, from the Isle of Urk.

(pausing to collect her thoughts, and then nodding her head for emphasis) "That was an experience! The Van Urks are a marvelous family, and they taught me a set of values which was . . . very different. I still write to them, and try to see them outside San Francisco, where they live now, whenever I go to the States. Before I lived with them, I believed that the most important thing was to do well in school. They taught me that what you do in everyday life--in associating with people, helping people, leading people--is more important. They are a religious family, very Christian, and this part of their values and beliefs impressed me deeply.

(pausing for emphasis) "Looking back, that year in Swarthmore with the Van Urks was the single most important experience in my life. That changed me the most, and influenced me the most.

"Of course, that was when I really learned to use English, there in Swarthmore. The subjects at the high school, such as mathematics, were very easy. But I could barely speak English then. English was the most important thing for me to learn.

"The Van Urks have two daughters, less than two years apart, and I came right in between. So the three of us were very close. Even so, the first two or three months were difficult--quite difficult for me. Their family was entirely different from mine, and I had to change myself and conceal part of myself, and really learn to be a different person to live comfortably with them.

"At home in Japan, I used to stay up until midnight to finish my homework. At the Van Urks, I had to go to bed at eleven o'clock. And I could not argue with my American parents (again, the mischievous smile) as I did in Japan, sometimes. I was their guest, in a way, and in the beginning, I didn't know how to say what I wanted to say. So I had to retreat. I am sure that they had to adapt to me in some ways, but I had to adapt and change much more. Since that time, whenever I have had to go into a new situation, it has not been difficult to adjust, to make new friends and get along with people.

"Also, I learned the frustration of not being a leader. In Japan, when I was with my school friends--girls or boys--I could lead them, persuade them to do what I wanted to do. In Swarthmore, I could not do that. Everybody was helpful and good to me, but I was always foreign, and I had trouble expressing myself. I had to be a follower, and it was very frustrating for me. I learned how people who are not leaders, who always have to follow, must feel. "

Comment: "Well, even though you learned so much, it must have been a great relief for you to come back to Japan when that year ended."

(looking very surprised at my comment, and thinking it over) ."No. I did not want to come back. At the end of my year with the Van Urks, I did not want to leave. I felt close to them, and I felt I was just beginning to learn something about America. And of course, I also enjoyed the material comfort of life in Swarthmore. Life in Japan was not as rich or comfortable in 1957-1958. When I left Swarthmore, I was wondering how I could get back to the U.S. for my university.

(in a lighter tone and smiling) "But after I got back to Japan, I was happy to be back. I had to go into a different class in high school, but that was not difficult, and I made a whole new set of friends. During the months after my return, I remember thinking many times that I preferred the American way of doing things--that Americans were more informal and direct. (laughing) While I was actually in the U.S. I am not sure I felt that way. But actually, when I got back home to Japan, I was very comfortable and happy.

"It is clear to me now that I had changed while I was in the U.S. It had strengthened me in many ways, and deep in my heart I was different afterward. I have been successful in hiding that change because of the adaptability I acquired. But people who know me now sometimes think I am very rash. That is when the change shows."

Question: "A few minutes ago, you said that at school in Japan, you were used to being a leader among your friends--both boys and girls. I have the impression, perhaps it is a stereotype, that school boys in Japan don't follow the lead of girls. Am I mistaken?"

"Well, in many schools the boys and girls were kept separate, and in that kind of school your impression is not mistaken. But in the schools I went to, girls and boys studied and played together, and it was not unusual for a girl to be . . . influential. If a girl was around the top of the class, the young men recognized it and respected her.

"Anyway, I adapted fairly quickly to Japan when I returned, except for one or two slips. In America, I had learned to speak freely to people senior to me, and to older people. One day, my mother took me with her on a visit to an older, important lady, and I just joined in the conversation, and I felt I could do it. (with an amused smile) Afterward, my mother gave me quite a scolding. I must have been very shocking."

TOKYO UNIVERSITY AND
THE 1960 TREATY DEMONSTRATIONS

"After I got used to life in Tokyo again, my last two years in high school went very smoothly. I liked the new friends I made and I enjoyed my school life very much--as much as before. I had a crush on some boy--as all my girlfriends did. The biggest change in my family life was that we had a TV at home. My parents had bought it while I was in the U.S.

"In early March of 1960, I sat for the examination to Tokyo University. I passed it and entered in April."

Question: "Isn't it a bit unusual to pass the entrance examination on the first try? Many of the Tokyo University graduates I have met only managed to get in after taking the test twice."

"Well, about half my Todai class of 2500 students passed the test on their first try. It was not that unusual. I did not expect to fail. Things worked out pretty much as I expected them to."

Question: "In your class of 2500, how many women were there?"

"We had about sixty women."

Question: "Did you feel somewhat isolated?"

(pausing to remember her feelings in 1960) "I don't think so. Maybe I have forgotten my feelings, but I don't recall feeling anything special. (continuing in a lighter tone) There was one problem. There was only one ladies' room on the whole campus. The campus for undergraduates in those days was the former Ichiko (First) High School, which had been a boys' school until after the war. When it became Todai, they converted only one washroom. It was an inconvenience if you had to cross the whole campus to reach it. But we girl students all got to meet each other there, and since we could not help but see each other there, we all became friends.

"I also knew the boys who had gone to my high school, so I had many friends, and I did not feel isolated. It is true that many of the freshman boys came from all male schools in the countryside, and they were not used to having girls at school. They seemed awkward when we were around. They did not talk to us--I don't think they knew how--and we did not talk to them. But I had enough friends from high school and from the new girls I met."

Question: "I have gotten the impression that getting into Tokyo University is the big hurdle, but that the university itself is not very difficult or demanding, at least not in the freshman and sophomore years. Was that your experience, too?"

"Yes, it was. Of course, I did some school work--almost out of habit--but I had a lot of time for other things, much more than in high school. I went to coffee shops with my friends. I played tennis. I spent quite a bit of time at the English Speaking Society. It was as much a social club as an academic club."

Question: "The year you entered Tokyo University was 1960--the year of the massive demonstrations in Tokyo against the U.S.-Japan Security Treaty. These demonstrations, some of which got out of hand and turned into riots, caused President Eisenhower to cancel a scheduled visit to Japan that summer, and also led to the resignation of Prime Minister Kishi. I realize that you began school in April, only a few months before the demonstrations and riots peaked, but did you get caught up in those events? What did you think about them?"

"Oh yes. I was involved, although not in a very active sense. Everybody in my class had to face that issue. There was a lot of turmoil on the campus, strong feelings, noisy meetings, demos (demonstrations). It was all new to me . . . all these political problems and social problems. In high school we were mostly from well-to-do families, conservative, very nice. The anti-treaty movement was something . . . well . . . entirely new, sometimes confusing, sometimes exciting."

Question: "Anti-treaty and even anti-U.S. feeling on the campus must have been running very high, and you had just spent a year at Swarthmore--a very important year--just a few years before. Did you feel torn in different directions?"

"I separated the American people--and especially my American friends--from the political issues. For me the anti-treaty movement was not anti-American. I liked America, especially the openness and generosity in the national character. For me, the movement was basically directed against the Kishi cabinet and Kishi's high-handed way of governing. So it was a domestic issue, for me, and for many others.

"I joined in some of the demonstrations, but I was not a very active demonstrator. I don't go to extremes or get very emotional. That is part of my personality. Sometimes I think it is a problem. Always in between, always moderate.

"There was a great deal of Marxist discussion going on at Todai, which was all new to me. So I tried to study it, in a reasonable way, and find out what it was about. I tried to be open-minded."

EXCHANGE STUDENT AT
NEW YORK UNIVERSITY, 1962-1963

Question: "When you reached your junior year, did you get serious about your studies again in preparation for the Higher Civil Service examination?"

"No. I was not sure what I was going to do with my future. I was very undecided. But something lucky happened. During the summer vacation in 1962, while I was walking on campus, I noticed an announcement about New York and Tokyo having a sister city program. It said they were going to exchange students. One to Tokyo. One to New York. Well . . . I casually thought that if I applied I might get it. And if I did, it would give me an extra year, an extra year to decide what to do. If I didn't pass . . . well, there was nothing lost. And it would be a change. So, I applied. The test was in August, just ten days after I read the announcement. I passed--just by sheer luck--and in September I was on my way to New York. The whole thing was so quick. So I went.

"I was pleased, but it was not like going to America the first time--not that exciting. It was so nice to see my American parents again. I spent almost ten months at New York University, living in the dormitory from September to June, and then I came back to Japan via Europe and the Middle East--a marvelous two and a half month trip--by myself.

"In New York, I lived in the N.Y.U. dorm, on the campus, at Washington Square, right in Greenwich Village--which was so lively and cultivated then, and not as . . . well, it is not as nice now. Although I had not been so serious about my studies that year at Todai, I found the courses and books fascinating at N.Y.U. (laughing) I got very interested in Western philosophy and in our class discussions. The rationality, the logic of Western thinkers, fascinated me. But don't think that I am a philosopher or well-versed in Western philosophy. I am a very simple person, really, and I just get excited when I see something new. I think it was that kind of excitement and not a deep, intellectual interest in philosophy.

"Probably the most important thing I learned from that year in New York was how to be a little bit demanding. I was not pro-tected, not living in a family, as I had been with the Van Urks. New Yorkers were . . . well . . . pushy and demanding. I learned that I couldn't get anything unless I was a little demanding, too. (slowly, with emphasis) That is so different from Japan. It was a difficult thing for me to learn, very difficult--and not always pleasant, but important.

"One of my friends at N.Y.U., at the dormitory, was Mitsuko Shimomura, who has become a famous journalist. We still see each other now and then in Tokyo.

"The person I remember the best, who impressed me the most, was an American woman who lived across Washington Square from my dormitory. She was a volunteer in the Tokyo-New York sister city arrangement. Her name is Mrs. Joe White, an Irish woman who came from Ireland when she was seven years old. Blue-eyed, very short, and very good and sweet. She is a retired schoolteacher--not at all rich, but devoted to helping others, and full of energy and interest. When she was entertaining people at her apartment, she often invited me over. She arranged for me to go to plays and musicals. Sometimes she took me herself, and sometimes her friends paid for my tickets. I lived on a very modest allowance, and I could not have enjoyed these plays and musicals without Mrs. Joe White's help.

"She knew that it was sometimes noisy in our dorms. Since she lived alone, she gave me a key to her apartment and said I should come there anytime I needed privacy or a quiet place. That was so . . . extremely kind and thoughtful. Just being with Mrs.

Joe White was an education in how to help people in simple, practical ways.

"I think she is in her eighties now. The last time I saw her--two or three years ago--she was on her way out of her apartment, carrying dinner to an aunt, older than herself, who lived in New Jersey. (shaking her head in admiration) I always try to see Mrs. White when I am in New York. We exchange Christmas cards. (ruefully) Hers always reach me before Christmas. But mine are always late. (smiling regretfully) I send my cards too late."

TRAVEL TO EUROPE AND THE MIDDLE EAST

"My room mate at N.Y.U. was a Jewish girl, a senior, who got married very soon after she graduated. She invited me to her wedding, that summer, but I couldn't attend because I had already left for Europe and the Middle East. She exposed me to some Jewish culture, which was also entirely new to me--and fascinating. When I was in New York, I saw the movie 'Exodus', which made me curious about the Middle East. So when I was traveling back to Japan that summer, I spent eleven days in a kibbutz, close to the Syrian border. People pointed out the Golan Heights to me, and further in the distance was Syria--a foreign country--whose army could invade. To me, as a Japanese, used to living on an island, that was . . . shocking. And I remember the signs of war . . . especially on the narrow road, winding through the mountains from Tel Aviv to Jerusaleum. I saw what was left of jeeps, blown up and wrecked in the 1948 war, still beside the road, turning brown with rust.

"Of course it was a serious matter. In a way I knew it. But I was also very young, and for me the trip was exciting and great fun. I got back to Japan much more confident and sure of myself. I felt as though I could go anywhere and get along."

Question: "Where did you go beside Israel? Where did you travel in Europe?"

(laughing merrily) "All over! France, Britain, Norway, Denmark, Sweden, Italy, Germany, Greece, Turkey, Israel, India, and Hong Kong. I had to do it with very little money, because there were strict limits then on sending foreign exchange from Japan. Half the time, I stayed with families, friends of the Van Urks. The Van Urks went to Europe often, and had a lot of friends there, and they helped me. I also stayed with some American Field Service friends who were Europeans. Where I didn't know any people, I stayed at YWCAs, or student dormitories that were open in the summer. Sometimes I stayed in very cheap hotels. I had to keep my expenses down. I did not take taxis. I walked everywhere, and I bought food at grocery stores and bakeries for lunch, instead of going to restaurants. But I was having a marvelous time--so much fun! I used English everywhere I traveled, and it worked.

"When I think of it now, it is amazing to me that my parents let me do that. I am not sure that I will have the courage to let my six year old daughter travel around the world by herself when she is twenty-one. (thoughtfully) I suppose I was quite insistent about doing it, and I was 100 percent certain that I would have no serious problems and would be able to do it well. And at that time, in 1963, I had no idea that I would be able to travel abroad as much as I have. I felt that I should use that chance to travel and see some of the world, because there would probably not be such a chance again."

THE HIGHER CIVIL SERVICE
EXAMINATION AND JOINING MITI

Question: "The world was a safer place for travel in 1963. I wonder if it will become that safe again by 2000, when your daughter will be twenty-one? Hmmm. Well, when you got back to Japan in September 1963, in the middle of your junior year at Todai, did you have a clearer idea of what you wanted to do?"

"No, not really. I was still undecided whether I was going to go to graduate school, which was . . . in a way . . . another excuse for not deciding what to do. At the same time, I realized that I was not the graduate school type. I cannot spend ten hours a day in a study or a library.

"The more I thought about it, I realized that I wanted to find a job where I would be treated equally with my male colleagues. It was not easy to find such a job then, or even now. It seemed to me that there was only one place where I could find such a job--in the government, in the Higher Civil Service.[3]   And even in the government, it depended on the ministry. Toward the end of my junior year (winter 1963-1964), I knew that I would not go to graduate school. I would take the Higher Civil Service examination.

"In MITI, I knew two women. One of them was a friend. So . . . the path was made for me in MITI."

Question: "Did you give any thought to any other ministry? What about the Ministry of Finance?"

"I did not try for the Ministry of Finance because there was nobody (laughing quickly) I mean there was no woman there. I was not that venturesome. It all comes from my moderate, upper middle-class background. I was careful and reasonable. "

Question: "MITI, Finance, and Foreign Affairs are the most powerful, prestigious ministries. When you were planning to take the examinations, were you thinking about where you might hope to exercise the most power . . . the most influence in shaping national policy?"

"I don't think so. Some of the men I knew at Todai were thinking and talking about that. But I was much more concerned to find a job where I could do work related to international affairs, and get equal pay and respect (little smile) without having to break new paths. So, I took the examination, passed it, and went into MITI in 1965, after I graduated."

MARRIAGE, FAMILY, AND CHILDREN

Question: "Your husband is also in MITI. Did you meet in the ministry, or did you know each other before?"

"We met at the ministry."

Question: "Then your marriage was probably not a traditional, arranged one, was it?"

"No."

Question: "How did you happen to get together? Did you

---

3. For a brief but useful description of the history, role, and recruitment of the national bureaucracy and the Higher Civil Service, see Robert E. Ward, *Japan's Political System* (Englewood, N.J.: Prentice-Hall, Inc. 1978), 163-67.

have similar backgrounds or share many common interests?"

(pausing very thoughtfully and seriously) "Not really. I am a city girl. He is from Kyushu. Hmmmm. How does one explain? It was not that we had so many things in common. (pause) I think it takes timing. The timing is very important. For example, I had a crush on a boy when I was sixteen, but I never thought of getting married then. It was out of the question . . . not practical. But after I entered MITI, we got to know each other well . . . and we were the right age. That is the way it happened. We were married just about four years after I joined the ministry."

Question: "As you know from the outline, I am working on the assumption that family life in Japan is more institutional and less romantic than in the U.S. Most of the future leaders I am talking with are so greatly occupied by their careers that they have very little time for family life. But to the extent that their families are a factor in their lives, they are a strong source of stability and support. Since you and your husband both work at MITI, I am somewhat at a loss to know how my assumption would apply to you."

"Well, working in the ministry gave us the opportunity to meet each other. But apart from that, we don't bring our official lives home with us. I mean we talk about our colleagues some time, or about MITI policy questions, but the fact that we work in the same ministry does not matter much in our marriage. At home, we talk more about ordinary, everyday things . . . about meals, or when and where to do something or meet . . . and the children. Now, he is on assignment in Geneva, but that is the way it is when we are both at home."

Question: "Yes. You have two children, six and seven years old. Since you and your husband both are at work all day, how have you raised them?"

"I have always had domestic help--women who I have counted on to help me raise the children. Right now, my help lives in, which makes it much easier. I also discovered, after I had my children, that Japan has excellent public nursery schools and day care centers. Until my children were one year old, they were at home with my helper. Then, from the age of one until six years old, from the time I left home in the morning until four-thirty in the afternoon, they spent the day at a nursery school. Since I was working and could not get them at four-thirty my helper would take the children home, care for them and play with them and feed them. Now, they are in elementary school, and after school in the afternoon they go to a public day care center until five, when they come home.

"I think this has been a good arrangement for my children-- maybe better in some ways than if I had been at home to raise them. In Tokyo, traffic is so heavy that most children cannot play outside as much as we did, or have many friends. Mothers have to watch over them so carefully that they keep them more at home, in the house, and it can be . . . a very narrow environment. In the nursery school there are good playgrounds and playrooms, other children to meet and play with, and good, responsible caretakers. There is usually about one caretaker for every three or four children. They are responsible, intelligent, supportive people.

"So far, things are going very well. Better than I expected. Since the children are six and seven, it is too early for us to worry about their academic work. Just so long as they are well and happy. That is what is important now. Of course, you can never know how children will turn out until they are grown up. I think that I am giving them a good childhood . . . certainly broader than many children receive, and they are adjusting to it very well. If later on they develop some traits that I don't like . . . well, even then, I could not be sure what shaped them. This question occurs to me, but I don't think it is worth worrying about."

Question: "I have read that many Japanese wives have jobs, but I thought that generally they went back to work when their children were well along in school. In the nursery schools for young children, what kind of jobs did the mothers have?"

"Your information is correct. The working women in Japan are an M curve. Their numbers are very high after graduating from school and before marriage. Then the number drops sharply, until the children grow up, and the number of working mothers curves sharply upward. But even in the lowest section of the curve, when the children are young, there are a considerable number of working mothers in Tokyo. Many of them are schoolteachers, or nurses, or switchboard operators . . . all sorts of jobs."

CAREER, MITI, AND
THE INTERNATIONALIZATION OF JAPAN

Question: "What you have told me about your family life
and your children is very helpful. I would like to discuss your career, your work at MITI, and MITI's role in Japan. I understand
that to a large extent, the general course of your career until now
(1985) was set when you entered MITI in 1965 with twenty other
successful candidates in the Higher Civil Service. I realize that
during the next decade your class of 1965 will be either promoted up
to bureau chief and higher, or will resign, and 'descend from heav-
en' into the private sector. At our first meeting, you made it clear
that you would not speculate on your future--which is entirely understandable. What would you like to tell me about your work in
MITI, and your career?"

"Yes. I am glad you put it that way. So far, I have done
what most of my colleagues have done. We have worked in various
divisions, in Tokyo and abroad. Between 1965 and 1970, I worked
in Foreign Exchange and Trade Finance, in the Minister's Office and
in the Minister's Secretariat. I have spent a great deal of time on the
international side of MITI. In 1972, I became a deputy division director in the International Policy Bureau. In the late 1970s, I
worked at the World Bank. Since 1980, I have been a division director in the Trade Policy Bureau, in the Agency for Industrial Science and Technology, and my job now is to head the International
Business Affairs Division in the Industrial Policy Bureau. From
1982 to 1984, I was on loan from MITI to the Cabinet Secretariat (in
the Prime Minister's Office). I was the councilor responsible for
comprehensive national security policy."

Question: "What has your work actually entailed? What has
it been like?"

"It has been fascinating and challenging. Of course, I have
usually only had a small piece of policy to work on. And sometimes
it has been hard for me to know whether my work has . . . had
much effect. But it is always challenging and stimulating. I have
been able to work on policy questions and policy making. Well . . .

at times, I have been able to see the whole process, to see the pieces being fitted together.

"Of course, there have been times when I found my work frustrating. Times when I have worked very hard, talked with people, written papers, and then it did not come off. Something happened, and my work was not used. But another issue or another task comes along, usually very quickly, sometimes the next week or the next day, and it is challenging work again. So, overall, it is a good life at MITI. Busy and demanding."

Question: "I think that the best known book in English about MITI is Chalmers Johnson's *MITI and the Japanese Economic Miracle*. Johnson attributes to MITI *the* major role in planning and guiding Japan's phenomenal industrial and economic growth, especially in the 1950s and 1960s. I wonder if he exaggerated MITI's role? Or do you think Johnson's view is basically correct?"

"Well, I have only read parts of Johnson's book. It seemed to me that he was very well informed, and that it is a good book. But the way in which he approached the subject almost unavoidably exaggerated MITI's role--whether it was intentional or not. He focused on what MITI did, and gave very little attention to others--to the Finance Ministry, or to banks, or business, or labor unions. So naturally, MITI was always in the foreground in his book and seemed to be the most important actor. (laughing)

"In trying to understand MITI today, Johnson's book could be . . . misleading. His history of MITI goes to about 1973 or 1975, just after the 1973 oil shock. The Japanese economy and MITI have probably changed more in the ten years since 1975 than they did during the twenty or thirty years before 1975--although those were years of very rapid growth. What I mean is that in 1969, for example, Japan's foreign exchange holdings were only about two billion dollars. Japan was a relatively small actor in the world economy. Now Japan is on the verge of being the largest creditor nation in the world. So, the kinds of issues and questions that must be dealt with now are very different than in 1973 or 1975--much more international. The Japanese economy is bigger and more complex, and also more interdependent--more tied in with the world economy.

"At the same time, MITI's authority is not as great as it was when industries were smaller and capital was scarcer, in the 1950s and 1960s. In those days, MITI could use its control over capital allocation to carry out its ideas. That was a power base. Now, the situation is different. Industry in Japan is more powerful and more independent.

"But even though MITI's role is changing, and its authority is not as great, I think that in a market economy there is always an important role which only a government can play. The market is not perfect. It can be improved with better information, with better foresight--better than most private companies can usually generate. The role of MITI is to supplement the places which the free market mechanism does not cover. Research and development is one. Basic R & D involves lots of risk and long lead times before anything comes out of it. Almost every government realizes this, and becomes involved to some extent in R & D.

"And another important role is in the foreign direct investment field--investments flowing out of Japan as well as into Japan. This investment is expanding, and it should grow even more. It requires more information--information about what host countries' policies are toward foreign direct investments.

"Well, MITI's effectiveness in questions like R & D and overseas investments, now and in the future, depends on whether people in industry think our information and ideas are reliable. If they think our sense of direction is correct, they will follow our guidance. Of course, we can still channel some resources, and influence companies in that way, but not very much compared to twenty or thirty years ago. Now it is much more a matter of intellectual leadership."

Question: "You have mentioned Japan's rapidly growing international economic involvement. How do you think this internationalization will work? Or what is needed to make it work? Former Foreign Minister Saburo Okita has told me that in order for the current trend of economic internationalization to continue to the year 2000, Japan will need many, many more people who have mastered foreign languages, especially English, and who are able to understand and deal effectively with foreigners."

"Oh yes. Now that we are expanding our role in international finance and investment, we do need many more people who can speak and do business with foreigners, and not on a simple level, but on a sophisticated level. For example, direct investment requires much more personal interaction--complex interaction--since people have to go abroad, live there and work with foreigners--than selling cars and electronic equipment. I think there are about fifteen thousand Japanese studying abroad this year, mostly in the U.S. Of course, we can never be certain how many of these people will become skillful enough at foreign languages and culture to really be able to do complicated international work. But certainly, sending many students overseas is the right direction to move. And we should bring many more foreign students and teachers into Japan. These are basic, long-term requirements for Japan's future.

"There is another requirement that is . . . maybe . . . (very thoughtfully, knitting her brows) . . . even more important, to some extent because it is not so well understood. (laughing) I am not sure that I understand this requirement myself. We need people . . . individuals . . . who think globally . . . who can be leaders on a global level. This is difficult for me to explain. I am still trying to formulate it. Japan's national interest is not as local or particular as it used to be. Let me put it this way. We need people who are completely Japanese, who are real leaders in Japan, and who at the same time are recognized as international leaders because they have ideas and plans that are good for other countries--or at least contribute to a more workable world economy. Up to now, we have accepted the world economy almost as a given . . . as a framework within which Japan had to work and compete. Now, I think, we need more people . . . leaders . . . who understand how Japan can use its capabilities to help create international structures that are good for Japan, and also good for the international community."

Question: "Yes. I think I see your point. There is obviously a great deal of complaining about Japanese insularity and selfishness, and this broader view of Japan's interests would help respond to these complaints. But I have lived enough years in Japan to realize how difficult this broadening or globalization of the Japanese perspective will be. In addition to a deeply ingrained Japanese belief that your country is resource poor, vulnerable, and weak, isn't there also a lingering doubt and fear among Japanese about your ability to be an international leader . . . in an acceptable, peaceful way? After all, Japan certainly assumed a position of international leadership before World War II, in China, in Asia, and in the Pacific. But obviously, that role was not welcomed, not accepted. Do you think that the disastrous failure of that attempt at leadership still inhibits the development of the kind of Japanese international leadership you have described?"

"Hmmm. Yes. I am sure it does. And there are also two other constraints. First, even though our international economic position has grown so much, our overall, political power base may still be too limited. It is not just a matter of having Japanese leaders who can think globally. Leaders in other countries have to feel that they should listen and give careful attention to these Japanese ideas and programs. I am not sure they are ready to do that.

"Another constraint is in Japanese society itself. I believe that internationalization is necessary for Japan's future, for our prosperity and security. But if it requires big changes in our values, in the way we do things on a day-to-day basis . . . well, I am doubtful about making such big changes. In some ways, we are not very flexible. We can change our goals, and learn new technologies, but it is much more difficult for us to change the way we relate to each other and the way we work. "

Comment: "It sounds as though you think that these various processes of internationalization are desirable and necessary for Japan, but that you are pessimistic about their success."

(laughing) "I sounded more pessimistic than I am. I was just trying to be realistic about the difficulties. But they are not impossible. After all, the problems facing Japan thirty or forty years ago looked much more impossible . . . and somehow, we did not do too badly."

BUSINESSMEN

Yotaro Kobayashi

YOTARO KOBAYASHI is president of Fuji Xerox Co. Ltd., one of the largest office machine firms in Japan, and the principal Xerox Group company in Asia. In 1980, two years after Yotaro Kobayashi took the helm, Fuji Xerox won the most sought after business award in Japan, the prestigious Deming Prize. In 1983, in recognition of his important role in Japanese business, his understanding of U.S.-Japanese relations, and his international stature, the Japanese government asked him to serve on the U.S.-Japan Advisory Commission, known as the Wise Men's Group. This group, composed of seven leading businessmen from each of the two countries, was formed to advise and counsel their governments on economic and business issues.

Fuji Xerox is a Japanese managed, 50-50 joint venture, established in 1962 between Rank Xerox of Britain and the Fuji Photo Film Co. Ltd. of Japan. It is worth taking a brief glance at the history of Fuji Xerox to understand how American technology and enterprise led to the creation of this successful British-Japanese joint venture, and also because it sheds light on how international business is conducted.[1]

In 1950, the Haloid Company, a little known manufacturer of photographic paper in Rochester, New York, started producing and leasing office copy machines that used an innovative electrophotographic technology called xerography, invented by Chester F. Carlson. In less than a decade, the word xerox became synonymous with office copy machine, and the reproduction of documents, which had been an expensive, laborious process, had been transformed into the inexpensive, simple operation that we now take for

---

1. Most of this brief historical account is extracted from *Fuji Xerox : The First 20 Years, 1962 --1982* (Tokyo: Fuji Xerox Co., Ltd., 1983).

A recent photo, with family.

Palace Courts, 1953.

Keio Elementary School (front left).

In college.

granted. In 1955, Haloid renamed itself Haloid Xerox, and in 1961, when it had become the largest copy machine producer in the world, it became the Xerox Corporation. In 1956, in the midst of the company's phenomenal early growth, President Joseph C. Wilson of Haloid Xerox, decided to start selling his booming new product on the world market. He was looking for a reputable, well-funded overseas partner. The Rank Organization in Britain, a large, powerful conglomerate that produced movies, owned theaters, and manufactured radio speakers and optical equipment, was looking for a promising investment opportunity. The Rank Organization funded Rank Xerox with three million dollars, and in return received Xerox patent rights and world marketing rights outside the United States and Canada.

In Japan, Setsutaro Kobayashi, president of Fuji Photo Film Co. Ltd., (and father to Yotaro) was keenly aware of the potential of the new office copy machines. In 1956, he and his colleagues decided to get into this promising new business. Their plan was to import the American technology into Japan under a licensing agreement, and then manufacture and sell the machines under their own company name. An American engineer from Haloid Xerox was invited to visit the Fuji Photo Film plant in May 1957. He was impressed by the scale, equipment, and technical expertise of Fuji Film, and a favorable report went to London. In fact, at that time Fuji Film was a larger firm than either Haloid Xerox or Rank Xerox. In July of that year, Rank Xerox got in contact with Fuji Film and learned that they wanted a licensing agreement. In October 1959, after more than two years of negotiating, President Thomas A. Law of Rank Xerox abruptly changed the terms of the negotiations and insisted that there must be a 50-50 joint venture or nothing. The Xerox business had become so attractive that Fuji Film quickly agreed to this tough new offer, and in November 1959, an agreement was concluded to establish Fuji Xerox. Then, it took more than two years for the technology and capital transfer arrangements in this joint venture agreement to clear the Japanese bureaucracy, and in February 1962, Fuji Xerox was finally established.

The story of Fuji Xerox since 1962 divides itself into three distinct chapters. Until 1970, Fuji Xerox held exclusive rights in Japan to Xerox technology, and in the absence of competition, it flourished by leaps and bounds. Its machines were basically Japanese adaptations of American designs and they were almost all sold in Japan.

In the early 1970s, after its exclusive patent rights lapsed, Japanese competitors such as Ricoh, Canon, Toshiba, and Sharp entered the market, and life became much more difficult. Fuji Xerox responded to the competition by extending its business beyond Japan into Asia, including Korea, Taiwan, Indonesia, and Thailand. The company also made an energetic effort to introduce its own innovative designs and technology into its new model copy machines, and began to diversify into facsimile equipment and computer peripherals. Despite these efforts, during the two years of economic uncertainty and rapid inflation that followed the 1973 Middle East War and the sudden increase in world oil prices, Fuji Xerox lost a substantial share of its market in Japan. In those difficult years, many of Fuji Xerox's customers decided to try less expensive, less well known copy machines and the customers liked what they found.

By 1978-1979, however, Fuji Xerox had regained much of its lost market share by resuming its technological lead in copy machines and at the same time holding down its prices. It was this successful rebound, based on improved quality control, that earned the Deming Prize in 1980. In the 1980s, Fuji Xerox has become a leader in design and technology in the worldwide Xerox Group, especially in desktop copy machines. It exports approximately 10 percent of its production to its Asian partners, and between 20 percent and 25 percent to Rank Xerox and Xerox Corporation.

I met with Yotaro Kobayashi in April and May of 1985, at his suite of offices in the Fuji Xerox Building in Akasaka, a thriving business district in Tokyo, and also at the International House of Japan, a few minutes away by car. At our first meeting, I was ushered into an office where he was working with his secretary, putting the final touches on a letter. He was in shirtsleeves, and he conveyed an unusual sense of energy and vigor. He is somewhat above medium height, athletic looking, ruddy faced, dark haired, and has keen, piercing eyes. He gave me a firm handshake and led me to a spacious, richly furnished conference room. On the way, Yotaro explained that he had two hours to talk with me on that day, and that he was ready to tell me about his family background and education. His English is clear and expressive, with a trace of a British accent. He began speaking somewhat hurriedly, but as we went on he gradually became more thoughtful and relaxed.

FAMILY BACKGROUND

"I was born on April 25, 1933, in London, England. You know that my father's name was Setsutaro. My mother's name is Chizuyo, and her maiden name was Chizuyo Shiose. I was their first child. I have two younger brothers and two younger sisters.

"My father comes from Hyogo Prefecture in western Japan. He was born in 1899, the second son of a fairly prosperous farmer. As a young boy, he did very well in school, and his parents had great hopes for him. But just about the time he graduated from grammar school, his father died . . . and the family suffered a financial setback. So, he was not able to continue with his formal education. Even though he couldn't attend school, he did the work for middle school on his own and earned the diploma. With that diploma in hand, he set off for Tokyo--just a teenager--with his mind set on getting into Ichiko. Ichiko was the Tokyo First High School, at that time the best in Japan. There was a difficult--very difficult entrance examination, and he got to work preparing for it. But before he could take it, he became ill--too ill to go on. I think he had a light case of TB. (pause) That was a . . . big disappointment for him.

"So, he had to go back home to Hyogo, and abandon his ambition to get into Ichiko. After he recovered his health, he went to Kansei Gakuin College, a private, Protestant school in Hyogo. He earned a degree there from the Commerce Department in 1923, I think it was. Anyway, Kansei Gakuin had an important influence on him. That is where he got interested in getting into business, overseas business, and also where he started picking up English. There were many foreign teachers there--ministers, I think. My father worked his way through school by helping one of these minister-teachers and living in his house.

"When he finished college, he had a strong desire to join the Suzuki Trading Company, at that time one of the fastest growing in the country. But again, just as he was about to take their examination, there was another . . . misfortune. Suzuki Trading Company went bankrupt. This delayed him for some time, but before too long the Iwai Trading Company grew out of the remains of Suzuki and he joined Iwai.

"The top management at Iwai seems to have taken a liking to my father--very quickly. He was an unusually hard worker. Very thorough and conscientious. A few years after he joined Iwai, about 1927, they sent him to work in their London branch. He worked there for seven years, became very good at English, and established himself as an expert young salesman. He was in charge of the sales of celluloid products made by Dai Nippon Celluloid. Now they are Daicel Chemical Industries. This selling of celluloid products is what led him into film and photograhic products.

"In the early 1930s, our government decided that for military reasons we should manufacture our own photo film here in Japan. So, the government subsidized a new division of Dai Nippon Celluloid to make photo film. In 1934, this new division split off and became Fuji Photo Film. When the company was formed, my father was asked to join them and head up their marketing division. Eventually, he worked his way up to become president. (smiling) I won't give you all the details. I can see you are wondering how I fit into all this.

"Well, before he joined Fuji Photo Film, while he was still working for Iwai in London, he returned to Japan for some months and got married to my mother. Then he took her back to London with him, where I was born. I was in London only about eight months before he returned to Japan to take his new job. So, I grew up here in Tokyo.

(speaking very thoughtfully and slowly) "What I remember most about my father--you know he died in 1977--is his belief in hard work . . . in competence . . . and the toughness of his character. The setbacks in his childhood probably taught him that life can be . . . harsh. About competence and hard work . . . he told us many times that there are geniuses and competent men. A genius is born that way. It is a gift of nature and nothing to be proud of.

Competence is something you acquire yourself . . . by application and work. He valued competence more than genius. That was the standard by which he judged himself . . . and others . . . including his children. And he was a tough judge.

"Also, his early years at Fuji Photo Film had an important influence on him, that he passed on to us. That was when he became uncompromising on quality. Even though the government was backing Fuji Photo Film in the thirties, the company had a hard time selling their product and almost failed. The film they made was poor. The customers were used to Kodak quality. Being in charge of sales, my father knew what the customers thought, and what they wanted. For quite a few years, he was in the position of constantly having to apologize for the poor quality. It was embarrassing. So, he developed a very, very strong belief in the value of a quality product.

"My father's hero was Henry Ford, and his favorite book was Ford's *Today and Tomorrow*. (going to the bookshelf, and bringing the book back to us) This was published in 1926. (opening to a full page photo of Henry Ford) Here, you see he autographed this for my father. (flipping through pages replete with margin notes and underlined passages) The ideas from this book that my father really made his own were first of all, that the customer is king. You have to serve them, and be honest and straight. In the end, you can't fool them, and they are the ones who make or break your business. He also believed that one's own employees ought to be one's best customers. His favorite part of the book is Ford's writing on technicians. Ford thought technicians were indispensable, but he also said that they excelled at thinking of thousands of reasons why you can't produce a new design, a new product. The most important job of the manager, he said, is to listen to all these reasons, makes sure he understands them, and then to tell the technicians that they have to do the new design--and make it work. (shaking his head and smiling) You know, he kept this book at his bedside until the last moments of his life.

"My mother is from Kyoto, and has a very different family background. Her family is . . . literary and intellectual. They are a Doshisha family. Doshisha is an old, private Christian school in Kyoto. My grandfather on my mother's side taught English there.

My mother has two brothers and three sisters. With the exception of one aunt, they all went to Doshisha, starting in middle school. My mother graduated from Doshisha Higher School. They were a very close-knit family, and Doshisha was a very close-knit sort of school. There were usually teachers and writers at her home when she was a girl. It was a very lively, entertaining home.

"Her marriage to my father was arranged. They had never met before he returned to Japan from London to marry her. (pausing and smiling) My mother told us that when she first saw him, my father's London clothes made a strong impression on her. She got along well enough with his family. My mother felt that marriage is . . . something you build and develop. She said that it was fine to get married to someone you know very well and are in love with, but that is not the only way. There could be a good arranged marriage if the husband and wife begin by respecting each other, and on that basis they build their marriage and learn to love each other over the years. That is what she did.

"My mother's Doshisha background is what influenced her to send us to Keio--which is also a private school, you know. She felt that a good private school is more cultivated, more liberal than a public school. Hmm. (very thoughtfully) You see, my mother had great respect for my father--for what he had accomplished, in spite of family hardship and setbacks. But I think she felt that his difficult life . . . his struggle to succeed . . . had left him too harsh . . . and that his way of measuring and judging people was perhaps too narrow and strict. She believed that a good, private school like Keio would give us a liberal education and broad, liberal values."

Question: "Was your education left to your mother to decide?"

"Yes, it was. My father was so busy in his work at that time that he left our education mainly in her hands. I think he favored the more competitive public schools, and felt that private schools might spoil us, especially the boys. But, he let her decide."

Question: "Since her father taught English, and she lived in England for about a year at the time you were born, I suppose that your mother was also good at English, and that helped you to learn English?"

(chuckling) "You might think so, but her English has never been that good. She has an active, lively mind . . . but I do not think my mother is a brilliant linguist. The marvelous thing about her is that she is such an . . . extrovert. She likes to mix with people, get to know them (laughing) no matter what their language is. (in an affectionate, admiring tone) She has never minded her own poor English. She has always gone right ahead and chatted . . . and really communicates effectively. Not at all shy. (pause) You know enough about Japan to realize how unusual that is . . . especially for a woman of her generation."

WAR AND SURRENDER

Question: "Would you care to tell me what you remember of the war years?"

"My memories go back to the late thirties, when I was in kindergarten, and the Sino-Japanese War was going on. We lived in the Omori district here in Tokyo, one of the better residential neighborhoods. (wrinkling his brow, thinking back) I have a clear memory of a neighborhood victory celebration, at night, with glowing lanterns. It was for our victory at Nanking.

"I learned years later how difficult things were at Fuji Film in those days for my father, but at home, we had . . . a very comfortable, secure life. My mother sent me to a kindergarten in Omori that was probably the first in Japan to prepare its students for the entrance examination to grammar school. Just a few boys and girls were chosen for this instruction--including me. So, I did well on the Keio Grammar School entrance test, and I got in even though I had no Keio relatives. In those days, about half of the Keio Grammar School had Keio relatives, so it was possible for an outsider to get in. (shaking his head and smiling) Nowadays, it is almost 100 percent Keio related students. Hmm. I liked grammar school, very much. I liked my teachers and the other boys.

"When I was in second grade, the Pacific War broke out. It didn't change my life much, not at first. But I remember the start of the war because until then, my family and friends called me Tony-- the name I had been given in England, as a baby. And we used to

call our parents Papa and Mama. But very soon after the war started, my father gathered us in our dining room--it was a western style
room--and told us that we must devote ourselves to making Japan
united and victorious. Hmmm. Being so international, I wonder if
he had his own ideas about the war? Well, if he did, he never
showed them. 'So,' he said, 'we must stop using English names
and words. No more Papa and Mama. From now on, you must
call us *Otohsan* (father) and *Okahsan* (mother). No more Tony.
You are Yotaro.' The boys at my school wore their hair fairly long.
My father looked at me and said, 'Go to the barber and get a short
haircut.' (smiling and shaking his head at the memory) I was
something of a rebel. I put off going. A few days later, he saw that
I still had long hair. He was irritated and took me to the barber
himself and had it cut--very short. In fact, he had my head shaved.
(both laughing)

"I was a happy-go-lucky type of boy, and a bit defiant,
while my father was a . . . disciplinarian. During the war, when our
school bus went by the Imperial Palace, we were all supposed to
bow toward it to show respect. But I didn't bow. He found out
about it and gave me some stern lectures.

"He also made it clear to me that as the eldest child, I had a
special duty and had to be more serious. My mother's eldest sister
and her family lived in Tokyo, also very comfortably. I was close
to her daughter and son, my cousins, and often stayed at their home.
One day, when my whole family was visiting with them, my aunt
jokingly said, as we were leaving, 'Tony-chan, you stay with us so
often that you are almost like one of my own children. One day,
why don't you become our child?' I liked my aunt and I wanted to
be diplomatic, so I said, 'I will think about it.' Everyone laughed.
It was a joke, and I was only about eight years old. But when we
got home, my father called me in to see him and scolded me severely. 'You are the eldest son. You have to think seriously about what
you say. This talk of joining another family is not funny--not a
subject for joking.' He was . . . extremely stern with me.

"In 1941-1942, in the early days of the war, I didn't take it
at all seriously. It was like an adventure . . . a movie. I was fascinated by the military--armies, tanks, and airplanes. When I was in
the third or fourth grade, in 1943, when I was nine, I noticed a

change . . . of tone. The radio was still reporting victories, but also reported heavy Japanese losses and casualties. My father's working hours became so long that we saw very little of him.

"In 1944, when I was in the fifth grade, the bombing in Tokyo started to become heavier, and the fourth, fifth, and sixth grade of Keio Grammar School were moved to Shuzenji, a hot spa resort on the Izu Peninsula. A very pleasant, scenic place. Tokyo hadn't been bombed much at that time, and when we left from Tokyo Station, we felt like it was an excursion. We were just a little sad, but only because we were going away from our parents. But they came to see us almost every weekend at Shuzenji, and to enjoy the spa. As the bombing worsened in Tokyo, there was very little hot water for bathing, and so when they came to see us it was a holiday for them, too. So, we were well off in Shuzenji, until the winter of '44-'45, when some of your planes even started bombing the towns around Shuzenji. Then, in January 1945, our school was relocated in Aomori, way up in northern Honshu.

"My father didn't want our family split up in different parts of Japan, so I didn't go to Aomori. I joined the rest of our family at my grandfather's house in Miyazu, another lovely seaside spot. (Miyazu is in Kyoto Prefecture, on the Japan Sea coast, close to Ama-no-Hashidate, one of the three most scenic places in Japan.) I stayed there until late 1945, the better part of a year. I went to the local school, along with about twenty other city boys whose families had come to Miyazu. School was a kind of . . . battleground, between the country boys and city boys. We were completely outnumbered . . . (laughing) but I was able to hold my own with the local boys because back at Keio, I had become good at a game they played. It was called 'pulling off the cap.' We all had red and white caps, and the object of the game was to take off everyone else's cap while you kept on your own. (smiling) Unlike most Japanese, the back of my head protrudes quite a bit, and it was easier for me to keep my cap on. (both laughing)

(pause and then in a serious tone) "I remember the Surrender on August 15, 1945, very clearly. My grandfather, my mother, one uncle, and my aunt were there in the room with the radio. The reception in Miyazu was bad. We could hardly hear the emperor's voice, there was so much crackling and static. But we all knew what it was. They all wept. About an hour later I was called to school and the Miyazu schoolmaster, also in tears, told us that the war was over. (pause) My own feeling was . . . just an emptiness. I could not weep. I was not surprised. There was talk of an American invasion, and my class had been called on to sharpen bamboo spears and dig some holes. The people around Miyazu were getting ready to move to caves, to keep on fighting. I didn't think we could fight very well . . . that way. But I didn't really understand what the Surrender meant . . . to lose a war. (long, thoughtful pause)

"Two months later, in October, we moved back to Tokyo. Most of the city was literally leveled to the ground by bombing. You have probably seen photos of it. (I nodded assent) Fortunately, our neighborhood in Omori was not badly hit. Our home and our street were . . . undamaged. So, unlike most people, we were able to move back into our home. Very fortunate."

Question: "Yes, that was unusual and lucky. Do you remember any shortages--especially a scarcity of food?"

"Hmm. Not in Tokyo. But the food in Miyazu, in 1945, had not been good. Very little rice. We had to eat potatoes most of the time . . . mixed with strange-tasting vegetables . . . that tasted like leaves. (pause) But there was enough, even then."

Question: "How do you think the war affected you-- your values and your perspective?"

(thoughtful pause) "I don't think it affected me . . . very deeply . . . compared to many others. I didn't suffer any real danger or hardship . . . personally . . . in my family or at school. The war may have had some effect on me . . . but not very much. (pause) We were . . . very fortunate."

THE OCCUPATION AND SCHOOL DAYS

Question: "How did your life go back in Tokyo, during the Occupation?"

"It was comfortable and smooth. Our family was well off, even then, and I don't remember any suffering. Fuji Film made a very quick comeback after the war, and my father was well off. We didn't lack food . . . or anything else.

"I went right back into Keio Grammar School. My homeroom teacher, who had liked me and had treated me as the class leader, treated me somewhat harshly for about two months. He criticized me for little things. You see, he was irritated at me for not sticking with the class when they evacuated to Aomori. But he got over that and in a short time our class became close and friendly again.

"When I graduated in 1946, I was the class valedictorian. My parents were very proud . . . but I think that at thirteen, I was a little too conceited. I took it for granted that I would be at the top of my class and the class leader. (thoughtfully) At the same time, being treated that way taught me to take responsibility for the whole class . . . to act like a leader."

Question: "How did the Occupation education reforms, the new teachings about democracy, affect your education?"

"Those reforms did not change things much at Keio. Even during the war, we had gotten a liberal, open-minded education. Our homeroom teacher, Mr. Kawamura, was a calligrapher. (smiling fondly) He was terrible at calligraphy . . . and weak at sports. But he was a cultivated, open-minded man. He was born in Kanda, an old, old neighborhood in Tokyo, in a family of traditional *geta* (wooden clog) makers. More than anything else, Mr. Kawamura was a patriot of Edo (traditional name for Tokyo), and he taught us a great deal about Edo history and art. He insisted that we write well. He also believed in being genuine and straightforward about . . . everything. He took us to visit every part of Tokyo--even the Yoshiwara redlight district. (laughing) One day each year, Yoshiwara was open to the public--to walk through. On that day, Mr. Kawamura marched us through, a class of eleven year old boys, to see this traditional Edo neighborhood. (both laughing) When he showed us old Edo prints, he used to leave some of Utamaro's pornographic pictures. Well, if our parents had known, they would have been . . . quite upset. So you see, our education at Keio Grammar School did not become noticeably more liberal under the Occupation. (both laughing)

"Then, I went into Keio Junior High School, which had become a three year course under the Occupation reforms. Again, I graduated as valedictorian. But it wasn't all study. (smiling at the memory) At that time, in the late forties, dozens of specialized movie houses opened here, showing English, French, and American films. I spent hours and hours enjoying those movies. My other hobby was baseball. I took up baseball and got quite good at it. We had a strong team--the Atoms. I pitched.

"Well, between study, baseball, and movies, the three years at junior high school seemed to go by quickly, and I went right on into Keio High School . . . in 1949. The classes in high school were much bigger than before. The three year high school had about 2700 students, about 900 in each year. The year I entered, we were divided into eighteen classes. So the atmosphere was much different from what I was used to . . . much more impersonal . . . and I remember feeling a bit lost there. The school was made up of three former middle schools. The main section were students preparing for college. A second section were getting commercial training, and a new third section were being trained for industry. I was the representative of the main section, and I served on the student government.

"About that time, my family moved to Setagaya, another comfortable neighborhood here in Tokyo. I helped to organize a neighborhood baseball team, a mixture of students, storekeepers, repairmen, vegetablemen . . . whoever was good at baseball and wanted to play. (smiling and shaking his head at the memory) My mother didn't like that. She said, 'Why do you have to mix with all these . . . people?' But you know, my father didn't mind. (pause and then in a pedantic tone) Yukichi Fukuzawa, who founded Keio, taught us that, 'Heaven has not created man above man. All men are created equal.' That is what I used to tell my mother. She used to frown at me and say, 'Yes. That is a fine saying. But in real life, it is not true.' (both laughing)

"In high school, I also took up tennis. I played in a private club my first year and got strong enough to make the Keio team in my second year. (chuckling) Your movies led me into tennis, you know. My friends and I found out that the most beautiful actresses, Gloria Swanson, Elizabeth Taylor--liked to play tennis. We saw photos of them on the courts in California. We talked it over, and we decided that if we learned to play tennis, maybe someday we would have a chance to meet them on the courts. (both laughing)

"Keio was the number one high school team in Japan in those days, and the year I joined we were expected to win the championship again. But we didn't. We got overconfident going into the semifinals. We were talking about how to win the finals, and not even thinking about the Osaka team that we had to play that day. Of course, they beat us. That was an important lesson. The next year, when I was a senior, we won back our title."

Question: "How did you do scholastically in high school?"

(laughing) "I didn't graduate as valedictorian. (pause) I was fourth or fifth in my class."

KEIO UNIVERSITY AND TOKYO LAWN

"From Keio High School, in 1952, I went straight into the college. I selected the Economics Faculty. I did reasonably well in my courses, but I was on the tennis team and I spent more time on the courts than on my studies."

Question: "What courses did you take?"

"Let me see. Basic economics, logic, math, English, and French."

Question: "Were you good at foreign languages?"

"Not especially. I found the grammar . . . boring. I didn't pick up on languages until later. I'll tell you what college life was like, and how that happened. Toward the end of my sophomore year, I became . . . discontent with the tennis team . . . actually with the coach. I liked tennis, and I was playing well, but the coach . . . gave too many orders. He even ordered us to cut classes when it interfered with our practice. I thought that was . . . going too far. (long pause, looking thoughtfully out the window) There was another reason. I had a girlfriend, a good tennis player, and I enjoyed playing tennis with her on the private courts. Our Keio team was not allowed to play on private courts, unless our courts were under repair. That was my . . . unofficial reason.

"I went to our team captain, and I said that it was wrong for the coach to order us to cut class. Of course, I sometimes cut classes on my own. But I didn't like to be ordered to play hookey. I said that unless the coach stopped giving that order, I would have to quit the team. (pause) So, I left the team. I stayed on friendly terms . . . and practiced with them sometimes. But I was off. At first, I thought I had done the right thing. But after awhile, I realized that the unofficial reason had been important . . . too important. (pause) That bothered my conscience.

"As it turned out, leaving the team made a big difference in my life . . . much bigger than I expected. After quitting the Keio team, I joined the Tokyo Lawn Tennis Club, in Azabu. The rule there is that half the membership must be non-Japanese. I think you know that club, don't you? It hasn't changed since the 1950s--including the clubhouse and the old showers. (both laughing) Well, at Tokyo Lawn I was exposed for the first time to an international crowd, including many foreign businessmen. My father had been urging me to get serious about studying English, but apart from going to foreign movies, I wasn't. At Tokyo Lawn, I found that I needed English to talk and play with the non-Japanese. Some of them were fine players, and I wanted to get on the courts with them.

"General Maxwell Taylor was an avid player at Tokyo Lawn, and he used to hit with several young officers who were really top flight. Men like Grant Golden, and Noel Brown, who was rated in the top ten. Pat Stranahan was there, in the army. He is from the Champion Spark Plug Family in Toledo. So was Don Gregg, who is now an adviser for George Bush. They were fine tennis players and fine fellows, and very friendly . . . as soon as I could speak English with them. We played a lot of tennis. (laughing). They were tennis nuts . . . and Ivy Leaguers--Princeton, Columbia--or other good schools, like Williams. Don Gregg is a Williams graduate.

"I also got a look at diplomacy and international politics at Tokyo Lawn, because quite a few diplomats played there. Don Gregg was in your embassy in those days. One of the non-Japanese I enjoyed playing with was George Rastrovof, who was in the Soviet embassy. George was a good tennis player, a lot of fun, and he was always around the club, even during the week. As a student, I had free time during the week, and I used to play with him. What I didn't know was that George was a colonel in the Russian army, a key man in their Far East espionage network, and a Beria man. After Beria's fall from power, George's days were numbered. Around Christmas of 1955, a Soviet ice skating troupe came to Tokyo. George found out that the head of this troupe was actually a KGB agent, whose mission was to take him back to Russia. This all came to light the day after the club Christmas Party, the biggest social event of the year. George was not at the party, and two other men I knew were also not there, an American and a New Zealand diplomat. It seemed odd. The next morning, it was on the front page of the Asahi newspaper--'Red Army Colonel Seeks Asylum in USA.' (smiling at the memory) Well, if I hadn't joined Tokyo Lawn, I wouldn't have had the chance to meet these people.

(shaking his head and chuckling) "My father had been encouraging me to think about studying in the States, but I hadn't really been interested . . . until I joined Tokyo Lawn and met men like Pat Stranahan and Don Gregg. They were a few years older than me, all out of school, and I looked up to them. Then, I decided that it would be a good idea to get a graduate degree in business administration at a good East Coast school. (both laughing) Well, my early choice was Harvard Business School. Pat and Don talked me out of that and convinced me to apply to Wharton. They advised against Harvard unless I first got some real business experience or took an American undergraduate degree in business. I didn't like the sound of that. I was afraid that if I took a job in Japan after Keio, I would have trouble leaving it to go to graduate school. They told me that for someone like myself, fresh from college and without business experience, Wharton was the best bet. I applied to Wharton, and at the same time to Williams College, to audit as an undergraduate for a year in case Wharton turned me down. But Wharton took me, and off I went . . . to Philadelphia.

THE WHARTON SCHOOL

"I traveled from Yokohama to Long Beach in June of 1956, on a passenger freighter--as the only passenger. That was a long two weeks! I read all the books on that ship, including the comic books. (both laughing)

"When we docked at Long Beach, I was met by my American sponsors, the Bushnells--of Bushnell binoculars. Dave Bushnell was the founder of the company. My father knew him because Dave had some of his binoculars made in Japan at a subsidiary of Fuji Film. I stayed some days with the Bushnells at their home in Altadena. (pause) I had seen a lot of American movies, and I thought I knew what it was like, but when I saw America itself for the first time--those California freeways and superhighways, full of big, fast cars . . . those luxurious, big houses in Altadena and Pasadena . . . I was . . . awestruck. That is the most accurate way to describe my feelings.

"I flew from Los Angeles to New York, where the Iwai people--from my father's old firm--met me. They took me out to dinner at the Stockholm, for smorgasbord. I remember the name of the place because I had never seen anything like it. The variety . . . and the quantity of food. My life had been affluent, you know (laughing) but at the Stockholm, I had the feeling that there were no limits. America seemed . . . unbelievably rich.

"I took the train to Philadelphia, and then a cab to my dormitory on the Penn campus. On the way, I was preparing myself in my mind for a completely American life--no Japanese to talk to. But on my first day at the Penn dorm, I ran into Osamu Toba, who I knew from Tokyo Lawn. (smiling) We were relieved to see each other.

"My adviser talked me into taking my summer school courses for credit--which was not my original plan. He told me my English was good enough and that it was a waste of time to audit. So, I did what he said. Then our professors handed out our reading assignments . . . and I was stunned. I had to read one hundred or two hundred pages a day, in English, to keep up. What a change from Keio. For a couple of weeks, I was up reading late every night, and sometimes into the small hours of the morning. Exhausting. I didn't know whether I was going to make it through. Then, I learned how to read the introductions and conclusions with some care, and to skim most of the rest.

"Toba had the same problem. When we both learned how to deal with the reading, we decided that we needed some tennis . . . to relax. We looked at a Philadelphia map and saw that there was a tennis club not far from the campus. It had a strange name--the Germantown Cricket Club. We took the train, changed a few times, and arrived at the place. It was a hot, humid day and we were casually dressed in slacks and short-sleeved shirts. Well, the Germantown Cricket Club is not like our modest, unpretentious Tokyo Lawn. It is a huge, opulent place with a fine clubhouse. It was . . . imposing. At the entrance, there was a very serious, formally dressed man, who looked like one of those haughty English butlers. You know, it was by accident that we picked the Germantown CC off the map. We had no idea that it was such a rich, prestigious club. Well, Toba and I decided that, after all, we had come this far, so we should at least go in and see if we could play tennis.

"The butler asked us politely what we wanted. We told him that we were from Japan, were members of Tokyo Lawn, and we wanted to play tennis. 'Oh,' he said, 'you must know Mike. He's from Tokyo, too. I think he's here now. Maybe he can arrange a game for you.' He asked us to follow him. So Toba and I walked along through the oak paneled clubhouse, looking at each other and thinking the same thing. 'Mike? We don't know this Mike. This butler thinks that all the Japanese in Tokyo know each other.' We came out onto the courts, and the butler called out to a Japanese man. 'Hello Mike. Here are two friends of yours from Tokyo.' Mike came walking over and of course, we did know each other (chuckling)..not very well, but we knew each other. Mike's real name is Sakaniwa, and I had met him a few times playing tennis at the Hokuyu Tennis Club, a small, select club established by the Mitsui family. He was in his thirties, a Keio graduate, and he had been in the States six or seven years by then. He knew everybody at the Germantown CC. He was very friendly and helpful, arranged for us to play tennis and introduced us to his Mainline friends. That worked out beautifully--for tennis and for socializing.

"In the summer of '57, Toba and I both got jobs in New York, on Wall Street, and we shared a nice apartment on Central Park West. My job was with the Bank of America, in their Foreign Department. Iwai Trading helped me to get it. Even though I was only there for about two months, the Wall Street experience was useful.

"Wharton School was hard work. I did well enough at my courses--nothing brilliant--and I took an MBA degree in industrial management in June 1958. I also became the second president of the Foreign Students' Club, after Tony DelRosario, from the Philippines. Tony was a year ahead of me. I saw him recently in Manila, where he is a top man in his government's energy policy.

"At the end of the spring semester in '58, my last year at Wharton, I had an oral examination scheduled about a week after the written finals. Well, the day after I finished my written finals, I came down with a very uncomfortable . . . disabling condition . . . a collapsed lung. I somehow got myself to the hospital. The doctor told me what it was, and said that all I had to do was stay in bed, keep calm, and it would get better in a week or two. It would probably never happen again, he said, because collapsed lungs recur only in about 10 percent of the cases. As it turned out, I was in that 10 percent. But I remained quietly in bed, and it did clear up in about ten days. When Toba came to visit me in the hospital, I asked him to go to my professor and arrange a make-up on the oral I had to take. Toba came back and reported to me that I was lucky. The professor was satisfied with my papers and my written finals, and had given me a waiver on the oral. So, I really relaxed and stopped worrying about it. As soon as I got back on my feet, I went to see this professor, to thank him for the waiver. He listened to me, looked at me . . . somewhat strangely, and said that Toba must have misunderstood him. There was no waiver. I had to take the oral. (looking dismayed at the memory) I was . . . really shocked. But the professor called a few other faculty, set up the oral right there on the spot--and I passed it."

Question: "Did your training at Wharton in industrial management turn out to be useful? Has it helped in your work?"

(thoughtfully) "Yes, it has. I was lucky to go to Wharton just when I did. The industrial management curriculum at that time was built around the idea of solving production problems--carefully defining the problem, looking at different solutions and comparing them, and getting good, hard data to check the results. They gave us courses in factory management, time and motion studies, and statistical quality control. It was very basic, nothing fancy . . . but these are the same ideas that Fuji Xerox, and the rest of Japanese industry, still use. (smiling) They are not very different from the teaching of Edwards Deming. (pause) Well, a few years after I graduated from Wharton, the emphasis shifted to marketing and finance. But now, after a quarter of a century, I think they have come full cycle, and are getting back to what they taught me . . . production and quality control.

"I remember two of my teachers very well. One was an older man of about sixty, Mr. Murphy. He wasn't a professor. He was a long-time lecturer in American business history and business policy. Something of an institution in the department. He was my counselor, and we met fairly often in his office. Whenever I was discouraged about this course or that, he had a way . . . of getting me going again. The other was a fairly young man, Professor Adrian MacDonaugh, who taught statistical quality control. I was really impressed by his lectures. I keep in touch with Adrian, and we usually get together when I go to the Advisory Board meetings at Wharton.

"After graduation, I wanted to take a look at the country, and on my way home to Japan, I took a leisurely trip to the West Coast. I stopped and visited with the Stranahans, in Toledo. I had made reservations on the old Red Zepyhr, which ran from Chicago to San Francisco, so I went up to Chicago to catch my train. I had a very comfortable roomette, and the view of the Rockies was . . . really spectacular and beautiful. In Los Angeles, it was great to visit with the Bushnells again. Some friends of theirs took us to Long Beach, to see the Miss Universe contest. (chuckling) That is the kind of unexpected treat that a young man appreciates."

CHOOSING A CAREER

"I got back to Japan in September, and I had until April of '59 to find a job. At Wharton, I had written a paper on the Japanese auto industry, and I was thinking of going into it. My father got me started with introductions. Toyota banked with the Mitsui Bank, and my father took me to see Kiichi Sato, who was president of the bank. This led to other meetings with automobile people. One evening, while I was in this process of looking around and making up my mind, I was visiting with my sister's father-in-law, Mr. Inumaru. He was about twelve years older than my father, a very kind man who was president of the Imperial Hotel. We started talking about what I should do, and he said, 'Why don't you work for Fuji Film?'

"Well, I had thought about that and decided against it. I told him that I was against nepotism. My father was president of the company. Also, I said that my father was a self-made man, and I thought that he preferred his children to make their own way. Mr. Inumaru listened to my reasons, and then he said, 'Your father has helped to build Fuji Film up to its present state, and I think that he wants to see one of his sons continue in his path. You know, he has given you a fine education, and this is a way you can pay him back. Of course, it will not work unless you do a good job. You know your father's standards. The advantage for you is that you may move up quickly and do some really interesting work.'

"Mr. Inumaru was a . . . very serious man. I had to think about his advice. In the end, I went to talk it over with my father. I wanted to make sure that he didn't feel that he had been . . . somehow pressed into taking me into the company . . . because I was his son. (pausing to think back, a faraway look in his eyes) He didn't say very much. All he told me was that there was no rule in Fuji Film against family members joining the company. And he also told me that if there was some other job I preferred to take, I should take it. That was it. It was up to me.

"Well, I decided that what Mr. Inumaru had told me made sense. I joined Fuji Film."

Question: "In your own mind, how did you resolve the issue of nepotism?"

(in a serious, thoughtful tone) "I knew that my father would not be easy on me. If I showed some hard work and competence, he would probably give me a chance to be in a responsible job, as Mr. Inumaru said. But then it would be up to me. It would depend on how I performed. If I should ever prove ineffective . . . he wouldn't protect me. (pause) I was convinced of that."

FUJI XEROX CO., LTD.

"In 1958, I went to work in domestic marketing at Fuji Film. At that time, about 90 percent of our sales were in Japan, but the company wanted to expand its overseas business. Because of my training at Wharton, I was soon moved over to Overseas Operations and put to work on the North American section. I was readying myself for an assignment to our New York office. That was in . . . 1961. You know that Rank Xerox and Fuji Film had already agreed on their joint venture, but the negotiations were still going on about the technology and capital transfers.

"Sol Linowitz, who later became an ambassador, was chairman of the board at Xerox Corporation, and handled their international negotiations. He was in Tokyo, working on Fuji Xerox. So was Tom Law, the president at Rank Xerox. They were both staying in the old Imperial. Well, at that same time, one of my brothers was getting married, and the reception took place at the Peacock Room of the Imperial. Naturally, my parents invited Sol and Tom to the reception and asked them to sit at our family table. My father told me to sit next to them and interpret and explain what was going on--which I did.

"After the reception, Sol Linowitz casually asked me to join him for a cup of coffee up in his rooms. (smiling at the memory) Before we even had a chance to sit down, he said, 'Why don't you come over and join Fuji Xerox?' I was surprised and . . . baffled. I didn't think he could be serious. It was too casual. He kept looking at me for a moment or two and said, 'Well, what do you say?' (both laughing) Well, I didn't know what to say. I was gearing up for my New York assignment, and I had never given a thought to working for Fuji Xerox. I didn't know anything about it. But I knew that my father thought very highly of Sol, so I was polite and tactful. I thanked him. I said that he was very generous to make me an offer, and that I would have to think it over."

(half jokingly) Question: "Yes. Isn't that the same kind of tactful answer that you gave to your favorite aunt?"

(smiling) "Yes. But this time I was really adopted. (both laughing) Actually, nothing was decided for about a year. That was just the first step. Sol came back to Tokyo several times and repeated the offer to me . . . and to my father. He said that Fuji Xerox needed someone with my educational background, that I would be useful to the company--a bridge between the two cultures. It took me more than a year to make up my mind, and it was 1963 when I moved over to Fuji Xerox.

"There was no single reason for my move, but two reasons were most important. I had a special respect for Sol Linowitz. Even before his offer at the Imperial, my father had spoken at home about Sol, and about Tom Law and Joe Wilson, the Xerox President. My father had done a lot of business with foreigners, and he said that these men were . . . special kind of people . . . the best he had seen . . . truly competent, smart and honest. He didn't say things like that lightly. So, I had a deep respect for Sol Linowitz, and I was . . . deeply honored that he asked for me. Secondly, I was just turning thirty, about the same age my father had been when he left Iwai to join Fuji Film."

Question: "How much of a break was it . . . moving from Fuji Film to Fuji Xerox? It sounds as though many of the people in this joint venture may have come from Fuji Film."

"Hmm. That was true of a small number of . . . key people . . . at the beginning. But for the most part, Fuji Xerox had to recruit and set up a new team--a team of Japanese managers and engineers. When I joined them at the end of September '63, my first assignment was in the Planning Department. (pause) I haven't forgotten the . . . shock of my first weeks. Their offices were beneath the Tokyo expressway, and not at all fancy. Of course, they were a new company, just building up, so I understood that. But one day soon after I started working there I was invited to an engineers' meeting. (pause) Well, it was . . . rowdy. It was a noisy, rude meeting. You would never have met people like that at Fuji Film. By that time, Fuji Film was a well established, first rate company, and hired its employees from only a few, select universities. Fuji Xerox was . . . a different matter. After the meeting that day was finished, I asked myself, 'What kind of company is this? Have I really made the right decision?' "

MARRIAGE AND LONDON

"Earlier that month, in September 1963, I married. My wife's maiden name was Momoyo Matsumoto. Her father was a professor of philosophy at Keio. Her grandfather was a law professor at Todai, and also a well known businessman. He was involved in drafting the postwar Constitution."

Question: "Oh yes. I think I remember the Matsumoto draft. Didn't General MacArthur reject it . . . as too conservative?"

(smiling) "That's the man. Joji Matsumoto. Have you read MacArthur's autobiography? He didn't write in very friendly terms about Joji Matsumoto. (laughing) By the way, Joji Matsumoto also headed the Manchurian Railroad at one time.

"Anyway, I met my wife through my sister, who was a year behind her at Sacred Heart. They were friends there and played tennis together. Our families had known each other for years, and that is the way we met. Of course, we had played a lot of tennis."

Question: (pause) "Was your wife . . . the unofficial reason you left the high school team?"

(laughing) "No, no. That was before I knew her. So, we married in September, when I had decided to change my job, but hadn't done it yet. We had been dating for about a year, when I proposed to her . . . and she accepted. But there were complications. Her parents were abroad at the time, on a two or three-month trip to Beirut and Rome. I had to write a letter to them asking for their permission. My wife had also agreed to take a job in Switzerland for a year, and had a contract with a firm in Zurich. So, she asked me to write to them, too . . . to disentangle her."

Comment: "I was going to ask you if your marriage was arranged. But obviously . . . you did all the arranging yourself." (both laughing)

"Well, we did have an official go-between, at the wedding. It was Mr. Kiichi Sato, the man from the Mitsui Bank. That was a traditional touch. And we had our reception in the Peacock Room at the old Imperial.

"Before I joined Fuji Xerox, I had agreed that we would go to London that winter, to work at Rank Xerox for about a year, learning the trade. So, my wife and I left for London in December and made it into a kind of honeymoon trip. We stopped to see friends in Manila and Bombay, spent some delightful days in Athens . . . and then on to London, where Tom Law and his wife were kind enough to meet us. Tom was a fine gentleman. His wife had found us a charming flat, a kind of penthouse, in the heart of West End, not far from Rank Xerox. We settled down there for what turned out to be a fourteen month stay.

"People said that 1964 was the best weather in Europe in one hundred years--warm and sunny--not typically English at all. (laughter) Thanks to my father and other friends, London was very open and friendly to us. We met all kinds of fine people, including some prominent people, and my wife and I really enjoyed it. Our English friends taught us to love the theater and music. Ronnie Leach was very kind to us. He was the head of Peat, Marwick, Mitchell & Company in the U.K., and handled the Rank accounts. He had not been knighted yet. (smiling and in a very happy tone) Sir Ronnie and Lady Leach took a liking to us, and treated us as though we were . . . their own children. And their children were warm and friendly to us, as well. We have remained very close to them. Lady Leach is . . . special. Full of energy, stamina and . . . fun. She told us that she was tired of being godmother to boys. She told my wife to have a girl . . . and she would be godmother to that girl. When we got back to Japan and had our first child, it was a girl, (laughter) and Lady Leach was as good as her word. (smiling warmly)

"I did a lot of work that year and learned something about the Xerox business. It was hard work, but enjoyable. The initial plan was to stay in London about nine months, but Rank Xerox decided I ought to stay on a few months longer and asked me to extend my stay. Well, I went to the Alien Office to apply for an extension on my work permit. After standing in a long queue, I finally reached the lady at the counter--a staunch British type. I told her that I wanted to extend my stay for another four months. She checked some records, looked hard at me and asked me where I was born. I told her London. She said, 'Yes. I thought so.' She stared at me for awhile longer and then said, 'Why are you here . . . in this building?' I explained, very patiently, that I needed an extension on my Alien Work Permit. 'Sir, you are *not* an alien. You were born here. You can work anywhere you like for as long as you like. Now, please stop wasting our time.'" (much laughter)

COMPETING IN JAPAN

"When I came back to Japan in 1965, I continued to work in Planning for a short time, and then in 1966, I moved over to Marketing. In '68, I became a member of our board, and the next year I took charge of Marketing, Planning and Publicity. In 1976, I was promoted to executive vice-president. Our president at that time was Mr. Yoshimura--Kazuo Yoshimura--a very fine, warm-hearted man, and a good leader. At that time, my father was chairman of both Fuji Xerox and Fuji Photo Film. Then, in 1977, he died very suddenly. He was just back from a summer holiday at Karuizawa, having an ordinary day. He had dinner with my mother, went to bed, and died in his sleep. (pause) Early in 1978, Mr. Yoshimura replaced my father as chairman of Fuji Xerox, and I moved up to become president. In 1980, Mr. Yoshimura retired from active management. The chairmanship of our board has been officially vacant since then, so I have been acting chairman."

Question: "What were the most important or influential experiences in your career--the ones that shaped your business outlook and values?"

(long, thoughtful pause, and then smiling) "You know, most of my career has been . . . uneventful. (laughter) No, no. That's true. It was mostly a smooth, upward path. I was lucky to join Fuji Xerox when I did. It grew so quickly . . . and I benefited from its rapid growth. Most of the time, I just had to work hard, avoid foolish mistakes, and things went quietly ahead . . . in the right direction.

"I'm not the kind of person who agonizes over his family background or whether he is really good enough. I concluded long ago that there is nothing one can do about such things. (smiling again) So, I just take things as they come, do my best . . . and hope they turn out well.

"There has been only one big challenge so far that I have had to face. That was after the Middle East War of 1973. It was just at that time that I found myself assuming quite a bit of responsibility in the company, and our future became very shaky . . . possibly disastrous. Until 1974-1975, we dominated the copy machine market in Japan. Our customers at that time used to say that Fuji Xerox is expensive, but it is the best. So, they were content with us, and we were getting on comfortably (laughing) a bit too comfortably. Then, the oil price crisis hit our economy. Many of our customers were caught in the price squeeze, and they decided that they had to cut their costs . . . even if meant giving up quality. When I met them in those days, they told me that to make ends meet they were going to have to switch temporarily to one of our competitors. Just for a year or two--until the economy got back on an even keel. When they could afford the best again, they would return to Fuji Xerox. (shrugging his shoulders) Well, what could we say? We told them we were looking forward to their return. But by 1976, we could see that they weren't coming back."

Question: "I looked over your sales and profits for the middle and late '70s, and noticed that while your profits slipped slightly in 1974 and 1976, your total sales were increasing moderately even in those years. Why did you feel that the future was so . . . shaky?"

(incisively) "Market share. Our market share was dropping year by year. That is the most important indicator.

"I heard what was happening from our old customers when I met with them, and I heard the same story from our marketing people. Our former customers had found that the inexpensive, supposedly low quality machines of our competitors were almost as good as ours . . . in some ways even better. They said, 'We like these machines. We like the quality and we like the price. Unless you drastically improve your product and get down your prices, we have no intention of coming back to Fuji Xerox.' (in a very serious tone) When you hear that . . . you know you have a serious problem.

"Well, in '76, I had just been promoted to executive vice-president. I was responsible not only for marketing, but planning and manufacturing . . . the whole thing. One of our executives, a very strong, honest man, had a frank talk with me. He told me that in order to get back on track, we needed to change our whole attitude, our whole way of thinking. He urged me to talk with Professor (Tetsuichi) Asaka of Tokyo University--a professor emeritus of mathematics and statistical quality control. This man had been working with us as a consultant in some limited areas of engineering and manufacturing, but I had never met him. He also worked with some very successful companies, such as Toyota and Bridgestone.

"Well, I went to see him and asked for his guidance and advice. (pause) Professor Asaka gave me the . . . brushoff. He was polite, but pretty clear. He said, 'I have never encountered a company that is as slow moving and as self-satisfied as Fuji Xerox. In fact, I was just about to stop doing consulting work for you . . . because it is harming my reputation.'

"I asked him to please change his mind and give us another chance, for at least six months. (pause) Professor Asaka taught me, and our whole company, some very basic lessons. First, he said we had to stop all our feuding and backbiting--upper management blaming middle management--middle management criticizing upper management. The upper management--including myself-- were responsible for hiring everyone in the company. We had to take full responsibility . . . and lead. That meant that we had to decide what needed to be done to make us an effective competitor again. And then we had to stick to that goal and that plan, and *not* let ourselves get sidetracked. Professor Asaka's strongest quality was . . . basic common sense. He said it would be fairly simple to decide what we needed to do. The problem would be to get everybody really working on it, in a single-minded way.

"I asked him to come to our next top management meeting. It was a review of our previous year's performance by our executive board members. He agreed, but only if there would be no other staff or secretaries. He wanted everyone to talk freely. Well, he listened quietly to all the reports--from marketing, engineering, personnel, and so on. When they were all finished, he said, 'Mr. Kobayashi, if you think this has been a real review of your past year . . . well, that is the basis of your problem. You all seem fairly happy with your reports. No wonder your company is in trouble.'

(smiling grimly) "I don't have to tell you that some of our directors were shocked and angry. 'What does this professor know about our business? Has he been making copy machines for fifteen years?' But Asaka was right. They were protecting themselves. I said that I agreed with the professor. He was right. We were in trouble, and if we really wanted to get out of trouble we had no alternative but to do the things he said and to work with him . . . if he would work with us.

"Professor Asaka got us to talk about what we needed to do to win back market share. Our marketing people knew the answer. So did I. The customers wanted a better product than they could buy from our competitors and they wanted it at a comparable price. Very simple . . . but painful. Looking at profit rates and at market trends, we could see that we had only a few years to make a comeback--to get a superior, price competitive product on the market.

"Those of us in marketing had a pretty good idea of what we needed. If we could give the customers a machine that would make 2400 copies per hour and was in the price range of machines that made 1500 copies per hour, they would want it and buy it. But other companies knew this too, so we had to get there first, way out ahead. We agreed that meant getting it on the market in two years. Simple enough . . . but our engineers said it was impossible. They had a four year cycle for developing a new product. They said that every step in that development cycle was essential. (pause) Of course, they could take short cuts . . . but then they couldn't answer for the results."

Question: "Yes. Again, protecting themselves?"

(laughing) "Exactly. (serious again) It was life or death for Fuji Xerox, and they had two years--not four. Well, we had three to four months of very tough meetings. The engineering people came around. I don't think it was our top management that convinced them. The market realities did it. While we were having these meetings, our market performance continued to worsen. They would have to do something drastic, or we would simply go down the chute.

"Well, some of the more aggressive, risk-taking engineers came up with a new design and a development plan. They had taken out all the extra margins they put in for delays and mistakes, you see, and they had a design, a development schedule and a production schedule that could give us the machine we needed, at the right price, in less than two years."

Question: "Did you have to make many personnel changes to bring this about?"

"Hmmm. I had to make a few, but not many. Basically, we had our same management team, at all levels, and our same work force, too. I made it clear that I was personally involved in this product. I was constantly visiting the development site, and so was President Yoshimura. We had a top management review session on its progress every week. It was a matter of . . . continuous prodding. But everybody from top to bottom knew that this new machine was top priority, and that the company's future depended on it.

"There was a period when we worked through the weekends, week after week . . . for some months. And there were times when our development group stayed at the plant overnight. At one point, President Yoshimura called to check on our progress and he found that we were working very late--in fact, staying at the plant that night. His health was not very strong, but he came to the plant from the head office in Tokyo, and stayed until the work was done.

"Fortunately, this product, the FX 3500, was a success. It came out in 1978, (smiling widely) and it was a smash hit in the market place. The customers liked it and they bought it. It was very fast, high quality, quiet, dependable, and well priced. (pause) It is the best-selling machine in our company history. The 3500 got us back on our feet."

Question: "Wasn't it also the 3500 that led to your company winning the Deming Award in 1980?"

"It was a big factor. When I became president in 1978, I told Professor Asaka that I wanted us to try for the Deming Award for Quality Control. He thought that if we could get the entire company, every factory, every office, up to the level of effectiveness we had reached during the work on the 3500, we might be able to compete successfully. We used the concept of Total Quality Control-- extending statistical quality control beyond manufacturing into every phase of our operations. (pause) You know, the Deming Committee inspects and cross-checks everything--every plant and office, to see how well it performs its function and also how well it coordinates with other parts of the company. Gearing up for the Deming competition was . . . as demanding and as much hard work as the 3500.

"My own feeling is that the key to our improved performance was this single-minded determination to get things right and team work--everybody helping everybody else. In developing the 3500 and holding down costs, the designers, engineers, and production people all worked together. They all listened to each other and they worked to get the machine we needed--at the price we needed. Basically, it is simply an extension of the idea of listening to the customers and meeting their requirements. The designers and engineers think of the production people as their customers.

(smiling) "Of course, our Japanese competitors have not been standing still watching us. They came along very quickly . . . to catch up. The competition is relentless. We have to keep pushing for better products and lower costs. There is always a point in the curve where it seems like you can't get more of both. Then you need a new approach, a new technology, a new material."

INTERNATIONALIZATION

Question: "What are the international dimensions of your business--of Fuji Xerox?"

"Our international business has two sides. One is in the Far East--in Korea, Indonesia, Thailand, the Philippines and Taiwan. This side accounts for less than 10 percent of our business. We export some of our products to them. But some of these countries--like Korea and Taiwan--have their own factories, and in addition to producing for themselves, the trend is to make some components and parts for us, as well.

"The other side is our business with Xerox and Rank Xerox. This accounts for between 20 percent and 25 percent of our business. We now export a large number of our machines and components to Xerox and Rank Xerox. These are our multinational accounts.

"Our relationship with Xerox and Rank Xerox has changed steadily changed over the past ten years. Before the late seventies, we were entirely at the receiving end. They furnished us our technology, management and marketing guidance and information, for which we paid royalty. But since '78-'79, we have been supplying them with certain machines--such as the successors to the 3500 and big facsimile machines . . . and even some management software on quality management.

"The FX 3500 was a turning point. Rochester and London were skeptical. The way we went about developing the 3500 went directly against their ideas of sound engineering and business. But when it worked, they accepted the results . . . very quickly. And I respect them for their honesty. They saw that we had cut the development cycle in half, from four years to two, and were producing and selling a high quality machine for $2000 per unit that they could not produce for less than $4000 per unit. Well, Xerox and Rank Xerox sent study teams here to find out how we did it. They have been able to adopt some of our methods. But it has been more difficult and slower than they expected. Differences between our cultures--national cultures and business cultures--and between the size of our operations have accounted for this. We employ about eleven thousand people, while Xerox employs about one hundred thousand. There is a lot of inertia in something that big . . . and it naturally takes more time to turn it around.

"Our relationship with Xerox in many respects is a microcosm of the Japan-U.S. relationship since 1945. In the sixties and seventies, Fuji Xerox was so small in comparison with Xerox, that whatever we did or didn't do, they didn't pay too much attention, and it didn't raise serious issues. Now, we are still much smaller, but we are challenging some of their capabilities and we are also an important part of their business. Our relationship now takes much more careful management . . . and sensitivity. Overall, both sides are better off . . . but there are many more frictions. For example, in 1983, the Rochester plant layed off some people. These people concluded-- wrongly concluded--that Fuji Xerox had put them out of work--that we were the villains. And on our side, we have to avoid sounding arrogant. (pause) I can tell you from my own experience that language problems aggravate these misunderstandings. In times like this, we need sophistication . . . and nuances. Often we don't get it. Not because of ill will, but language problems give us . . . oversimplifications.

"On the Far Eastern side, we have a different set of issues and we have to think differently. Countries like Korea and Taiwan, the NICs (newly industrialized countries), are coming up very fast and quickly gaining confidence in their ability to produce and compete. They know they can produce some things better than we can. They are sometimes very . . . nationalistic . . . even at the cost of economic common sense. They are very sensitive about pressures and orders from Japanese. (pause) I think that we have to be sympathetic with them. And we have to be honest and straight. No tricks, no funny stuff. We have to show them that we want to work together, to cooperate for the long-term future.

"Our business in the Far East is closely tied in with our suppliers here in Japan, who have been making 60 percent to 70 percent of our parts. As we go off-shore for more and more components, we don't want to damage our Japanese suppliers. We have had long, productive, happy relationships with them. So, we are looking for ways to work together with them in going to places like China and Taiwan, or Singapore. I think we will be able to work that out."

Question: "Based on your own experience in doing international business, how do you define the term internationalization?"

"Hmm. For me . . . it is fairly simple. Internationalization is the process of understanding the differences between your own culture and way of doing things and foreign cultures and behavior, and then deciding when you should adopt or conform to their ways and when it is better to stick to your own."

Question: "Yes, that sums it up very well. Japan and Fuji Xerox have been engaged in this process very intensively and successfully. Do you expect the process of internationalization to continue on into the next century, or do you see obstacles and possibly reverse trends setting in?"

"I see our internationalization continuing--with more and more Japanese being exposed to the non-Japanese world and learning to deal with it. (pause) But the process will not be as smooth as it was in the past. (emphatically) That is very clear to me. It is just a matter of relative capabilities . . . and size. When Japan's capabilities were weak, as they were in fifties and sixties, it was easy to see the superiorities of American technology, for example, and it was simple, common sense to see the advantages of learning that technology. And in those days your country was an enthusiastic teacher and model for us . . . because we were not seen as a competitor. Our output was so small that we had . . . an insignificant impact on other countries.

"Now our capabilities are closer and it is not always as easy as it was to decide whether to follow a foreign model or whether to create our own. And because our capabilities and our impact have grown, we Japanese are expected to bear more responsibility for the whole international economy--for what is going on in other countries.

"It is easy to talk about these abstractions, but these changes create very serious and painful . . . psychological problems. The Japanese are so used to being a small fish in the pond, just scrambling to stay alive, that it is very difficult to accept international responsibilities. And some people in America and Europe just won't accept Japan's achievements in a positive way. They insist on seeing Japan as a threat, a dangerous threat. Well, in these circumstances, the process of internationalization is bound to generate disagreements and frictions.

"The main problem, it seems to me, is how to manage these natural disagreements and irritations--not to let them get out of hand. (pause) You know that Fuji Xerox lives in a highly competitive world, and I am not against competition. But I sometimes worry these days that competition and competitiveness can be carried too far and can become . . . childish and destructive. This is true on both sides of the Pacific. Our economic achievements have led some Japanese to act . . . arrogantly . . . like someone who has won a big game, you know. And some Americans are acting as though they lost the big game . . . and are trying to prove that the other side cheated. Of course, international business and economics don't work that way.

"Well, I am repeating a point, but I don't mind making it again. I am confident that we can keep building our relationship into the future, and that both our countries . . . and other countries as well . . . will continue to benefit, if we avoid getting carried away with these . . . childish oversimplifications."

Tokio Kanoh

TOKIO KANOH is a general manager in the Tokyo Electric Power Company (Tepco), which produces 32 percent of Japan's electrical energy and is the largest privately owned power company in the world.[1] After the United States, Japan is the second largest energy consumer in the world, but its pattern of consumption is different than the American pattern. The Japanese use slightly less than half as much energy per capita, and electricity plays a bigger role in Japan. In recent years, about 20 percent of the total energy consumed in Japan has been electrical, compared to 15 percent in the United States. In industrial energy use, the divergence has been even more pronounced and is growing. Japanese factories get 26 percent of their energy from electricity, while in the United States the figure is 18 percent.[2] The main reason for these differences is that Japan has been more rapidly reducing its dependence on fossil fuels--which are virtually all imported (99 percent)--by using its water power to the full and by rapidly developing nuclear energy. Water power and nuclear power translate into electricity. Moreover, this trend is part of a larger, cooperative industrial policy sponsored by the government and private industry, which is moving Japan away from energy-intensive heavy and chemical industries toward knowledge intensive, sophisticated electronics. As Japan moves into the 21st century, electricity is expected to become its most important form of energy.

When I interviewed Tokio Kanoh he was the director of the Electric Power Pavilion at the Tsukuba Expo 85, an elaborate international science fair set in the midst of the rice fields, about an hour

---

1. *Electric Power Industry in Japan 1985* (Tokyo: Japan Electric Power Information Center, Inc., January 1986), 3.
2. *Energy Balances of OECD Countries* (Paris: International Energy Agency, OECD, 1985), 77, 121.

A recent photo.

With Tokyo University classmates, 1953.

Back row: Kenji (second son), Nobuko Katoh (elder daughter), Naoko (second daughter), Ayako (wife). Front row: Mr. and Mrs. Katoh (son-in-law's parents), Yachiyo (mother), Takao (elder son), Tokio Kanoh.

by train and cab, north of Tokyo. Mr. Kanoh was one of the planners and organizers of the Expo. He chaired two of its committees and worked actively on five others, ranging from Site Planning to Uniform Design. I met with him at his airy, spacious Expo offices on a sunny, breezy day in May 1985. Outside the full-length, second-story windows, the Expo was teeming with thousands of visitors, most of them neatly uniformed school children who had come on class trips from all over the country. There were also a number of foreigners visible, including a half dozen middle-aged Chinese industrial planners who were sipping tea in the Electric Power Pavilion VIP lounge, while one of Mr. Kanoh's executive staff discussed power plants with them.

Tokio Kanoh has the tanned, ruddy complexion and the lithe, energetic bearing of a middle-aged sportsman. His expression is open and direct. He smiles often and speaks in a deep, musical voice. It is easy to picture him as a sociable, popular student at Tokyo University in the 1950s, organizing and singing in the Midorikai Chorus. His classmates liked him so well that they elected him conductor for life of the Midorikai Old Boys' Chorus, a position that he greatly relishes. He is a good mixer.

Beneath the tan and the charm, however, there is another Tokio Kanoh--a meticulous, industrious executive who has worked his way up through the Tepco ranks, and now sits on the influential and prestigious energy and scientific committees which are sponsored by the ministries of Foreign Affairs, Finance, and International Trade and Industry (MITI). From 1978 to 1980, Mr. Kanoh was an advisor to Prime Minister Masayoshi Ohira, and served on his Policy Research Committee. He is also vice-chairman of the Technical Committee on Energy Conservation of the International Energy Agency of OECD, and an active member of the Energy Task Force of the Pacific Economic Cooperation Committee. Moreover, Mr. Kanoh is author, co-author, or editor of ten books. Most of them are on energy related topics, such as *Proposals for the 21st Century* (1978), and *Energy Strategy for Japan* (1981), both of which he wrote. Finally, he is a college teacher. He regularly offers courses on international relations and energy policy at Todai, and in 1980 he was invited to teach at Harvard for a semester.

In several crucial respects, Tokio Kanoh's background and experience are typical of Tepco's senior executives. He attended a prestigious Tokyo higher school and graduated from the Todai Faculty of Law. He worked his way up steadily and patiently through the executive ranks, and keeps in touch professionally and socially with his old boy colleagues. The government seeks his advice and assistance on energy policy. However, his international experience and connections, as well as his writing and teaching, are exceptional, and they also mark the beginning of a trend in the company toward internationalization. When he joined the company in 1957, there were no Tokio Kanohs at all in the upper ranks of Tepco. Generating and selling electric power was an essentially domestic, local operation. Fuel to fire the generating plants had to be imported, but that was the business of petroleum firms and trading companies. Since the 1973 Middle East War and the OPEC oil embargo, however, the electric power companies in Japan have recognized that their own local fuel stockpiling, crisis management, and future development are inextricably connected with events in the Middle East, the Pacific Basin, and the OECD. It is important for them to have executives who can participate in the international energy planning that takes place in New York, in Singapore, and in Paris. They want executives who can tell them what is going on in the international energy world, and can use that knowledge to help make company policy.

FAMILY BACKGROUND AND CHILDHOOD

Tokio Kanoh was born in Tokyo on January 5, 1935, to Yoshio and Rieko Kanoh. I explained to him my interest in his family and local ties.

Question: "Perhaps we could begin by looking at your father's side of the family. Could you tell me about them, where they lived, what they did for a living?"

(in a matter-of-fact tone, without sadness) "I don't know. My father died when I was five years old, in 1940. It is a pity that I don't remember him, but I hardly knew him. He was on the staff of the Asahi newspaper. They are a big, national newspaper, you know, and he worked at their Osaka office. I lived in Tokyo with my mother and older brother. We only saw my father sometimes on the weekends, or on holidays, when he had a chance to come home. There was no Bullet train then, and it was a much longer trip from Osaka to Tokyo. It is too bad . . . but it is not so unusual in Japan, even now, for fathers to live away from their family because of their job. We call it *tanshin funin*.

"I hardly had a chance to talk with him, or to know him, and I know almost nothing about his family. His parents were already dead. I have only a few cousins on my father's side, and we are not . . . close friends. He died of a stomach disease. He must have worked too hard. Maybe he drank too much sake. But I don't know the details. I only remember the funeral.

"Our family is still connected with the Asahi newspaper. My older brother succeeded my father, and is on the Asahi staff. "

Question: "I see. That is sad. I am sorry. I had no idea that your father had died so young when I asked about him. (pause) Is there anything else that you would care to tell me about your family?"

"Hmm. (pausing thoughtfully) My mother's maiden name is Masunaga. According to our family tree, they were samurai, related to the Genji (making a mock frown) a very old and noble family. (laughing) I don't believe it. I think the Masunaga were a family of rich Edo merchants. They were millionaires who used their money to become samurai. Maybe my great-grandfather bought that family tree.

"But they did have much money. They owned fine property and a big house in the Aoyama district of Tokyo. I remember going there as a little boy. I enjoyed sailing on their boat, on a lake right in the middle of Tokyo. But they lost everything. I think some of my ancestors almost bankrupted us with their extravagant way of living, and then World War II finished off their fortune. So, I don't boast about my ancestors. (smiling and looking directly at me) I don't think about them too much, except for my mother. She is a strong, firm woman. She is seventy-seven years old."

WORLD WAR II

Question: "You were six years old when the war began in the Pacific, in the first grade in elementary school, I expect. Do you have any clear memories of that time?"

"Yes. Some very clear memories. I was in the Aburamen Primary School, which was founded by the local government of Meguro-ku. That was my school from 1941 to 1947. And the war, well . . . the war was the most important part of my childhood.

"In 1944, I was evacuated from Tokyo to Yamanashi Prefecture, to avoid the bombing. I was mostly in Yamanashi for the fourth and fifth grades. But even then, in 1944-1945, I came back to Tokyo now and then. I happened to be there for one of the heaviest air raids. It was on March 10, 1945. And I was there for many other bombing raids. (in a matter-of-fact tone) It was beautiful the way the planes flew over, high, high up . . . and the anti-aircraft fired at them . . . like fireworks. (in a sad, pained tone) Then the bombs hit the ground, and it was . . . very terrible . . . explosions and fires. Almost everybody's homes were burnt to the ground. I escaped from the fires. I ran here and there, anywhere to get shelter. Many friends and relatives were killed--most in fires. I went to downtown Tokyo, and there I saw many, many dead bodies--many burnt bodies. Horrible. It was . . . miserable. (in a firm tone) So, I hated the war. (pause) But it was Japan's fault. We attacked Pearl Harbor . . . and we were repaid."

Question: "Did you have enough to eat, in Tokyo and in Yamanashi?"

"No. We did not have enough food--either in Tokyo or in Yamanashi. Once I caught a frog, and I was so hungry . . . that I ate it. I was often sick, and so were my friends, because we didn't get enough calories, enough nutrients.

"In Tokyo, my mother made us cut away all the flowers in our garden, and we cultivated potatoes, tomatoes, wheat, and other food crops. I even ground our wheat to make bread. I had to learn to do that. But it was not enough. We were weak and we became sick easily, because there was not enough food. (smiling) Now, we have the opposite problem. We eat too much. We have to diet to be healthy.

(pausing for reflection and speaking slowly and quietly) "My childhood and the war . . . that whole time . . . was a series of shocks to me . . . and losses. First, I lost my father in 1940. Then, in 1945, I lost my country . . . in a way . . . when Japan was defeated. It could never be the same. (pause) Thirdly, I lost confidence in my teachers . . . and they had been . . . very important for me. Until the end of the war, I believed my teachers. They taught us that the U.S. is a hateful enemy--Yankee devils--and that Americans wanted to kill all the Japanese people. We were supposed to grow up and become soldiers to defend Japan against this hateful enemy. That is what my teacher said, and I believed him.

"Then, when I was ten years old, the war ended, and my teacher changed his attitude . . . immediately. So easily. He just said, 'I was wrong. The U.S. is a good, democratic country. It is a very kind country. We must learn from the U.S.' He told us to cross out all the bad words and sentences about the U.S. in our textbooks, with India ink.

"Well . . . I lost all confidence in my teacher--all respect for him. I will not tell you his name. He is alive, and is still connected with education. He had been a soldier and had been dispatched to my school by the army to teach. When the war ended, he changed-- just like that. He joined a union, and became a member of an educational committee and became the head of that committee. (frowning, in a disapproving tone) He is not an example to follow. (pause) I don't hate him, but I cannot respect him. He is still powerful. That is why I cannot tell you his name."

Comment: "So, your childhood in the war made a skeptic of you."

"Skeptic? . . . Maybe. I still believe . . . but not absolutely. I wrote a book recently in which I made the point that there are no absolute truths. But I argue for some kind of truth. I recommended many religions--many gods--polytheism. This is good philosophy, and also good energy policy. We should not expect to find all the truth in one place, and we should also diversify our sources of energy. (smiling) It is very dangerous to be dependent on one god, on one teacher or one source of energy. Well, that kind of thinking comes from my childhood in the war."

MIDDLE AND HIGH SCHOOL IN OCCUPIED JAPAN

Question: "Yes. I can see how your childhood in the war shaped these ideas. You had to learn to adapt to shocks and losses. How about the postwar period, especially the Occupation years, from the end of the war until 1952?"

"Hmm. Those were almost the same years as my middle and high school. I went to Shiba Middle School from 1947 to 1950, and then to Shiba High School from 1950 to 1953. For me those were good years--entirely different than the war and the bad year after the war. You know, Japan was still very poor and our family was poor, but in 1947 my life changed. It became better. When I was twelve, in 1947, I took the examinations for middle school. I was accepted at Azabu and Shiba. After the Occupation education reforms, there were three first-class middle schools left in Tokyo. They were all private schools--Azabu, Shiba and Kaisei. My older brother was already at Shiba, so that was the school I entered.

"At Shiba Middle School we were also taught democracy. The Ministry of Education said that the student class leader must be elected by the students, and not appointed by the teacher . . . as they used to be. The class elected me. (grinning) So, I thought democracy must be very good. (both of us laughing, and then in a more serious tone) In primary school I had been appointed class leader by the teachers because my grades were high. But for me, people and friends were more important than high grades."

Question: "Did the teachers continue to influence the elections very much?"

(laughing) "The teachers had some influence. That is true. But they didn't control the election. I think my classmates really picked me. They elected me as class leader every year, all through middle school and high school.

"About the same time I was learning about American democracy at school, I also met my American cousin. He was a

soldier in the Occupation. You know, I have relatives in Chicago--
people who left Japan years before the war. By the time of the war,
they were second-generation, *nissei*. They were born in America. I
am related to them through my cousin Chieko Onoda. Chieko's
mother is my mother's sister. My aunt became a designer in
Chicago. Chieko teaches at the University of Illinois in Chicago.
Her specialty is nursing. Her husband, Sam, is a lawyer. He
works in the labor relations section at the Indiana Steel Company.

"Well, one of my American cousins, Katsumi Neeno, who
is now a medical doctor, was a soldier in the Occupation forces. At
that time he was a student preparing for medicine. He was drafted
and sent to Japan. I was . . . very impressed when I met him. He
spoke only a little Japanese, but he was very kind to me. It was . . .
hmmm . . . strange. I was just a boy, but I was a . . . defeated,
poor Japanese and he was a rich American soldier. When we went
on the train, we had to sit in different places. American Occupation
soldiers here. Japanese over there. (shaking his head in dismay at
the memory) I didn't like that.

"But this man was so talented and sociable that I liked him.
I liked him even though I envied him. I could see that he had a good
life, and also that he was a man of . . . culture. So, after I met him I
had the idea of going to the U.S. to see what it is like. I didn't go
until years later, after I graduated from the university. I don't want
to exaggerate, but meeting him had some influence on me. My
cousin Katsumi was only in Japan for six months. I saw him fifteen
or twenty times and he visited us maybe two times. We only spoke
with each other in broken Japanese.

"I should also tell you two other important things about my
school years at Shiba. When I passed the examination for the middle school, that meant I would also be admitted, without an examination, to Shiba High School. So that examination when I was
twelve, was a turning point in my life. My father was dead and we
had no money. Compulsory education ends after middle school.
But since I did well at Shiba Middle School, I was given a scholarship to Shiba High School, and it is a very good school. Many
Shiba graduates enter the best universities and jobs. The director of
the Fujitsu Electronics Pavilion here at the Expo is a classmate of
mine from Shiba. Hiroaki Eguchi is his name. And there are many

others. We are going to have a Shiba class meeting here at Tsukuba this weekend, with twenty-six of our classmates. Golf and a party. All good friends. I am responsible for organizing these meetings. I am the secretary of the Shiba Alumni Association. I am also chairman of the Shiba PTA, because my two sons go there now. So, since I entered there in 1947, my whole life has been connected with Shiba School.

"Another thing is that Shiba is a religious school. The religion was part of our teaching. It is Johdohshu Buddhism--Pure Land Buddhism. The essence of it is that everyone may commit errors, scandals, bad things in their life. But if one believes in the Buddha and prays sincerely to him, everyone can come back to the Pure Land. (very pleased at this prospect, and shaking his head for emphasis) That is a good vision. (Mr. Kanoh saw that I was nodding in agreement and smiling, and he laughed) No, no. I have no terrible scandals to pray about. Just little things. When I was a student, I was not serious enough. I made good grades, but I wasted time. I enjoyed gambling--at horse races, and poker, and mahjong. I liked to drink beer and whiskey, even when I was sixteen and seventeen years old. The teachers prohibited such things. But they were not so terrible. I learned hospitality and friendship when I was gambling and drinking."

Question: "Did you start studying English more seriously after you met your American cousin?"

"No. I didn't do any extra work on languages until I entered the university. In high school I did my school work, including the English course, but I didn't learn much English there. I was in the debating society--in Japanese--and I played on the baseball team. Also I went to a music school and played piano.

"Music is important to me. I began to study piano when I was four years old, and I always enjoy making music and being friends with musical people. One of my classmates from music school is Kyoko Edo, who is a famous pianist in Japan. She is really talented, and a good person. You know, Shiba School is an all boys school and I hardly knew any girls in high school, except for the ones in my music school. Anyway, there are some musical genes in my family. My mother's brother, my uncle, Ichiro Fujiyama--his original name is Takeo Masunaga--is still a popular singer, even though he is getting old."

TOKYO UNIVERSITY

Question: "Did you give much thought to college and a career when you were in Shiba School?"

"Hmmm. Not very much. Maybe I should have, you know. But actually I didn't. I was very happy in school, and I was . . . happy-go-lucky, not worrying about the future. In my senior year, since I had good grades, I took the examination for Todai, and also for Keio University, and for the Defense Academy. I passed all of them. I went to Todai, still on a scholarship, because we had no money."

Question: "I see. So you passed the entrance examination for Todai on your first try?"

(laughing) "Yes. You know that many of the students who go to Todai take the examination two times before they are admitted. I remember feeling very . . . junior . . . very young, when I first entered Todai, because so many of my classmates were one or two years older than me."

Question: "Under what faculty did you study?"

"I went into the Law Faculty. I had no clear plans, but I was a good student, so the Law Faculty seemed to be . . . natural."

Question: "Most of the Todai graduates I have met tell me that they were relaxed about their studies in the first two years, and then became more serious in the last year or two. Was that true for you?"

"I was relaxed and I enjoyed the first two years and then . . . (thoughtful pause) I relaxed and enjoyed the last years." (both laughing)

Question: "Didn't you have to keep your grades high to hold your scholarship?"

"Yes . . . and I did. But the school work was not too demanding."

Question: "Were you a member of the English Speaking Society? That seems to have been a popular activity in the 1950s at Todai."

"No. (laughing) I was too busy . . . doing other things. I was the leader of the Student Council, and that took a lot of time. But I began to study foreign languages. I went to the Athénée Française, to a German school, and to an English language school. I think that all the students at Todai in those days were studying foreign languages and conversation--especially English. We all thought that we should learn English--really learn to speak it. The U.S. was the country to catch up to, and we needed English to do it."

Question: "It must have been quite a heavy work load, doing all three of those languages at about the same time. Is your French and your German as good as your English?"

(laughing and shaking his head in a self-deprecating way) "My English is not that good. I can speak . . . yes . . . but I know it is . . . still clumsy. In the last few years it has improved. Anyway, I cannot speak German as well as English or French. I think English is my best foreign language. The reason is that I belonged to an English conversation class that was taught by a beautiful and elegant lady. The class met every week for two years. And I never missed a class. (both laughing) Also, I used to write letters in English to my cousin in Chicago, Chieko Onoda--about every two weeks--and she would correct my English. She was a big help to me."

JOINING TEPCO

Question: "Did you give any thought to your future career while you were at Todai?"

"In my senior year, yes. Then I thought about what job I should take. (thoughtful pause) It was a serious question for me."

Question: "I see. What considerations were on your mind? Did you give any thought to becoming a bureaucrat, or a journalist, or anything else?"

"Hmm. Not very much. I did not have such a favorable idea about the government ministries when I was young. (smiling) Even now, I sometimes have doubts about them--although some bureaucrats are my close friends, and they are very good people, hard working public servants. (after another pause and some hesitancy) A big consideration for me was the salary. This was also true for others at Todai in the 1950s. Compared to later, not so many wanted to become bureaucrats because the bureaucrat's pay was less--about two-thirds the pay in a big, private company. I think the best student in my class joined Sumitomo Metals, not a ministry. Well, I was not rich, you know. After the university, there were no more scholarships. I had to make a living and be a responsible member of my family.

"In those days, Mitsui Petrochemical gave the highest salary. Nippon Ginko (Bank of Japan) was second, and Toden (Tepco) was third. Steel companies, automobile companies, and electronic companies like Sony and Matsushita were not big and rich yet--not until later. The textile companies were still prosperous, but they were about to decline. I studied all these companies--their salaries and future possibilities, and that influenced me.

"I was also influenced by Mr. Kazutaka Kikawada, who was the vice-president of Tepco, and also the chairman of *Keizai Doyukai* (Committee for Economic Development). He was in his forties then, a very energetic, intelligent leader. What he said had a strong appeal for me. I wanted to make a good salary, but I did not want to be entirely selfish. I wanted to work for the good of society. Mr. Kikawada used to criticize many big companies for being too selfish, interested only in profits and money. He said that was the bad side of capitalism. He appealed to all companies to have social responsibility--to be as eager to contribute to society as to make profits. He was not a Socialist, but a semi-Capitalist. A pure Capitalist is interested only in profits. Kikawada used to say, even then, that the power companies must reduce the sulphur dioxide and nitrogen dioxide in the air.

"I liked his ideas. I was very eager to join his company, and I asked him to recruit me. Two of my teachers at Todai recommended me, and helped me to join Toden--Professor Sasaki and Professor Oka. Professor Oka is still alive. He is an authority on bureaucracy, and we had some hard debates when I was a student. (noticing my questioning look) Yes, I used to sometimes debate with my professors. But even though I disagreed with him sometimes, he was a great help. So, I was able to join Tepco after graduation, in 1957. I did not start as an executive, but as a staff member. Even university graduates started as staff members."

EVENING SCHOOL AND CORRESPONDENCE COURSES

"Not being an executive in my early years at Tepco had . . . some advantages. Executives often work late. But in those days I usually finished by six o'clock, and I could take courses in the evening. I started a correspondence course in the Economics Department at Keio in 1958, and I used to go there to study after work, and sometimes to have a discussion with a professor. I completed the degree at Keio in 1964 . . . with honors. In 1960, I took another evening correspondence course at Japan Management School--a business school. They gave courses in statistics, game theory, business math for financial analysis and some computer programming. I finished their course in . . . 1962. They were good, useful courses. I enjoyed them."

Question: "You were doing both these evening correspondence courses at the same time from 1960 to 1962, in addition to your work at Tepco? Wasn't that . . . exhausting? Didn't you get overtired now and then?"

"Oh no. It was a busy time, but I enjoyed it. It was not too difficult. I went from my company to Keio early in the evening and worked on their courses. Then, I would go to my home and do an hour or two on my correspondence courses on math. I liked those math courses. There was enough time for everything--to work, to eat and sleep and to talk with people."

Question: "When you were going to the Keio campus in 1960, did you take an interest in the anti-U.S.-Japan Security Treaty movement and demonstrations that were going on that spring?"

"I went to a few meetings. But I was too busy with other things to get involved very much."

Question: "What were your thoughts at the time about the whole issue of the Security Treaty?"

(thoughtful pause) "My feelings--basic feeling--was that it was most important to have close ties with the U.S. This or that clause in the treaty seemed . . . secondary to me. We had a . . . choice. Japan could have a market economy, or a centrally planned economy. I did not want us to have a centrally planned economy. The free market economy is . . . not perfect . . . but much better. The centrally planned economy is very bureaucratic--excessively bureaucratic--and not good for us. I felt that the U.S. was the leading free market economy, and that if we kept close ties then we could have a market economy--and we could participate in the international market economy. I believed that was most important for Japan."

Question: "Why were you critical and negative about centrally planned economies and bureaucratic control? Where do you think that came from?"

"Hmmm. That is very difficult . . . but I think there were some reasons. (smiling) Part of it is . . . temperament. There is something . . . unpleasant to me about all bureaucracy . . . even though it cannot be completely avoided. Also, going to two private schools, Shiba and Keio, had some effect. In private schools the students were not so fond of bureaucracy. In the public schools-- like Todai--they are much more fond of bureaucracy. Private schools--the teachers and students--favor business more and market economics.

"There is some misunderstanding on this, I think, in your country. Many Americans get to meet Japanese officials and talk with them, and they get some wrong ideas. These officials are often good, able people, and somehow, Americans think that all the best students want to be officials, bureaucrats . . . that the bureaucrats are the most able people in Japan, and lead and govern the rest of us . . . who were not good enough to become bureaucrats. That is wrong and foolish.

"I was in Washington D.C. a couple of weeks ago, and one American talked with me and said that he heard from some Japanese that MITI has the most talented people, and that MITI arranges everything and gives orders to the top industrialists and bankers. That is an error. A complete error.

"There are some good people . . . top people in MITI, whom I know well . . . and also some who are not so good. You know, there were sometimes scandals in MITI, and sometimes mistakes (smiling) silly mistakes. (pause) The same is true of company executives and politicians . . . and academics, too. But, the most important point is that in Japan, the private sector, the ministry officials, the politicians, and some academics work together. No one sector steers everything or is in charge. We bear the same burden. However, we have different functions. Some are planning--the officials. Some are governing--getting elected and making laws. Some are creating and producing. That is the function of the private sector, of business and industry. The system requires that we work with each other.

"Sometimes officials say that they must decide things because the private sector is too selfish. Usually . . . most of the time, that is not true. We find a way to do what is good for our company and for the whole economy. We have social responsibility."

ENERGY POLICY

Question: "One of the reasons I hoped you would be in this study is that many Americans think of Japan as an exporting giant, an industrial economy that is threatening to inundate American and world markets with its automobiles, chips, electronic equipment, steel, and so on. We give very little attention to what Japan has to import, and it seems to me that the biggest, most essential, and most expensive of Japan's imports is fuels--fuels for energy. Would you care to discuss energy policy? What is Japan's situation, and what do you think should be done?"

(going to a file cabinet and returning with a folder of notes and colored graphs) "I gave a talk at an energy seminar in Tokyo last week that was mainly on oil production and oil imports, but it also included the whole energy policy. One of the main points I made is that even though we Japanese have diversified our energy sources somewhat in the last ten years or so, we are still much too vulnerable. Our diversification is not yet close to adequate.

"Please look at these charts and figures. (taking charts from folder and passing several over to me) I use your country as a model for Japan to aim at. Of course, you have much more of your own energy resources, but still, you have made more good changes in some parts of your energy policy than we have. In 1977, on this chart (studying the chart together) the biggest foreign suppliers of oil to the U.S. were: (1) Saudi Arabia, (2) Nigeria, (3) Libya, (4) Algeria, (5) Iran. All of them except Nigeria in the Middle East, the most insecure source of oil. Now, please look at 1984. In 1984, the biggest foreign suppliers of oil to the U.S. were: (1) Mexico, (2) Canada, (3) Venezuela, (4) United Kingdom, (5) Indonesia. Not one Middle East country in the top five. All top five sources much more secure than the Middle East. (smiling and reaching over and to shake my hand) Congratulations. The U.S. has done an excellent job in improving the security of imported oil supplies. You should get a gold medal in the international energy Olympics. (both laughing)

"By 1984, only 10 percent of U.S. oil imports came from Middle East. Only 30 percent of the oil consumed in the U.S. was imported, and oil accounted for 40 percent of total energy consumed in the U.S. This means that if there is a crisis or war in the Middle East, and Middle East oil supplies are cut, only 1 to 2 percent of total U.S. energy supply is cut. (shaking his head, very impressed) Of course, you start off in much better position than Japan . . . but still, this is Olympic champion performance.

"Now, please look at Japan. We made some improvements from 1977 to 1984. But we are still 100 percent dependent on imported oil, and oil still accounts for 60 percent of energy consumed in Japan in 1984. We reduced our dependence on Middle East oil from about 85 percent to 70 percent. We worked hard to do this, but our position is still . . . not satisfactory . . . not at all good. We are still much too dependent on insecure imported energy. If Middle East oil is cut, it still means that Japan loses 40 percent of its total energy supplies. Just like that. We have built oil stockpiles, yes. But if the oil cut is extended for one year, Japan faces economic disaster--a 40 percent cut in energy supplies." (shakes his head emphatically in disapproval)

Question: "Yes, I see how vulnerable Japan is to disruption in oil supplies. What do you propose to do about it?"

(ticking off answers on fingers of left hand) "First, we must keep working to improve energy efficiency and to conserve energy. That is essential, and depends entirely on our own efforts. We must get the most use of every drop of energy--no waste. There is still room for great improvements in energy efficiency--in industry, in heating, in transportation.

"Secondly, we must try to import more oil from secure sources. I always argue that we should keep pressing, again and again, for the U.S. to let us buy oil from Alaska. (shaking his head for emphasis) I understand the U.S. case for not selling Japan Alaskan oil--but it is not a strong case, and you can change your laws. Laws are made by men. If you sell Alaskan oil to Japan, you can quickly make a sizable cut in your trade deficit with Japan. We Japanese want to be more dependent on the U.S. for oil, not so much on the Middle East. But you don't let us. (shaking his head again for emphasis) This makes no sense.

"Third, we must continue to shift more to LNG and to coal. We have used up almost all our water power, but we must do what we can there, too.

"Fourth, and maybe most important, also because it depends on our own decisions and work, is to build more nuclear power plants and develop fast breeder reactors. You know, we import our enriched uranium from the U.S. Nuclear energy will not make Japan energy independent. But it will be more secure than fossil fuels. We have been doing this, with some good results. Please look at this page. Nuclear energy in Japan has increased from 1,780 megawatts in 1973, to 24,520 megawatts in 1985. Now it is as much as 27 percent of our electrical energy. We have about twenty more nuclear plants under construction or soon to begin construction. They will double our nuclear power capacity in the next ten years."

Question: "Yes. I can see your logic. But Japan has earthquakes. Can you protect nuclear reactors and fast breeders against earthquakes? Couldn't you have a Three Mile Island here, or even worse? What about storing nuclear wastes? How will you do it? Nuclear energy seems to have become much more expensive in the U.S. than was expected. Don't you also have to worry about costs?"

"Oh yes. We have to worry about all those things. But we can protect nuclear power plants against earthquakes, and we can store waste safely. It is technologically possible. The problem is cost. We must bring down the cost of safe nuclear power . . . by improving technology. (pause, in low, intense tone) I think we can do that. You know, our nuclear plants are maybe the most efficient in the world. But there is still room for technological improvements--much room."

Question: "Do you know Hisahiko Okazaki--the diplomat who is now your ambassador to Saudi Arabia? He said very similar things to me in 1977, about nuclear energy. He was a member of a group that was advising Prime Minister Fukuda on energy policy."

"Oh yes. We are close friends. He graduated from Todai, oh, about five years before me. We worked together as assistants on energy policy for Prime Minister Ohira. Most of that team was from the ministries--like Okazaki, and some people from MITI. Two or three of us were from the private sector--like myself and Jiro Ushio (chairman of Ushio Electric Company, and adviser to Prime Minister Nakasone). We came to have strong ties, and get together often to discuss. We have a kind of alumni club from the Ohira days, called *Kengyukai*. (laughing) *Kengyu* means a studying cow. Did you know that dead cow was a nickname for Mr. Ohira?"

Comment: "Mmmm. I can see the connection. He had a very broad, impassive face. And he was . . . somewhat bloated. Still, that is a strong nickname." (both laughing)

"Well, maybe someone should do a study of Japan's energy policy based on the Studying Cow Society. No, no. That is no joke. The Studying Cow Society is a . . . fairly influential alumni association. Maybe these alumni associations are the government of Japan." (both laughing)

MARRIAGE AND FAMILY

Question: "Would you mind if we talk for awhile about your marriage and family?"

"Not at all. I married in . . . 1961, when I was twenty-six years old. We have four children, two sons and two daughters. I have had only one wife (laughing) not two or three."

Question: "Well, that simplifies matters, doesn't it? Was your marriage a traditional, arranged marriage?"

"Well, yes . . . but not in the sense that we were introduced to each other by a go-between--a *nakohdo*--at a formal, marriage interview--a *miai*. I knew her since we were children. My wife is the sister of my older brother's classmate--a kindergarten classmate--at Ochanomizu. So, my mother and my wife's mother are very old friends. And that helped to bring us together. My wife's name is Ayako. Her family name is Hirata. She is six years younger than me.

"She went to Joshi Gakuin Girl's School. So did my my wife's mother, Chieko Onoda's mother, and also our two daughters. Now, Naoko, our younger daughter, is studying at Joshi Gakuin High School. (smiling) On the female side of my family, they all have the Joshi Gakuin connection--just as we are all Shiba School on the male side. My wife graduated from Ochanomizu University in Tokyo. She specialized in food chemistry. For awhile before marriage and after, she worked as a researcher for the Kokusaku Pulp and Paper Company.

(looking over the outline of biographical topics that I had prepared and grinning at me) "Now, I have a question for you. In this outline you say that your assumption is that, 'marriage in Japan has more of an institutional and social component than in America and it is an important source of support and stability in career.' I don't think that marriage is such an important factor in a man's work or career. What do you mean by this?"

Comment: "Well . . . I mean that usually in Japan, people are less romantic about marriage than in the U.S. The Japanese believe that it is important to marry and have a family, not just for personal happiness, but also because their parents and . . . society expect them to. They do not usually marry so much on the basis of love--romantic attraction. They see their marriage as a social institution as well as a personal matter. So, husband and wife tend to be more tolerant of each other, and they are also, in a sense, more separate. The men work hard at their jobs, and the women work harder at being mothers. Because of this, there is less divorce in Japan than in the U.S. Marriages are more stable. I meant that this stability is a source of support and strength in your life and in your career. I didn't mean that the wife or her family arrange for the husband's promotions."

"Hmmm. (mock seriousness) That is allright. That is a satisfactory answer. (both laughing) I agree with you. Marriage is changing in Japan, but still we are . . . suspicious of quick marriages . . . love at first sight and then rushing to get married. If young people marry that way they often base their marriage on mutual misunderstanding . . . and then they base their divorce on mutual understanding. That is happening now in Japan, more often than it used to. But it is hard to make strict rules in these matters. Sometimes, the American style works very well. But it is more risky.

"I don't think that all the formalities of the traditional marriage are necessary. The important thing is that the boy and girl have many things in common . . . that they are friends and are realistic about each other . . . and have the understanding of their families. My older daughter, Nobuko, will marry this autumn. She has known her boyfriend for four years, since she was eighteen. He was the leader of the Midorikai Chorus at Todai, and my daughter is a soprano in a women's choir. He is good, reliable, and kind. He graduated ahead of my daughter and joined the Dai Ichi Kangyo Bank--the top bank in Japan. They are in love, but also good friends, and their love is not based just on first impressions. That is important.

"In the traditional marriage, the go-between used to really arrange things. In my marriage, we had an honorary go-between, a *nakohdo,* who was master of ceremony. In my daughter's wedding also they will ask someone to be honorary *nakohdo.* I have been this kind of *nakohdo* many times--about ten times. (warm smile) I enjoy being the master of ceremony when a very nice boy and nice, sweet girl are married."

CAREER

Question: "What factors do you feel have been most important in advancing your career? How much importance would you give to hard work, or to brains, to family and school ties, or to luck . . . or whatever else you think should be included?"

"My career is not complete. It is unfinished. So, there is no success to explain. I love my job. I am happy to do it. (pausing) But I have no ticket for future assignments or promotions. (shaking his head and half smiling) I am not even sure that I will have a job with Tepco after the Expo closes in the fall. We shall see. (Mr. Kanoh was promoted and is still at Tepco.)

"But I know what you mean. I will try to answer. I work hard, but that is normal in Japan. By Japanese standards, I am a medium hard worker. My family is . . . medium level. Some of my wife's side are successful in academia, and my mother's brother is successful in music. But we have no big successes in business. School ties are good. Not unusual, but good. There are other men with faster, more accurate brains. My brain is . . . OK, but not top quality. (grinning) You see, I am a medium quality, medium cooked Japanese steak. (both laughing)

(more seriously) "I have been lucky. Tepco grew very quickly after I joined the company. The 1960s were the most rapid years of economic growth in Japan. Industries and people needed much more power, and much more electric power. So Tepco expanded, and became the biggest private company in Japan, and the young men on the staff had many opportunities. (When Nippon Telephone and Telegraph (NTT) became a private company in 1985, it surpassed Tepco in total assets.) Even now, we are lucky. Electric power will continue to be important in the information society. Secondly, I was especially lucky that I worked for successful, fine bosses. Mr. Kikawada was not my direct boss, but he gave me the chance to enter this company, and I always admired him and wanted to work for him. Mr. Masami Kadota was my direct boss. He is now president of the Electric Power Development Company, a semi-public company, and he was appointed by the cabinet. He taught me how to practice crisis management. I owe him a lot. Mr. Gaishi Hiraiwa, who is the board chairman of Tepco, was also my boss for a time. He is now the deputy chairman of *Keidanren* (Council of Economic Associations, the most influential of the industrial interest groups). He was the man who asked me to work at the International Energy Agency (IEA), and to enlarge my international experience. I have had successful bosses, and they have been able to give me fine opportunities."

Question: "You mentioned crisis management. Has that been an important part of your work at Tepco?"

"Important? (laughing) It has become my life work. Energy crisis management was my job on the Technical Committee of IEA, and also for Prime Minister Ohira. In the two years I worked for Mr. Ohira, I was sent to the IEA meetings in Paris eighteen times to work on energy conservation and fuel switching--that is how to convert primary energy from oil to other sources. Most of my books and articles are about some aspect of crisis management.

(seeing that I was unsure what he meant) "What I mean by crisis management is first, detection of potential crisis--such as abnormal oil stockpiles, or spot prices, or political changes in the Middle East. Second, to prevent the crisis, as much as possible. That is the most useful step. Third, to minimize the damage from the crisis. Well, you know, the whole energy policy I discussed with you is energy crisis management. This policy gets me into some controversy in the electric power companies. Many of the bosses and managers want most of all to promote electric power, to sell more in order to make more profits. My approach is that overall energy conservation is most important for Japan . . . to reduce vulnerability . . . to prevent energy crisis. It is good to switch to electric power, but only if there is conservation of total energy use.

"My friends in MITI agree with this, and together we created the Energy Conservation Center of Japan. My boss, Mr. Hiraiwa is now the chairman of the center. Mr. Shoh Nasu, who is the president of Tepco, and also my former direct boss, assigned me to work on conservation policy. So far we have done pretty well in the OECD countries, including Japan. In 1974, before conservation began, the total primary energy use for OECD countries was 3.5 billion metric tons of oil equivalent. There were some ups and downs, and in 1983, we were still at 3.5 billion--even though there had been significant economic growth. For Japan, the energy picture is also like this."

Question: "I can understand the importance of energy conservation, but how can switching to electricity help in crisis prevention or management?"

(shaking his head and smiling indulgently) "I can see that you have not studied this question. Electricity is a secondary energy. It can be produced from a variety of primary energies--oil, coal, LNG, nuclear power, solar energy, falling water, tidal currents and so on. If we have a large electric power system that can be fueled by many different primary energy sources, then we can shift from one primary energy to another--to prevent crisis, or to limit the damage. (grinning) Many gods and many devils is safer.

"Energy crisis management is what I was asked to teach at Harvard by Professor Ezra Vogel. It is what I do on the Pacific Economic Cooperation Committee. It is . . . my life's work."

INTERNATIONALIZATION

Question: "What does the word internationalization mean to you?"

"I think of internationalization in terms of individuals--of what it takes for a person to be internationalized. To become internationalized, a person must first of all have a deep, strong knowledge and sympathy with his own country and people. Some people who become interested in foreign countries and languages are trying to escape from their own culture. They will not become internationalized--not in the sense that I mean. We must stand in our own culture and extend our hands from there to shake hands with foreigners. A person who can do that is truly internationalized."

Question: "Do you think that Japan has enough internationalized people to serve its present and future needs for getting on in the world?"

(thoughtful pause) "It is not possible to give a straight yes or no answer to that. Up to now, since 1945, we have been getting along in the world. We have been doing business--peacefully and productively. I don't know how many internationalized Japanese we have. It could be a few hundred or a million, depending on the exact definition of internationalization. Whatever the number, we will need more of these people in the future (thoughtful pause) and the whole process of interacting with foreigners may have to . . . change . . . become more intimate. Hmmm. Yes, intimate. That is the word I want.

"Up to now, some Japanese have learned foreign languages and cultures, and have been skillful at dealing with foreigners. But we have remained, basically, an isolated island people. Japanese marry Japanese. Japanese almost never invite foreigners into their homes and families. Germans, Swedes, Americans, English, Italians, and French have many relatives in each other's countries. They are related by blood. Their homes are more open to foreigners.

(very seriously) "That is so important. When I was invited to teach at Harvard or to attend a symposium there last year, my American friends took me into their families to stay. I joined them in their family meals. We had long discussions, late into the night, about everything. That is the way to really learn about other cultures. The language is only a tool for this real cultural learning.

(more lightly) "I have a few Japanese relatives in Chicago, you know. But I want relatives all over the world. We must have more marriages with foreigners. (laughing) Japanese men have to fall in love with foreign ladies and marry them. Like my good friend at Todai, who married a French lady. Now his French is better, and he is often invited to lecture at the Ecole Nationale de l'Administration. It is too late for me to make an international family, but I open my house to foreigners, and I tell all my staff people to do the same. My American friends stay in my home, and take meals with us--and find out what Japanese are like. I send my children for summer holidays in the U.S. to take summer school courses--even though it is very expensive. (shaking his head in dismay at the cost.)

"It is also important that we work together and do practical things together with foreigners. That is why I opened this pavilion to all nationalities. We have recruited not only Japanese people to work here, but two Koreans, a Chinese, an Indonesian and one Canadian--my secretary, Karen Mingay. They are all very good, and we get along very well.

"There are two reasons why I take this approach. First, I know from my experience in international energy planning that these intimate, informal friendships are important and helpful. 'Know who' is as important as 'know how.' Secondly (thoughtful pause) our behavior should be changed from how to learn from other countries, to how to contribute and share with them. We will not be able to contribute and share . . . unless we are friends . . . unless we have a network of intimate ties . . . unless foreigners feel comfortable with us. If we go on, in the future, just learning technology from foreigners and selling them our products, they will come to hate us.

"It is very difficult for Japanese to become more open and friendly. (pause) But somehow, we must learn to do it."

THE FUTURE

Question: "How do you think the world is going to look during the next ten to twenty years? What will Japan's position be? How do you think U.S.-Soviet relations will develop?"

"Let me discuss U.S.-Soviet relations first. The Strategic Defense Initiative (SDI) is a big issue, and I think it will continue to be one for some years. Now, the SDI is still in the research phase, and I think the U.S. should not give it up--not yet. The U.S.S.R. until now has been racing hard to build up its offensive nuclear forces, intercontinental missiles and also many intermediate range SS-20 missiles against Japan and Europe. They have been doing this to frighten us. The meaning of the SDI is that the U.S. may be able to cancel out this Soviet offensive threat. That is why the Russians are so upset about SDI. I think your country should continue research on SDI until the Russians sit down and negotiate a real cut in offensive nuclear weapons--both intercontinental and intermediate range.

"I hope the Russians will see that it is better for them to be more . . . cooperative . . . not just on nuclear weapons, but also on technology, on food, and in energy policy also. They are too . . . suspicious. They think everyone is their absolute enemy. Of course, there are enemies, and national conflicts . . . but there is room for more cooperation.

"The U.S.S.R. is a big, powerful country, but they have serious weaknesses and defects. I have been studying them for the last few years as part of my research and writing. Their industrial management is . . . deficient. Their big industrial projects usually fall far behind schedule because of bad planning, lack of parts, lack of information. Quality control is not good. Their buildings fall apart. Their machinery breaks down often.

"I calculate that the Soviets will also have energy shortages in the next ten years--unless they change their energy policy and learn to make better use of their coal and natural gas. They need better energy technology.

"Their most serious weakness is that they do not know how to grow enough food. They want to be completely independent--so that no country can put pressure on them or threaten them, but they cannot feed themselves. (shaking his head in dismay)

"Well, I hope the Soviets will change their attitude . . . that they will sit down at the table and really negotiate. If they do, maybe we can all benefit. There would be less fear and less nuclear weapons. We can share peaceful technology with them, including energy technology. They would be better off, and we would too.

"As for Japan, I think we will be one of the leading countries in the free world. We might be able to contribute to a real improvement in superpower relations. We have no attacking forces. We do not threaten the Soviets, or the Chinese, or any country in the world. If the U.S.-Soviet political climate improves, and the Soviets decide to be constructive, we Japanese could cooperate with them on industrial projects and energy development. (pause) In the meanwhile, however, we should cooperate somehow with the U.S. on SDI research. It includes research on advanced electronics, computers, lasers, optic fibers, and we Japanese should get in-volved--on the government level and on the business level, too."

Question: "What do you think the future prospects are for U.S.-Japanese relations--both economic and security relations? What do you think the implications are of the basic changes that have taken place in our economies? In 1955, for instance, the U.S. produced 40 percent of world's total GNP, while Japan produced 2 percent. Now, the U.S. produces 20 percent of world production, and Japan 10 percent. In 1955, it seemed natural for the U.S. to provide for Japan's military defense. How does it look to you now?"

"I can only tell you my own ideas on what we should do. (laughing) I am not in charge of these policies. To my feeling, Japan should have bigger defense forces. We should not be afraid to spend more than 1 percent of our GNP on defense. That is a silly limit. We should build up our defense forces by buying large com-puters and more fighter aircraft from the U.S., off-the-shelf items. This would improve our defense and also our trade balance with the U.S. A larger air force of fighter planes is defensive, and would not threaten any country."

Comment: "Yes, I see. But Defense Minister Kato, and most of his cabinet colleagues, want Japan to continue building American fighter planes here in Japan, under licensing agreements, and they seem reluctant to increase the number of planes."

(firmly) "I don't agree with them. They are not flexible enough on these questions. I am not talking about a major rearma-ment. But we should be more willing to build up our air defense, and to buy off-the-shelf items of American equipment.

"On the future of U.S.-Japanese economic relations, I have two comments. First, the U.S. should let us buy oil from Alaska. We could buy a million barrels per day from Alaska at $28 per bar-rel. At current prices and exchange rates (May 1985) this would amount to about $9 billion per year. That would help the trade bal-ance.

(hesitantly, with a smile) "It is not polite to say this--please forgive me--but I would like to give an idea to my American friends. In order to deal with the trade imbalance between our countries, I ask Americans to please study the Japanese market. Please send people to Japan to study our markets carefully, and to live and work here for a long time. Then you will be more successful in selling in Japan. You know, when I was young I owned a Chevrolet for five years--and I was very proud of it. (shaking his head ruefully) Even though I liked that car so much, it was not convenient. The steering wheel was on the wrong side. When it had engine trouble, I had to wait months and months to get replacement parts. Finally, the rising gasoline prices caused me to change to a more efficient Japanese car. (pause) That is only one item. If you study our market . . . I think you can do better, and then we will be able to buy your products."

Yuzaburo Mogi

YUZABURO MOGI is a managing director of Kikkoman Corporation, a member of the board of directors, and also first executive vice-president of both Kikkoman International, Inc. in San Francisco, and of Kikkoman Foods, Inc. in Walworth, Wisconsin. He is the key international actor in a three hundred year old family business whose main product is a traditional Japanese food seasoning--soy sauce.

The Kikkoman Corporation is one of the oldest manufacturing enterprises among the two hundred largest industrials in Japan, and it is the largest soy sauce producer in the world.[1] In 1985, international operations accounted for 27 percent of Kikkoman's total business. It is true that in the 1930s, before World War II, 10 percent of Kikkoman's sales were overseas. But those overseas sales were almost entirely to Japanese living in Manchuria and North China, and to Japanese-Americans in Hawaii and on the West Coast. Since the 1950s, however, Kikkoman has greatly expanded its market to non-Japanese consumers. It has been sold in North America as an all purpose, international seasoning rather than one limited to Oriental cookery--and it has sold very well.

Internationalization went hand-in-hand with diversification. In 1949, the company produced seven branded products, almost all directly derived or related to brewing soy sauce, which was far and away its leading product. By 1980, Kikkoman sold more than three

---

1. For a detailed account of Kikkoman's history and recent operations, see W. Mark Fruin, *Kikkoman: Company, Clan and Community* (Cambridge, Mass.: Harvard University Press, 1983). Most of the data in this introduction was derived from Professor Fruin's excellent study.

A ski trip with friends.

At a Kikkoman plant.

dozen branded food and food related products, ranging from Del Monte tomato ketchup and Disney brand fruit juices, to Ragu spaghetti sauces and Mann's wines. Soy sauce accounted for 58 percent of its sales and is expected to drop to no more than 50 percent during the next decade.

The decisions to internationalize and diversify were reached in the mid-1950s, when Kikkoman's management concluded that the Japanese home market for soy sauce was flattening or going into a decline. As it turned out, between 1952 and 1972, Kikkoman increased its share of the Japanese soy sauce market from 14 percent to 33 percent, largely by means of vigorous marketing and advertising, and thus more than compensated for the anticipated shrinkage of domestic soy sauce consumption. Nevertheless, it was pessimism about the future of the domestic market that led Kikkoman to plunge into an American advertising and marketing campaign.

During the 1956 Presidential race between Dwight Eisenhower and Adlai Stevenson, American TV viewers saw their first Kikkoman soy sauce advertisements, and Safeway stores began to carry the product. In 1957, Kikkoman International was established in San Francisco to handle business in North America. For its first decade, it registered annual sales increases of close to 20 percent, and has since continued to grow at between 10 percent to 15 percent annually. In 1973, Kikkoman opened a soy sauce factory in Walworth, Wisconsin, just in time to avoid an American embargo on soybean exports to Japan in 1973. The Walworth plant greatly strengthened Kikkoman in North America by eliminating overseas shipping costs of soybeans to Japan and soy sauce back to North America. It also continued a three hundred year old family tradition of brewing the soy sauce beside the soybean fields, which is the way the business was started in the agricultural village of Noda, northeast of Tokyo.

Yuzaburo Mogi's father, Keizaburo, was the leading advocate and planner of the 1956 plunge into the American market. As president from 1962 to 1974, Keizaburo directed Kikkoman's internationalization and its diversification. Yuzaburo Mogi was mainly responsible for siting and building the Walworth plant. Since the Walworth plant was built, Yuzaburo Mogi has spent about three to four months each year in the United States, helping to manage Kikkoman's business in this country.

The Kikkoman building rises nine stories in the old merchant neighborhood of Kanda, overlooking a busy freeway in bustling, downtown Tokyo. I first met Mr. Yuzaburo Mogi there in his executive suite on a gray, rainy April morning in 1985. The conference room in which we met was large, richly and tastefully furnished, and dominated by Japanese wall hangings and prints. Mr. Mogi is a tall, vigorous, carefully groomed man in thick spectacles. His dark hair is receding, but his face is fresh and smooth. He speaks English with a distinct Japanese accent, but fluently and very expressively. He emanated good cheer, and it was apparent that he was enjoying his work and his life. He was born on February 13, 1935, in the town of Noda, in Chiba Prefecture, the ancestral family seat, to Keizaburo and Toki Mogi.

FAMILY BACKGROUND

Mr. Mogi took the initiative in discussing his family.

"If you don't mind, I'd like to start with my family. You may know that the Mogi and Takanashi families were already in the *shoyu* (soy sauce) business even in 1630, in Noda. They used to ship their *shoyu* to Edo on river barges, like the one on that print (pointing to a colorful wall print). Well, in the second half of the 19th century and early 20th century, the business began to change more quickly than ever before because of the technology we imported from the West. We found new methods for brewing soy sauce, and we began to ship by railroad instead of barges. So, it became possible to make much more soy sauce in our new factories, and to sell our product everywhere in Japan.

"In the late 1800s and before 1917, there were eight Mogi-Takanashi family businesses in Noda, making soy sauce and competing with each other. Then, in 1917, these eight families merged to establish Kikkoman Corporation. They realized that in the new, much bigger national market, it would be better if they stopped competing with each other and merged. This would also give them more capital to improve technology and equipment--which was becoming more large-scale and expensive. So, that is what they did.

(pausing, rubbing his chin and smiling) "You know, even though that merger was a good business idea, it had some disadvantages . . . it created problems. For instance, Kikkoman Corporation needed only one president and one set of managers. Many former presidents and executives who lost their good jobs had unhappy feelings. There could have been problems because of those unhappy feelings, but they could not let their feelings show, because at that same time, in the 1920s, labor problems were becoming so bad. We had to stick together, be united. We had no time to fight with each other.

"Labor problems became so severe that in 1927-1928 we had a strike of 218 days, one of the three longest strikes in Japan before World War II. That was a very bad time. There was even some violence. However, as a result of that strike, we learned how to get along with our labor union and work together."

Question: "What do you think caused such a severe, long strike?"

"Well, there were so many changes after 1917 that many foremen and workers became uneasy . . . and anxious. Their pay and working conditions in those days were not good . . . but it was not getting worse. However, their jobs were being changed . . . almost every year, it seemed, and they worried about these changes and the future. Our management did not give enough attention to these problems. Too aloof. Bad communications. So, the labor people became desperate . . . and bitter. That caused the long strike."

Question: "How did you learn about this strike? Was it discussed at home?"

"Oh yes. My father used to sometimes tell us about the big strike. He was a graduate of Hitotsubashi University (a prestigious Tokyo school that has graduated many business leaders) in 1926. By that time, the Mogi family was deeply worried about the labor struggle, and they asked a famous professor at Hitotsubashi, Professor Teijiro Ueda, to help them. He was a labor relations expert. Well, Professor Ueda sent two good students to the Mogi family. My father was one of them."

Question: "So, he was not born in the Mogi family?"

"That's right. He was born Katsuji Iida, in the town of Asahi, also in Chiba Prefecture. He worked for Kikkoman all through the strike, and helped the company. Then, in 1929, he was adopted into the family when he married my mother. He became Katsuji Mogi, and when his father died, he became Keizaburo Mogi II. He was president for twelve years, from 1962 to 1974, and then he became chairman of the board for six years, until he retired in 1980. Now, he is president of Japan Soy Sauce Brewers Association. He is still active--has lots of energy, even though he is eighty-six. (laughing and nodding his head for emphasis)

"My mother's father, Keizaburo Mogi--the man who adopted my father--was an . . . unusual man in some ways. When he was young, he decided to become a politician and he went to Kaishu Katsu. Katsu was a famous politician at the time of the Meiji Restoration in 1868. Well, my grandfather requested Katsu to become his follower, so he could enter politics. (laughing) Katsu told him to go back to the family business. Then he decided to give his family soy sauce business to his sister and to start a new business and a new cadet branch of the Mogi family. He was . . . innovative. He introduced the newest equipment and technology in his factory, and he did quite well. He was a somewhat restless, energetic man."

Comment: "Well, I think it is worth noting that while Kikkoman is a family business--even now it is largely run by the Mogi family--the family adopts talented outsiders to help them keep up the quality of its leadership."

"Yes, yes. (nodding vigorously) That is right. Since 1917, there have been eight presidents of Kikkoman. Two of them were adopted. But, you know, the Mogi family itself is vigorous and open-minded. Even though we have strong traditions, we are ready to try new things. For instance, we took our product to the World Exhibition in Vienna, even in 1873 . . . when it was not so common for Japanese to travel to Europe. A few years after that, in 1886, one of the Mogi sons, Nobutaro was his name, was sent to London to study. But he died soon after he came back to Japan. Shinzaburo Mogi went to the U.S., to Denver, in the 1890s, and made soy sauce there. He was the forerunner of our Wisconsin plant. I think they had an . . . enterprising, venturesome spirit."

CHILDHOOD AND WAR IN NODA

Question: "Did you grow up in Noda?"

"Oh yes. I went to elementary school in Noda, starting in 1941, and then to middle school in Noda from 1947 to 1950--to the ordinary schools in the town. In 1950, I entered Ueno High School, in Tokyo, but even then I continued to live at home in Noda. I commuted every day to Ueno on the train. It was a five hour commute. But conditions were still so bad in Tokyo that it was better to live in Noda."

Question: "I know you were only ten years old when the war ended, but could you tell me what you remember of the war and the early Occupation period?"

"Well, in the early years of the war, when I was a small boy in elementary school, I wanted very much to become a naval officer and fight in the war. That was my ambition. (shaking his head and smiling) The navy officers had the best looking uniforms. (both laughing)

"By 1945, when Okinawa fell, I was about 10 years old, but we school boys in Noda began to think that Japan might not win the war . . . that maybe we would lose. Our teachers all told us that Japan was the land of the gods, and could not be defeated. But I began to doubt that it was so. We were not bombed in Noda, and there was no war damage. But at night, we could see the glow in the sky from the terrible fires in Tokyo, about twenty-five miles to the southwest. We knew that Tokyo was being bombed and destroyed. It was frightening, you know. But we were in no direct danger. Noda remained peaceful, even during the worst days of the war."

Question: "Did you have enough to eat in Noda?"

"Yes. Almost as much as we wanted. (laughing) We could not stuff ourselves as much as we liked. But we had enough. We were very fortunate. Noda is in good farming country. Of course, the food was plain and simple--not much variety--no meat. But enough rice and good vegetables, and sometimes chicken and eggs. We did not suffer from lack of food."

Question: "Hmm. By 1945, you began to suspect that Japan might be losing the war, and yet your teachers were telling you that Japan was invincible. What did you think of your teachers? How could you believe them, or trust them?"

(thoughtfully) "They had . . . no choice. We knew that they had to say that--that Japan was winning. So . . . I did not hold that against them. Perhaps they no longer believed it themselves. But my teachers were not bad. They were good people. I especially remember two of them. There was Mr. Shozo Tanaka in first grade of elementary school. He gave us many, many writing assignments. We had to write a story or composition for him almost every day. He trained us very well. I also admired my fourth grade teacher, Mr. Shiro Kawano. He was more the athletic type, frank and cheerful and a very strong guy. You know that type. I remember him as a very good teacher. In our elementary school, there was no military training. But Mr. Kawano used to teach us sports.

"Then, on August 15th, 1945, during our summer vacation, the war ended. I was only ten years old, but it was a . . . shock . . . sort of bewildering. During the war we were told bad things about the Americans, and now they were coming to Japan. But even within a month, we heard that the Americans were friendly, and not to worry about them.

"The last year of elementary school, right after the war ended, was confusing. We had all the old textbooks, that were printed before the war, and there was nothing else to use. But, we had to cross out . . . oh, about 50 percent of what was printed in them-- cover them with black ink. Well . . . that is what we had to do. (shrugging his shoulders, smiling, and shaking his head)

"In 1947, I entered the middle school in Noda. If it had not been for the war, I would have gone to a good private middle school in Tokyo, and lived in Tokyo. But in 1947, the city was still in ruins, and food was short, so it was better to remain in Noda. Another thing that happened because of the war and Occupation reforms in education was that they took away the entrance examination for middle school, because middle school became compulsory. Well, when I was in fifth and sixth grade of elementary school this was not yet changed, and I studied very hard, thinking that my future depends on that entrance examination. (laughing) Then, in 1947, when I was ready to enter middle school, there was no longer any test, and I just went right in. That seemed . . . strange to me."

Question: "Did you make good friends with the other boys in the public schools in Noda?"

"Oh yes. (laughing merrily) Certainly. We were good friends, you know, but then I went to high school in Tokyo, and we did not see each other for many years. But about twelve years ago, we formed a Junior Chamber in Noda, and some of us got together again. (warm smile) They are now the shop owners and business-men in Noda. They elected me to be the first president of the JC in Noda. "

Question: "Did you see Americans in Noda during the Occu-pation? What do you remember about them?"

"Well, very few American Occupation officials or troops came to Noda--even though it was just a couple of hours from Tokyo. Most of the Americans I saw were in . . . our house. Now and then, my father brought American people to visit with us, as guests. Well, of course, they were very pleasant, good people. Naturally, I had a very good impression of Americans."

HIGH SCHOOL

"In 1950, I entered Ueno High School, in Tokyo. That was a good quality school that sent many graduates to top universities. I wanted to live in Tokyo, you know, but I could see that it was still not a good idea. Even in 1950, five years after the war, food and housing in Tokyo were . . . not so good. So, I commuted five hours every day, except Sunday, back and forth from Noda to Ueno. It took two hours and twenty minutes to go in, and two hours and forty minutes to return home. At first . . . that made me very tired (laughing) Gradually, I became used to it. I had to get up at five every morning, and leave my house at six, to catch the train. It was very crowded in the morning, with businessmen going to work in Tokyo. I usually had no seat. In the evening, I got home at 5:30, except on Saturday, when we had a half day at school, and I came home at three o'clock. But the ride home was easier. The train was not crowded, and I could get a seat and read and study. At home, I would have dinner, study for another hour or two, and get to bed around nine. It was a busy schedule.

"You see, that commuting was . . . important for me. I'll tell you why. I had two brothers. One of them was an older brother, who died just after he was born. That made my mother and father very careful about the health of their children. They took care of me . . . too much, when I was a young boy. Whenever I had some small cold or slight fever, they would say, 'You better stay home. We will call the doctor and get medicine.' and so forth. So, I could not become strong. In my high school days, it was different. I went to school every day, even if I was a little tired or sick. Gradually, I became healthier . . . and I started to have confidence in my health and strength. I felt that even though I have to do some tough work . . . I can do that. That kind of feeling, from getting up at five in the morning, winter and summer, was important. It helped me later at Columbia Business School, when I had hard reading assignments in English and could get only a few hours sleep. (laughing merrily) I knew I could do that. It was allright."

Question: "I imagine, then, that you had very little time in Ueno High School to make friends or play sports?"

"Yes. Very little time. But I joined a baseball team with my classmates, and managed to play a little in the summer. I played first base, but I was not such a strong hitter. I was sixth in the batting order. But you are right. I had very little time to chat and make friends at school. You see, I always had to catch my train. (both laughing) So, my best friends were the students I rode with on the train in the morning. I used to change to the new electric Joban line at Kashiwa, about thirty minutes from Noda. Many students used to ride on that train. I saw a few of those guys almost every morning for three years, and we became close friends (laughing) a sort of Joban commuter club."

Question: "Were there any teachers or classes at Ueno that left a strong impression on you?"

"Hmm. (pause) You know, I just studied hard . . . and tried to memorize what I needed to pass the tests. (laughing) That was all I had time to do."

Question: "Yes, of course. That five hours a day on the train. Did you give any thought to your university education or future career while you were in high school?"

"Oh yes. I wanted to enter Keio University. It is a good university, and several men in our family had gone there. I also liked Keio because of the founder, Yukichi Fukuzawa.[2] He is a good model for young Japanese . . . even now. You know, he learned Dutch when he was a student in the Tokugawa days, and was very venturesome and went overseas to America in the 1860s. He knew Japanese must learn from the West and get along with other countries . . . and still be true Japanese. Even though he was from a samurai family, Fukuzawa taught that Japan must be good at industry and business.

(pause) "As for my future career, I did not talk about it too much. I knew that I was part of Kikkoman . . . and that I was expected to go into the company. Yet, in the early 1950s, Japanese business conditions were unstable and uncertain. The future did not always looks so promising. Sometimes I thought that maybe I would enter some other business. My parents did not say anything to me about this. (pause) Sometimes I felt that Kikkoman was too old fashioned . . . kind of out-of-date, you know."

Comment: (laughing) "Well, I understand your point, but it seems amusing to me, since Kikkoman has been so enterprising and adventurous. Maybe it was the idea of making soy sauce, which is certainly a traditional seasoning." (both laughing)

"Yes, yes. That was part of it. (smiling agreeably) But high school boys are not so realistic, you know. Anyway, I studied hard at Ueno High School, and in my senior year, in 1953, I took the entrance examination for Keio, and I was admitted."

---

2. Yukichi Fukuzawa was one of the most famous, influential and colorful figures of late 19th century Japan. For more detail on him, and his ideas on Japan's modernization and Westernization, please see Carmen Blacker, *The Japanese Enlightenment: A Study of the Writings of Fukuzawa Yukichi* (Cambridge: The University of Cambridge Press, 1964).

KEIO UNIVERSITY

"It was a good change for me to leave home and live in Tokyo. In those days, Keio had one campus in Yokohama, for freshman and sophomores, and the main campus in Mita, Tokyo, for juniors and seniors. First, I lived in a boarding house in Tokyo, close to Yokohama. Later, I moved to another place closer to Mita. I used to go home about twice a month . . . with all my laundry to give to my mother. (both laughing) Otherwise, I stayed in Tokyo."

Question: "How was your student life? Did you have to study hard? Did you have a generous allowance, and live . . . oh, more comfortably than the average student?"

(laughing long and hard) "You see, Mother was quite strict. Not an easy mother. She never gave me much money. She felt I would not study if I had any money to spend. (pause) Of course, she was right. (both laughing)

"After I entered Keio, I wanted to join extracurricular activities and make friends. You know, I had no time for that when I had to commute to Ueno. So, I tried to make up for it at Keio. It was such a . . . different life. I joined the Journalism Club and the Student Council. I worked hard at the Student Council. That was a sort of democratic, elected student government. For some time, I became the secretary-general. We used to decide on the money for the student activities. So much for the rugby team and the baseball team. So much for the Singing Club. It was good experience.

"The living conditions were . . . not at all like today, you know. Some of our classrooms in Yokohama were still in quonset huts, with no heat in winter. We wore a heavy coat to class, and still it was cold. There was no regular bath in the boarding house, and I went to the public bath. Food was . . . so-so. In the student dining room, curry rice was ¥40. But one curry rice was not enough for anyone. So we used to always buy two curry rice for ¥80. It was only a curry sauce, you know, hardly any meat.

"The classes were not so easy at Keio. It took some work. However, the most impressive book I read when I was at Keio is not a college text book, but Peter Drucker's book on management.[3] It was translated into Japanese and was very popular in Japan in those days, and at Keio. When I read that book, I really became interested in business administration and management. Peter Drucker is . . . very smart . . . and a good writer.

"When I was a junior, I also took a course on labor relations taught by an American professor from the University of North Carolina. His name is Whitehill. He taught in English. There was a translator at his lectures, but I tried to understand his English."

Question: "How was your English then?"

"Well, I had studied grammar and so forth in middle school and high school, but I was just beginning to study . . . well, what I would call real English. In my junior year at Keio, I attended English conversation classes--outside of Keio--two or three times a week. The teachers were Americans or British. That was helpful."

Question: "Did you belong to the English Conversation Club at Keio?"

"No. I did not think that was such a good way for me to learn English. You know, they had few Americans or British to teach them in that club. They used to practice English talking to each other, but it was not always such good English. Another thing that helped me to study English was the conversation class every morning on NHK radio. The program was from 6:30 to 6:45, except on the weekend. I used to listen every morning, and I tried to remember each sentence. And I tried to read something in English every day. That also helped."

Question: "Why did you develop this interest in learning English in your junior year?"

(firmly, with emphasis) "I decided I wanted to go abroad-- to America. When I read Peter Drucker's book and attended Professor Whitehill's class, I got the idea that I should study business administration in the U.S. I was very impressed with your country's approach to business administration.

"So, I visited the American Cultural Center in Tokyo, and they had some information . . . some catalogues of business

---

3. Mr. Mogi is referring to Peter F. Drucker, *The Practice of Management*, (New York, N.Y.: Harper and Row, 1954).

schools. Then I wrote to Columbia, and three or four other famous schools, and asked them for more information and for admission applications. I liked Columbia the best. My mother thought it was a good idea, but my father . . . had some worries. He knew some bad stories about young Japanese studying abroad. He was not so happy to see me go to New York. We had one Kikkoman person in San Francisco, but nobody in Manhattan. But, eventually, he agreed.

"I'll tell you why Columbia was my first choice. (ticking off the reasons on his fingers) You know, New York is *the* business center, and I thought the professors at Columbia might have some practical experience and would know how business really works. I also heard that there were many foreign students at Columbia, so it would be . . . easier to adjust. The third reason is that I liked their teaching method--a mixed method of case studies and lectures."

COLUMBIA UNIVERSITY

"I was lucky to go to Columbia. The most popular subjects there around 1960, were marketing and finance. Those were important for Kikkoman. Marketing--in a systematic way--was a new concept in Japan--including international marketing. I took my MBA in general management with a minor in marketing and international business. Also, there were several good professors at Columbia. Men like William Newman, Charles Summer, and Joel Dean. They were famous professors--especially in management and business economics.

"I especially remember Professor Dean. He passed away. His class was on Monday, and he gave us a quiz every week, so we had to always do his assignment. (laughing) He was a tough guy. His quizzes were tough . . . and his final was tough. (smiling at the memory) Oh, I used to study hard for his class. When we finished his final, I talked with other students--American students. Most of us felt . . . we had not done well. Then, Professor Dean posted the grades, and I got an A. (beaming and nodding in happy reminiscence) There were very few A's, you see. Maybe five or six, and seven or eight flunked in a class of thirty-five to forty. I was quite happy, because it took me so long to read his assignments. My English reading was slow in comparison with that of the American students. Maybe half my Japanese reading speed. So, I had to stay up half the night to finish his assignments. Professor Dean also sent a letter to each student who got an A, a letter of congratulation on the fine work. That is a good way to run a course. Have tough grades and a reward for good work. I still have the letter he sent to me. I really wanted to do good work in his course.

"The toughest course for me was human relations. That included a lot of psychology and sociology. It was so different from Japan--the way people think and act in Japan."

Comment: "But professors of psychology and sociology think that they are working on science--on subjects that are universally valid, in any culture."

"Hmm. Maybe. But it did not seem that way to me. (laughing) Anyway, even though it was hard to understand, the human relations course was important, (serious tone) because that is the way American companies and businesses really think. So, if we are going to do business in the U.S., we have to know the American way. It is very different from Japan. But we have to understand these American ideas."

Comment: "Yes. I see your point. That helps to explain why Japanese have been so successful in promoting their exports. They really try to find out what the foreigners want--what they value--and then produce it and sell it to them. They do not just take successful Japanese products and say, 'Here. We Japanese think this is a great product. Now you can buy it, too.' " (both laughing)

"Yes. And this understanding of Americans is also very important when you want to set up a business in the U.S., like our plant in Wisconsin.

"Another thing of importance I learned at Columbia is business English. This is a special kind of English, but it is used in businesses in many countries around the world. It is a kind of international language.

"I told you that at Keio, I spent a lot of time on extracurricular activities and chatting with friends. Well, I liked that, and I wanted to do that at Columbia, too. But I was very busy--just doing my course work in English, in the library or in my room at John Jay

Hall. So, I tried to pick on an activity that was not so time consuming. I picked the Toastmaster Club. It was a dinner meeting, every week, and I had to have dinner anyway. Each week, every man had to speak on a subject given by the topic master. That was fine English practice . . . and we had fun there, too. I also joined the International Business Club. They had a meeting about every two weeks or so, from 3:30 to 4:30 in the afternoon. Usually, we had a New York businessman come and give us a talk about his experiences in business. I also joined the Business Fraternity, and the International Student Club. You know, they had a tea every afternoon on the campus, at the Business School. Some professor's wives used to serve the tea, and there were good cookies and sweets. I used to sometimes take a break from my studies and walk over there. So I was able to make some good friends--Americans and also people from other countries. Some of my Columbia friends are now my consultants and business friends.

"Malcolm Pennington, who was one of my classmates, is my advisor and consultant. (smiling) One Toastmaster friend, Tom Crouse, married a Japanese woman, and I was his go-between, his *nakohdo*. (laughing) He sent me a letter saying he wanted to marry a Japanese woman, but he must have something called a *nakohdo*. (both laughing) So I was drafted, you know. And there are many other friends and business associates from Columbia. I am on the Dean's Advisory Council, so I go there twice every year for the meetings.

(pause, then in a thoughtful tone) "You know, when I went to Columbia in 1958, I did not expect to go into international business. I expected to work mainly in Japan. But while I was there in the Business School, I started to become internationalized . . . to become more open to different cultures. Also, New York was important . . . because it is an international city. So, my studies at Columbia Business School were a . . . very big step for me. I think it had more impact on me than I planned. In addition to all the things I mentioned, I gained *konjo* at Columbia. Do you know *konjo?* It is difficult to translate, but it means something like spirit and confidence."

KIKKOMAN

"When I completed my MBA, in the summer of 1961, I traveled back to Japan through Europe. I spent about a month in Europe--had a very relaxing, good time. Then, I came back to Japan, to really start my work. I was given the training for a new employee. I worked in the factory at Noda for six months, learning how we make soy sauce. I had to do all sorts of jobs--including manual jobs--like any new employee.

"Then, I was assigned to do clerical work in the Accounting Department. I also participated in introducing computers to Kikkoman. I did not study computers at Columbia, but I read about them. The company set up a committee for introducing them. That computer committee consisted mostly of young people, including myself. Well, I worked for a year and a half at introducing computers to Kikkoman. I attended the IBM computer introduction course here in Tokyo, to learn something about them. When I finished working in Accounting in 1964, I started to work for Corporate Planning. I also got involved in New Products and also in Organization Planning."

Question: "Could you give me some specific examples of the plans and products you proposed, or initiated?"

"The idea of having a factory in the U.S.A. came up. In 1965, when I was in Corporate Planning, this idea came up and the top management told us to make a cost study of a factory in the U.S., with all the data and calculations. Well, it was still too early to open a factory, but our study showed that freight costs to the U.S. were very high. So, to cut freight costs, we found a good bottling company in Oakland, California. We started shipping our soy sauce to them in bulk containers and they bottled it. That was in 1967. After this, our sales in the U.S. kept steadily increasing, and by 1970, our company realized it was a good time to look again at the possibility of having a plant in the U.S.A. So, in 1970, I was moved to the International Operations Department, to work on this. We did another feasibility study, that took about six months. Finally, in March 1971, it was decided we should build a plant in the U.S."

Question: "How did you come to select Wisconsin?"

"Well, that came later. First, we compared the East Coast, West Coast and Midwest, and picked the Midwest--because it was convenient for distribution, for shipping. Chicago is the center for the railroads and highways. Also, raw materials, soybeans and wheat, are in the Midwest. Those were two key reasons. Then we compared sixty locations in the Midwest, and finally picked Walworth, Wisconsin. I only visited the top six locations. Mr. Malcolm Pennington, my old friend from Columbia, checked all the locations and narrowed the choice. In September 1971, we picked Walworth as the place to build. It had good rail and highway connections, very good quality workers--hard workers, and a peaceful, stable atmosphere.

(pause, thinking back, stroking his chin again) "Well, we were ready to build . . . but then we realized that there was a . . . big difficulty. There was much, strong local feeling against us . . . up there, around Walworth. They did not want us. At first, I thought it was because we are Japanese. I went there myself to see. But that was not true. They were worried about pollution, and they were against any factory. It was farming country, pure farming country, you know. Even now, you can see only farms from our factory.

"So, I went to the town board meeting, and the county board public hearing. I tried to explain that soy sauce is pollution free. There is no . . . industrial pollution. Our soy sauce is a natural food product. Some companies make a kind of artificial *shoyu,* but Kikkoman makes natural *shoyu.* I talked with them for more than two months. We established a good base for understanding . . . for trust. We became . . . close friends.

"We also decided to hire local people as much as possible. Of course, we had to bring our soy sauce makers--biochemists, technicians, and production manager from Japan. No one in the U.S. knew how to make our soy sauce. At first, in 1973, we had fifteen Japanese there. Now, it is eight. We employ about four hundred and fifty people in the U.S.A. There are about one hundred American workers in the Walworth factory. You see, soy sauce brewing is now very capital intensive, technology intensive-- not labor intensive.

"You know, I learned some things from that Walworth plant. The farm people who work there are hard working and quiet. If they don't know you, it is hard to talk with them. (shaking his head) It can be very hard. But after they get to know you . . . they are very good, very kind people.

"People from farms make the best factory workers. In farming, they learn . . . the whole production process--tilling, planting, to harvesting. Everything must be done well . . . or there is no crop. So, they do good work--conscientious work. They have the farm work ethic. That is what I call it. This lasts for three generations, from when the grandfather leaves the farm to go into the factory, through his son and grandson. The grandfather and father teach it. Then, it seems to disappear.

"I think this is also the case in Japan. Our factory workers in Japan are still good because they are mostly within three generations of the farm. I asked many of them, and almost all say their father or grandfather was a farmer. So, in twenty or thirty years, this may be an important question for Japanese industry. How to have a good urban work ethic?

"Well, several years after the Wisconsin plant opened, in 1977, I was promoted to general manager of International Operations. In 1979, I was put on the board of directors. In 1982, I was promoted to managing director, in charge of International Operations and Accounting and Finance."

Question: "How would you compare your position, your job, to one in an American corporation?"

"Hmm. It is like being a senior vice-president and at the same time, a member of the board. However, in the U.S.A., the senior vice-president is hardly ever a member of the board. In our company, we have seven managing directors, and the president, and the board of eighteen members, which includes the managing directors and the president.

"As for my work, I spend about 40 percent on management, general management, and about 60 percent on international business and other responsibilities."

MARRIAGE AND CHILDREN

Question: "If we could go back some years, I know that you are married and have children. Could you please tell me when you married?"

"Oh yes. It was in 1966. My wife is the daughter of a medical doctor."

Question: "Was your marriage a traditional one, with a formal meeting--a *miai*--and the traditional arrangements, with a *nakohdo*, and so forth, or was it more modern?"

"It was fairly traditional. We had a regular *miai,* and a formal meeting of the two families. But before the marriage was decided, I saw her about fifteen times. So, we had a good chance to talk to each other, you know, and get to know each other. In the old days, usually there was not much chance for that. But otherwise, it was traditional.

"My wife's family name is Sato. She was Atsuko Sato, and she was brought up in Kamakura, not far from Tokyo. She went to college at Seishin (Sacred Heart), here in Tokyo. She studied English, and speaks quite well. We have three children--two boys of eighteen and fourteen, and a daughter of sixteen. (rubbing his chin thoughtfully) Well, let me see. (pause and then with a pleasant smile) You know, there is not much else to tell about my wife and children. We are . . . well . . . a normal family."

TRANSLATION AND WRITING

"You know, ever since my graduation from Columbia, I have participated in study groups, to work on translations and do some writing. Some of these are team translations of American books on business . . . such as H. P. Maynard's *Top Management Handbook,* and Richard Barber's *The American Corporation.* I have also written several books in Japanese. Two of them are general business books--*Introduction to International Business*, and *Accounting and Finance*. The other two are more on my personal business experience--*How to Make an Overseas Plant*, and *The Day Shoyu Made It To America's Tables*.[4] (both laughing)

Question: "Has the government called upon you for advice on international and overseas business activities?"

"Yes. I have been a member of several committees set-up by MITI on overseas investment and international communication."

INTERNATIONALIZATION

Question: "How do you define internationalization? What does it mean to you?"

"To me, it is a . . . process, with several steps. The first step is for Japanese to realize the big differences between our culture and attitudes, and foreign cultures and attitudes. (pause) That is not so difficult. Almost all Japanese do that. The second step is to . . . learn what you need to bridge the difference. That means to learn the foreign language and culture. That is a hard step. I think only a small percentage of Japanese do that. The third step is to . . . actually bridge the difference--to deal effectively with foreigners, and to become . . . comfortable with them. That is the most difficult.

"You know, if they have to do it, I think many more Japanese can learn foreign languages, even though it is hard. But most Japanese can get along without it. They don't need it for their everyday life here in Japan.

"In our company, this is a practical question. When we opened the Wisconsin plant, it was difficult to get our Japanese bio-chemists, soy sauce brewers, and production managers to go to America to work. I picked the first fifteen people to go, mainly because of their production skills not because they were good language students. You see, twelve of those fifteen people would be responsible for the quality of our soy sauce. And when they joined Kikkoman, they expected to work only in Japan. The sales people expect sometimes to work overseas, but not the production people.

---

4. The Japanese titles of Mr. Mogi's Japanese publications are: *Kokusai Business Gaku Nyumon*, (1969); *Keiri Zaimu*, (1966); *Kaigai Genchiseisan no Susumekata*, (1975); and *Shoyu ga America no Shokutaku ni Nobotta Hi*, (1983).

"So, I organized an eight month English study program for these twelve people before they left Japan. They studied English full time. I hired some special teachers for them, and divided them into two classes--one for beginners and the other for intermediates. Well, they all studied hard and did quite well. And when they got to Wisconsin, they were able to get along . . . in practical English. They more or less . . . you know . . . internationalized.

"Their attitude was good. That is the most important ingredient for the third step. They wanted to learn about America . . . to understand American ways, and to get along there. They were flexible . . . not arrogant.

"Before the war, Japanese did not do so well in business overseas. (laughing) They had too much confidence in themselves, and in the Japanese way of doing things. They did not want so much to learn. After the war, they became more humble. That helped us to do business overseas, and to internationalize. You know, America is not like Japan before the war. (both laughing) Very different. But on this one point, Americans are like prewar Japanese. They are sometimes . . . too confident, overconfident, and not eager to learn. (pause) That is natural for a victorious country. But it is not good for internationalization.

(thoughtful pause) "Of course, since we Japanese have rebuilt our country and have become more rich and comfortable, we are becoming confident again. (smiling) So, we have to be careful that we do not become overconfident."

Question: "I wonder if it might not be easier for a Japanese to learn how to live and do business in the U.S., than for an American to do that in Japan? It seems to me that America is more business-like and open, while Japanese society is more personal, hierarchical, and closed."

"Hmm. There is some truth to that. Americans want to know the product and the price. But there is also . . . (shaking his head for emphasis) . . . a lot of personal relations . . . of knowing people. It takes a long time and a lot of work with people to build a business in the U.S. It took us more than sixteen years.

(In a thoughtful, pleasant tone) "I think if Americans work hard at learning Japanese and doing business here, they will have a good chance for success.

(pause) "Maybe the hardest thing to learn is the difference of marketing and distribution in Japan and in the United States. There are two main differences. One is that marketing in Japan is more affected by personal relations. Personal relations are important in America, but they are even more important in Japan. Americans tend to be more business-like and impersonal. Another difference is that the distribution in Japan is vertical, while it is horizontal in the U.S. In Japan the wholesalers are the customers of the manufacturers, and the retailers are the customers of the wholesalers. But in the United States, manufacturers, wholesalers, and retail stores are horizontally positioned, and the consumers seem to be their only customers.

"By the way, since the Vietnam War, I have watched your country to see what they would do . . . after their setback . . . after their confidence was damaged. I am still not sure how it will turn out. When you suffer a setback, you can react in different ways. You Americans are still rich, so you might become like an old-time aristocrat, and stop working and just enjoy yourself. You know, consuming more than you produce, always going into debt with the merchants to buy luxuries. Nowadays, that does not work so well. Or, you can work hard, and prove to yourself that you . . . have learned something, and that you are . . . really good."

Schunichi Hiraki

SCHUNICHI HIRAKI is deputy general manager of the Business Development Department, Industrial Bank of Japan (IBJ). The IBJ is the largest of the three long-term credit banks in the country, which also include the Long-Term Credit Bank of Japan and the Nippon Credit Bank. It is essentially a wholesale bank, whose customers are other banks, many of Japan's and the world's largest corporations, and governments, including the Japanese government. It began life in 1902 as a semi-governmental institution authorized to issue government-guaranteed bonds with the primary purpose of financing the building of Japanese industries. In 1952, largely as a consequence of the American Occupation, the IBJ became a private institution, held by the public and listed in the Tokyo Stock Exchange. For its first fifty years, it was essentially a domestic bank. Beginning in 1956, however, when it opened an office in New York, the IBJ became internationalized. By 1987, it had six overseas branches (New York, Chicago, London, Paris, Hong Kong, and Singapore), an agency in Los Angeles, twenty-three overseas offices, and ten foreign bank subsidiaries, including IBJ Schroder Bank and Trust Company, which was acquired in 1986. It is heavily engaged in energy development and is financing industrial projects around the world, including petroleum development in Bohai Bay, northern China, coal development in Blair Athol, Australia, and liquified natural gas in Indonesia, Malaysia, and Australia.[1]

The IBJ is the only Japanese bank that has a triple A rating from Standard and Poor's and from Moody's Investors Services. It is the sixth largest bank in Japan and the seventh largest publicly held

---

1. The Industrial Bank of Japan, Ltd., *IBJ: The Fact Book, 1986*, 72-82. Also see *IBJ: Annual Report, 1986*, 10.

At left, first year of high school.

Office photograph (center, with glasses).

bank in the world, ranked by size of deposits.[2]

Sohei Nakayama, the president of the IBJ from 1961 to 1968, "and probably the greatest go-between of modern Japanese business," personifies the bank's role and its influence.[3] In the late 1960s, when Japan was in the early stages of "liberalizing" its economy, which meant opening it to foreign competition, the Ministry of International Trade and Industry (MITI) had a plan for large-scale mergers in the steel, automobile, machine tool, computer, petroleum refining, petrochemical, and synthetic textile industries. The MITI plan aimed at creating Japanese corporate giants able to compete with U.S. Steel, General Motors, IBM, and Krups. There was strong resistance in many of the targeted industries, however, and their leaders formed an Industrial Problems Research Association known as *Sanken*, to respond to MITI's merger plans. Nakayama headed *Sanken*, was instrumental in negotiating workable compromises between MITI officials and industrialists, and strengthened the IBJ's links to both. Sohei Nakayama also aggressively led the IBJ into international finance and started the practice of training some of the bank's best qualified young officers to handle its international business. One of the first of Nakayama's internationalists was Schunichi Hiraki.

I met with Schunichi Hiraki five times between February and April 1985, usually at his large, comfortable offices and in the bank's tasteful executive dining room. The IBJ is a fifteen-storied, sleek, brown building in the Marunouchi district, one block from the Imperial Palace grounds in central Tokyo. Most of the big Japanese banks have their headquarters in this neighborhood, including the three largest banks in the world, the Dai-Ichi Kangyo Bank, Fuji Bank, and Sumitomo Bank. The buildings are meticulously maintained, and the wide sidewalks are crowded with dark-suited bankers and clerks. Marunouchi is one of the world's principal financial centers, on a par with Wall Street and the City in London.

---

2. *American Banker*, July 30, 1987, 48.

3. Chalmers Johnson, *MITI and the Japanese Miracle*, (Palo Alto, Calif.: Stanford University Press, 1984), 277. For a more complete account of Sohei Nakayama, please see Ralph Hewins, *The Japanese Miracle Men*, (London: Secker and Warburg, 1967), 382-396.

Schunichi Hiraki is a stocky, energetic man in his mid-forties, dark haired, smooth-faced, and bespectacled. His eyes are large and expressive and frequently twinkle with humor. His English is fluent and relaxed. His voice is strong, and when he becomes enthusiastic or intense, which he often does, he raises it. In conversation he is lively, quick-witted, even ebullient. He was born to Toshiaki and Toshiko Hiraki, on June 9, 1941, the first of their three children.

FAMILY BACKGROUND

"I was born in Kobe, one of the two largest ports in Japan. My father was a shipbuilding engineer. He graduated from the Imperial University in Kyoto, and he worked for Mitsubishi Heavy Industries. His family is from the countryside near Osaka. Way back, I think they were samurai. But in the civil wars of the 1600s, they were on the losing side and became farmers. They became prosperous, bought land, and by this century they were fairly rich landlords. But my father's father died at an early age, and that was very bad for them. They had to sell most of their land, and the family's assets were . . . almost wiped out. My father's family name is Kitano. (pause)

"My mother's name is Hiraki. So you see, when they married, my father took the Hiraki name. That is not . . . normal . . . but sometimes we do that in Japan."

Comment: "I understand how these adoptions work. Your mother's family probably wanted him to take their name because he is such an able man."

(smiling and shaking his head at me) "Well, he did have a good education. (pause) But I think my father decided to join the Hiraki family because the Hirakis were much wealthier than his family. I think it was his idea.

"My mother's father had been very successful in real estate. He had bought quite a bit of farmland in what became the central part of Kobe City, and after the First World War, when the city grew so quickly, it became residential and business real estate. You can imagine how the value shot up. He did so well that he was appointed to the Kobe City Council. In those days, that was an honorary post--no pay and no authority--but some influence. It was a recognition of his business success and his wealth. You know, I still have some memories of my grandfather, but not much. He died in . . . 1945. I remember that when he visited us, my parents would always call me to come and greet him, and that he would hug me and be very affectionate. (smiling) So, they are nice memories."

Question: "What did your mother's family do before her father struck it rich?"

"They were prosperous farmers and petty landlords in Kobe . . . for a long time, for several hundred years. We have Buddhist temple records of the family that go back to about 1600, and there are family tombstones that go back earlier than that. Some of the Hiraki were chosen to head the local farmers, as deputies to help govern the area. In those days, Kobe was directly under the Tokugawa family rule.

"The Hiraki family is still basically a Kobe family. That is where most of us live. (smiling) When you look at these tombstones in the graveyard of the Buddhist temple, you can see the good times and bad times of the family. In some generations the stones are big and rich . . . and in others . . . pretty small. (laughing) Some of the smallest are barely visible . . . nominal tombstones." (both laughing)

Question: "When your father took the Hiraki name, did he become the heir to the family?"

"No. My mother has a brother who is two or three years older than my father. Her brother became the head of the family. My mother has five sisters and this one older brother. She is the youngest. Of course, her brother was cherished by the family . . . even spoiled . . . because he was the only son. But he has done pretty well. He is a Keio (University) graduate, and he became a managing director of the Taiyo Kobe Bank--eighth largest in Japan-- before he retired. Then, he took after his father and went into real estate (smiling) and did well at that, too.

"My grandfather's younger brother went to England after the First World War--the family financed his trip--and studied textile manufacturing there. He brought back some special spindling technology, built a factory in Kobe, and made a small fortune. Then he used some of his money to build a privately owned toll road about thirty kilometers long, from Ashiya (a Kobe suburb) to Arima hot springs. Well, when my uncle retired from the Taiyo Kobe Bank, he took over that toll road, improved it, and then was successful in developing the mountainous land in that part of Ashiya--it is really steep--into residential real estate." (smiling and nodding his head respectfully)

Comment: "Well, I can see that you come from a family of entrepreneurs."

(laughing) "Yes. There is some entrepreneurial blood in the family. But that is fairly common around Osaka and Kobe, where we have a long commercial tradition. (with his half humorous twinkle) Who knows, maybe someday I will retire from banking and become an entrepreneur myself."

WAR AND OCCUPATION

Question: "Since you were born in 1941, you were only about four years old when the war ended. Do you have any memories of the war?"

"Hmm. (thoughtful pause) Not too many . . . but I have some."

Question: "Do you have any recollection of the air raids on Kobe?"

(nodding affirmatively) "Yes. Yes, I do. Even though I was only a small child, I remember the B-29s and the bombing. (pause) It must have been the last year of the war. (pause, thinking back) The air raid sirens went off in the middle of the night and woke me up. My mother and father were waking up my younger brother and sister. We had to get to an underground shelter. My brother and sister were too young--just babies and toddlers. They couldn't walk well enough, and they were half asleep, so my parents carried them. I was the eldest . . . so my mother and father kept saying, 'You must walk yourself. You are a big boy.' (serious pause and then a small smile) I didn't feel like a big boy. I was . . . terribly sleepy."

Question: "And frightened?"

(pause) "It was not really frightening. I don't remember being frightened. We heard the planes and explosions . . . but they were not that close. The heavy bombing was down on the waterfront, in the Kobe Harbor district where there were shipyards and factories. We lived three miles away at the foot of Mt. Rokko. Only a few bombs fell in our neighborhood, probably by accident. I remember that once some houses on the next block were hit--probably by an incendiary--and burned down. It was windy and even our house caught fire--a small fire. My father put it out. Our house is still there, and although it is repaired and repainted, the scars from that fire are on the house."

Question: "You actually remember that fire? It isn't something you learned about later?"

"I remember that fire. I saw it. (pause) But it was not terrifying--not at the time. Maybe I was so young . . . I didn't know enough to be frightened."

Question: "Do you remember food shortages or hunger?"

"Well, I don't remember starving . . . or any food shortages like that. It seemed to me there was enough food. But in Kobe, it seemed that we were almost always eating some kind of . . . pancakes made from flour, and only sometimes a meal of rice mixed with barley. No meat, and very little fish. My father had to stay in Kobe to work, and my mother used to take us to stay with our relatives in the countryside for some days. We went back and forth on the train. In the countryside we ate more vegetables and rice . . . and eggs. Then we would go back to Kobe to be with my father, but the food was not as good.

(a reminiscent pause) "I recall that in Kobe, I was sick with a cold. And because I was sick, my mother gave me a special treat--eggs mixed with rice and soy sauce, *tamago gohan*. That was delicious. A great luxury.

(pausing and wrinkling his brow in thought) "Hmm. I really can't be sure if that was in 1945 or 1946 or so. I don't remember the end of the war in 1945. There was no sharp break between the war and the beginning of the Occupation--not in my memory. But I remember having that cold and the *tamago gohan*.

"My memories of the early Occupation are . . . mostly vague. There was a gradual improvement in our life . . . in food and clothing. I saw very few Americans or foreigners. Just a few Occupation troops in downtown Kobe when I went along shopping sometimes with my mother.

"My first really sharp memory of that time is when I was about six or seven. A beautiful young woman--a Japanese in her early twenties--came in our house to use our phone. Only a few houses in our neighborhood had telephones. She brought an American soldier with her, in a fine uniform with medals. She was beautifully dressed and . . . very striking. And . . . she was talking over the phone and talking to this soldier in some language I could not understand. It was English. That was the first time I heard English . . . and it was a remarkable event for me . . . to hear her talk and to see this American soldier so close, in the same room.

"I heard later that she was a secretary for the Occupation and that she married her American fiancé. (pause) You know, I think that incident was an . . . internationalizing influence. Even though I was so young and didn't know what was going on, I thought it was . . . glamorous. This beautifully dressed young woman and her American fiancé--and speaking in a foreign language. I was really impressed with that.

(pause) "Another memory I have from those years is also about foreigners--White Russians. They came from Siberia after the Communist Revolution and went into business, and some did very well. They had villas close to ours, in the Kitano foreign settlement. But they were wiped out by the war, left without anything and some of them were . . . penniless during the Occupation. When I was about six or seven, at that same age, I remember seeing some of these White Russians in old, tattered clothes, begging . . . in the cold weather . . . begging in our neighborhood. (shaking his head) That was pitiful.

"Then, toward the end of the Occupation, when I was a fifth grader, in 1951, my father went abroad for six months. Things were much better by then, and Mitsubishi sent him to study ship-building technology with Westinghouse in Pittsburgh and Philadelphia, and then to Switzerland, with Sulzer, who makes ship's engines. He sent many, many letters and picture postcards home. I read them and studied them, thinking how great it must be to travel around the world like that, to all these cities. (shaking his head and smiling) I wanted to go, too."

Question: "Did your father speak English and German?"

"Well, he could speak a little of these languages. He had studied some English and German in his school days and before he took this trip he went to English classes at the Kobe YMCA, and learned more conversational English.

"So he was able to get along . . . certainly for engineering work.

"My father flew home during the summer of my fifth-grade vacation, and my mother took me up to Tokyo with her to greet him at Haneda Airport. (smiling warmly) That was my first trip to Tokyo, and I was so happy to see my father (grinning) maybe because he brought me bananas. (both laughing) That's right. Bananas. They were very precious at that time."

Question: "Well, when you think back on it, what effect or influence did the war and Occupation have on your values . . . your way of looking at life? Do you think it was an important, strong influence?"

(thoughtful pause) "You know, I was one of the lucky ones in my generation. My father was building warships for Mitsubishi, so he was not drafted and he was able to support us and look after us pretty well. We could travel easily to our relatives in the country and get better food. When we came back to Kobe, our house was there. Even after the Surrender, my father's company kept him at work, and we didn't have any great hardship. (pause) Compared to the way people live now we had very little, but I could see that we were much more comfortable than many other people. I know that. (pause) So, compared to these people, the war did not have such a heavy influence on our family . . . and on me.

(looking at me very seriously) "But it had some influence. I know how different our life then was from . . . the affluent life we have now. I know that cities can really be bombed. I don't think about these things very often. But I think they made a difference, an important difference."

SCHOOL IN KOBE

"We lived in Kobe until I was fifteen, so I went to grammar school and junior high school there. The grammar school was an ordinary, public school--not special or attached to a university like Keio or Tokyo Education University. Nothing spectacular, but reasonably good."

Question: "Were the students almost all from well-to-do families, or was it more mixed?"

"Oh, it was very mixed. The children came from all different kinds of families--shopkeepers, laborers . . . a carpenter's son, office workers. All kinds. Our neighborhood, at the foot of Mt. Rokko, is called Hyogo-ku, and it is really part of Kobe City, not a suburb. You know, Kobe is very narrow, stretched between the Mt. Rokko range and the Gulf of Osaka. There is the port and the docks, the business section behind it, and then you are at the foot of Mt. Rokko, where it is more residential."

Comment: "Yes, I have been to Kobe. It is an attractive city, even though it is narrow, as you say. Reminds me of San Francisco, the way it swoops up from the harbor."

"Well then, you know how beautiful Rokko is. Our backyard was the foothill of Mt. Rokko. I used to play in it with our two dogs. (thoughtful pause) You know, I was very fortunate . . . compared with my child . . . who is living in a concrete jungle.

"Well, after six years in that grammar school, I graduated and went to Nada Junior High School in Kobe, which is one of the best in the country. It is a private school, and nowadays Nada and Azabu, and Kaisei in Tokyo, send the most graduates to Todai. When I was accepted to Nada it was good, but not as competitive as it is now."

Question: "Did you have to pass a test to get in?"

"Yes, and once you passed that test you were automatically accepted to Nada High School as well . . . as long as your work was fairly good in the junior high. I don't think the test was very difficult. (smiling) Probably because I had been well prepared. I was number one or two in my grammar school, and my parents pinned a lot of their hopes on me. In my last year of grammar school, when I was twelve, they hired a private tutor to prep me for the Nada test. The first tutor got TB and had to quit, and they got another. So you see, I was well prepared . . . and I was not very worried."

Question: "Is Nada a boarding school?"

"They had students from other parts of Japan, and some arrangements for them to live there, but it is not like an American boarding school. Of course, I lived at home. Also, Nada school is not terribly expensive either, even though it is a very fine private school. It has a large endowment that was established by the Nada sake breweries. You must have heard of them. They make the best sake, and are very big and successful. So, the campus is pretty big and the buildings are very fine, and the school is well supported.

"At Nada, they combined the three year junior high and three year high school course into five years. We did the usual subjects-- math, Japanese, English, history, science, and so on. Then, in the sixth year, they concentrated on preparing the students for the university entrance exams . . . for the best schools . . . Todai or Kyoto University."

Question: "How was the training in English? Did you learn much of your English at Nada?"

(shaking his head and laughing) "Not so much. I think the training there was . . . inadequate. The English courses were mainly grammar, reading and some writing. But they are aimed at passing the university entrance exams, and they were very good for that (laughing) but not at teaching practical English. As a matter of fact, my teacher at Nada, Mr. Mohri, was famous in Japan for writing a book on how to pass the university entrance English tests. That is a special skill.

"You know, one of the easiest ways to improve our English training is to change the university entrance exam--to make it more realistic and practical. Because the students will work to master whatever they have to do to pass that test.

(grinning) "Well, I know you are going to ask me about my school work and my grades. Right? (both laughing) I didn't work hard at junior high school--just enough to pass. I was in the lower half of my class. We were about 175, and at my best I ranked between 80 and 90. Sometimes I slipped as low as 120. I was really devoting myself to judo. (noticing a look of surprise on my face) Yes, to judo. I am a little heavy now, but I was strong and well built at that age, and I spent most of my time after class at the gym-- usually about three hours a day--practicing hard at judo. So when I got home in the evening I was so hungry and tired I used to eat and go right to sleep. No time for homework.

"Judo is a big activity at Nada school. The founder of Nada was related to Jigoro Kano, who started Kodokan Judo. So it is a special tradition at Nada."

Question: "What did your parents think of all that judo and your mediocre grades?"

"They didn't oppose my judo, not in my first two years. In fact, in the first year or two of junior high, when I was thirteen and fourteen, they encouraged me to exercise and practice. But in the third year, my grades really dropped. I was about 150 in the class, and I think they were worried. (pause) Then, just at that time, I got an injury behind my right knee during judo practice. I still feel it sometimes in cold weather. Between that injury and my poor grades . . . well, I was forced to quit judo. I was very discouraged . . . but only for a short time. Because after the spring semester of my third year, my father was transferred to Tokyo, to the Mitsubishi Heavy Industry head office. (The school year in Japan begins in April.) We moved during the summer vacation. Nada had a special arrangement with Azabu school, and I was able to transfer into Azabu without taking any entrance examination. That was a lucky move. It gave me a chance to . . . how do you say . . . to turn over a new leaf."

AZABU HIGH SCHOOL IN TOKYO

(reminiscing in a thoughtful tone) "Hmm. You know, I missed judo practice. I was fairly good at *newaza*, wrestling on the mat, and I liked being on the team at Nada. So, in the back of my mind, up in Tokyo, I was thinking, 'Someday, I will get into judo again.' I didn't do it at Azabu High School, but afterward, at Todai, I tried again. (smiling in a self-deprecatory way) I was . . . very confident. Too confident. I thought that the Todai judo wrestlers

were not as strong as our team at Nada. But I was wrong. And I
was out of practice. I was thrown away on the mat. I couldn't keep
up with them . . . so I stopped."

Question: "But you turned over a new leaf, at Azabu High
School, as a student?"

"Oh yes. You know, my grades at Azabu . . . well, they
surprised me. (both laughing) I graduated as one of the *yutosei*, in
the top 5 percent. The standards at Azabu were the same as Nada,
but since I stayed away from sports and clubs, I just pitched into my
school work . . . and my grades went up."

Question: "Were there any teachers or subjects that made a
lasting impression on you?"

"Math and Chemistry were my strongest subjects. I was
able to get top grades in them just doing the homework every day,
exercise by exercise and page by page."

Question: "I see. I have the feeling that you may not have
been deeply interested in your school work, even though you were
good at it. That it was . . . work you had to do. Am I wrong?"

(thinking over the question and then with a mischievous
twinkle) "You are partly wrong . . . and partly right. Thinking
back, I tried to act as though school work was just something I had
to do . . . that I was an indifferent but obedient student. Some boys
are like that, you know. It was a kind of pose. But to some extent,
I was interested in math and chemistry. I liked the logic, and I liked
the lab work in chemistry, doing experiments. I was thinking that I
might go into chemical engineering in the university, until I studied
economics with my social science teacher, Mr. Fukuda. He was
very good at introducing us to general equilibrium and the price ad-
justment mechanism. That influenced me to think about studying
economics. I asked my father about this, and even though he is an
engineer, he left it up to me. And I decided on economics."

Question: "Were you planning even then, while you were
still in high school, to go into business or banking after the university?"

"Business, banking, or maybe the government bureaucracy.
I didn't make up my mind until later, during my last year at Todai.
My most important goal when I was in high school was to enter To-
dai. At Azabu, the people with the best grades almost all tried for

Todai. So it was the natural thing to do. And at home, well it was just understood that I would go to Todai or Kyoto University."

Question: "Yes, but even some of the people with high grades don't make it. The competition is very tough. At the time, when you were finishing high school and getting ready for the entrance exams, what were your thoughts about that?"

(thinking back and then looking at me very directly) "Well, I was ready to compete. I was confident. So I took the Todai entrance exam in 1960, when I was about to graduate from Azabu, but I didn't pass it . . . not that first time. It was not such a terrible shock. As you said, even some of the best students don't pass the first time. Then, I went into a preparatory school for the entrance exams for one year, really worked at it, and in 1961, I passed and enrolled at Todai. In 1960, I took only the Todai exam. (smiling) In 1961, I hedged. I also took the exams for Keio, Waseda, and the Tokyo University for Foreign Studies--just in case."

Question: "I know this is a hypothetical question, but if you had been one of the people who did not get into Todai, and you had gone to the other schools you mentioned, how much difference would it have made in your life?"

"Of course, I can't be sure, but I don't think that is too difficult to answer. In some ways it would have made a great difference. Practically speaking, I would have had less chance to get into the elite of business. I would have had less . . . interesting work, less prestige. And maybe less money, (laughing) but maybe not. Maybe I would have made more. (both laughing) But if I had done my best, I would be allright . . . inside myself. You are born with a certain amount of ability or talent, and you should use it. (pause and then in a bright, affirmative tone) The important thing is to do the best with what you have."

TODAI AND CHOOSING A CAREER

Question: "When you got to Todai, how did you find the life there? What influence did Todai have on you?"

"I became a little more independent . . . from my parents. They thought that was a good idea, and so did I. (thoughtful pause)

My biggest interest at Todai was the English Speaking Society--a student club. When I was a student, between two and three hundred freshmen joined the society, and then most of them . . . well, faded away during the year. By the end of the school year, we used to have a total membership of about fifty people. I was one of the steady, regular members. I used to go to our club room everyday, and go on all our trips and activities. The society was my . . . focal point.

"To a large extent, I think it was because of my father, although he never told me what to do on these matters. It was his example. Anyway, I wanted to learn English. I thought that whatever career I enter, I want to really learn to speak it, because it is the international means of communication. With a command of English, I would be able to work and travel all over the world. That was the main reason I spent so much time on the English Speaking Society. But there were also some girl students in the club, and it was one of the rare places to meet girls and talk with them. (smiling) That was a . . . fringe benefit. And in fact, some of the girls were really good at English, much better than me, and I learned something from them. We had a few speech contests and debates with teams from some of the women's colleges

"I was so active in the society that in my sophomore year I was chosen vice-president, and in my junior year, president. The seniors were too busy job hunting to take care of the club. That is when I met many of my best friends--including Kosuke Nakahira and Yoriko Kawaguchi. Yoriko had already lived in the States, and she was really fluent in English.

"Some of the other members were also pretty good English speakers, and I was way behind them. I was unhappy about that. I felt that I had to catch up. So, I took the NHK TV English program every evening, and used their textbook--it was only ¥150, about forty cents at that time--and I did all the exercises. That was the biggest help for me. There was no language lab at Todai in those days, and our English courses were mainly reading and writing."

Question: "Did you practice everyday on campus, with the other members when you met them?"

"We were supposed to do that (shaking his head and smiling) but we mainly talked to each other in Japanese. But on each school vacation--spring, summer, and autumn--we rented some To-dai facility in a resort area and took a society trip. Then, we spoke only English. Every time someone used Japanese, they had to pay a ¥10 fine. That was an effective teaching aid. (both laughing)

"Another thing that was very helpful was that some kind people from the British and American embassies--some of them wives of diplomats--came to our club room and tutored us once a week. They were not paid, you know. We invited them to our student parties to show our gratitude. Sometimes they joined us on our vacation trips.

"I also used to go to the American Cultural Center in Tokyo, oh, about once a week, to borrow books and talk with people. For a while, I took an English conversation course there.

"In my junior year, when I was president of the club, (British) Prime Minister Home came on a state visit to Japan, and he came to Todai. We were asked to have a discussion with him. (laughing) We didn't say very much . . . but he was very pleasant, and it was good English practice.

"In my sophomore year, a German student, Herr von Benckendorf, came to see us when I was vice-president. He was representing the International Association for Students in Economics and Commerce-- called AIESEC--which is the abbreviation of the French--and pronounced like the name Isaac. He wanted us to help form a chapter for AIESEC at Todai and at three other universities, Hitotsubashi, Keio, and Waseda. I was already so busy that at first I was kind of lukewarm about his idea, but Mikio Kato of the International House--I think you know him--was enthusiastically helping von Benckendorf, so we and the students from the other universities joined in and set up a new chapter of AIESEC. Well, that turned out to be very lucky for me. Part of the AIESEC program was setting up international student exchanges . . . using internships for vocational training. A Todai-Northwestern student exchange was set up, and in my senior year I worked as an intern at the Continental Casualty Insurance Company on State Street, in Chicago. That was from . . . September to December in 1964. (happy grin) So, there I was . . . in your Midwest."

MIDWESTERN INTERLUDE

"It was my first visit . . . my first time outside of Japan . . .
and I learned a great deal. (shaking his head, smiling broadly at the
memory) I also had a . . . great time. It was almost accidental that it
worked out so well. Before I left Japan, I knew that I would be
employed by the Continental Casualty Insurance Company as a kind
of trainee and that their salary would cover my expenses. But I
didn't make any plans about where to live, or even where to stay
overnight when I landed in Chicago. I was just a student, and I
thought I would go to a Y, or an inexpensive hotel, or some place
like that.

"I was told that someone from the Chicago area AIESEC
would meet me at the airport. It turned out to be James Salvatore,
Jr. He was vice-president of the Chicago area AIESEC, and a first
year student at the University of Chicago Business School. Well,
when Jim heard that I had no hotel reservation for that night, he invited me to stay with his family. They live on Glenlake, in a Chicago suburb just a few blocks from Evanston. Of course, I said yes.
I wanted to see how it was in an American family . . . in a real
American home. (smiling warmly) They were very open and kind
to me . . . even at our first meeting, just after I landed at O'Hare.

"Well, I had no other ideas of where I wanted to live, so I
asked the Salvatores if they would mind if I lived with them for
three months. I would pay for my food and expenses, whatever
they thought I should pay. They knew that I was getting only a
small salary as a trainee at Continental Casualty. They have a fairly
comfortable, roomy house in Glenlake and only one son. So, the
Salvatores asked me to stay on as their guest. They were . . . so
friendly and kind.

"I commuted everyday by the elevated to State Street, to
work from nine to five at Continental Casualty. Jim Salvatore and I
became pals. In my free time, he introduced me to his friends . . .
and to his girl friend . . . so I learned how young Americans act
with each other. So, for three months in the fall of 1964, I was totally immersed in the American way of life . . . on a regular, family
basis. That really made me feel at home in your country.

"I am still in touch with the Salvatores. They visited with me in Tokyo, and whenever I go to Chicago, I visit them . . . or at least call from the hotel or the airport to say hello, if I am too busy. (smiling warmly) They are a really . . . fine family . . . good people."

BECOMING A BANKER AND A HARVARD MBA

Question: "How did the three months as a trainee in Chicago fit in with choosing your career? Aren't most of the students at Todai who are going to join a company recruited during the fall of their senior year--just about the time you were in Chicago?"

"Yes, that's the way it usually works, but it is not that . . . rigid, and it was somewhat more flexible back when I was a student. I think nowadays there are more restrictions about when employers and students can begin formal contacts. In the summer vacation of my senior year, in 1964, I went knocking on the door of the personnel department at several banks in Tokyo, getting in contact with them."

Question: "Did you write first or send a resume? Or did one of your professors introduce you?"

"Not in my case. Some people did that, but I just went to their personnel department, told them I was a Todai student and that I wanted to apply for a position with them. Hmm. That was not such an unusual way to job hunt. Other students were also job hunting that way."

Question: "Yes, I see. Had you decided by that summer that you were not going to become a civil servant and that you would go into banking?"

"Yes. I decided that summer. The Higher Civil Service Examination was scheduled for some time in late August and the interviews in early September, and if I wanted to go to Chicago, I had to leave in late August. I decided it was more useful to spend the three months in the U.S. (thoughtful pause) At that time, it was a rare opportunity for a student to be sponsored to go to the U.S. Of course, I could have taken the government examination, but my mind was pretty much made up to go into banking. I was talking with IBJ, the Mitsubishi Bank, and several other banks. Hmm. It was not . . . a very calculated decision. (smiling) I had a good feeling about the prospects in banking . . . and especially about IBJ. My father introduced me to the people at Mitsubishi Bank, since he worked for Mitusbishi Heavy Industries, and I took the entrance examination for Mitsubishi Bank and for IBJ. I passed them both, and then I decided I wanted to work for IBJ.

"The main reason I picked IBJ was that they told me they were starting a program for sending a few young officers overseas to attend universities, including American universities. Mr. Nakayama was our president then, and it was his idea. IBJ was just beginning to get into international banking, and Nakayama-san thought overseas business would expand and that the bank would need people with international training."

Question: "Did the Mitsubishi Bank, or other banks, offer similar training overseas?"

"Not at that time. IBJ was the . . . pioneer. It was the first bank to train its people overseas this way--to pick them and cover their expenses itself. Before IBJ started its program, a few Japanese bank officers had studied in the U.S. They had gone on Fulbright Scholarships. They had applied for scholarships on their own, and the scholarships covered their travel, their education expenses, and even their living costs. The banks just gave these Fulbright scholars a leave-of-absence. Of course, that saved our banks some money, but it was not a reliable way to train people. The Fulbright committee decided who to send and the number of bankers was very limited. Well, in the 1960s, Nakayama-san thought that IBJ should have its own overseas training program, so that we could make sure our bank had enough people with international training.

"Of course, I had no guarantee when I joined IBJ in 1965 that I would be picked for overseas training. They told me it was competitive . . . that first I would have to join the bank and work there for a year or two and then it would depend on my tests and my attitude in the bank. Well, between forty and fifty young bank officers applied for the program. We took an English test and we were also screened on the basis of our . . . contribution to the bank. Four were chosen. One went to Cambridge in the U.K. One went to Germany. And two to the U.S.--MIT and Harvard Business

School. That is how I got to Harvard Business School. IBJ sent me there from 1967 to 1969, and I completed the MBA degree."

Comment: "It seems to me you took a pretty big gamble when you joined IBJ. The odds were about ten to one against IBJ sending you to Harvard."

(laughing) "Mathematically, you are right. But when I joined IBJ, I had . . . a good feeling about my chances. I thought that all my work in the English Speaking Society and my experience in Chicago would probably pay off. (grinning) Anyway, that was why I decided to join IBJ, and it worked. Two years after I joined the bank, I went to Harvard Business School."

MARRIAGE AND FAMILY LIFE

"When I got back from Harvard Business School in 1969, I was twenty-eight--a good age to get married. (smiling) That is what my parents told me, and also my friends at the bank, and I agreed with them."

Comment: "I imagine you were . . . a prime candidate for marriage (both laughing) with your Todai, IBJ and Harvard credentials."

"Well, in a way, yes. But the bank kept me so busy that I didn't have time to associate with the ladies. I was an economist in our Economic Research Department. I had to keep up with daily statistics, write reports, and so I was always busy and working until late in the evening. (pause, and then in a musing, nostalgic tone) In part of my mind, when I thought of marriage in those days, I used to daydream that somehow I would meet a beautiful girl . . . we would fall in love, you know (laughing) and live happily ever after. Actually, I had no time for that kind of romance . . . or for chasing after girls.

"So instead, I had arranged meetings with young ladies-- *miai*. For almost two years, I had a *miai* every week or so. (noticing that I was surprised at the frequency of his marriage interviews and chuckling) Yes, almost every week I had one. I was given the resumé and the family history of many fine, young ladies and asked to meet them. My parents and their friends would say, 'If you can spare the time this weekend, we would like to have a *miai* for you. Please come to our house at such and such a time.'

"For about a year, I was . . . just agreeable to most of these requests. But I wasn't really serious. I went to meet almost all these young ladies, and I chatted with them . . . and that was all. I was so absorbed in my work that I didn't think much about these meetings. I was concentrating on being a banker, and acquiring basic techniques such as financial cost/benefit analysis, and preparing myself for what I hoped would be an overseas assignment to the Asian Development Bank or the World Bank. But after I turned twenty-nine, I realized that I ought to take these *miai* more seriously, that I ought to marry and settle down by the time I was thirty.

"Then, before too long, I met my wife at a *miai*. It was arranged by a mutual friend of my mother and my wife's mother. I knew that Michiko was a graduate of Waseda University. She had majored in English literature, and I wanted a wife who could speak English. I found that Michiko shares my hobbies. We both like to listen to music. She plays the piano . . . pretty well and enjoys it. She also plays tennis . . . but not that well."

Comment: (jokingly) "You usually win in your tennis matches?"

(both laughing) "Yes, yes. My wife doesn't try too hard to beat me. So you see, we were compatible. We went to concerts, played tennis, got to know each other, and decided to marry."

Question: "Did you take your wife's family background into account?"

"To some extent, but it was not a major factor. Michiko's father is a professor at Japan University. His name is Fumio Momose. He teaches nutrition in the Agro-Medicine Department. He is a Todai graduate. Her mother is a former high school teacher. They are not wealthy, but are oriented toward education. (pause) If I had been . . . a real calculator, I would have looked for a family with strong banking connections. (smiling) But I wasn't . . . and I am happy in my marriage.

"We have one child, a girl of twelve, just beginning junior high school. Her name is Ayaka. We would like to have more children, but somehow we haven't. (thoughtful pause and then in a matter-of-fact tone) Family life is not always so easy. A few years after we married, we went to the World Bank in Washington for three years and a half. It has been nine years since we got back, and my turn for another overseas assignment may be coming. My wife wants us to build a house. We bought a lot in a Tokyo suburb some years ago, so we have the land for a house. But who will take care of a new house for us if we go overseas? So, we keep living in an IBJ apartment. It is only thirty-five minutes from my office, which is convenient, but it is only sixty-nine square meters (about six hundred and forty square feet), very, very small by American standards. Sometimes, I take close American friends to our apartment to show them the reality of Japanese housing. But our place is not suitable for entertaining business friends. So you see, even though I have a good salary by Japanese standards, housing is enormously expensive and difficult in Tokyo. If my family or my wife's family was really wealthy, then we might be able to afford a bigger apartment, maybe one hundred square meters (about nine hundred square feet) in central Tokyo. That would probably cost about ¥100,000,000 (about $720,000).

(looking directly at me and smiling) "Well, my wife and I talk a lot about houses and apartments and we don't always agree. But we get along. And we manage to have a reasonable standard of living. Our daughter is fond of music, too. We send her for piano lessons and for ballet lessons. And she has started playing tennis with my wife.

"My wife's mother is a baptized Christian, and she used to teach at Sacred Heart High School for girls, here in Tokyo. Michiko is not baptized, but she attended Catholic mission schools and she likes to go to the Catholic church now and then and she usually takes our daughter. Our daughter goes to the public school in our neighborhood.

"We are not such a religious family. I don't go to church. But occasionally I do Zen meditation . . . to renew myself. In my student days at Todai, I was deeply impressed by an American missionary--Father Dwight Johnson, a Lutheran minister. When I was a freshman, I went to his bible classes at Denenchofu Lutheran Church, and I enjoyed them and felt attracted by many things he said. There was a good group there of boys and girls, all about nineteen or twenty. It was comfortable and wholesome, you know, and we felt very good there. Father Johnson wanted to baptize me, and I thought about it very seriously and talked it over with my father. In the end, I decided not to do it. But I felt that some of the things Father Johnson taught us . . . are true and important. People are weak and sinful. It takes discipline and you have to really work at it to be a decent person. And he also used to say that, 'God helps those who help themselves.'

(thoughtfully, in an appreciative tone) "In a way, Father Johnson got me thinking about religion . . . about how a person should act and believe. After awhile, that is what led me toward Zen Buddhism. When my father died and we gave him a Buddhist funeral service, I also realized how deep and strong Buddhism is. (pause) So nowadays I go and do *zazen* (meditation) at a small temple near my home. In the summer, for a few days, I go to a Zen Temple in Chiba Prefecture, and try to learn more. (thoughtful pause) Maybe I could not really appreciate the Christian idea of sin. But I understood human weakness . . . my own weakness . . . and that it is good to focus and to concentrate. That is an important kind of self-control and strength that you can learn.

(thoughtful pause) "You know, when I sit back like this and think about my life, my family life and marriage . . . they have been basically good and sound. And my family life and my work have meshed smoothly. I know from some of my American friends that this is . . . not always the case with them, that now and then their family life and their career are in conflict. Things are changing in Japan--the newspapers say that these days some middle aged wives get fed up with their husbands and leave them--but this family and career conflict is not so common here, yet. (smiling) So, in this sense, I am a fairly typical Japanese."

CAREER

Question: "I know that you have already touched on your career in the IBJ. You are now (summer of 1985) a manager in the Business Development Department, working primarily on energy projects. Your overseas experience with IBJ has included your graduate work at Harvard from 1967 to 1969, and your three years as a seconded officer at the World Bank, in Washington, from 1973 to 1976. What would you say have been the most important and formative experiences you have had as a banker--as a Japanese, international banker?"

"Hmm. (pause) Before I answer your question, let me tell you what my basic attitude is about my career . . . otherwise you may have some mistaken ideas about how I see my job and the IBJ. I am not such a devotee of Japanese business practices . . . of lifetime employment and the seniority system. Quite a few of my American friends from Harvard Business School have changed firms two, three, even four times since we graduated, and some of them have done very well. A few have successfully founded their own companies or investment firms. Well, I have been impressed by what they have done. (thoughtful, serious pause and then looking at me keenly) If some firm . . . maybe a multinational . . . comes along and makes me a very generous offer (lifting his eyebrows expressively) I might take it. Also, if sometime in the future, I see a good chance to start up a new business, well, I might do that too."

Comment: "I am not too surprised to hear this. I had the feeling from our first meeting at the Aspen seminar that you are an entrepreneur." (some laughter)

"Well, yes, perhaps you were right. But what I have said doesn't mean that I'm unhappy at IBJ. (smiling) You know, the literal translation of this bank's name is the Japan Entrepreneur Bank. That is why I'm with IBJ. (laughter) So far, my career has been satisfying . . . what I hoped it would be. But still (smiling at me) I am not sure that I am a lifetime employee.

"This year is a fairly important one for me. Up to now, the forty-six men who joined IBJ in 1965, have moved up the ladder almost as a group. There was some difference when we were promoted to the rank of manager about five years ago. About thirty-five of us were promoted in the initial screening. The others were promoted the following year. Now, we are all up for promotion to the deputy general manager level. This is not an automatic promotion. Not everyone will get it. But if all goes well--and I think it will--I should get promoted this summer." (In June 1985, Mr. Hiraki was promoted to deputy general manager, Business Development Department, and invited me to a dinner to celebrate the occasion.)

Question: "I know that you will not predict your own future in the bank, but I do wonder if the top officers all rise up through the IBJ hierarchy, or do some of them come in from the outside?"

"Almost all of them are IBJ people. Every now and then an exception may be made . . . for a retiring bureaucrat from MITI or the Finance Ministry, for a few years as an advisor. But the very top management people are all IBJ.

"Here. Let me sketch the structure for you. (pulling over a pad and drawing an organizational chart) If I get promoted to deputy general manager, I will be . . . let me see . . . four or five steps (smiling) big steps down from our president, Mr. Nakamura. In order to reach the top, I have to get promoted to general manager, to director, to managing director, then to vice-president and then (grinning impishly) who knows. (seriously) But you should know that there are only about twenty directors, fourteen managing directors and two vice-presidents. I know that in American banks the size of IBJ, you sometimes have two hundred vice-presidents, but we only have two. So, the promotion ladder gets very, very steep--from now on.

(thoughtful pause) "A few years after I got back from Harvard, after I married, I spent a year and a half in our Osaka Branch, mostly negotiating corporate loans. That was standard, necessary bank work. (looking at me keenly) I knew that, but still, I couldn't help but wonder why the bank was not using my international training."

Question: "What did you think the reasons were?"

"Well . . . all the young bank officers have to be treated in a basically equal way. There can't be any special favors or special treatment. Otherwise it is bad for morale. I knew that . . . but I was a little restless. Anyway, the Osaka deputy branch manager, Mr. Mori, asked me to stop by his office one day. I did, and he told me that depending on final clearance from the World Bank in Washington, D.C., I would be assigned there within a few months. (shaking his head and smiling happily at the memory) I was . . . astonished. I was hoping for some foreign assignment, but . . . the

World Bank! (smiling broadly) That seemed like an impossible dream.

"I knew that the three IBJ officers who had been seconded to the World Bank before me had done well afterward . . . they had become managing directors or were about to be promoted to that level. So, I felt then that all the work I had done, first to get to Chicago, and then to go to Harvard for the MBA, meant something after all. (pause) So, you see, in some ways all the young officers have to be treated alike. But naturally, only the people with overseas training and enough English could be considered for the World Bank. Mr. Mori told me that usually the World Bank interviews foreign officers at its Washington head office before their appointment. But because of the Harvard MBA, they did not think it was necessary in my case. Well, even though I missed a free trip to Washington, when I heard that I really appreciated Harvard." (laughter)

Question: "I know that Finance Ministry officials are regularly seconded to the World Bank, but what is the basis for IBJ officers going there?"

"We are the leader among Japanese banks in syndicating loans to the World Bank. We are their main commissioned bank in Japan. So we have to understand each other's operations. This has led to a kind of special relationship between IBJ and the World Bank. After my assignment in Washington, two other IBJ men followed. Now, Mr. Ouchi, one of our managing directors, is vice-president in charge of cofinancing at the World Bank.

"You know, our relationship with the World Bank is in many ways the story of Japan's economic achievements. Up to 1956, we borrowed a lot of money from them, to build the first Bullet train and then the Tokyo-Osaka toll highway--two big, expensive projects. Those loans were guaranteed by our government and the IBJ was not much involved. But starting in the 1960s, Japan began to lend money to the World Bank--the money that IBJ syndicates. For the last few years, we have been the largest contributor.

(Nodding his head for emphasis) "But you know, even though we have sent a total of six officers to the World Bank, including Mr. Ouchi, we have not been as strongly represented as we should have . . . in light of our contribution. The World Bank has been . . . hmmm . . . an Anglo-Saxon stronghold ever since it was founded.

"Well, anyway, my career with IBJ has been working out the way I hoped it would. When I came back to Tokyo in 1976, I became an energy economist. Since I was in Washington during the Middle East War in 1973, and during the first energy crisis in 1973-1974, I had started working on resource energy deals. IBJ wanted me to continue that work, and it became a very hot issue again in 1979, when the Shah's government collapsed in Iran and we had the second energy crisis. And I've been working on energy questions, in one way or another, ever since."

Comment: "I noticed that the IBJ is deeply involved in energy loans and energy development all over the world. So this is also a major, perhaps the major item in IBJ's operations."

"Well, Japan has very few energy resources. Our industry, almost our whole economy depends on imported energy. So, we have to do what we can to develop energy resources all over the world. That is the sensible way to make sure that we can get enough energy at reasonable prices--expand supply and diversify supply.

"In a sense, you know, the IBJ is doing the same job now for the world that it was established to do for Japan back in 1902. Then, we financed long-term, basic projects necessary for Japan's industrial growth. Now, we lend money to the world and help to select the most promising energy projects, not only for Japan but for the other countries as well. We try to be the honest broker and the honest agent.

"Well, this international energy economics and financing is just the kind of work that I wanted to do. It is important, useful work--for Japan and for our bank. And I have to travel and do business frequently--almost every month each year--in your country from the Powder River Basin in Texas up to the Alaskan North Slope, and now and then over to Europe and the Middle East as well. In your country I have been working recently on natural gas and steaming coal. I also have been working in the Middle East on our petroleum related projects--in Kuwait, Saudi Arabia and Abu

Dhabi. I have gone to these countries . . . oh, six or seven times during the last five years.

(twinkle in his eye) "Remember, I said when I was a little boy in Kobe, I was jealous of my father when his company sent him to Europe and America--that I wanted to go to all those places. Well . . . . (gesturing with his hands, both laughing)

INTERNATIONALIZATION

Comment: "It seems to me that your experience with Christianity may indicate how you balance internationalization and your identity as a Japanese. You studied the Christian Bible, gave serious thought to certain basic Western values and ideas, and then blended them into your own life and into your practice of Zen."

(laughing) "Well, I haven't thought of it like that--balancing internationalization and being Japanese. But yes, there is something to what you say.

"I don't think there is much danger that internationalization--the increasing interaction between Japanese people and the people in other countries--will lead to the destruction of our culture or most national cultures. All these national cultures will keep changing, but they will not disappear. I can see on my travels that climate and geography is so different in different countries that people must have different ways of living and looking at things. The problem is the other way around. It is to understand enough about other countries and cultures so that we can get along and do business with them in a practical way.

"My own experience in business matters and in personal interactions is that most Japanese learn some good, useful things from foreign cultures, but they also . . . well, they can't agree or accept everything. So, we keep many Japanese ways of acting and thinking. What is important is getting exposed to the rest of the human race and learning to somehow get along with them in practical, everyday business terms. So, we Japanese should have open minds, even if we don't like or accept some foreign values or culture. That is just common sense.

"You know, I feel very comfortable in your country and when I am with my American friends . . . but I don't agree with everything Americans believe, or accept all of their values. Hmm. On my trips to Kuwait, Saudi Arabia, Bahrain, and Abu Dhabi, I can see that the differences between Japanese and Americans are not as great as I used to think sometimes. Most of the time my work in these countries goes smoothly because their bankers and top officials have studied in America or England. So we do our work in English and we base our contracts on your business laws. They don't try to do business in Arabic or based on Muslim law. (smiling at himself) But I had to learn to adjust and to . . . tolerate some things that were . . . well, surprising to me.

"On one trip to Kuwait, I had a hotel reservation and when I got there my room was taken away by an upper echelon official from a neighboring country. (lifting his eyebrows) I had to sleep on a sofa in a waiting room. (half-humorous, half-serious indignation) That was outrageous. Also, I was shocked to see men--adult men in these countries holding hands, walking in the streets holding hands. Well, I had to learn to tolerate such things in order to do business there. That's the way it is. They have different ways.

"Of course, these were minor, personal discomforts. But some cultural differences spill over into politics and economics and are much more serious. For example, IBJ is the main bank on a big Iranian petro-chemical project that goes back to the days of the Shah. Well, last week the Iranian Congress resolved not to service the debt--even though we are prepared to renegotiate. (pause) Well, from a Japanese standpoint--and from an American standpoint, too-- that is wrong and outrageous. And it is. But as a practical matter, we have to hold back our anger and keep trying to resolve this in a business-like way. This Muslim fundamentalism is very emotional and intense, but eventually they will have to be practical again. Over the long term--I mean ten to twenty years--I think we will be able to resolve problems like this. They must sell their oil and we will continue to be a major customer. So, we will keep working patiently at these problems."

Question: "What are your views on future relations between Japan and the U.S. and Japan and Europe? In the U.S., in particular, there seems to be a growing sense of irritation with Japan, over the persistent U.S. trade deficit."

"Well, you are right about this growing irritation in your country. (serious pause) This irritation is . . . a fact. But I wonder how reasonable it is. We are in a period--I don't know how long it will last, maybe another ten years or so--when Japan is the most efficient, successful manufacturing country. Great Britain was in that position for a long time before World War I. Your country held that position from World War II until the 1970s. Now, Japan seems to be in that position, but I don't think it will last too long unless Japan can keep ahead of the rate of technological and economic changes. Anyway, I don't think that this is some kind of dangerous, terrible problem.

"Japan is following close to the U.K. and U.S. pattern. We will have a trade surplus for some years and we will also have big capital outflows. We will use the surplus to invest around the world . . . and a great deal in the U.S. But Japan is not taking over other countries . . . or threatening them in some terrible way. (pause) This is the way the market economy is supposed to work. In fact, Japan's overseas investments--which are growing rapidly--will eventually end our trade surplus. The yen will appreciate and Japanese goods will get more expensive. Also, our overseas investments will make industries in other countries more competitive.

"So, I don't think that Japan's trade surplus is such a terrible economic problem . . . or something abnormal. (serious, thoughtful tone) I hope that the U.S. regains its competitiveness. You have great natural advantages in resources, including human resources, and space. Hmm. It would really be a serious problem, for Japan and for the whole world, if your economy goes into a serious decline. We don't want that to happen."

Index

About the Author

MARTIN E. WEINSTEIN has the Japan Chair and is the Japan Program Director for the Center for Strategic and International Studies, Washington, D.C. He is the editor of *Northeast Asian Security After Vietnam* and the author of *Japan's Postwar Defense Policy, 1947-1968*.